An Introduction to
Town and Country Planning

The Built Environment Series

Series Editors

Michael J. Bruton, *Professor of Planning in the University of Wales Institute of Science and Technology*
John Ratcliffe, *Dean of the Faculty of the Built Environment, South Bank Polytechnic, London*

Introduction to Transportation Planning   *Michael J. Bruton*
The Spirit and Purpose of Planning   *Edited by Michael J. Bruton*
Theories of Planning and Spatial Development   *Philip Cooke*
Conservation and Planning   *Alan Dobby*
An Introduction to Urban Renewal   *Michael S. Gibson and Michael J. Langstaff*
An Introduction to Regional Planning   *John Glasson*
Politics, Planning and the City   *Michael Goldsmith*
Policy Planning and Local Government   *Robin Hambleton*
An Introduction to Town and Country Planning   *John Ratcliffe*
Land Policy   *John Ratcliffe*
An Introduction to Town Planning Techniques   *Margaret Roberts*
Citizens in Conflict   *James Simmie*
The Dynamics of Urbanism   *Peter F. Smith*
Welfare Economics and Urban Problems   *Bruce Walker*
Planning for Public Transport   *Peter White*

In association with the Open Univeristy Press

Man-Made Futures   *Edited by Nigel Cross, David Elliott and Robin Roy*

An Introduction to Town and Country Planning

John Ratcliffe
Dean of the Faculty of the Built Environment,
Polytechnic of the South Bank, London

**THE BUILT
ENVIRONMENT**

Hutchinson

London Melbourne Sydney Auckland Johannesburg

Hutchinson & Co. (Publishers) Ltd
An imprint of the Hutchinson Publishing Group
17-21 Conway Street, London W1P 6JD

Hutchinson Group (Australia) Pty Ltd
30-32 Cremorne Street, Richmond South, Victoria 3121
PO Box 151, Broadway, New South Wales 2007

Hutchinson Group (NZ) Ltd
32-34 View Road, PO Box 40-086, Glenfield, Auckland 10

Hutchinson Group (SA) (Pty) Ltd
PO Box 337, Bergvlei 2012, South Africa

First published 1974
Reprinted 1975, 1977 and 1978
Second edition 1981
Reprinted 1982 and 1983

Set in Times

Printed in Great Britain by The Anchor Press Ltd
and bound by Wm Brendon & Son Ltd
both of Tiptree, Essex

British Library Cataloguing in Publication Data
Ratcliffe, John
  Introduction to town and country – 2nd ed. –
  (The built environment).
  1. City planning   2. Regional planning
  I. Title   II. Series
  711   HT166
ISBN 0 09 144020 3 cased
     0 09 144021 1 paper

Contents

Part Four: Development and control

Preface to the first edition

The principal purpose of this book is to provide an introductory text for students preparing for the examinations of the Royal Institution of Chartered Surveyors, especially the town and country planning syllabus, although certain aspects of the urban economics syllabus have been included where appropriate to the general theme. It has also been compiled with a view to fulfilling the same function for the various diploma and degree courses in estate management that qualify for exemption from the Institution's examinations. It is further hoped that it will serve as preliminary reading for both under-graduate and postgraduate town planning courses. In addition, it has been conceived with a view to catering for the recent development in modular unit degree courses, specifically those which offer some aspect of town planning within their range of options. At the present time this includes certain science, social science, engineering, carto-graphy and construction courses. Having been actively involved in the teaching and preparation of courses in town planning for both planners and estate managers I am only too aware that no single publication currently satisfies these respective syllabus demands.

An attempt has been made to produce a simple and economic review that encompasses the historical development of town planning, its recent emergence, the existing organization and management, some modern trends, certain popular techniques and predominant problems. This general objective is on the one hand ambitious, aiming to cover in a comparatively comprehensive manner a wide range of subjects falling within the broad sphere of planning, and on the other relatively modest, seeking merely to introduce the selected topics, forsaking any pretence at great depth or special authority in particular areas. Naturally in such an ever changing and increasingly all-embracing discipline the contents of a text as restricted as this one are bound to be somewhat arbitrary in their selection and from time to time inevitably reflect the author's own views, limitations and prejudices. In seeking to draw together the many elements and aspects that together constitute the history, development and practice of planning this book cannot hope to rival in chosen fields more specialist publications, and for the interested reader further detailed references are supplied. The choice of the title itself presented certain difficulties epitomizing the inherent problems surrounding a subject which can mean all things to all men. I opted for *An Introduction to Town and Country Planning* purely for its simplicity, fully recognizing that strong and cogent arguments can be advanced for adopting any one of a number of other descriptions as valid alternatives.

Part One seeks to define and explain the nature and context of present-day town planning, at the same time outlining the professions that practise or participate within it. It also sets out to describe the emergence and development of the subject, highlighting the most illustrious personalities and summarizing the most salient occurrences. Particular attenton is paid to the legislative framework that supports the planning system and the way in which the various agencies at different scales attempt to implement policy.

The implicit complexity of the planning process has predicated the need for a variety of methods with which to comprehend and predict the forces at play in determining the quality and performance of the environment. Part Two outlines some of the most popularly applied techniques of appraisal. Because the book is not intended for practitioners, or even for advanced study, the detailed mechanics of the surveys and techniques reviewed, the scope of which is by no means exhaustive, is not set out. The various selected approaches are merely introduced. A separate chapter, however, is devoted to explaining the need for the evaluation of alternative strategies, a much neglected field of study.

Town planning frequently appears in the form of contentious or controversial public issues such as the topical debates concerning pollution, public participation, conservation and traffic congestion. Part Three sets out to explore a number of these problems and attempts to indicate the role of the town planner in tackling respective solutions. With a growing emphasis being placed upon the social, economic and political aspects of urban and regional affairs it has become strangely *passé* to devote much attention to the regulatory, physical and legislative facets of the planning spectrum. Part Four tries to recognize their continuing relevance in allocating land between competing uses and controlling the impact of resultant development.

Although every effort has been taken to ensure that the incorporated material is accurate and up-to-date the usual *apologia* has to be made for the effluxion of time, the inadequacies of authorship and the speed of change. Writing on town planning has been repeatedly likened to painting the Forth Bridge, and as I watch the introduction of new techniques, the floating of new ideas and the pursuit of fresh strategies, I am only too aware how apt is the analogy.

Throughout my studies and my career to date I have been exceptionally fortunate in both my teachers and my colleagues. It would be inappropriate, not to mention invidious, to single out the many individuals who have on different occasions contributed the necessary advice and stimulus. I must, however, acknowledge the debt I owe to Dr Gerald Burke, who first instilled in me an interest in town planning, and to Michael Bruton, whose experience, guidance and encouragement has proved invaluable during the course of preparation. A book of this kind is actually written by innumerable people whose contribution is recognized, albeit inadequately, by the copious references throughout the text and without whom the task would have been utterly impossible.

Finally I would like to thank my wife Vivien, to whom I dedicate the book, which is little enough repayment for the patience and understanding she has constantly shown me in all my work.

Preface to the second edition

Looking back at the decade that has passed since I began the task of producing the first edition, I am astonished at the pace of change. A new system of development plans has become established, local government reform has taken place, we have experienced booms and slumps in the property market, the community land scheme came and went, public participation waxed and waned and the whole issue of the inner city crisis has been brought into sharp relief. The problem has been to know where to start and when to finish, but the objectives and coverage remain much the same as before. I only hope that readers will forgive the many omissions that still persist.

Part One
The nature and development of town planning

1 The need to plan

What is town planning?

The persisting process of urbanization, the worst excesses of an industrial society, and the explosion in population growth and car ownership, have all contributed towards a heightened awareness, and ultimate acceptance, of the need for the introduction of some form of regulation regarding the distribution of land between competing uses. The expression, profession and practice of town planning, with its multi-disciplinary nature, comprehensive perspective, changing character and continued self-questioning, is extremely difficult to define. It has been variously described as 'the art and science of ordering the use of land and siting of buildings and communication routes so as to secure the maximum practicable degree of economy, convenience, and beauty'[1]* and as 'an attempt to formulate the principles that should guide us in creating a civilized physical background for human life'[2] whose main impetus is thus '...foreseeing and guiding change'.[3] Put another way, however, it is concerned with providing the right site, at the right time, in the right place, for the right people.

Control over the layout and design of urban settlement has been exercised since time immemorial. The early civilizations that congregated in the valleys of the Tigres and Euphrates demonstrated an ability to impose order upon comparatively high-density community living, and established an elementary system for the provision of services and facilities, as did the Inca and Maya cultures of South and Central America. Hippodamus of Miletus is generally given the accolade of being the first town planner with his 'chequer-board' or gridiron layout of Piraeus nearly 2500 years ago in Greece. The distinctive hallmark of Roman colonial expansion was the dispersion throughout their empire of standardized uniform town plans. Not only has planning a long history, however, it can also be said that to some extent all development is planned. The individual

*Superior figures refer to the References on pages 473–81.

dwelling is constructed so as to maximize efficiency in terms of function, daylight, outlook and convenience. Similarly a block of offices is designed to facilitate movement, management and servicing. There is little difference between the planning of separate dwellings and that of whole towns; it is only the scale and the interests involved that vary.

Perhaps the most important single justification of a formal system of town planning concerns these very interests, for planning is a reconciliation of social and economic aims, of private and public objectives. It is the allocation of resources, particularly land, in such a manner as to obtain maximum efficiency, while paying heed to the nature of the built environment and the welfare of the community. In this way planning is therefore the art of anticipating change, and arbitrating between the economic, social, political and physical forces that determine the location, form and effect of urban development. In a democracy it should be the practical and technical implementation of the people's wishes operating within a legal framework, permitting the manipulation of the various urban components such as transport, power, housing and employment, in such a way as to ensure the greatest benefit to all.

Town planning aims at securing a sensible and acceptable blend of conservation and exploitation of land, as the background or stage for human activity. This involves the process of establishing the desires of the community, formulating them in a manner that facilitates comprehension and discussion, preparing a policy for their adoption, regulating the degree and proportion of public and private investment, guiding the provision of public services, initiating action where necessary, and continually examining the effect of the adopted policy, making adjustments if required.

The very expression 'planning' is now applied to almost all kinds of human activity, and consequently tends to mean all things to all men, being comprehensively defined as 'the making of an orderly sequence of action that will lead to the achievement of a stated goal or goals'.[4] The practice of town and country planning in particular, however, implies the introduction of a strictly spatial component in addition to other social, political or economic considerations. This sequential and goal-oriented character overtakes the more traditional stages of 'survey–analysis–plan' put forward by Patrick Geddes in the 1920s, and largely adhered to until the 1960s, whereby information relating to a chosen area was collected and examined for prevailing problems and indications of change and a plan subsequently produced for a given future period based upon decisions at that point in time. Now planning is seen as a cyclical process subject to continuing scrutiny and change. Though criticized for demonstrating a somewhat partial physical land use attitude, a useful threefold ideology of planning, illuminating the spatial aspect of the discipline, has been suggested as being 'to reconcile competing claims for the use of limited land so as to provide a consistent, balanced and orderly management of land uses . . . to provide a good (or better) physical environment for the promotion of a healthy and civilized life . . . and providing the physical basis for a better urban community life'.[5] In the light of the current crisis facing many inner urban areas, and because of what is contended to be a lack of understanding of urban processes and a promotion of predominantly middle-class values by planners, a more radically political school of thought has evolved believing that planning should seek to attain more redistributive goals in order to redress alleged social injustices which have taken place in the city, arguing that invariably it has been the already poor and disadvantaged who have again borne the costs of planning policy and suffered successive setbacks.

Planning is also said to be the application of scientific method to policy making, but again this definition can be applied to most activities, and in many ways it only serves to camouflage the essentially political nature of urban planning, for though attempts are sometimes made to divorce planning from politics the two are inextricably interwoven. Almost any planning decision is to some extent concerned with the allocation of resources so that some people gain while others lose, and for this reason it is misleading, if not downright dangerous, to conceal the overtly political complexion of planning policy.

Planning and the market

In the absence of town planning, land would be apportioned between competing uses by the price mechanism and the interaction of demand and supply. In this free-market situation, land would be used for the purpose which could extract the largest net return over a foreseeable period of time, but experience has shown that, unfettered, the market can consume resources in an ill-conceived and short-sighted way, creating almost insurmountable problems for generations to come. Moreover, the competition engendered in the private sector where *laissez-faire* conditions prevail can all too often breed waste. The private sector developer seeking to maximize his personal profit frequently neglects the provision of both social services and public utilities. The very need for planning arose out of the inequality, deprivation and squalor caused by the interplay of free-market forces and lack of social concern prevalent during the nineteenth century. Furthermore, unplanned, these forces combine to produce the fluctuating booms and slumps that epitomize private-sector instability.

Planning, therefore, has properly been identified as 'a concern of government and a field of public administration'[6] because inherently it is involved with political choice rather than market transactions, so that public agencies have been established to control the operation of markets in the interests of the community and supplant markets in the provision of certain kinds of goods and services. A number of reasons justifying the exercise of political choice through planning intervention are advanced for this,[7] including the provision of 'public goods' such as roads and defence that are supplied to all; the existence of other goods and services which produce side effects upon those not involved in their consumption; the need to supply certain high-cost, high-risk goods and services unattractive to private enterprises, such as electricity and aerospace, which are best placed in the care of national monopolies; the necessity to control certain complex operations such as land assembly for comprehensive redevelopment, where public regulation secures a better overall outcome than would private-market transactions; and the desire to protect or preserve particular activities or resources that are considered beneficial to society at large, such as historic buildings, open space and leisure facilities.

The market, operating alone, does not provide the most appropriate location for what are generally described as the non-profit-making uses of land, such as transport termini, gasworks, roads, fire stations and sewerage plants. Nevertheless, the correct siting of these non-profit-making uses of land can render the profit-making uses of land more profitable. Proximity and accessibility to these various services and activities are often essential to commercial viability. Thus planning assists the market in becoming more efficient.

At a time of ever-accelerating social, technological and political change, planning seeks to direct and control the nature of the built environment in the interests of society as a whole. In doing so it is unlikely to please all the people all of the time. There can be little doubt, however, about the need for some degree of intervention in private-sector decision-making, despite occasional frustration, fault and delay. Although there exist violent political and philosophical schisms regarding the ownership, management and return from land, the needs of traffic management, for example, demand far wider comprehensive layout and design than can be provided by the private sector. Central area reconstruction is another instance where large-scale corporate acquisition is more effective than fragmentary private purchase. Despite the obvious merits implicit in some form of control and guidance over the nature and function of the built environment, ensuring economic efficiency, social justice and physical quality, the application of comprehensive land use planning does not always meet with universal acclaim. Strong undercurrents, favouring a great deal less formal planning and a freer interplay of market forces, exist in a number of quarters. Planning and planners are often accused of setting themselves up as arbiters of public taste, frequently in blissful ignorance of consumer demand. The model or plan that they produce, which aims to achieve balance, symmetry and order among the various elements and systems of urban organization, does not always cater for changes in taste, habit or preference. A case in point is the recent trend towards out-of-town retailing, extremely attractive to the shopping public, but not popular, it appears, with the planner. This intransigent policy, with its innate conservatism, can lead to the charge of social engineering of the kind least befitting the spirit and purpose of town planning. It is possible that the restriction of residential development and the control of densities against prevailing demand, even when adequate services are available, could preserve the social status and property values of current residents, without due consideration being given to the welfare of potential future residents. In this way, the planner becomes the protector of existing social class structure on a selective basis, as opposed to being the guardian of the well-being of society at large. Furthermore, the reactionary nature of the planning process is said to stifle initiative, and the conformity that is introduced lacks the incentives required to stimulate experimentation and change. One can scarcely imagine a proposal to build the equivalent of a latterday Brighton Pavilion or Albert Memorial endearing itself to a modern town planning committee, let alone meeting the many building regulations and planning standards imposed.

In a similar vein, the machinery of town planning is criticized for being excessively preoccupied with the trivia of urban development such as advertisement control, the siting of vending machines, the design of private houses, and the provision of car parking. It is a matter of regret that in the minds of many the term 'town planning' has become synonymous with 'development control'. Planning in all spheres of life, and throughout all professional activities, can easily become obsessed with scrutinizing the detail of every tree in the wood, and lose sight of the shape, size and significance of the wood itself.

Another aspect that detracts from the total success, and complete acceptance, of comprehensive land use planning is the inadequacy of the statutory system providing the legal framework within which it is forced to operate. Often, by its very nature, a particular plan or policy will depreciate the value of certain individual interests. This might be caused by the construction of a nearby urban motorway, airport or school. The law of the land is at present incompetent totally to recompense this loss or blight.

Despite the above deficiencies it can be said that the twin forces of the free market and the planning process tend to act as a beneficial corrective, one of the other. The planner has to operate alongside the market, directly influencing, and frequently assisting, its functioning, but in a manner that takes account of both public and private interests. Increasingly he depends upon private–sector development for the implementation of a large proportion of planning proposals, not only city centre redevelopment, where high costs virtually prohibit public investment alone, but also residential, industrial and commercial undertakings of all kinds. Moreover, there is a tendency towards the use of free-market methods by planning agencies, such as the introduction of parking charges to ease the congestion of traffic in towns. Compromise solutions and joint developments are becoming the order of the day.

Categories of planning

At different times and by different people the organization and management of the human environment has been variously described as town and country planning, town planning, physical land use planning, development planning, social and environmental planning and even simply planning. Distinctions have been drawn between economic, physical and social planning. In essence planning is merely a process which evolves a method for doing something, economics is the science of the management of resources, physical means pertaining to the world of material things, and social is concerned with the condition of people. The stewardship of the environment is all these. The dominance of one aspect above another is essentially one of scale rather than method. The construction of a new urban motorway, or the establishment of a new university, within a town, obviously affects the environment and has economic, physical and social repercussions. The degree of importance or consideration given to each respective element largely depends upon the level of planning, whether it is national, regional or local.

Economic planning, for example, is often considered to be a national and regional approach, calculating and controlling the allocation of resources, ignoring physical and social implications, and is primarily concerned with facilitating the working of the market. Physical planning is more closely associated with the regional and local scale, intervening in, and controlling, the market mechanism, reconciling public and private objectives, and is directed towards the spatial qualities and relationships of development. Although divorced from any particular scale, social planning is commonly held to suggest some form of idealistic or utopian engineering detached from practical feasibility and economic sense, but is more appropriately seen as the organization of resources to combat problems such as poverty, discrimination or deprivation. The endless comparing and contrasting of these supposedly separate subjects is both invidious and fruitless. Without the framework of national policy, which is after all meant to be the political expression of the community, the distribution of resources to geographical regions, public and private sectors, selected industries and social groups could not be contrived and co-ordinated in such a way as to permit realistic regional and local planning. Thus social considerations should determine the nature of national economic policy while physical planning is very much the material expression of that policy at the local scale. The different elements cannot, therefore, be separated; they are part of the same process, interrelated and interacting. This does not mean to say that they always attract the attention they deserve, but if one element, be it economic, physical or social, is neglected, it is not necessarily planning that is bad, but merely bad planning. It is evident that national economic policies such as the location of industry, office decentralization, housing subsidy, education and hospital expansion programmes are bound to be put into practice within the local context, having an inevitable reaction upon all other local activities, which in turn may require treatment in a physical or social planning sense. The barriers between these different areas, so strong in the 1950s, are at last breaking down. It has finally been recognized that it is impossible to prepare a plan for a community without the assistance of a number of contributory disciplines. The role of the town planner cannot be confined to land use allocation alone, it must also include consideration and co-ordination of associated activities bearing upon the human and physical environment. This synoptic view is succinctly put by Gordon Cherry who describes the purpose of town planning as being

to promote a physical environment which is harmonious, pleasing and convenient; a related social objective is to assist in securing for man some of the means of individual personal satisfaction and happiness. This is a wide field, but the interrelated aspects of total planning practice as at present conducted fall into place: for example, determination of land use and a communications pattern to secure order and convenience; the planned provision of distribution and facilities design to secure aesthetic qualities in the physical environment; regional planning to promote effective growth patterns in the national interest and to equalise economic opportunity, and so on. The role of social planning is the third part of the total planning trilogy, supporting the other fields of physical and economic planning.[8]

A further dimension to the categorization of planning, however, is the ecological. Following the timely warnings of writers like Rachel Carson there is a growing awareness of the need for man to come to terms with nature, but it is exigent that we improve our understanding, respect and management of the world's life-sustaining systems.

Concepts of town planning

There are probably as many concepts of planning as there are planners, possibly more. Most would accept, however, that planning is concerned with taking an objective and rational view of future conditions, assessing what society desires its destiny to be, forecasting the amount of change, estimating the degree of control required, and formulating a policy to take account of this destiny, change and control.

While this book does not attempt to provide any particular insight into the highly academic field of planning theory, a brief mention of the extremes of thought is perhaps pertinent. To begin with, a distinction is often drawn between the 'normative' and the 'behavioural' theories of planning, whereby a normative approach implies a concern with how planners ought rationally to proceed in an ideal world, whereas a behavioural approach concentrates more upon the actual limitations that circumscribe the pursuit and achievement of rational action. Without indulging in abstruse and unproductive argument, it seems evident that reality lies somewhere between these two extremes, for most plans aim at some kind of rational solution, but with a recognition that they will be affected by and modified in the light of changing circumstances. Another way of approaching this apparent dichotomy in planning thought is exemplified by the utopian as opposed to reformist philosophies. The utopian view deems it desirable and possible to both aim for and achieve an optimal end state, advocates a rationally deduced set of means to achieve this end and believes that planning should be comprehensive in its approach rather than disjointed. Reformism, on the contrary, considers that a concentrated effort should be made to correct existing problems, proposes a piecemeal 'incrementalist' path to societal change, and suggests that planning is incapable of pursuing a rational comprehensive ideal and is only able to adopt a series of limited disjointed actions. Strict utopianism has been largely discredited, not just for its obvious naïvity but also for its authoritarian flavour, and though the planner may retain idealistic concepts at the back of his mind, he is essentially concerned with solving present problems, some may say too much so.

Yet a further way of expressing these divergent views is summed up in the comparison of what is called 'blueprint planning' with 'process planning'. Blueprint planning adopts a comprehensive approach towards planning and is ideally portrayed in the system employed until fairly recently in the United Kingdom. It has developed from the technical professions of architecture, surveying and engineering, and has consequently produced solutions to urban problems that are predominantly physical in character, such as land use maps, zoning, density controls, building regulations and planning standards. It acts through the medium of a 'master plan', hence the description 'blueprint', and operates upon a rigorous established administrative structure. The overall desires of the community, otherwise known as the goals and objectives, are given, having been previously decided by the political representatives, and do not therefore form part of the procedure of planning. Although it attempts to influence or direct all the activities connected with the physical environment, and is founded upon the notion of public benefit and amenity, it is singularly ill-equipped to deal with the majority of social issues and is at times incompatible with economic expediency. While exercising great control over the environment, it is subject to considerable delays between the political decision, the preparation of the plan, its implementation, and any subsequent review and amendment. The exact nature of the problems encountered in this country are discussed later.

In contrast, process planning sees planning as a continuous task, distinct from a static policy prepared at one particular point in time. Great premium is placed upon the incorporation of social and economic planning within the physical framework. Constant review is maintained regarding the performance of the plan and adjustments made whenever necessary, thus reducing delays to a minimum and preserving the relevance of the policy in the light of prevailing circumstances. The realization of recent years, in this country, that the complex problems of urban structure and organization require an approach more akin to process planning has led to fundamental changes in both the theory and practice of town planning. This again is described in later sections.

A note of caution must be struck with so much mention of 'plans', for it has been said that 'plans cannot usefully exist in themselves, their role is as the policy element in administrative systems focused on the control of change'.[9] In other words, it is the subsequent executive decisions that determine action and the actual control of change, not the mere statement of policy. For although an appreciation of the problems and procedures of implementation, or the putting of policy into practice, must be part of the united formulation of planning policy, it is important to recognize that plan making is only one part of planning.

The practice and problems of town planning

In practice, the town planner is expected to be able to operate to secure adequately related activity in the various parts of the framework of a comprehensive town and country planning system involving the local, urban, metropolitan, regional, rural and natural resource fields. Furthermore, this traditional role of controlling and allocating the use of land among competing activities has been substantially enlarged to take account of social and economic factors. In addition, he is expected to assist in the selection of overall goals for the welfare of the community at the policy-making level of local government, and in the organization and management of local government itself.

These wide terms of reference call for peculiar skills and present many problems. First, on the one hand the professional town planner attempts to direct, guide and influence the formulation of a plan and exert pressure to gain its acceptance and implementation. He theorizes on bigger and better ways of planning. He seeks to establish policy, co-ordinate departments, set goals, outline objectives and control development. On the other he is charged with discovering, examining and acting upon the wishes of the local community, and translating their dictates into a feasible plan through the application of professional skills, techniques and judgement. He is thus faced with a situation where he is both master and servant.

Second, he is expected to undertake a comprehensive appraisal and detailed analysis of all problems related to the physical environment. He must grapple at the same time with transport, housing, education, commerce and recreation, and consider them in their economic, social and physical contexts, bearing in mind their national and regional as well as local connotations. With each component, in each context, and at every level he is attributed with exceptional proficiency. Thus the planner is made both generalist and specialist.

Third, he is repeatedly confronted with the problems of poverty, deprivation, loneliness, old age, discrimination and unemployment. Yet all too often he is forced to reconcile these contentious and controversial long-term aspects of town planning with short-term financial and political expediency. He is thus asked to provide both social and economic planning expertise.

Fourth, the town planner is presumed to possess taste and judgement in aesthetic and environmental matters. Being vested with powers of conservation and protection he is taken to be the guardian of heritage and the arbiter of architectural and historic interest. Increasingly, however, he is placed in situations which require a methodical and scientific approach, based upon a thorough training in numerate disciplines. In this way he is asked to bridge the gulf between the arts and the sciences.

Fifth, one of the planner's principal accredited skills is that of communication – communication between the planner and the planned, the professional and the politician, one department and another, and from one scale of operation to another. Despite this there is a marked tendency towards the excessive use of 'jargon' which inclines to confuse what is otherwise clear and over-sophisticate what might well be straightforward. The theories and expressions involved are not only often 'lifted' from other disciplines, but also used inaccurately and out of context. He is therefore portrayed as both articulate and esoteric.

Last, there are a number of other areas of practice where the town planner is placed in a difficult position, frequently full of conflicts. He is assumed, for example, to reconcile the impact of private and public costs and benefits; at the same time it is often necessary, in order to secure the proper performance of the plan, to stimulate in the short run the degree of private investment and therefore entrepreneurial reward, sometimes at a long-run loss to the community. These days he is also charged with ensuring that full consultation and liaison with the public take place at all stages of the planning process even though this very participation and discussion of alternative strategies can spread blight like a great plague over the face of the land.

From the all-embracing nature of the complex task relating to the organization and management of the physical environment, it can be seen that it is impossible for the town planner to tackle all aspects, cater for all attitudes, and deal with all dimensions involved. He must be appreciative and selective; where he specializes he must consider the wider repercussions of his decisions; where he acts on behalf of one group, sector or agency he must be aware of the interests of others; and all the time he must direct himself towards the study of uncertainty and the consequences of change – the very essence of planning.

The professions in planning

The process of planning is an extremely complex and comprehensive operation and therefore demands a variety of skills on the part of the people who participate in it.

While planning is unquestionably an essential function of modern society, it can be argued that there is no such profession as planning, not can there be; for lacking a discernible rigour or discipline, and a clearly identifiable client relationship, it has been defined, perhaps rather unkindly, as a hodge-podge of unrelated social sciences, dissipated further by a superficial understanding of inadequate quantitative techniques, whose proponents are people who appear increasingly to know less and less about more and more. Another, and even more pejorative view, has been expressed as 'The planner has become a monster, a threat to society . . . a callous technocrat, a law unto himself . . . outside the process of democratic control.'[10] Such criticism of planning and planners, together with the introvert self-questioning of planning by planners, has already led to the profession attempting to formulate a theory *of* planning rather than an application of better practice *in* planning. Moreover, certain elements within planning are now becoming concerned not only with the framing of policy advice but with the politics of adoption and implementation, and the day has also dawned of the advocate planner, who is at least overt and recognizable, and, more insidiously, what has been described as the 'bureaucratic guerilla', operating clandestinely within planning authorities, who is not. But such are the polemics of current planning. In seeking, therefore, to identify the precise role and function of the various disciplines contributing to the organization and management of the built environment, probably the most difficult of all to define is the town planner. He is increasingly required to discover a wider variety of solutions to an expanding number of problems. Because of this there is clearly a place for other specialist professions injecting their knowledge and expertise as and when appropriate. General categories of contribution are distinguished by McLoughlin[11] who groups them into 'activity contributors' such as demographers, economists, and persons with a knowledge of specialist activities such as extractive industries, recreation and tourism; 'space contributors' such as architects, landscape architects, engineers, land surveyors, valuers, argiculturalists, geographers and geologists; 'communications contributors' such as transport engineers, specialists in air traffic, telecommunications and public transport. There are also 'channel contributors' which include engineers of many kinds as well as architects, and finally other contributors providing a general service, such as sociologists, political scientists, systems analysts, mathematicians, computer programmers and management consultants. In this way urban and regional planning can be seen to embrace almost enyone with the slightest interest in the human environment who wants to take part.

Those who are widely accepted as playing a leading role and generally merit professional recognition, in addition to the membership of the Royal Town Planning Institute, are surveyors, architects, landscape architects, economists, engineers and sociologists.

The surveyor

The general practice surveyor concerned with estate management and valuation has his origins in the measurement of land; this was extended first to the value of buildings, then to their cost, and more recently to the effects upon urban development of various activities. The introduction of comprehensive land use planning in 1947 placed heavy demands upon the existing professions, particularly the surveying profession, who bore the brunt of the responsibilities conferred by the Act of examining their local authority area, analysing the results, and preparing the development plans. To this day many senior town planners are also chartered surveyors; there is a close relationship and a natural progression between their respective disciplines. With a knowledge of construction techniques, economics, law, town planning and valuation, the surveyor is made well aware of the physical, administrative, legal and financial constraints that beset the management and condition of the built environment. Within the sphere of town and country planning he currently performs the following functions:

1   He acts as an adviser and advocate for persons affected by planning decisions and proposals.
2   He works as a member of planning teams not only in a general capacity as a surveyor/planner but also frequently as a specialist quantity surveyor, valuer or building surveyor.
3   In the field of land economy he plays a prominent part, possessing an ability to comprehend market forces and measure, predict and control their effect.
4   The 1968 Town and Country Planning Act placed great emphasis upon the survey and analysis of the economic characteristics of an area, a subject the surveyor is singularly equipped to supervise.
5   Traditionally, the task of conducting shopping surveys, the calculation of retail catchment areas, and the assessment of shopping floorspace requirements has fallen to the chartered surveyor. To a lesser extent the same is true of office and industrial development, for with his understanding of the property market and his appreciation of planning criteria he is in an excellent position to undertake these tasks.
6   The techniques of measurement and evaluation employed in professional surveying practice provide one of the few absolute measures of performance available to town planning, that of return upon investment. Although not always appropriate, particularly where there are a large number of intangibles, most schemes possess substantial elements that can be costed and compared. This facility can, however, be a drawback, and many

valuers acting as members of a planning team adopt an over-cautious approach, for whereas the planner is permitted to generalize, and the architect portray his designs in outline, a valuer's figures often appear too specific and rigid. This can be overcome by the use of certain operational research techniques such as sensitivity analysis and probability distribution.

7   The surveyor in town planning must increasingly be prepared and practised in the use of a whole range of comparatively new techniques including cost–benefit analysis, critical path analysis, gravity models, linear programming and discounted cash flow, and be conversant with the capabilities of a computer.

8   Town planning as a profession appears blissfully unaware of the nature and importance of land tenure as a determining factor in the urban environment. This view is eloquently put by Switzer: 'Without ownership of rights in land – a system of tenure – no physical development can take place. Tenure is the bridge from intention, resources and technical skill to realization. Knowledge of tenure and the ability to understand its legal, financial and social implications is fundamental to effective and efficient land use, and I regard it as being the surveyor's special and basic contribution.'[12]

9   With an ever-increasing proportion of investment in connection with the built environment being undertaken by public agencies, it is vital to the planning of the nation's resources to be able to forecast, guide and regulate prospective development on a national and regional as well as local basis. Again the surveyor has a considerable contribution to make.

10   Specific topics within the overall planning process where the surveyor's expertise is much in demand include central area redevelopment, cost benefit analysis, rehabilitation projects and conservation schemes.

The landscape architect

This discipline has experienced the fluctuations of professional favour over the last 100 years or so. Before the middle of the last century landscape architects such as Repton and Loudon were accorded a status closely akin to that of the architect. The advent of the landscape gardner, however, relegated him to the lowly position of an 'external decorator'. Since the First World War and the estab-lishment of the Institute of Landscape Architects in 1929 and particularly over the last ten years he is now accepted as a specialist in the planning team in his own right, whose term of reference is 'the whole of the outdoor environment in both town and countryside' and whose attention is directed to a wide range of diverse problems starting with 'the small scale where we include pavings, fencing, the detailing and planting of open spaces in towns and around buildings. . . . At the other extreme are the problems of conservation and management of coast and countryside, and in between comes the full range of design and layout tasks for recreation, industry, town development and the like'.[13] These all-embracing skills concern town and country planning in the following areas:

1   The landscape architect prepares, as a preliminary to the project of development, a plan of the site, examining the contours, geology, soil conditions, availability of water, local microclimate, existing vegetation and general surroundings, all of which might influence the scale and design of the scheme.

2   Having appraised the nature of the site he is further occupied with the task of relating this to the designated function. In doing so he must consider the possible movements of vehicles, pedestrians and utilities, the proposed density of development and any potential hazards, all the time searching for ways in which he can facilitate development, promote safety and enhance the environmental quality.

3   The landscape architect by propitious planning can alleviate the incursion and imposition of noise, fumes and unsightly appearance.

4   He is responsible for the provision, selection and location of outdoor furniture and fittings such as seats, benches, plant holders, street lamps, litterbins and signposts.

5   The singular expertise of the landscape architect makes an invaluable contribution to the design and implementation of urban renewal projects. The choice of simple yet attractive materials, the tasteful refurbishing of the fabric of the dwellings, the pleasant and effective closure of streets, the clever use of space and proportion, the skilful planting of trees and bushes and the consideration of cost, management and maintenance, are part and parcel of the art of landscape architecture.

6   Although the value of landscape can, in all probability, be evaluated both economically and socially, this has yet to be done. Techniques for conveying the feel or aesthetic quality of a place

have, however, been developed using a sort of 'bird's-eye' plan of a space, and plotting with symbols what can be seen from various points. This technique is called ISOVIST and has been used by the Central Electricity Generating Board in the siting of power stations. A similar approach was employed in the planning of the Durham sections of the national motorway network where visual corridor maps were drawn up defining those areas most visible. This was conducted in varying weather conditions and a general limit of three miles on either side was established within which blemishes were selected for special treatment. In the same context, Gordon Cullen has devised a landscape notation system for Alcan in analysing and describing landscape. Likewise, Kevin Lynch in the United States was more interested in people's reactions to their surroundings; he got them to describe routes they followed, naming landmarks, and prepared maps showing what individuals thought about their city.

The economist

With both economics and town planning pursuing the same study of the allocation of resources there is inevitably an affinity between them. Economics, however, places greater emphasis upon the maximization of efficiency and production, whereas town planning seeks to maximize the welfare of the community. The economist, with his tools of analysis, knowledge of markets, and understanding of location can assist the process of town planning in the following areas:

1 In that town and country planning is largely the physical expression at a regional or local scale of national economic planning, the economist has a significant part to play in the translation of national policy into a local context.
2 The 1971 Act charges local planning authorities with the responsibility in preparing their development plan of paying regard to 'the economic planning and development of the region as a whole'. The economist in the planning team must, therefore, be prepared to examine the repercussions of individual local policies upon surrounding areas.
3 Regional planning provides the level at which economic planning predominates, perhaps to the exclusion of other social and physical aspects. The planning techniques employed in regional

survey and analysis are mainly those of the economist, namely input–output analysis, economic base and the technique for area planning.

4   At the stage in the planning process where alternative plans are compared and contrasted, the evaluation stage, the economist again comes into his own. Cost benefit analysis, the planning balance sheet, cost effectiveness and threshold analysis are approaches derived from economics.

5   The construction and use of mathematical models and their application at all levels of the planning process have advanced enormously over recent years. Many of these are either essentially economic models or require a substantial amount of economic data.

6   In relation to the specific topics of industrial location and employment the economist is required to provide a broad indication of policy, need, distribution and degree so that the other members of the planning team can decide more precisely the type of manufacture, the amount of floorspace, the design, the exact siting, and the supply of ancillary services, utilities and residential accommodation.

7   The introduction into certain problem areas of planning of the economic methods of allocating resources among competing uses, and of regulating demand and supply, via the mechanism of marginal cost pricing, has received considerable support of late, particularly in respect of transportation and recreation planning.

The sociologist

The application of social aims and objectives to the philosophy and design of urban form has a long and distinguished tradition. Underlying religious, moral and political themes in the creation of communities can be traced back as far as Aristotle, Plato and Socrates, through Aquinas, More and Savonarola, to Owen, Buckingham and Salt. With a few notable exceptions such as Howard, Corbusier and Lloyd Wright, the role and practice of social planning was virtually eclipsed by early Public Health, Housing and Town Planning Acts which tended to equate social concern with physical condition. Recently, however, the theoretical division between the character of the built environment and the nature of the human environment has been broken down, and the inextricable relationship between social planning and physical planning has at last been recognized. The contribution of the sociologist is increasingly welcomed in the planning process. Sociology is a behavioural as opposed to physical science, but social behaviour and attitudes frequently determine the use of land. Planning can therefore be seen as a form of urban ecology engaged in the study of the interrelationship of living things and their environment, with sociology an integral discipline. Social analysis assists the planning team in the following ways:

1 The sociologist is concerned with achieving and maintaining equality of opportunity. Cherry describes this aspect as 'developing the full potential of all communities by a process of maximization of opportunity and a widening of choice'.[14] This often involves the protection of minority interests such as the poor, the underprivileged and the immigrant.

2 He assesses the provision and performance of social services and facilities from the public's point of view and integrates their organization, management and location within the local authority development plan.

3 He identifies the desires, demands, priorities and problems of individuals or groups within the community in an attempt to establish the goals and objectives which will guide the formulation of a planning policy. In doing so he must balance the need for the efficient organization of society with the preservation of individual freedom, thus providing 'planning with a human face'.

4 The sociologist is called upon to describe the intricate pattern of social relations and the way of life of the inhabitants of areas likely to be affected by planning activity. This may range all the way from describing the social patterns in local 'neighbourhood' groups[15] to an examination of such problems as those caused by colour, class and creed, the disturbance of family ties, the journey to work, high-rise living, and migration to new estates and new towns.

5 As a preliminary step in the preparation of any plan it is therefore necessary to conduct a social survey identifying the values and attitudes held by various sections of the community. The sociologist is equipped to prepare, implement and analyse such a survey.

6 Certain social processes, or forces, influence the nature of the urban environment, causing crisis areas and community breakdown. Chapin isolates and defines three such major social

processes that affect land use and command the attention of the sociologist and planner alike; he calls them 'dominance', 'gradient' and 'segregation'.[16] Dominance is the control of one area over another, gradient is the degree of dominance, and segregation is the related process of clustering. Thus, the central business district is one centre of dominance possessing a certain gradient or influence over surrounding residential areas, which could result in the segregation of lower-paid service workers' dwellings and in urban decay.

7   With the growing awareness of the need for public participation within the process of planning both urban and rural areas, the sociologist's task of ascertaining community desires takes on a more important role – that of acting as advocate on behalf of the inhabitants of an area.

8   The upsurge of demand for greater recreation facilities owing to increased leisure time, higher standards of living and greater mobility places a further duty on the sociologist, ensuring that the development plan reflects individual preference in this respect.

9   It is also his responsibility, with others, to make forecasts and predictions regarding the future state of society given existing demographic, social and economic trends.

10   Finally, it lies with the sociologist to comprehend the purpose and performance of the planning system. Increasing, sociological analysis is being focused on the process of planning itself, not just on the effect of the physical environment upon human behaviour.

The architect

Traditionally the architect has always been associated with the design, development and ordering of towns. Alongside surveying the contribution made by the architectural profession to the organization, management and practice of town planning has been considerable. His role in the planning team can be summarized as follows:

1   He provides a three-dimensional perspective to two-dimensional plans.

2   There exists a strong similarity between the process of designing for the space and movement within and about dwellings and the process of planning the distribution of land uses and the communication between them.

3 The architect frequently finds himself responsible for the preparation of detailed planning schemes, and the production of planning briefs specifying permitted forms of development, their limitations and restrictions as to size, height, density, construction, materials, access and parking. In other words he is called upon to assist in compiling a detailed framework for commercial proposals within the context of the development plan in order to stimulate private investment.

4 As the finished product or end result of the majority of planning proposals takes the form of a building, it is inevitable that the profession exclusively concerned with the built form should be represented and consulted at every stage throughout the process of determining the context within which building should take place.

5 In recent years great emphasis has been placed upon the role and function of the 'urban designer' who falls neatly between the respective professions of architect and town planner and is likely to be drawn from both. His attention is directed towards not only the impact of individual buildings but also the physical repercussions of groups of buildings, the space around them, the movement between them, and the forces that direct the planning and development processes – a hybrid animal indeed!

6 The architect is also involved in the preparation of detailed planning schemes such as town centre development, and the construction and organization of major building complexes such as hospitals and universities.

7 The expertise of the architectural profession is particularly valuable at the local scale. All too frequently, however, the practice of development control is carried out as a matter of routine, and rather uninspired, administrative procedure. The greater participation of architects at this stage might provide a more imaginative implementation of the development plan proposals and a more respectful recognition of planning in general.

8 The future of the profession within the planning process has been described, perhaps rather generously, by the Royal Institute of British Architects' own steering committee on the architect in planning reporting in 1965 in the following manner: 'Architects have a contribution to make at all levels of planning. In national planning they have a consultative role; at regional level they should be members of the planning team; at local level, however,

where town design and redevelopment should form a large sector of the work, the design skills of the architect must play a decisive part.'

2 The emergence of modern town planning

From earliest times man has striven to attain a perfect physical environment. The Egyptians expressed themselves monumentally but statically, the Greeks created a more varied and dynamic urban style which the Romans standardized in their functional manner, the Middle Ages achieved the unlikely state of harmonious cacophony, the Renaissance contributed unsurpassed beauty and magnificence, the Baroque 'a planned achievement' as opposed to the ideal plan, and the Age of Enlightenment a conscience as well as a concept.

England has been particularly fortunate in its urban heritage. The Romans were well versed in the layout, organization and management of towns, every general being said to carry an 'army issue town planning scheme in his knapsack'.[1] The Normans were experienced town builders. The Middle Ages were free from the internal strife that ravaged continental settlements, while the seventeenth and eighteenth centuries were rich with fine examples of urban development, notably the work of Inigo Jones, Christopher Wren, John Nash, Robert and James Adam, John Wood, Dobson, Grainger and James Craig.

The nineteenth-century philanthropists

The nineteenth century witnessed the climax of the industrial revolution, and the worst of its anomalies. The process of urbanization had become a stampede, the uncontrollable influx of the rural poor flooding towns in search of employment reached alarming proportions.

The growth of both population and towns during the nineteenth century was dramatic. Between 1801 and 1901 the population of England and Wales grew from 8.9 million to 32.5 million, by the time of the 1851 census over half the population was classed as urban, and from 1821 to 1851 over 4 million people moved to the towns, a problem that would severely tax the abilities of present-day town planners. The resultant conditions were almost indescribable – verminous, filthy, insanitary, disease-ridden back-to-back hovels, squalidly assembled in overcrowded uniform ranks.

It is little wonder that at a time which echoed the militancy of the Paris Commune and when the clamour of revolution rang throughout Europe, a fear regarding the collective power of the poor, and a concern over the creation of a nation divided, should reverberate through the establishment. It is reflected in the writings of Disraeli, Marx, Chadwick and Chalmers who advocated the splitting up of poor communities, and Canon Barnett who urged Oxford undergraduates to live as 'settlers' in the East End of London thus setting the scene for Lady Henrietta's Toynbee Hall.

This despoliation of the town and exploitation of the industrial labour force did not go entirely unheeded. The century was distinguished by a number of 'utopian socialists', a term coined by Karl Marx to describe a group of social thinkers whose attitude was unscientific and idealistic and who hoped to improve working-class conditions by individual benevolence, philanthropy and enterprise. These reformers concentrated on the development of separate new communities outside urban areas, and there emerged a succession of plans based on a variety of political, social and philosophical ideas.

First, and perhaps foremost, amongst these philanthropists was Robert Owen (1771–1858) who proposed the creation of agricultural villages of between 800 and 1200 persons catering for all the social, educational and employment needs of the community.[2] His plans, submitted to the parliamentary committee looking at the problems of the working classes in 1817, and to the County of Lanark in 1820, envisaged these 1000-strong communities having residence near their place of employment, communal living for the older children, central heating, and private lodgings only for families with children under three years old, and being agriculturally based but including some industry on the outskirts. Owen himself set the example by establishing an industrial complex at New Lanark, which provided excellent working and living conditions, cheap but unsubsidized shops, and an adult education centre. It is worth noting that he also increased output and made substantial profits.

Owen's influence is clearly detectable in the writings of James Silk Buckingham (1786–1855). His ideas on co-operation and association are set out in his book *National Evils and Practical Remedies* published in 1849. He proposed the development of a specially planned, socially integrated community, which he called Victoria

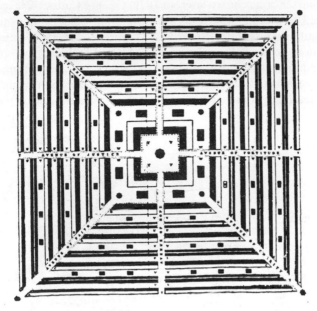

Figure 1 *Victoria*

(Figure 1) in deference to the Queen. It was to be built in open country, a mile square, with a population of 10,000 housed in numerous buildings arranged on a quadrangular basis, larger in the centre and gradually becoming smaller towards the outskirts, surrounded by 10,000 acres of agricultural land, and owned and managed by a public company with the inhabitants as shareholders. Whereas Owen practised a form of paternalistic communism, Buckingham preached integration and temperance. His plans contained strong moral and religious overtones, for in Victoria there was to be no tobacco, no alcohol and no weapons of war. His schemes were never carried out owing to a lack of financial support.

The concept of attempting to improve the working-class environment continued to flourish throughout the nineteenth century. In 1853 Sir Titus Salt moved his factory and workers away from the appallingly grimy and congested conditions of Bradford to a green field site outside the town where he constructed what was considered to be a model industrial community, Saltaire, on an admittedly dense, uninspired, monotonous gridiron pattern but with easy access to the open country.

A quarter of a century later, in 1879, George Cadbury, faced with the need to provide new premises to allow for expansion, built the more suburban town of Bournville (Figure 2) outside Birmingham which was open to all workers irrespective of their place of employment. Shortly afterwards, in 1888, William Lever, a soap manufacturer, constructed Port Sunlight as a model village for his employees just three miles south of Birkenhead. It consisted of most pleasant

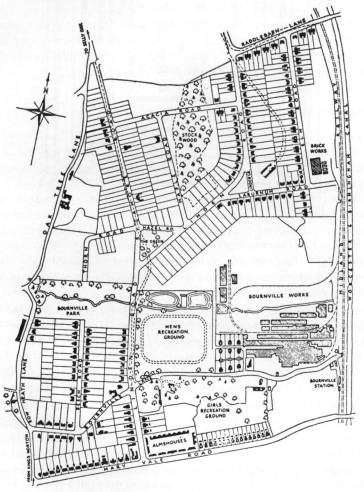

Figure 2   *Bournville in 1898*

Source: R. Bell and C. Bell, *City Fathers: The Early History of Town Planning in Britain* (Barrie and Rockcliff 1969).

cottages with small back gardens, open front gardens and allotments in the centre of housing blocks. In essence it portrayed the same brand of paternalism as existed in Saltaire and New Lanark, and reaped the same commercial rewards.

In this way, the nineteenth century can be seen as probably the most prolific era for radical utopianism as the Owens, Levers, Cadburys, Salts and others strove to realize their idealistic constructs, for New Lanark, Port Sunlight, Bournville, Saltaire and many other utopian settlements were much more than simple industrial housing schemes, being attempts at creating a planned and organized alternative society. Their success, such as it was, has exercised a profound effect upon modern British town planning.

Public health legislation

As a method of administering the nation's resources in a local context with a measure of equity for all classes, town and country planning as we know it today has its roots in the public health and housing legislation of the late nineteenth century.

Most towns and cities had only the most elementary arrangements for providing water, disposing of sewage, clearing refuse or treating mass epidemics, and many had none at all. The average expectation of life was 41 years in 1841 but only 26 years, for example, in Liverpool; infant mortality rates ran at levels of around 250 per 1000 in most northern industrial towns, yet today we become alarmed at a level of over 25 per 1000.

By the 1840s urban conditions were so appalling, politicians so alarmed by continental upheavals, and the climate of opinion so favourable, that a series of legislative measures were enacted to combat the growth of disease and squalor caused by the lack of adequate sanitation and standard of accommodation. Two major official reports, of the Select Committee on the Health of Towns in 1840, and of the Royal Commission on the State of Large Towns in 1845, both recommended that there should be a single public health authority in each local area to regulate drainage, paving, cleansing and water supply. The Public Health Act of 1848 was passed at a time when an epidemic of cholera had killed 54,000 people in England and it founded a Central Board of Health which through a series of local boards exercised functions similar to those of the Poor Law commissioners. Through unpopularity it was abolished in 1858. The 1848 Act was followed by the Housing Acts of Shaftesbury (1851),

Torrens (1868) and Cross (1875), which were consolidated in the major Public Health Act of 1875. This Act introduced a set of codes or standards in respect of the level, width and construction of new streets; the structure of houses, their walls, foundations, roofs and chimneys; the layout of buildings and external space requirements, and their sanitary facilities; as well as providing powers for closing down dwellings thought to be unfit for human habitation. To implement these regulations the country was divided into urban and rural sanitary districts, themselves responsible to the Local Government Board established in 1871. Much of the credit for these advances lies with Sir Edwin Chadwick the politician, and Sir John Simon the administrator. Although conditions in towns were undoubtedly improved, a wider range of facilities provided, and a great awareness of the need and requirements of the working class induced, the primary concern had been with hygiene and sanitation, as opposed to equity and increased opportunity.

Urban sprawl

Probably the most distinctive feature of the last quarter of the nineteenth century, and one also destined to mark the twentieth, was the phenomenal spread of urban growth outwards from the town. The growth of the railway, the evils of central area congestion, the emergence of a mobile middle class, the development of other cheap forms of public transport, the rapid construction of relatively inexpensive housing estates outside the town, and the active social support for the erection of 'model dwellings' in residential suburbs to improve living conditions, were all factors combining to accelerate the outward suburban movement. Between about 1870 and 1914 nearly all British cities obtained a cheap and efficient public transport system, but one of the problems was that many new suburban districts were developed outside existing public health authority boundaries and it was recognized at the time that the advantages of country air were being offset by faulty building, bad drainage and an insufficient water supply. Conditions quickly improved, however, as changes in local government boundaries, tighter public health legislation and an enhancement of the income and social standards of the suburban dwellers occurred. A number of privately sponsored experiments took place in the years between 1875 and 1914, such as the construction in 1877 of Bedford Park on the western edge of London, the operations of companies such as the Tenant Co-operators Ltd which developed a number of private suburban estates around the turn of the century. The most notable venture at about this time was the formation of the Hampstead Garden Suburb Trust, instigated by Henrietta Barnett, and strongly influenced by the emergent writings of the garden city movement. Between the two world wars the whole process of growth and decentralization began to speed up owing to further developments in the public transport system, relatively inexpensive building costs, an aspiring lower middle class and the availability of mortgages. The effect upon London, in particular, was enormous, for it has been observed that whereas the population of the capital grew from 6.5 million in 1914 to 8.5 million in 1939 the built-up area expanded threefold. Much of post-war planning policy has, therefore, been directed at controlling urban sprawl and attempting a more orderly approach to the creation of new urban settlement.

The garden city movement

Towards the end of the nineteenth century the various philanthropic concepts were drawn together and embodied in one plan by Ebenezer Howard (1850–1928). In his book, *A Peaceful Path to Social Reform*, published in 1898, he set out his plan for a satellite town called a Garden City which he portrayed on a grand scale. It would comprise 6000 acres, 32,000 inhabitants, a central area of 1000 acres, individual plots 20 feet by 130 feet, with a gross density of 30 persons per acre. There would be six boulevards each 120 feet wide extending radially from the centre; these would assist in forming six wards which would provide the basis of local government and community services. The 'city' would be self-sufficient in terms of employment, possessing its own industry, commerce, shops and agricultural production. Howard envisaged a whole molecular infrastructure of garden cities clustering around a central city of about 50,000 population. His philosophy was almost certainly influenced by the writings of William Morris, particularly in respect of the necessary reorganization of society along collective socialist lines and a basic distrust of the existing city. Physically he appears to have incorporated several of the ideas of Robert Pemberton, who designed in 1854 a settlement in New Zealand which he called Happy Colony.

A great deal of criticism has been levelled at Howard's plans as being unrealistic in their adherence to geometric proportion, but he presented his design of concentric circles of varying land use as a

universal rather than as a particular model, the actual plan being
drawn once the site had been selected (Figures 3–6).

In 1899 Howard formed the Garden City Association, the forerunner of the Town and Country Planning Association, with the
intention of putting his theories into practice. A company called the
Garden City Pioneer Company was registered in 1902 with the
express purpose of finding a site. After a brief survey one was found at
Letchworth in Hertfordshire and, in 1903, the First Garden City
Limited was in business. Letchworth was designed by the architects
Raymond Unwin and Barry Parker in 1904. Owing to financial
constraints its development was slow, but it was entirely privately
sponsored. Unwin and Parker also drew up the plans for Hampstead

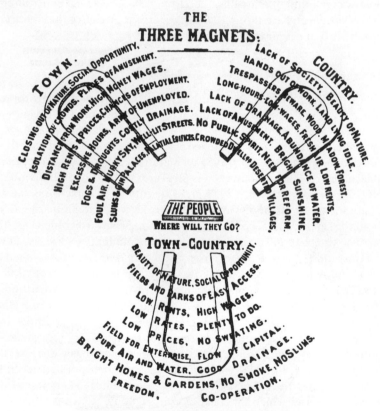

Figure 3   *Howard's 'The Three Magnets' – demonstrating the respective
advantages and disadvantages of both town and country and the amelioration of
the drawbacks in the garden city ideal*

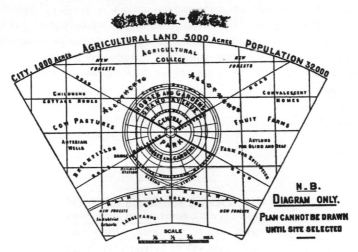

Figure 4   *The garden city in a rural setting*

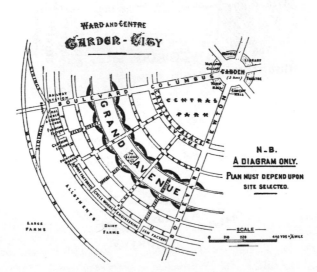

Figure 5   *Section showing a ward and the centre of the garden city*

Garden Suburb, the concept of Dame Henrietta Barnett, in 1907. After the First World War, Howard and his associates attempted to consolidate the garden city movement at a time of post-war construction, and in 1919 Welwyn Garden City was begun. Welwyn attempted for the first time to secure a 'social balance' by a skilful integration of varying socio-economic groups, but like its precursor Letchworth its growth was hampered by financial constringency.

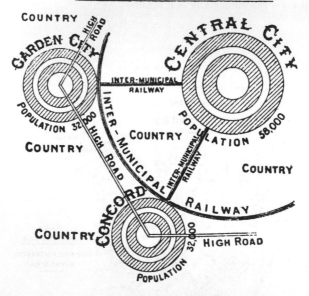

Figure 6   *City growth*
Source: Ebenezer Howard, *Garden Cities of Tomorrow.*

The linear city

The medieval linear village with development on either side of a single road, and the proposal for a linear new town propounded by James Craig for Edinburgh in the late eighteenth century, found expression in Don Arturo Soria y Mata's Ciudad Lineal put forward in 1882 and illustrated in Figure 7. He suggested a town for 30,000 people based

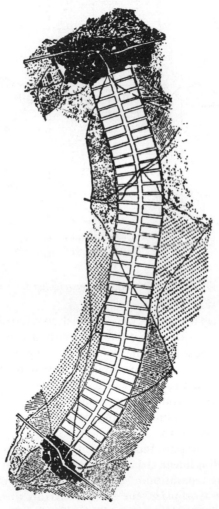

Figure 7   *Don Arturo Soria y Mata's proposed linear city*

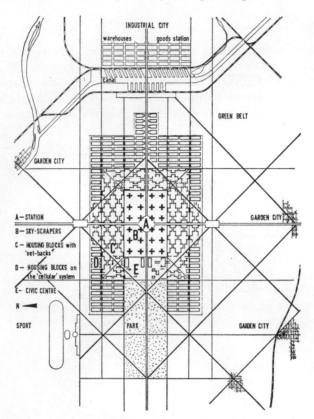

Figure 8   *An outline of Le Corbusier's master plan for Chandigarh*

upon the principal transport route which would take the form of a street 500 metres wide and of infinite length, depending upon urban growth. All services would be channelled along the street and other community facilities would be grouped at regular intervals along its course. The residential area would be limited to 200 metres either side, beyond which would lie the countryside. Soria y Mata envisaged these urban chains linking existing cities with a cobweb of development. Shortly afterwards, in 1901, Tony Garnier, a French architect, published plans for his Industrial City which possessed a definite centre but with a linear structure and placing great emphasis upon zoning and the separation of various urban functions.

In 1933 Le Corbusier, the great Swiss architect, planner and visionary, author of *Urbanisme* (1923), *Towards a New Architecture*

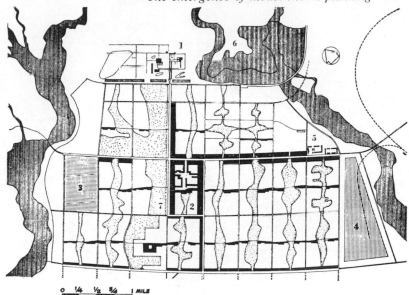

Figure 9 *More detailed plan for the northern sector of Chandigarh*

1 Capital complex 5 Grain and timber markets
2 City centre 6 Lake
3 University 7 Town park
4 Industrial area

Source: Frederick Gibberd, *Town Design* (Architectural Press 1970).

(1925) and many other notable works, designer of Unité d'Habitation (1945), an 18-storey tower block box of homes, and Chandigarh, the new capital of the Punjab, proposed cities La Ville Radieuse and City of Tomorrow, based on a linear system, seeking to ease congestion by the use of skyscrapers and elevated roads. In his City of Tomorrow, designed for 3 million people, there would be subways for servicing, a co-ordinated transport system, a high-rise business and entertainment centre surrounded by five- to seven-storey residential blocks, and then detached dormitory garden city suburbs. In Ville Radieuse, planned for 1.5 million, there would be extremely high densities with skyscrapers on the periphery of the city as well as in the centre. Le Corbusier also planned Chandigarh in the early 1950s along a linear approach (Figures 8, 9).

In the footsteps of Soria y Mata and Le Corbusier, the Modern Architectural Research (MARS) Group worked out a development plan for London (Figure 10). Although prepared in 1937 it was not

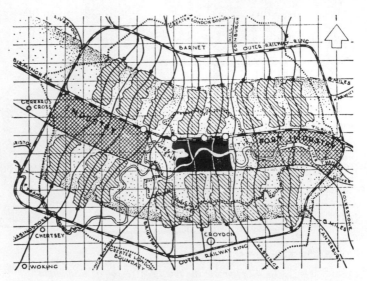

Figure 10   *The MARS Group plan for London*

published until 1941. It applied the linear concept to the complete redevelopment of the metropolis in the form of a herringbone layout with the backbone providing access to the administrative and commercial centres, and fourteen districts of 600,000 persons each set at right angles to it. A main arterial and an orbital railway were included in the plan, as well as a hierarchy for social organization based upon a unit of 1000 persons, six units forming a neighbourhood, about six neighbourhoods to a borough, and approximately twelve boroughs to a district. This original and far-seeing master plan was far too revolutionary and has sadly lapsed into this historical perspective.

The most recent developments adopting a linear approach have been the plans for Cumbernauld prepared in 1958 by Hugh Wilson, and the scheme for Hook New Town published in 1961 by the London County Council. The advocates of the linear plan list its advantages as:

a simple economical form of traffic segregation

a pattern of movement and location comprehensible to the average
   citizen

the town centre grows in proportion to the demands of residential
and industrial expansion
subsequent possibility of expansion to absorb a larger population.[3]

Its critics are more numerous and its defects more apparent:

accessibility to central area is impaired
separation of arterial and local traffic is exceptionally difficult to
achieve
services have to be provided over a longer distance and are therefore
more expensive.

The neighbourhood unit

The social upheaval of the nineteenth century, the physical repercussions upon urban form, and the reaction of reformers all
contributed to the concept and creation of model communities to
accommodate the working class, some by dispersal to satellite towns
and others by the establishment of urban villages. A common theme
runs through all attempts to formulate standards for residential area
layout and town design, that is the search for the ideal size of population which relates to both the provision of services and the retention
of identity. Robert Owen considered 800 to 1200 persons to be the
appropriate size, James Silk Buckingham thought 10,000; in France,
Fourier designed 'Phalansteries' for about 1800 inhabitants and
Ebenezer Howard divided his garden cities into wards of around
5000, aiming to provide social services, integration of classes, and a
sense of community.

In America, two architects, Henry Wright and Clarence Stein,
having toured and studied the work of the English garden city movement, developed the idea of a neighbourhood unit even further. They
set up the City Housing Corporation in 1924 to build an American
garden city. Their first attempt was at Sunnyside, New York, which
owing to local regulations was constructed on a gridiron pattern, with
large lawn-covered courts leading off the streets. Probably its most
notable inhabitant was Lewis Mumford, who lived there for eleven
years and described it as being 'framed to the human scale'. Clarence
Stein was particularly impressed with Raymond Unwin and Barry
Parker's low-density cul-de-sac layout, and in 1928 he prepared the
plan for the ill-fated town of Radburn (Figures 11, 12). The projected
population was to be 25,000, divided into three neighbourhoods of
around 8000 each, the size required to support an elementary school.

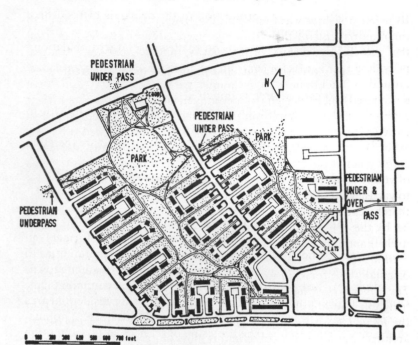

Figure 11   *Radburn*

Source: J. Tetlow and A. Goss, *Homes, Towns and Traffic* (Faber 1968).

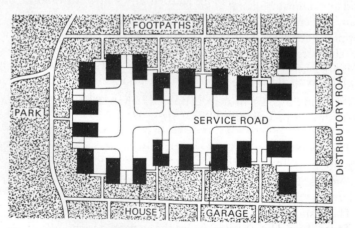

Figure 12   *Service road in detail*

Source: J. Tetlow and A. Goss, *Homes, Towns and Traffic* (Faber 1968).

Its prime objective was to take the garden city concept and adapt it to the requirements of the motor age, segregating the pedestrian from the vehicle by means of footpaths, underpasses and bridges, providing rear access for cars and grouping residential 'superblocks' around a backbone of continuous parkland. Wright and Stein considered their design to be universally applicable, but their experiment was criticized on the grounds that having developed so close to existing built-up areas they had in effect extended suburbia, exacerbated commuting problems, neglected to provide local employment opportunities, ignored the entertainment requirements of young people and, by the nature of the house type, displayed a bias towards white-collar workers and white Anglo-Saxon Protestants, thereby causing local dissension. The City Housing Corporation was hit by the depression and forced into liquidation in 1933, Radburn itself remaining uncompleted.

Many of the ideas incorporated in the plan for Radburn were originally put forward in 1910 by Clarence Perry in his publication *The Wider Use of the School Plant*. It was he who first coined the term 'neighbourhood unit', which he explains in some detail in vol. VII of the *Regional Survey of New York and its Environs*. Perry was not an architect but a social worker and is more closely associated with the green belt towns developed in the 1930s than with the actual construction of Radburn. In proposing what he described as 'a scheme of arrangement for the family life community' he saw the neighbourhood unit as ensuring that all residents were 'within convenient access to an elementary school, adequate common playspaces, and retail shopping facilities. Furthermore, their districts will enjoy a distinctive character because of qualities pertaining to its terrain and structure, not least of which will be a reduced risk from vehicular accidents.'[4]

Perry laid down six principles upon which the design of neighbourhoods should be based:

1 The size should be related to the catchment area of an elementary school.
2 The residential area should be bounded on all sides by arterial streets; there should be no through traffic.
3 There should be ample provision of small parks and play areas.
4 There should be a central point to the neighbourhood containing the school and other services.
5 District shops should be located on the periphery, thus serving

approximately four neighbourhoods.
6   There should be a hierarchy of streets facilitating access but discouraging through traffic.

These precepts were taken up by Wesley Dougill in his writings about the use of school buildings as the foundation for neighbourhood planning, and in his examination of Wythenshawe, near Manchester, as an example of neighbourhood units in practice. Along the same lines was the notion of 'precinct' planning, put forward during the Second World War by the Assistant Commissioner of the Metropolitan Police, Sir Alker Tripp. He too stressed the need for a hierarchy of arterial, sub-arterial and local roads. The sub-arterial roads would bound and create residential, commercial or industrial areas which would be known as 'precincts'. His work was significant because it recognized the separate functions that are provided by different roads, and was the forerunner of Professor Colin Buchanan's noted work, *Traffic in Towns*.

At about the same time the National Council of Social Service produced a report that looked at the social needs of residential areas. It stated that in existing residential development the journey from home to work was too long and there was inadequate provision of community facilities. It suggested that a greater degree of social balance should be achieved in future urban development, and that community facilities should be located at the centre of a neighbourhood area, no further than 10 to 15 minutes' walk away from the population of 7000 to 10,000. Methods of obtaining social balance were considered by the Dudley report a year later, in 1944, which also criticized the existing density zoning as being too inflexible as well as noting that there was insufficient variety of dwelling types. It too favoured a population of approximately 10,000 for each neighbourhood, which should be no more than 10 minutes' walk away from the community centre. The area of the neighbourhood would be 168 to 482 acres depending upon the topography and appropriate density, and to link residential blocks a continuous park, footpath and playground network was suggested. Once again the primary school was advocated as being the focal point of the neighbourhood, but unlike Perry the report suggests that the shops would also be similarly situated. The report's findings were generally accepted by the Ministry, apart from the fact that they thought the size of the population should be 5000.

New towns

Drawing upon the experience of the garden city movement, and prompted by the Town and Country Planning Association, the government started to display interest in the notion of new towns during the 1930s. After Howard and the other nineteenth-century reformers, the idea gained momentum with the reports of the Committee on Unhealthy Areas (1900), the Committee on Garden Cities and Satellite Towns (1935), and, most important of all, the Barlow report (1940). The Barlow report analysed the factors affecting the distribution of the industrial population, with particular reference to the disadvantages of allowing further concentration of industry, and suggested possible remedies. It hinted at dispersion and suggested the formation of a research body to consider solutions, while a minority report fervently advocated the establishment of satellite towns and garden cities. No action was taken until after the Second World War, when Lewis (later Lord) Silkin was appointed Minister of Town and Country Planning. He was a firm believer in the new town philosophy, and in 1945 the New Towns Committee under Lord Reith was set up to consider 'the promotion of new towns in furtherance of a policy of planned decentralization for congested urban areas'. Its recommendations were embodied in the New Town Act of 1946. It placed great weight upon attaining a satisfactory social balance of self-contained communities, probably as a reaction to the drab, monotonous, one-class, pre-war London County Council (LCC) estates such as Becontree and Dagenham. The time was ripe for a positive policy in this direction, there still existed a strong control over the economy from the war, there was a Labour government willing to exercise it, and London had suffered terrible destruction and required redevelopment; Abercrombie's plan for London propounded the dispersal of 1.25 million persons, 0.5 million to be relocated in new towns whose sites were suggested. Since the 1946 New Towns Act some twenty-eight new towns have been designated including three, Northampton, Peterborough and Warrington, that strictly rank as town expansion schemes (Figure 13).

Between 1947 and 1950 the first phase had been designated, fourteen towns in all; eight in the London ring, Basildon, Bracknell, Crawley, Harlow, Hatfield, Hemel Hempstead, Stevenage and Welwyn Garden City; two in the North East, Peterlee and Newton Aycliffe; two in Scotland, Glenrothes and East Kilbride; and one,

Figure 13   *British new towns*

Figure 14 *The original plan for Crawley New Town showing the physical separation and separate identity of neighbourhoods*

Cwmbran, in Wales. These are sometimes described as the Mark 1 or first-generation new towns. Unlike their garden city predecessors they aimed to achieve a 'social balance' in both the individual neighbourhood units and the community as a whole. For example, Crawley strived to reflect the class characteristics and social balance that existed throughout the country (Figure 14). Thus, when there was found to be 20 per cent 'middle class' nationally, they planned for the integration of 20 per cent 'middle class' in the neighbourhood units as well as in the town at large. In practice this is difficult to achieve because people tend to segregate themselves at the local level. The very concept of neighbourhood units was held in great esteem. In Stevenage, for instance, the original town centre formed the nucleus for the first neighbourhood of 10,000 persons and five more of similar size were grouped around. From social survey and research it would appear that the neighbourhood unit is a useful planning tool for designing and provision of community facilities, but inhabitants tend to associate themselves with very much smaller residential areas such as streets, blocks or wards. It has been suggested that the concept of neighbourhoods as envisaged in the development plan had little significance in Stevenage.[5] Even when the neighbourhoods did seem to work, at least from a functional point of view, it was found that they did so to the exclusion of the town centre. In Harlow and Basildon people seemed either reluctant or unable to travel from one neighbourhood to another, which weakened the various community organizations and led to individuals possessing a very small circle of friends. This, in part, is said to account for that mysterious but malignant ailment, the 'new town blues'. There was a temporary halt in new town construction between 1951 and 1961, largely as the result of a change of government. The 1952 Town Development Act directed attention instead towards the expansion of existing towns, providing financial support and encouraging local authorities to agree amongst themselves regarding the planning and management of overspill schemes.

Expanded towns were developed on a much more varied base and shared little uniformity in target size. The scale of the operation largely depended upon local circumstances, and some arrangements made under the Town Development Act were as small as 1000 to 3000, some even less. At the other extreme, such schemes as those agreed between London and Basingstoke, Swindon and Wellingborough almost matched the character and scale of new towns. Swindon, in fact, has virtually become one of the largest twentieth-century town developments in the country. Most of the larger schemes were related to London overspill, and, whereas the average distance of new towns from their 'parent' city is between 12 miles and 35 miles, that of London's town schemes is 77 miles with an extreme of 230 miles, though provincial expanded town arrangements are generally closer. As already mentioned, the underlying principle of expanded town policy was essentially one of encouraging local authorities to tackle the overspill problem resulting from the redevelopment of existing congested urban areas themselves. Authorities wishing to 'export' surplus population were expected to enter into 'orderly and friendly' arrangements with neighbouring authorities whereby development could be undertaken by either, and assistance in the form of subsidies would be made available by central government. Such schemes were often little more than simple housing arrangements; they did not guarantee self-containment or social balance, there was no careful examination of sites, scant regard was paid to their true role and function, poor provision of additional facilities was frequently made, and generally less variety of jobs or services were offered than would be found in new towns. The biggest problem was found in the short distance overspill transfer schemes, where development tended to follow the lines of least resistance and a repetition of earlier urban sprawl took place.

Only one new town was designated between 1952 and 1959, Cumbernauld, in 1956, which was the first of a new generation of new towns commonly referred to as Mark 2. It represented the movement away from seeking social balance by complete integration, and its community structure was far less physically determined than the first generation of new towns. There was less adherence to the formal idea of an architecturally designed neighbourhood unit and less physical division of the town. By allowing for a higher density, more concentrated population grouped around a hill-top town centre, and almost total pedestrian–vehicle segregation, and ensuring that everyone was within walking distance of everyone else, it was hoped that social intercourse would be facilitated. In similar vein the London County Council put forward proposals for a new town in the South East called Hook (Figure 15). Although it was never built, the plans, often referred to as the 'Hook book', envisaged a strong dominant town centre, high densities, and great accessibility to community facilities.

The 1959 New Towns Act, enacted in the light of the apparently successful economic performance of the immediate post-war towns, gave fresh impetus to designation and development. The new towns of the early 1960s, however, were largely unconnected with London, concentrating instead on Birmingham, Merseyside, the North East and Scotland. They were, in order of designation, Skelmersdale, Livingston, Telford, Redditch, Runcorn (Figure 16), Washington, and Irvine. Shortly afterwards took place the designation of North-ampton, Peterborough and Warrington, where development under New Town Act powers is to occur on a partnership basis between the development corporations and the existing local authorities. In all these later new towns, increased mobility and planned accessibility have tended to invalidate even further the idea of a fixed residential neighbourhood size. Moreover, the notion of separating various functions such as employment, shopping, education, recreation and

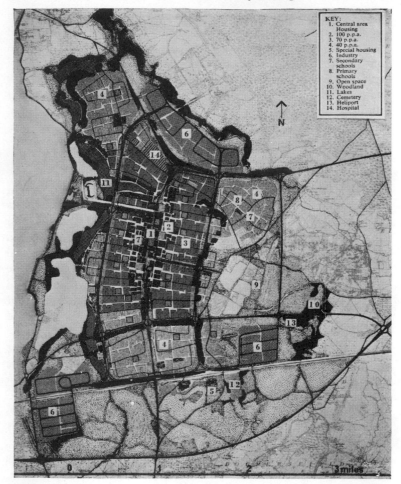

Figure 15   *Proposed Hook New Town demonstrating the integrated high-density linear approach*

Source: Frederick Gibberd, *Town Design* (Architectural Press 1970).

residence has also been questioned, and in Washington, for example, where a basic 'village' unit of about 4500 persons can still be discerned, shops, primary school, pub, and employment are provided in the local village centre. The unit is thus a convenient size for all daily needs and contained to the extent where the residents will have a sense of belonging. The planner now aims to introduce greater flexibility into his schemes by designing for the 'group', which is a very small social unit of up to 50 families, then for the 'place' which is the successor to the neighbourhood unit but still gives a sense of identity, being up to 500 families strong, then to the 'village', which consists of several places, and finally to the town itself.

The original new town concept of a population size between 20,000 and 60,000 was found to be too small to stimulate the necessary economic growth and balance of employment. The ultimate size of

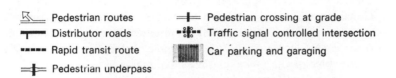

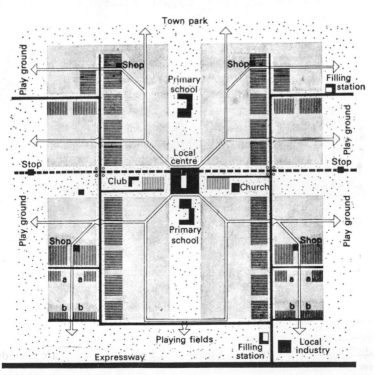

Figure 16   *Diagram of the community structure at Runcorn, comprising 8000 people divided into four neighbourhoods of 2000 persons each*

Source: Runcorn Development Corporation.

most towns was therefore increased, and later designations were in respect of 'new cities'. These were Milton Keynes in Buckingham-shire (Figure 17), with a planned size of 250,000, and the Central Lancashire New Town in the Preston–Leyland–Chorley area, originally expected to grow to 430,000. Other new town innovations are the 'in-town' development by the Greater London Council (GLC) at Thamesmead, intended to accommodate 60,000 Londoners of various socio-economic groups, and the more limited satellite towns of Newcastle, Cramlington and North Killingworth.

Considering that the early new towns were designed in the absence of any previous theoretical study or practical research it is perhaps surprising the degree of success they have obtained and the relative insignificance of the mistakes they have incurred.

Undoubtedly a large number of people have discovered a fresh and more acceptable way of life since transferring from the congested

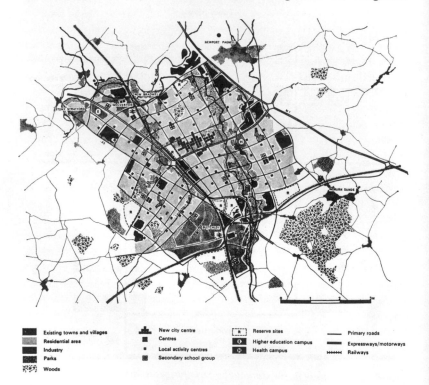

Existing towns and villages	New city centre	Reserve sites	Primary roads
Residential area	Centres	Higher education campus	Expressways/motorways
Industry	Local activity centres	Health campus	Railways
Parks	Secondary school group		
Woods			

Figure 17   *Milton Keynes, illustrating the dispersed low-density chequerboard design*

'twilight' areas of the cities. It is unwise, however, to exaggerate the impact of new town development. Up to 1968, after twenty years of new town policy, their total population had only grown to 554,000, representing approximately 1 per cent of the population of the country, and currently stands at rather less than 1.8 per cent. Although certain development of peripheral areas and expansion of existing towns proves comparatively inexpensive by ensuring the full economic use of existing services and facilities, it has recently been suggested that owing to higher direct costs of improvement, costs associated with greater distance, inflexible public utility and trans- portation systems, together with increasing obsolescence in the conurbations, new town construction presents a cheap and viable alternative. Nevertheless, even under such circumstances, total cost per capita has appeared to rise with growth, and in any event cost minimization only makes sense if profitability is fixed. In attempting to steer growth away from existing congested urban areas the new towns, particularly those around London, did manage to attract industry to their new estates. The accompanying workers, however, were all too often the key, skilled, relatively well-paid employees whose numbers were scarcely significant as a remedial measure to counteract congestion in the cities, and whose predominance militated against the establishment of a socially integrated com- munity in the receiving new towns.

The creation of a well-integrated socially balanced community has traditionally been a prime objective in the establishment of new towns. They have, however, been found to attract people by their apparent characteristic of 'social exclusion', whereby the very poor are offered little encouragement to move. Studies have shown that in British new towns higher income groups tend to leave and a distinctive segregation between neighbourhoods within a town occurs. Housing difficulties are presented because the 'filtering' process, whereby low-income groups are accommodated in stock made cheap by age, conversion or division, does not exist in new towns. Either substantial housing subsidies are required or these low- income groups are excluded altogether. The Burns report describes the new towns as catering for the 'middle man', discouraging the poor and immobile and failing to attract the executive. In the same context the new towns have traditionally sought to achieve 'self-contain- ment'. During their first ten years the early new towns possessed a relatively self-contained structure but despite an overall balance between jobs provided and workers employed there has been an increasing amount of work travel between each town and the older established towns around. The jobs ratio, that is the number of jobs supplied per 100 employed residents, has increased. Within the eight London new towns, for example, the ratio went up from 98.6 between 1951 and 1961 to 132.8 between 1961 and 1966. Throughout the country the Mark 1 new towns remain comparatively balanced communities, however, possessing an overall average job ratio of 102.8. The employment expansion in the early 1960s following the experience of the initial decade of development tends to suggest that new towns have job deficiencies in their early stages, but once the basic social and industrial structure has been established employment growth gains in momentum and proceeds to outrun the growth of population. This in turn increases the number of people who travel in every day and this creates a wider, more dependent hinterland. A survey by Ogilvy, reported in the *Town Planning Review*, 1971, put the actual increase in numbers travelling in at over 60 and those travelling out at approximately 17 per cent. This cross-movement has reduced the self-sufficiency of new towns, although at Welwyn Garden City, which it can be argued is at a more advanced stage of development than the others, the trend has stabilized.

The objects of self-containment, integration and balance may result in certain economies but may also give rise to a lower level of productivity, a risk of instability, a curtailment of adaptability, and the problem that periods of decline can have more serious repercussions on smaller urban areas than larger ones. A closed labour market is also very difficult to maintain; witness the fact that for every ten workers who find employment within the early British new towns another seven commute out every day. Conversely, in the more recent Scottish new towns another trait has developed; large numbers of workers are preferring to return to the old cities to live and are travelling out to the industrial new town estates every day to work.

The investment in new town development is also favoured as a method of stimulating investment and growth in the economy at times of decline by promoting demand. However, the time lags between the recognition of economic problems and the implementation of growth policies is often too long to allow such new town investment to be used as a counter-cyclical device. Furthermore, any such effective economic measures must be able to be used in the opposite way, but slowing down growth at times of new town development with its 'front-heavy investment' could be disastrous to private enterprise's cash flow. The notion that new towns could provide a kind of domestic *détente*, intercepting migrants from rural areas and thereby giving a breathing space to the cities, has never been an important factor in this country, and has virtually disappeared since rural migration has fallen to a mere trickle, playing a decreasing role in metropolitan growth. Perhaps one of the most forgotten aspects in favour of a new town development policy is that it permits and facilitates the public ownership of land, thus allowing the community to automatically recapture the 'unearned increment'.

Another theoretically attractive claim for adopting the new town approach is the proposition that it acts as a kind of urban planning laboratory. Because of the control over development, timing, programming, magnitude and location, the stimulation and planning of construction, layout and investment policy can be made on a more rational basis. The infrastructure can be provided more effectively and efficiently and the resultant performance more accurately assessed. An interesting example of just such experimentation can be seen at Le Voudreuil, one of the eight French new towns attempting to deflect commercial growth away from existing urban areas. Situated near Rouen, it is one of the smallest, with a planned population of 140,000, but is being designed from its earliest stages to control air, water, noise and visual pollution, thus providing a test bed for innovation.

Private enterprise in new town development

At various times it has been suggested that private enterprise should play a greater role in new town development. After all, Letchworth and Welwyn Garden Cities were established on private finance. The United States has experienced a number of such ventures ranging from the commercially motivated 'company towns' like Pullman, to the more utopian green belt towns that were constructed during the depression of the thirties on garden city principles and let at low rents. The accent appears to have been on the provision of accommodation to the detriment of social amenities and community services as at Radburn and Sunnyside. The worst example of this manifestation is Levittown on Long Island, New York, where 50,000 people live in identical homes and scant regard has been paid to local employment, the town becoming a glorified 'commuterville'. The developments at Columbia and Reston appear to rectify these deficiencies.

Apart from Howard's exploits there have few such attempts in this country. One that never got off the ground was British Petroleum's proposal in 1955 to construct a new town of 25,000 population called All Hallows on the Isle of Grain in Kent principally for the employees of their oil refinery. They were refused planning permission by the Minister on the ground that the scheme appropriated too much agricultural land. One of the most recent attempts was that at New Ash Green, again in Kent, where Span developers undertook to build a small self-contained community of about 7000 persons in co-operation with the Greater London Council (GLC) as an alternative to urban sprawl. The GLC withdrew their support after construction had started, and Span were financially unable to continue. Bovis, another large developer and builder, took over responsibility but on a very different and more conservative basis.

Naturally a great deal of private investment of a commercial industrial and residential nature goes into existing government-sponsored new towns and the general policy is to induce more. There is, indeed, a speculative swing towards a more total commitment by developers in the construction of new communities probably on a comparatively small scale and in conjunction with local authorities.

The administration of new towns

Once a new town has been designated by means of draft order and any consequent local public inquiry has been held, a development corporation is established to take overall responsibility for the management of the town and the implementation of the plan. Although their powers are fairly comprehensive, the local authorities and statutory undertakers are still liable for administering such services as health, education, sewage disposal, gas, water and electricity. Where necessary the development corporation can assist either technically or financially. As one might expect, the relationship between them is not always harmonious. The corporations are wholly financed by the exchequer who, with other central government departments, must approve all expenditure and be assured that a reasonable return can be expected. Thus, on the principle of 'he who pays the piper calls the tune', new town policy is directly controlled by Whitehall. Once the development of a particular new town nears completion, its assets, liabilities and responsibility of management are transferred to the New Towns Commission, an *ad hoc* public body set up for the purpose. The Commission will then set up a local executive in the town to fulfil its administrative duties; this has normally comprised the old corporation's staff.

A realization of the desperate plight facing the inner urban areas of many major cities, and a consequent search for remedial measures, has contributed to a policy change by government in respect of new towns. A total reduction of 380,000 in population targets was announced in early 1977 and the development corporations in Bracknell, Skelmersdale, Redditch, Runcorn, Basildon, Corby, Harlow and Stevenage are to be wound up by 1982; many designated planned extensions have been scrapped and proposed population target rises at Basildon, Corby and Runcorn have been refused. The cut-backs have been felt most acutely by the last-generation new towns created since the mid-1960s, such as Peterborough, Milton Keynes, Northampton, Warrington, Telford and Central Lancashire. In Central Lancashire particularly, the reversal of policy represents a serious blow; an expected population growth of around 200,000 has been reduced to a derisory 23,000. A direct connection between new town growth and inner city decline is a difficult and somewhat contrived one to establish, and a halt to the new town programme is in itself unlikely to contribute greatly to arresting the flow of people and jobs from the large cities.

A balanced industrial structure

The severe unemployment that spread throughout the country between the two world wars caused the government to give serious attention to the role and location of industry. The effects of the depression hit some regions harder than others, and a direct link between unemployment and industrial structure was discerned. A scheme to retrain redundant labour from declining industries was introduced in 1928, and following a number of studies into the problem four *special areas*, in South Wales, the North East of England, West Cumberland and Clydeside, where unemployment was particularly acute, were designated under the Special Areas Act 1934. Commissioners were appointed under the Act to assist in improving the prevailing social and economic conditions. It was not until 1936 and the setting up of the Special Areas Reconstruction Association, however, that financial assistance was made available to prospective firms considering development in the special areas. Even then it was limited to small businesses, until the Special Areas Act 1937 extended it to larger concerns as well as introducing a system of tax incentives on a regional basis. It also attempted to encourage the unemployed from 'depressed' areas to retrain and move to other parts of the country. This policy was largely ineffective because of the high level of unemployment throughout the nation.

A major landmark, in terms of town and country planning as well as industrial location, was reached in 1940 with the publication of the report of the Royal Commission on the Distribution of Industrial Population under the chairmanship of Sir Montague Barlow. The Commission had been charged with inquiring 'into the causes which have influenced the present distribution of industrial population' and to 'consider what economic or strategical disadvantages arise from the concentration of industries' and then 'report what remedial measures, if any, should be taken in the national interest'. The Commission proposed the creation of a central agency to oversee the redevelopment of congested areas and assist in the decentralization of industry and population. It recommended that dispersion should be directed to garden cities and satellite towns which would be equipped with trading estates. Because the outbreak of the Second World War mopped up surplus labour for military service and wartime munition production, no immediate action was taken. The stage was set, however, for comprehensive planning at national, regional and local levels, and it is only recently that the policies advocated by the Barlow report have been questioned.

The 1944 White Paper on employment policy, and the subsequent Distribution of Industry Act 1945, again focused attention on the need to achieve balanced industrial development in special areas and a degree of control over industrial location was exercised by means of *building licences* and the designation of *development areas* which were approximately the same as the special areas. At the same time the Board of Trade was empowered to establish industrial trading estates and to build factories on them in order to attract firms to the areas of concern.

The Town and Country Planning Act 1947, besides reforming the entire system of planning, introduced the *industrial development certificate* (IDC) for premises over 5000 square feet as a successor to building licence control in directing the location of industrial development. It also extended development area status to North East Lancashire, Merseyside and parts of the Highlands. Between 1947 and the Local Employment Act of 1960 few measures in respect of industrial structures were enacted. Because of a general 'upswing' in the economy the post-war situation to 1960 was comparatively healthy, and development areas received over 50 per cent of new industrial building.

Since 1960 a wider and more sophisticated range of controls and inducements has been introduced and this is reflected in the current situation.

Recent policy

Two broad categories of measures aimed at obtaining a balanced industrial structure and alleviating unemployment exist today – first, the negative controls preventing expansion in locations deemed unsuitable, such as planning permission itself and IDC requirements, and second, positive inducement to industry to locate where development is required, such as grants, tax concessions and subsidized sites. The areas of concern are classified generally as *scheduled areas* and comprise special development areas, development areas and intermediate areas (Figure 18).

Special development areas were designated in 1967 and consist mainly of the coalmining parts of South Wales, Northumberland, Durham, Cumberland and Ayrshire. *Development areas* are the declining regions first identified in 1945, replaced by development districts in 1960 and selected on the basis of having an employment level above 4.5 per cent, and in turn superseded in 1966 by development areas under the Industrial Development Act. They are not now selected on such strict unemployment criteria and the larger area covered allows industrialists a greater freedom to choose their own location. Almost the whole of Scotland and Wales, large parts of the North of England and sections of Cornwall and Devon are included in this category. The *intermediate areas* were introduced in 1969 following the report and recommendations of the Hunt Committee. They are sometimes described as the 'grey areas' and represent areas of slow natural growth as opposed to actual decline. They were found notably in parts of North West England, Yorkshire and Humberside where reasonably low unemployment rates concealed major structural economic problems, high net out-migration, low activity rates and poor physical infrastructure.

Apart from what has been described as a brief interlude of anti-policy in 1970–1, government assistance has generally been extended throughout the 1970s. Special development area status was extended to Clydeside, Tyneside and Wearside in 1971 as well as intermediate area status to Edinburgh. Moreover, in 1972 the Industry Act re-

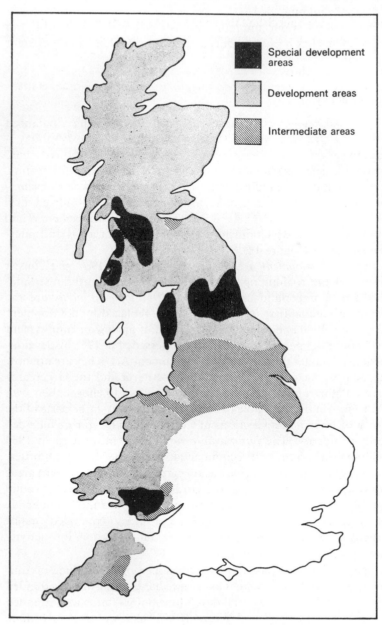

Figure 18   *The assisted areas*

introduced generous levels of grant aid; extended intermediate area status to the remaining parts of the North West, Yorkshire, Humberside and Wales; abolished the need to obtain industrial development certificates in the development and special development areas, and relaxed the threshold elsewhere; and set up new, regionally based, industrial development boards to assist in the allocation of aid. Apart from further changes to the certificate threshold, amendments to the regional employment premium, the extension of development area status to Edinburgh and Cardiff and special development area status to Merseyside and parts of North West Wales, so that more than 40 per cent of all Britain's employed population is contained in assisted areas, and the setting up of the National Enterprise Board and the Welsh and Scottish Development Agencies, the principal policy measures to have been introduced over the past few years in respect of attaining a balanced industrial structure have been directed towards the problems of employment in the inner city, which are discussed separately in a later chapter.

There is still a need, however, to integrate national, regional and local planning more effectively, possibly by means of more powerful regional development agencies. These could co-ordinate the efforts of individual organizations, separate (and all too often competing) local authorities, as well as interpreting national economic policy in a more local physical context.

Green belts

As a restriction on urban growth the notion of a green belt has always occupied an important position in British planning theory. At various times different practical, political and philosophical arguments have been advanced for limiting growth in this way:

1   It prevents the loss of a town's identity.
2   It ensures the economic use of urban land and facilities.
3   It prevents ribbon development.
4   It ensures that adequate recreational facilities are within everyone's reach.
5   It combats air pollution.
6   It preserves the environment.
7   It prevents the erosion of agricultural land.

In 1962 the Ministry of Housing and Local Government produced a pamphlet *Green Belts* which places them in their regional context.[6]

The problem is to reduce employment in the heart of the conurbation and to encourage its growth in towns which, though partly dependent on the great city, are independent to the extent of providing sufficient local employment for the people who live there, as well as shops and opportunities for entertainment and recreation. Looked at in this way, a green belt is seen as a means of shaping the expansion of a city on a regional scale and not just an attempt to combat the forces making for growth.

Thus it implies city regional planning: in fact, Lewis Keeble refers to green belts as 'a faint substitute for regional planning'.[7]

Their origins lie as far back as Greek theory on ideal city size, whereby a town would grow to a predetermined and physically constrained size after which expansion should be catered for in a new settlement on a fresh site. Attempts to encircle London with a girdle of land to conserve its environment and prevent its further growth also have a long history. In the reign of Elizabeth I a proclamation was delivered in 1580 prohibiting the erection of any dwelling within three miles of the City boundary, declaring that 'a city of great multitudes needs restrictions to prevent crowded housing and great poverty'.[8] Elizabethan policy failed, and it was not until the advent of the nineteenth-century reformers that the concept of a green belt was revived. In nearly all of the periods, utopians envisaged new towns of a chosen size set in the countryside surrounded by protected open space. A green belt policy was implicit in the writings of Ebenezer Howard, and in 1919 the Garden Cities and Town and Country Planning Association openly advocated the imposition of rural belts around urban areas. In 1901 Lord Meath, inspired by Chicago's 'green girdle', suggested a similar scheme for London consisting of a chain of parkways set five to nine miles out from the city connecting existing open spaces. Shortly afterwards, in 1910, G. L. Pepler proposed a London ringway 326 feet wide, ten miles out, and in 1914 the London Society produced a plan for the capital which included a circular structure of open spaces even closer in. Further consideration was given to the idea during the 1920s and 1930s, most notably by the Greater London Regional Planning Committee who retained Raymond Unwin as consultant. He put forward two alternatives: first, that a flexible barrier approach should be adopted which could retreat through time with growth, with certain special areas being preserved; second, which he did not recommend, that a fixed permanent open space should be established in which no development should take place. Despite Unwin's reservations it was the latter suggestion which survived to Sir Patrick Abercrombie's Greater

London Plan and was the forerunner of our present metropolitan green belt.

During the 1930s both the Middlesex and London County Councils bought land for the provision of regional open space and in 1947 they obtained the power to designate land for such purposes without having to purchase it. Towards the end of the Second World War, in 1944, Abercrombie produced his Greater London Plan in which, reinforced by the findings of the Barlow Commission relating to the control of growth, he proposed the application of four rings of population growth to limit development. The inner two referred to residential density but the third ring defined a green belt within which no new settlement would occur and where expansion of existing communities would be very restricted. Despite the continued growth of London the green belt has largely survived intact, although a bit 'dog-eared'.

The respective county plans prepared under the 1947 Town and Country Planning Act proposed a green belt slightly smaller than that contained in the Greater London Plan. Their submissions were greatly influenced by central government, and in 1955 Duncan Sandys, then Minister of Housing and Local Government, in Circular 42/55 extended the principle of green belts to provincial centres for the following reasons:

to check the further growth of large built-up areas
to prevent neighbouring towns from merging
to preserve the special character of a town such as Oxford, Cambridge, York or Norwich.

Wherever practicable a green belt was to be several miles wide so as to ensure an appreciable rural zone around the built-up area concerned. Within a green belt, approval was not to be given, except in very special circumstances, for the construction of new buildings or for the change of use of existing buildings for purposes other than agriculture, sport, cemeteries, institutions standing in extensive grounds, or other uses appropriate to a rural area. A further circular laid down the procedure for establishing a green belt and drew the attention of authorities to the need for drawing up a positive development control policy with particular regard for visual amenity within a green belt. In the late 1950s and early 1960s substantial extensions were proposed to London's green belt, the principal statutory green belt and a model for all others, effectively increasing it to over 30 miles wide in places. Different authorities viewed the green belt in varying ways, however, for the London local authorities saw it principally as a means of maintaining recreation land and rural scenery, whereas the surrounding county councils saw it as a method of preserving open agricultural land and halting the spread of London suburbs, thereby retaining their sovereignty. The reorganization of London government in 1964 altered the balance of interest when a significant part of the green belt came under the control of the new local authorities at the expense of the counties.

In 1962 the government published a comprehensive review of green belt policy and its implementation, dealing with such aspects as building restrictions, use of land, definition, descriptions of London and provincial green belts, implications, maintenance and improvement (Figure 19). This review not only reaffirmed the basic belief in green belt policy but also expanded upon the need and implications for future designation. In particular it stressed the desirability of controlling city expansion and encouraging the more efficient use of land within existing urban areas. Despite these avowals, however, a study of planning appeal decisions for the period indicates a divergence between theory and practice, and the 1963 White Paper on London's employment problems and their consequences on land and housing programmes suggested that while a green belt policy should be retained, some of the lower-amenity-value land should be released for housing development. Similarly, the White Paper on South East England in 1964 called upon local authorities to review their proposals for extending the green belt in the light of the need for more housing land, and the theme of relaxing absolute green belt restrictions was continued in the same year in *The South East Study* which called for a greater emphasis to be placed upon an appreciation of the more positive aspects of the policy. The subsequent document *A Strategy for the South East* in 1967 made little impact on the London green belt concept apart from supporting the approved green belt and proposing the use of selected 'country zones' in preference to any further extensions, and the 1970 Strategic Plan for the South East also accentuated the importance of more positive protection for valuable areas of countryside. Moreover, while the 1969 Greater London Development Plan had strongly supported the concept of a metropolitan green belt the panel of inquiry were less enthusiastic, suggesting that it did not appear to be a strong planning tool for conservation and that some land within the green belt would in any event have to be released for housing. Disenchantment continued with two government circulars in 1973 on housing, which though

Figure 19   *Green belts in England and Wales as at 1 May 1962*

restating an adherence to green belt policy called upon local planning authorities to find 2000 acres of land from within it for urgent residential development. Nevertheless, the revised Strategic Plan for the South East also reiterated support for the preservation of the green belt and recommended tighter controls in what they called 'areas of restraint'. More recently a comprehensive study of the London green belt was published in 1976, confirming the relative success of green belt policy but observing that a large amount of housing and employment had taken place as an unfortunate precedent within the belt, that much of the open green belt land close to the urban fringe was of poor appearance and that insufficient open-air land for recreation had been made available. The study recommended that there was a continuing need for the green belt to serve its original purpose with an updating to include strategic regional and environmental planning policies; that such strategic regional policies should encourage development in designated growth areas and provide recreation facilities; that environmental planning policies should be adopted to deal with green belt areas in a manner similar to ordinary countryside planning policy; that varying areas of green belt may require different treatment, with the crucial inner areas needing careful protection of the vulnerable green wedges adjacent to the urban fringe, and the outer areas requiring a careful control of recreation and other uses to protect agricultural viability. A second report by the Standing Conference on London and the South East in 1977 concerned itself with the improvement of green belt policies, noting that structure plans cannot define the boundaries of the metropolitan green belt, which should therefore be implemented by county or district council local plans. It also recommended a 'countryside fringe policy' and the adoption of 'landscape development strategies' to secure the development of visually acceptable landscapes.

It can, therefore, be seen that while the green belt policy is one of the most simple and famous of all planning concepts its implementation is far less straightforward. The approval of 'unfortunate development', the pressures for housing land, the conflict between recreation and agriculture, changing central and local government objectives, and the lack of positive landscape treatment have all combined to erode the effectiveness of green belt policy. Nevertheless, current reassertions of support and recommendations for improved performance in fact promise quite well for the future of the green belt.

Regional planning

The nature and role of regional planning springs from the criticism that central government policy is often too remote and local government administration too parochial. The need emerges for an intermediary at the regional scale to provide a meeting place for national economic planning and more local physical land use planning. The overall expression of a national plan should not be exclusively concerned with merely securing, for example, 5 per cent economic growth, but should also seek to provide an appropriate framework for the planning of such elements as country parks, motorways, water catchment and mineral resources. Although as yet there is no common approach or accepted procedure, it is the regional scale that best lends itself to initially translating economic policy into physical form.

The concept of regional planning is thus largely based upon national economic planning and the need to translate this into a physical context that both defines the problem and facilitates the implementation of solutions. The overall management of a country's resources by central government involves a certain degree of interference with market forces to ensure that no one part of the nation, or sector of the community, benefits unduly at the expense of another. It also implies, however, a distribution or redistribution of assets in such a way as to benefit the whole and every sector of the community. At its outset, therefore, any attempt at a rational approach towards comprehensive regional planning is beset by divisions in interest and attitude.

Two principal aspects of regional planning can thus be identified, economic and physical. It is with the latter, the physical aspect, that this section is concerned, although it cannot be emphasized enough that its nature is largely determined by the former with its roots firmly planted in location theory and the philosophy of the hierarchy of settlements.

The puzzle of defining a region for planning purposes has caused much research, debate and controversy. A region is capable of meaning all things to all men and no special classification exists to assist definition. The following categories of regional scales amply portray the problem:

Physical. A regional identity can be discerned by a particular topography, such as the Lake District; or a form of agriculture, such as vineyards, hopfields and sheep farming; or a distinctive landscape, like the Devonshire lanes or Cotswold cottages; or by an area of water catchment.

Economic. A region might relate to a certain economic sphere or influence like a market town, shopping centre, or focus of employment whose tentacles of commuting delimit the boundaries. Similarly it might be identified by a common economic problem such an unemployment in coalmining.

Ethnic. Probably one of the most obvious influences of regional identity is a common heritage, tradition, accent or language. People are often only too anxious to attach labels such as North Walean, Lancastrian or Man of Kent to themselves.

Administrative. A more recent developments is the selection of a region for the purposes of administration or management. This can relate to local government, as with metropolitan administration by the Greater London Council, or to statutory undertakers like the various regional electricity, gas or water boards.

Regional scientists have traditionally classified these aspects under three differently styled, but similarly conceived, headings. First, the *homogeneous* region that relates to a natural, and often static, combination of physical, social, ethnic or other characteristics. Second, the *nodal* or *polar* region which is based upon more dynamic and economic activities grouped around a central place. And third, the *programming* or *policy-oriented* region, almost identical to the previously described administrative region. Usually it is a form of pragmatic compromise that actually determines the nature of a region, with a large degree of overlap between the respective categories.

Perhaps the first attempt at land use planning on the regional scale was Sir Patrick Abercrombie's London Plan in 1944. London's influence has since been more widely discerned, and the Strategic Plan for the South East published in 1967 looks at the physical problems of accommodating a projected population increase while at the same time checking excessive growth. Another instance of regional planning in this country is the *South Hampshire Study* which investigated the future requirements of the Southampton–Portsmouth region. This, however, is closer to the scale that is more commonly described as 'sub-regional', which is employed in the implementation of strategic planning when all elements of the planning process are to be considered, and there is a need to transcend existing local authority boundaries. It is represented by the *Teesside Study* undertaken by private consultants and published in 1969, the *North Gloucestershire Sub-Regional Study* initiated in 1966 and published in 1970, and the *Coventry, Solihull, Warwickshire Sub-Regional Planning Study* which also reported in 1970.

Early attempts to control the use of land in this country were almost exclusively local in application. The first Town Planning Act in 1909 did not so much as hint at the fact that demand for land should be reconciled on a basis less parochial than the existing local authority boundaries, let alone on a regional scale. It was not until the 1920s and 1930s with the southward drift of labour, the disparity of earnings, rising unemployment in the north, combined with steady and occasionally spectacular growth in the south, that any great concern was displayed regarding the imbalance of regional resources. In a period of what we consider to be serious unemployment, it is worth remembering that the number of unemployed in Jarrow in 1934 was almost 70 per cent. The first legislative attempt to combat the worst excesses of the depression was the Special Areas Act of 1934 which defined certain areas, including South Wales, the North East, Glasgow and the areas around Barrow-in-Furness, as warranting special financial assistance to stimulate industrial growth and thus employment. Although some potential demand was deflected, the 'boom' continued unabated in the South East. In consequence the government set up a royal commission to report on the distribution of the industrial population (the Barlow report, published in 1940). This set a pattern for future regional planning policies by calling for a balanced distribution and appropriate diversification of industry and employment throughout the various areas of Great Britain. With the onset of the Second World War little was done immediately but the report remained as a blueprint for future action. Despite the Minister being charged with 'securing consistency and continuity in the framing and execution of a national policy with respect to the use and development of land throughout England and Wales' in 1943 there was little conscious endeavour towards an integrated regional policy implicit in the 1947 Town and Country Planning Act. The 'never had it so good' reflationary period during the 1950s delayed the need for concerted government action. The reappearance of unemployment in the less favoured regions combined with the increasing obsolescence of development plans in the early 1960s focused attention on the problem of regional imbalance. As a result a series of regional studies were instituted. They were conducted jointly by the Ministry and the

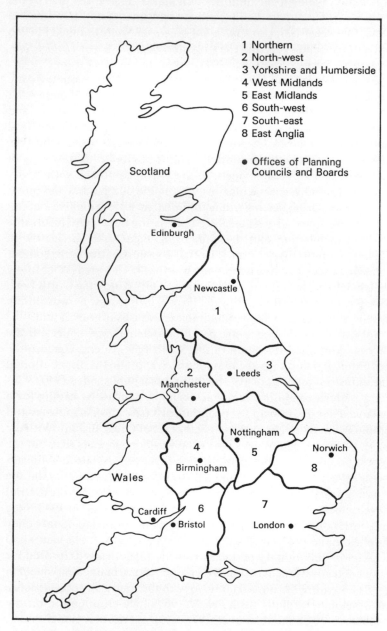

Figure 20   *The planning regions*

constituent local authorities, and were first directed at the South East, the North West and the West Midlands. *The South East Study* was produced in 1964 and demonstrated an unprecedented scale of physical planning, with proposals for whole new cities in the Solent, Milton Keynes and Newbury areas, together with new town development and expansion of existing towns like Peterborough, Ipswich and Swindon, all intended to act as counter-magnets to the insuperable growth of London.

Nevertheless, *The South East Study* was still severely criticized for undertaking its investigation, and putting forward its recommendations, in isolation, not placing enough weight upon the need and condition of other regions. The pressure for consistency in physical planning at the regional level and continuity with national economic policy encouraged the Labour Government in 1965 to transfer the responsibility for its direction to the ill-fated Department of Economic Affairs. At the same time ten regional economic planning councils were set up, eight in England and one each in Scotland and Wales (Figure 20). The councils comprise individual members of the public selected by the Minister and drawn from such fields as industry, politics and the universities. They act in a purely advisory capacity, having no executive power to implement their proposals. They are supported by regional planning boards which are staffed by civil servants representing the various ministries concerned with regional matters.

The creation of this regional planning machinery was intended to provide a framework for the execution of national policy and thus set broad objectives for each particular region and to generate a climate within which these objectives could be achieved. Owing to the lack of administrative authority, disenchantment has spread among members of the various councils who have felt a certain impotency and frustration at being relegated to what has been described as merely the role of regional stocktakers. Not only have the councils as a whole been left in a vacuum, but they have also acted in isolation, one region often competing with another for industrial favours and growth.

While they have not always dovetailed in the manner expected, it should, in all fairness, be said that they have provided a more comprehensive and flexible machinery for the operation of physical planning and the allocation of national resources between regions. The keynote of their policy, in the form of a plan, will therefore be primarily concerned with broad strategies regarding future commercial expansion, general accessibility, urban growth, and perhaps large-scale recreation facilities. The plan should not be fixed and rigid but aim to stimulate the adoption of its strategic proposals at the local scale. Because regional planning should express national policy it is greatly affected by the various tools of economic planning such as industrial development certificates, tax concessions, investment incentives, loans, grants, and so on. Perhaps too much emphasis is placed upon industrial employment, and more consideration should be given to other aspects such as planned decline, leisure facilities, agricultural production, and service industry.

One further feature of regional planning merits attention and that is the development of the theory of 'growth points' or 'growth poles' which aims at focusing economic activity on particular points within a region. These need not necessarily be existing centres but would have a latent potential for exceptional growth that can be stimulated by the introduction of certain industry, or services, or by the upgrading of a particular road system. This would release the latent growth potential and produce beneficial multiplier effects throughout the region.

3 The foundations of town planning legislation

Historical development

The foundations of modern town planning legislation were laid in the Public Health and Housing Acts of the nineteenth century which set out to ameliorate the 'monster clots of humanity' where 'the working man is pacing the low, dim swampy habitation good enough for the creation of wealth'.[1] Stimulated by Ebenezer Howard's example, and spurred on by the pressure of influential bodies advocating the adoption in this country of the powers available to municipal authorities in Germany to plan the extensions of towns in advance and control the subsequent development,[2] the government introduced the Housing, Town Planning etc. Bill in 1909.

The Housing, Town Planning etc. Act 1909

The powers provided by this Act were essentially permissive, allowing local authorities or landowners to prepare schemes for land close to towns 'in such a way as to secure proper sanitary conditions, amenity and convenience', and confined itself merely to listing the most important elements of a scheme as: streets, roads and other ways, and stopping up or diversion of existing highways; buildings, structures and erections; open spaces; the preservation of objects of historical interest or natural beauty; sewerage, drainage and sewage disposal; lighting; water supply; and ancillary works. It did not relate to land already developed or unlikely to be developed, and the administrative procedures were tortuous and complex, requiring a local authority to obtain permission from the Local Government Board before it could even begin to prepare a scheme, let alone take any action to implement it. They were also obliged to give all parties likely to be affected by the proposals extraordinary rights of consultation and objection at every stage, and the general provisions of each scheme had to be laid before Parliament. It was criticized at the time for being too timid an enactment, and many leading proponents of the fast emerging town planning movement were greatly disappointed at its cautious and uncertain approach. Owing to the voluntary nature and limited scope of the Act, the onerous and virtually unworkable compensation provisions, the slump in estate development and the First World War, only thirteen schemes were formally submitted out of an authorized 172, and only a handful actually implemented in the first ten years up to 1919. The introduction of statutory town planning was, therefore, a comparatively modest affair and has been described as follows:

Its application was an option exercisable only in the face of deterrents; it applied in any case only to a small proportion of land and a narrow range of conditions; and it was concerned only with the physical layout of land and buildings; the social considerations which might guide that layout were left either to be disregarded or to be sought empirically for every separate scheme. Statutory town planning was no more than a halting advance, not a conclusive victory.[3]

The Housing, Town Planning etc. Act 1919

This Act removed the necessity of obtaining the consent of the Local Government Board before preparing a scheme. It also enabled two or more authorities to prepare joint schemes for planning purposes, thus providing the first glimmerings of regional planning. It did, however, make the preparation of schemes for all land in the course of development, or likely to be used for building purposes, obligatory upon all boroughs and urban districts with a population of over 20,000. The Act also introduced the idea of 'interim development' whereby the Minister was empowered to permit development to proceed while the scheme was being prepared even though it might not eventually conform to the policy. In practice an interim development order was issued by the relevant local authority, which if not obtained could seriously jeopardize a developer's right to compensation if subsequent action was taken to implement the schemes.

The Town Planning Act 1925

For the first time town planning was separated from housing and although no new provisions were enacted all existing legislation was consolidated in this one measure.

The Local Government Act 1929

This Act introduced county councils into the hierarchy of planning authorities. They were given wide-ranging highway responsibilities, as well as being empowered to act in place of a county district council which had neglected to prepare a planning scheme when required to do so. They were also entitled to be represented on joint committees, the formation of which the Minister could direct together with the proportion of each constituent authority's representation. Any urban or rural district council was entitled under the Act to voluntarily relinquish its planning powers to the county council.

The Town and Country Planning Act 1932

All existing legislation relating to town planning was repealed and a new code, including the reference for the first time to country planning, was enacted. Many important changes were made, the most notable of which were:

1 It extended the power to make schemes to land already built upon or never likely to be built upon. This advance heralded the onset of comprehensive planning.
2 It extended the provisions for interim development control.
3 The necessity of obtaining the Minister's consent for a planning scheme was reimposed. It also had to be laid before Parliament for twenty-one days following the Minister's consent.
4 The imposition of a fixed date upon local authorities by which schemes had to be prepared was repealed.
5 Some degree of flexibility to allow for the modification and amendment of schemes was introduced.
6 Increased power was given to local authorities to secure the retention of amenities, including the protection of trees and woodland, and the control over hoardings and advertisements.

The Minister of Town and Country Planning Act 1943

The responsibility for planning had rested with the Minister of Health until 1942 when it was transferred to the Minister of Works and Planning. In 1943 these powers and duties were assigned to a separate minister who was charged with 'securing consistency and continuity in the framing and execution of a national policy with respect to the use and development of land throughout England and Wales'.

The Town and Country Planning (Interim Development) Act 1943

Although the changes made by this Act were few, they were none the less important. The principal measure brought all land throughout England and Wales for which no planning scheme had been made under *interim development control*; thereby any person wishing to undertake development had first to obtain permission, otherwise the development could be removed without payment of compensation if it did not accord with any subsequent scheme.

The Town and Country Planning Act 1944

This Act, which was hailed as introducing an element of 'positive planning' for the first time, authorized local authorities to acquire land which had suffered extensive war damage, sometimes called 'blitzed' land, or which suffered from bad layout or obsolete development, sometimes described as 'blighted' land. Procedures for compulsory purchase were expedited, the powers of acquisition, management and disposal widened, and the basis of compensation adjusted to the 1939 value.

The Town and Country Planning Act 1947

This Act provided a landmark in the history of town planning legislation. It repealed all other enactments and inaugurated comprehensive planning. Its main provisions can be grouped under two headings, financial and physical planning. The financial provisions are dealt with elsewhere.

In respect of the administration of physical planning in England and Wales, the responsibility was vested in county councils and county borough councils, taking the place of the 1400 previous local authorities. These new authorities were required to prepare and submit a *development plan* for their area to the Minister within three years from 1 July 1948. These plans indicated how they proposed that the land in their area should be used. They were intended to be subject to revision every five years. Having drawn up the development plan no owner of land, with certain exceptions, was allowed to 'develop' his land without first obtaining planning permission from the local planning authority. Appeal against a local planning authority's decision lay to the Minister. Wide powers to control development and enforce their decisions were granted to the new authorities. It is impossible to exaggerate the importance of the 1947 Act for it provided the most comprehensive and radical framework for the control of land use in the world. The development plan and development control systems it established operated without any significant change for over twenty years, and during that time this machinery for planning administration and policy implementation has, despite its shortcomings, been the envy of the world.

The present position

No sooner had the Town and Country Planning Act 1962 been passed, consolidating existing legislation, than pressure was exerted to review the planning system and consider possible change. Criticism was levelled at the prevailing procedure on the following grounds. It was said to be based upon development plans that were too certain, fixed and rigid, which inexorably led to a stultification of the planning system and an inordinate number of appeals. They were said to reflect local land use rather than integrated planning policy. The entire process had become overloaded, cumbersome and slow, there being in the region of 400,000 applications for planning permission each year, of which over 12,000 went to appeal. Delay, then as now, brought planning into disrepute. While the notion of development control was considered essential to effective land use planning, the plan upon which it operated appeared to stress the negative aspects of control as opposed to providing a positive stimulus to the creation of a good environment. The administration was over-centralized, general principles of a strategic nature were concealed by a host of detail; consequently the Minister required on average about three years to consider the submission of a development plan, by which time it might well have become out of date. There was said to be little or no co-ordination between contiguous authorities which seriously detracted from the practice of effective regional planning. Further, it was stated that there had been inadequate participation by the public in the planning process, and insufficient regard paid to their interest.[4]

All these defects, and more, were described in the report by the Minister's Planning Advisory Group which was set up in 1964 to review the future of development plans. Published in 1965, the report made a number of proposals which were introduced in the 1968 Town and Country Planning Act, and now appear re-enacted in the 1971 Town and Country Planning Act.

The Town and Country Planning Act 1968

This measure introduced a development plan system possessing a new form, content and procedure. It created a two-tier hierarchy of plans, aimed at providing a broader and more flexible range of plans at a strategic level, and yet a more certain, pertinent and detailed picture at the local scale. These provisions are now included in the 1971 Town and Country Planning Act. As and when the Secretary of State for the Environment was satisfied that a local planning authority was of the appropriate area, and suitably staffed, they were allowed to adopt the new procedures. This entailed the preparation of a *structure plan* and subsequent *local plans* for its area. Together these form the *development plan*.

The structure plan

This is basically a written statement accompanied by any necessary supporting diagrammatic illustrations and is designed to introduce a large measure of flexibility into the system. The structure plan is intended to translate national and regional, economic and social policies into a local context, and in doing so provide a framework for the implementation of local plans. While establishing the general aims and proposals for the area it should also contain the overall development control policy which can then be applied in particular circumstances at the more detailed and specific local plan stage. Whereas the 1962 style development plan had, to a large extent, failed in integrating the various land use systems and the agencies responsible for them, the structure plan will provide a basis for co-ordinating decisions between the various local authority departments and committees, as well as between the planning authority itself and the various constituent authorities and statutory undertakers who possess an interest in different aspects of the plan. Moreover, the planning of these various systems will often entail a certain degree of overlap between neighbouring authorities. Co-operation and co-ordination between them in terms of aims, policy, standards and survey material is therefore imperative.

One aspect where the structure plan is intended to improve on the past performance of the 'old style' development plans is in respect of those areas that have a high priority for comprehensive and intensive treatment. Because of their magnitude, the cost involved, and a lack of urgency the old *comprehensive development areas* conceived in the

1947 Act and perpetuated in the 1962 Act were all too often abortive or still-born. In an attempt to remedy this situation the new procedure allows for the indication of *action areas* which must be included in the structure plan. Another element that has been much neglected is the role that can be played by forces other than the local authority, and it is important that the structure plan should have regard to degree and proportion of public and private investment implicit in the respective planning policy and the contribution that various external agencies can play in its implementation.

Structure plans are not geared to a specific date, for different elements in the plan will require different time scales. Rather it will draw attention to those aspects that demand treatment in the short run, such as action area programmes and new housing development. It will outline the various stages at which particular policies will be put into practice. The projected population in 1981 and 1991 will be indicated so as to establish a basis upon which the housing, employment, communication and public facility needs can be judged. Some objectives of the plan will not be related to any precise date but will denote the long-term strategy for the area. Unlike the quinquennial reviews of the old style 1947 and 1962 Act development plans, structure plans will be subject to continual review depending upon the changing needs and conditions of the community.

Format

Naturally the exact nature of the structure plan will largely be determined by the individual characteristics of the area concerned. There will, however, be certain features common to all plans. They will all relate to national and regional policy as well as taking into account the strategies of neighbouring authorities. They should also contain:

1 A descriptive analysis of the social, economic and physical characteristics of the area.
2 A critical appraisal of the success or failure of existing policies and a summary of any commitments that might affect future policy. Moreover,
3 A county structure plan should define the authority's position in respect of adjoining areas and identify any mutual sub-regional spheres of influence. It should also examine the main planning issues in the countryside, such as journey to work, employment, population growth or decline, agriculture, forestry and conservation.

4   An urban structure plan should also examine the links it has with surrounding authorities and assess the nature of its hinterland. It will describe the principal functions of the town, whether they be industrial, commercial, marketing or associated with tourism. It will examine the pattern, distribution and nature of activities throughout the town and identify any problems that arise therefrom such as obsolescence, traffic congestion, lack of open space and outdated layout.

5   From this appraisal the authority should state its aim in terms of the area's efficiency and environment. This will provide a broad indication of what the plan is seeking to achieve.

6   The crucial stage of the structure plan is the formulation of the strategy which co-ordinates the aims of the plan and sets out the way in which it is hoped they will be accomplished. The plan will normally explain how the strategy was selected from the various alternatives that presented themselves, and illustrate the more detailed proposals and policies for particular areas and specific subjects.

The following subjects or elements would be appropriate for individual attention within the structure plan.[5]

population	shopping
employment	education
resources	social and community services
housing	recreation and leisure
industry	conservation
commerce	utility services
transportation	minerals

Process

The process for preparing a structure plan is based upon the statutory requirements contained in the 1971 and 1972 Town and Country Planning Acts and the 1972 Local Government Act, together with subsequent regulations made under the 1971 Act and supplemented by various circulars, directives and guidance notes issued by the Department of the Environment (DoE). Though local authorities are not constrained by any set procedure for the preparation of structure plans, apart from certain legal requirements concerning public participation and the report of survey, a roughly similar approach towards the task was initially adopted by most authorities, strongly influenced by 'systems theory' and a DoE publication *Management Networks – A Study for Structure Plans* issued in 1971. Some of the various stages by which a structure plan is prepared and approved can be summarized as follows:

1 Plan preparation commences with the production of a project report by the local authority setting out the scope of the plan, a programme of those studies that have to be undertaken, a time-table of the work involved, an outline of how the local authority intends the work to be performed and an indication of the manpower implications. This report acts as a basis for preliminary discussions with the DoE, neighbouring councils and other government agencies, and project reports have now been prepared for all areas of England and Wales.

2 At the same time as the local authority starts work on a structure plan the regional office of the DoE sets up an 'appraisal team' consisting of administrative and professional planning staff and supported by representatives of other relevant government departments. This appraisal team follows the plan through until approval, initially monitoring the plan's preparation and later being responsible for briefing the panel at the examination in public, having also drawn up the DoE representations for the examination. Finally, the appraisal team has an important role in formulating any modifications which are made to the plan.

3 Work on the actual structure plan itself naturally begins with a study of the existing situation and an analysis of the findings. In practice this stage has proved to be complex and time-consuming. Forecasting change is always a problematical exercise, and, despite government advice on possible ways of measuring and predicting growth or decline, no standard procedures have been evolved. This has led to considerable dispute at examinations in public about conflicting forecasts. Because of what appeared to be the excessive amount of time taken over surveys and analysis the DoE advised local authorities in a 1974 circular not to be preoccupied with the analysis of data or the use of sophisticated techniques which might make only a marginal contribution to the choice between alternative policies.

4 The local authority then has to identify the various strategic policies available to it. This involves deciding on the likely size and possible location of future growth or decline so as to minimize the potential problems and maximize the opportunities indicated in the

initial studies and forecasts. These series of alternative strategies then form the basis for consultation with neighbouring authorities and the first public participation exercise. Subsequently these strategies are evaluated in the light of the consultative and participatory procedures and a single basic strategy for the structure plan evolved. The policies and proposals for the implementation of this preferred strategy are then brought together and presented in a draft written statement.

5   This draft plan is then publicized and the public are encouraged to comment upon it as a second obligatory stage of participation. The plan is also submitted to the regional office of the DoE and discussed at a non-statutory 'presentation meeting', the aim being to clarify matters of possible doubt and to alert the local authority to matters which the DoE feels might have to be reconsidered and revised. When the public participation exercise has been completed and any necessary revisions have been made following public comment and the observations of the DoE, the structure plan is submitted to the Secretary of State and the formal administrative review procedure begins.

6   Having determined that the submitted document fulfils the statutory definition of a structure plan, the DoE prepares for the plan's *examination in public*. The introduction of this new method of appraising planning policy was designed to accelerate the process of public discussion and provide guidelines for central government review. Although the examination is held in public it does not constitute a final judgement on the plan, being primarily a forum to clarify which parts of the plan require modification. It is not a free-ranging discussion for further public participation, and the DoE is responsible for determining the issues to be discussed and the participants to be heard. The panel for the public examination consists of an independent chairman, an officer from the DoE regional office not previously involved in the preparation of the plan, and an experienced planning inquiry inspector, who are all supported by a secretary and a technical officer from the DoE. There is a code of practice for the conduct of the examination, setting out the basic criteria for consideration and stressing that the examination 'will be directed to the matters which the Secretary of State considers need to be further investigated . . . it is the occasion for covering in public the matters to be examined . . . but not for endless arguments or for pursuing points for their own sake'.[6] The main matters to be discussed are any clashes between national policies and the structure

plan, compliance with existing regional strategy, and consistency with the policies of neighbouring authorities. The policies contained within the plan are also examined to ensure internal consistency and the availability of sufficient resources to effect implementation. The appropriateness of the structure plan as a context for local plans is scrutinized to make sure that sufficient information is provided to guide local plan preparation without supplying so much detail as to usurp the districts' local planning function.

7   When the examination in public is over the panel prepares a report which is 'an assessment of the selected matters in the light of the discussion which has taken place at the examination and will contain recommendations'.[7] The recommendations relate to such matters as the size and location of growth strategies, the policies for a particular issue or area, the level of generality or detail, the approach and methods of the plan makers, and changing conditions since the plan was prepared. Recommendations have been made, for example, changing a growth strategy deemed to be too low (Solihull), incorporating a revised pattern of housing demand (Birmingham), allowing for a faster decline in birth rate (Suffolk), withdrawing a by-pass proposal (Teesside and Cleveland), and providing for gypsy sites (Birmingham). The panel's reports typically take from about three to six months to prepare, and are submitted to the Secretary of State so that he can then decide whether to reject or approve the plan, with or without modifications. In this he is assisted by a detailed list of points prepared by the DoE appraisal team highlighting any matters which they feel have not been dealt with in sufficient detail, the implications of the report on other stated government policies, and how the recommendations can best be put into effect by way of either reservations or modifications. A preliminary decision letter is then compiled and circulated to relevant government departments for amendment. Eventually a final draft analysis and decision letter is given to the Secretary of State for final consideration and approval; he, following service of a tentative notice of his intentions upon the local authority (for further discussion), publishes formal notice of approval. To date this final stage has been extremely long, lasting a matter of three or four years, owing largely to the novelty of the system and the early complex grouping of examinations; however, the DoE hopes that the review process can be streamlined to last fifteen to eighteen months from submission to approval.

Appraisal

Critics of structure planning and structure plans have been numerous, and among the many castigations of the process are that:

1   Regional policy is neither clear nor effective enough as a proper basis for the preparation of structure plans in a coherent pattern for a region.

2   In their present form the plans are essentially growth-oriented instruments requiring additional application of resources to secure implementation.

3   The plans are potentially very sensitive to changes in social, economic or administrative policy.

4   The DoE appears to adopt the role of co-ordinating planning policy as opposed to promoting and innovating, so that national policy is itself diluted to being merely a low level of common consensus, avoiding obvious contradiction.

5   There has been a preoccupation with techniques of analysis and prediction, particularly in the early stages of the process, which attempt to refine the appraisal of such factors as population change, housing need and economic trends beyond their capacity.

6   Delay has been an endemic feature of the system. While it is perhaps unfair to refer back to 1968 as the introduction of structure planning, given the reorganization of local government operative from 1974, it is nevertheless the case that twenty-six commencement orders were made before 1974 when the commencement order for the rest of the country was introduced, and by April 1978 only forty-two of the seventy-nine proposed structure plans for England and Wales had been submitted, of which eleven were approved and a further twenty-two examined in public. Even the DoE stated in 1974 that structure plans should be submitted not later than 1 April 1978, intimating that authorities themselves thought this attainable, and now aspires to 1982 as a final date for the functioning of a fully approved fretwork of plans.

7   Many early structure plans tended to dwell on detailed matters inappropriate for that level of plan.

8   They do not always make clear exactly what the particular authority is trying to achieve, making it difficult for other agencies, particularly those involved in implementing the policy, to act on them in a desired fashion.

9   It is difficult to link structure planning as portrayed by the early

plans with the emergent corporate management approach being adopted by many authorities.
10 Proper public participation has proved to be a particularly intractable task.

A partial recognition of some of these problems was demonstrated by the DoE in 1974 in a circular[8] which abandoned the idea of structure plans being all-embracing policy documents, and encouraged local authorities to consider the character of their own area and then only include in the structure plan those 'key' issues requiring most urgent attention. The circular envisaged that housing, employment and transport would be key issues in most plans, but that other issues would vary between different areas. This advice can reasonably be interpreted as a central government endorsement of a shift in planning thought away from the comprehensive approach to what has been described as a 'mixed scanning' approach, which attempts to identify selected priority problems of policy demanding early and close attention. A later circular,[9] issued in 1977, not only confirms the notion of concentrating on key issues but also reduces the status of *Development Plans: A Manual on Form and Content* by suggesting that it should only be used as a guide. Nevertheless, considerable latitude is afforded to individual structure planning authorities in the devising of their own particular plan, and one county council has taken advantage of this to produce an interesting and attractive variant. East Sussex felt that the production of a structure plan was required as quickly as possible in order to provide a framework for more detailed planning in the county, and, therefore, by concentrating on the key issues, they decided to produce a plan within a year and subsequently revise it on an annual basis. It can be argued that in breaking away from traditional blueprint planning the East Sussex approach, which has now gone through several annual cycles, represents a much more realistic view of the planning function. It recognizes that important omissions have to be made at times – a much needed major study of rural transport, for example, was delayed for a couple of years – but it also has the advantage of linking both short- and long-term planning policy with available financial resources determined by an annual budget.

The scope, format and function of structure plans is still evolving, and as the production of both additional structure plans and the more detailed local plans takes place the relationships between the various scales of planning may become clearer. For commentators and critics of the structure planning process, however, it is all to easy to recall the words of Max Beerbohm that 'There is much to be said for failure. It is more interesting than success'.

Local plans

There are three different types of local plans:

District plans, intended for the comprehensive planning of large areas

Action area plans, for comprehensive planning of those areas indicated in the structure plan for improvement, development or redevelopment, starting within the next ten years

Subject plans, which deal with particular aspects within the structure plan.

All of them consist of a map together with other diagrams, illustrations and a written statement. Although a local planning authority may undertake the preparation of local plans, and embark upon the various steps involved in public participation, they cannot become statutorily enforceable until the structure plan has been approved.

The overall purpose of local plans is to make the new system of development plans more adaptable to changing circumstances, being more detailed and more certain in character while at the same time being more flexible in application. The very nature of local plans is expected to vary according to prevailing circumstances in different areas. There is, therefore, a wide range of possible local plans with no standard form of presentation or procedure for implementation. There is no specific scale set down for them, apart from a minimum scale of 1:25,000 for rural areas, 1:10,000 for villages and towns in counties, 1:10,000 (but more usually 1:25,000) for district plans of large towns, and 1:1250 for central area plans. Because they are likely to get out of date more quickly than structure plans, and great weight is attached to their currency, they do not require the Secretary of State's approval, and the responsibility for their review, alteration, repeal and replacement lies with the local planning authority. In exceptional circumstances the Secretary of State may direct that the plan shall not have any effect unless it has his approval.

There are four major functions common to most local plans:

1   They apply the strategy of structure plans.
2   They provide a detailed basis for development control.
3   They provide a basis for co-ordinating development.
4   They bring local and detailed planning issues before the public.

Not only must the local plan relate to the structure plan, indicating the method whereby overall objectives are translated into more specific policies and proposals for the area they cover, but it must also be consistent with other local plans. This presumes that full consultation between the local planning authority and the constituent local authorities, together with the appropriate measures to ensure full citizen participation, take place.

The 1972 Local Government Act had a significant influence on the new two-tier system of local planning authorities formally created in 1974. The relevant functions of each type of authority are outlined in the Act and district councils are designated as the authorities with the primary responsibility for the preparation of local plans. In so doing, the Act provides for the preparation of *development plan schemes* to be drawn up by county authorities to:

designate the planning authority to prepare and adopt each local plan
specify the title and nature of each plan with an indication of its scope
specify the area covered by each plan
set out the programmes for the preparation of each plan
indicate the relationship between plans for an area, stating those to be
    prepared concurrently with the structure plan.

A subsequent circular was issued by the DoE in 1974 in the absence of specific regulations covering development plan schemes. It urged speed in preparing schemes so as to remove uncertainty from the situation and to bring out priorities for more urgently needed plans. In suggesting that it was not necessary to include all possible local plans at first instance, the circular also stressed that the capacity of the local district authority to prepare local plans should be considered, and where it was inadequate, and the scope of the plan could equally be applied to a wider area, such as a subject plan, then the county authority should be responsible for the preparation. The Town and Country Planning (Structure and Local Plans) Regulations 1974 were also introduced with the aim of providing further guidance on the form and content of local, as well as structure plans which include those aspects to be covered in a local plan, together with the procedures a local authority should employ to ensure final adoption of the plan.

District plans

These local plans are prepared for the comprehensive planning of relatively large areas, usually where change will take place in a piecemeal fashion over a comparatively medium- to long-term period. According to the development plans manual this relates to parts, or the whole, of a town and to rural parts of counties. In selecting areas for district plan preparation, priority should be given to those areas which are under pressure for development or re-development and where there will be a greater need for control. The functions of a statutory district plan can be summarized as:

in general, to set out the planning policies for each area, to restate and amplify the long-term planning intentions of the structure plan, to describe specific proposals, and to lay down development control criteria

in urban areas, to apply the structure plan policies for environmental planning and management

to contain policies for the management of the environment, which includes action that does not fall within the definition of development and is therefore not under planning control.

The size limits for a local district plan were originally set at between 5000 and 75,000 people, which seems to indicate that central government did not intend metropolitan districts with populations of around 250,000 to use them for the comprehensive coverage of their entire area, although this is exactly what has happened in a number of cases. District plans can, therefore, cover a wide range of issues in respect of specific areas and detail the policies for change of a local authority in those areas. Such plans form by far the greatest proportion of local plans contained in current development plan schemes proposed by county councils.

Action area plans

These plans are intended to guide the comprehensive planning of areas suitable for treatment within ten years, and as such are the leading instrument for short-term change. If the preparation of an action area plan is thought apposite for a particular area it must initially be indicated in the structure plan. Once this is done the plan must then be prepared as soon as is practicable.

The essence of these plans is their urgency, for they are intended to replace the comprehensive development area plans initiated by the 1947 Town and Country Planning Act, which tended to reflect the optimism of local planning authorities ideals rather than the pragmatism of their abilities. The action area is, therefore, more tightly drawn and is concerned with intensive investment and innovation. It may relate to a whole range of proposed development, city centre, district centre, old and new residential areas, industrial, civic, commercial, shopping or recreation uses. Further, they may be concerned with the reclamation of derelict land, conservation areas or country parks. The action proposed need not relate exclusively to that taken by public agencies but might include private development or perhaps a combination of both.

Subject plans

Where matters require a detailed development policy, but are not suitable for inclusion in the comprehensive district plan, a subject plan may be prepared. This will generally relate to issues that cover a wide area, such as the reclamation of derelict land in a number of places within a county, the visual treatment of a motorway corridor, or a policy towards footpaths throughout a local authority area.

Subject plans should be concerned with 'a consideration of a particular description of development or other use of land in the area' and are often used to give effect to administrative procedures associated with structure plans, such as the powers and grants available in green belt areas. The development plans manual outlines certain criteria upon which a subject plan should be based:

1   The subject should have limited interaction with other planning issues, so that it can be planned in isolation.
2   The subject should cover an area wide enough to warrant separate treatment.
3   Local policies and proposals are not required in advance of a comprehensive plan in areas where the structure plan may provide a framework for development control.

The DoE envisages that most local planning can be dealt with in district and action area plans, while subject plans should be reserved for occasions where there is an urgent need to develop a particular policy. Such is the restrictive nature of subject plans, therefore, that very few have, in fact, been prepared.

Appraisal

The local planning process is still in its infancy, and although little analysis has so far been undertaken, and consequently little published research is available, much of what has been written has been largely critical. Among the main criticisms are:

1   That, rightly or wrongly, many district planning authorities are acting against the guidance of the development plans manual and developing different approaches towards the nature and function of local plans and the process of local plan preparation. Some are following the manual's approach and preparing plans from a limited policy viewpoint, while others are adopting a much broader approach, identifying and responding to issues regardless of whether they fall within the statutory planning remit.[10] This is said to lead to confusion and uncertainty.

2   The further criticism is also levelled at some local plans that they place too much emphasis upon physical aspects. The Home Office report on deprivation,[11] for example, evidences the argument that in the past planners have tended to see urban deprivation in physical terms, and framed physical solutions to the problem such as *Housing action area* and *housing improvement area* programmes.

3   As a corollary, few district authorities are now likely to prepare a district plan that contains only land use proposals, particularly if the county structure plan, as previously observed, concentrates on a number of key issues. While central government still retains an ordered view of the levels of planning, it is becoming increasingly clear in practice that the division of respective responsibilities between county and district, and therefore structure plan and local plan, is neither simple nor explicit. It may be possible to achieve a successful bond between strategy and tactics within the existing procedures, but, in some authorities, district plan making powers are either expended in the preparation of a surrogate structure plan or inadequately underpinned by more partial subject plans or action area plans.

4   Because of a growing policy orientation in local planning there is a distinct danger of losing the necessary local environmental framework required for implementation and development control. The likelihood is, therefore, that there will emerge a tendency towards the production and use of informal plans with all their inherent capriciousness.

5   It is often said that local plans are too narrow in their format, being prepared predominantly by the town planning department of a local authority and viewed by other departments as having but a

marginal impact on their activities. In the same context, difficulties are experienced by most local authorities in local plan preparation by the problems of interagency negotiation between central government, local authorities, and the entire range of public and quasi-public services and utilities.

6 The local planning process is alleged to be too slow, largely as a result of its statutory dependence upon the production and approval of a structure plan for the area, but in many cases even the procedure for producing the local plan itself has demonstrated long gaps between the survey of the area, the recognition of particular problems, and the preparation of an appropriate local plan.

7 Some of the most serious questions surrounding local planning efficacy are those relating to the execution of the plan. Despite continual pleas, not to mention legislation, for the propagation of positive planning, local plans remain as passive if not negative control mechanisms. They provide neither short-term palliatives nor long-term solutions in respect of the *execution* of planning policy. Too few local plan preparatory documents demonstrate a satisfactory understanding of the private-sector development industry and its associated agencies, which probably reflects inadequate consultation in this direction. In many problem areas, local plans need to be vehicles for marketing the local authority to the various implementation agencies – presenting opportunities, providing initiatives, and giving undertakings of procedural performance. However heretical it may appear, many authorities sadly lack the necessary entrepreneurial aggression to bring their plans to fruition.[12]

8 One of the stated statutory functions of any local plan is to bring local and detailed planning issues before the public. Public involvement is a problematic exercise, however, and a number of issues can be identified pertaining to community participation in local planning. To begin with, the very concept of a community view, or a set of complementary views, is an illusive one; fruitful participation can be extremely expensive; the more extensive the consultative procedures, and the wider the range of proffered alternatives, the greater the degree of uncertainty and blight engendered; false aspirations are often evoked by the presentation of possible futures, and eventual disappointment often breeds further disillusionment with planning; the admittedly imprecise art of handling public response to participatory invitations is still in its infancy; and, perhaps debatably, the role of elected representatives is frequently undervalued. One

illuminating discovery drawn from a number of exercises has been that many issues of public concern and complaint relate to problems such as the efficiency of public transport, the standard of education, and the level of public health, which are the province of agencies not central to what is conventionally deemed planning.

Despite these criticisms the focus of planning activity is likely to be fixed on the local scale for the forseeable future, and there is growing evidence that there is already a greater sensitivity to the production of economically realistic plans which have also been prepared in response to genuine local demand. This is discussed more fully in the section on corporate planning and area management.

4 The organization and administration of town planning

Central government

The need for a common policy, philosophy and framework regarding the management of national environmental strategy, local government and regional planning, combined with the desperate urgency to combat pollution, congestion, urban decay and a housing shortage, spurred the Government in October 1970 into taking a bold and novel step. What were previously the separate and relatively autonomous Ministries of Housing and Local Government, Public Building and Works and Transport, only loosely grouped under Anthony Crosland, were combined together as the Department of the Environment, and their legislative, financial and administrative powers concentrated under one person, the Secretary of State for the Environment. Three ministers are directly responsible to him:

1 The Minister for Transport, who is responsible for general transport policy, roads, railways, ports, freight movement, inland waterways, road safety and vehicle licensing.
2 The Minister for Planning and Local Government, who is responsible for land use and regional planning, land policy, new towns, minerals, local government structure and finance, countryside policy and water and sewerage.
3 The Minister for Housing and Construction, who is responsible for the policy and finance of the housing programme, the construction industries, the Property Services Agency and building research and development.

The Department of the Environment is also concerned with such responsibilties as the co-ordination of work on the prevention of environmental pollution, with special reference to clean air and anti-noise functions. Furthermore, it undertakes research through bodies such as the Building Research Station, the Construction and Housing Research Advisory Council and the Planning and Transport

Research Advisory Council. The rationale for the 1970 reorganization was set out in the White Paper on the machinery of government (Cmnd 4506), which stated the aims as to:

improve the quality of policy formulation and decision taking in government by providing ministers, collectively in Cabinet and individually within their departments, with well-defined options to the contribution they can make to meeting national needs

match the field of responsibility of departments to coherent fields of policy and administration

ensure that the government machine responds to new policies and programmes as these emerge.

This remodelling is in line with current trends in management techniques and decision making and was not only applied to those ministries relating to the environment but formed part of a complete reordering of central government responsibilities. The Board of Trade, a large proportion of the Ministry of Technology and part of the Department of Employment and Productivity were incorporated as the Department of Trade and Industry. To formulate and examine national strategy and determine priorities a new Central Policy Review Staff was set up in the Cabinet Office. To assist in its unification, support its common purpose, and ensure a greater degree of flexibility, the Department of the Environment (DoE) moved its headquarters to a single building in Marsham Street off Horseferry Road. It is perhaps ironical that a department pledged to secure and improve our environmental heritage is itself housed in such a monstrous monolith. The very size of the Department must itself present problems; the sheer logistics involved in running an establishment of over 70,000 staff must be enormous.

The functions of the department

The Secretary of State is still charged with the duty of 'securing consistency and continuity in the framing of a national policy with respect to the use and development of land throughout England and Wales' as set down in Section 1 of the Ministry of Town and Country Act 1943. He thus preserves the ultimate authority for all policy relating to the control of land use, and is the chief executive for the organization and management of planning in this country.

It is difficult to summarize the Secretary's, and therefore the Department's, wide powers of policy formulation and instigation, but in general terms he holds all the statutory powers previously held by the three separate ministries. His prime interest is with matters of a strategic nature regarding overall policy and programming, and in particular co-ordinating the fight against environmental pollution. Many countries abroad are expressing a similar concern in respect of the environment. France has appointed a minister who is charged with pleading its cause against all other departments who threaten it. The President of the United States is informed on these aspects by high-ranking and influential advisers. Nowhere, however, are such a wide array of powers as exist within the DoE available to one minister.

The Minister, now the Secretary of State, has always held the responsibility of approving the individual development plans submitted by local planning authorities. It is in this way that he has secured consistency and continuity of land use throughout the country. Under the 1971 Town and Country Planning Act, authorities operating under Part I of the Act are required to submit the structure plan for the Secretary of State's approval. Any persons wishing to object to the plan may do so to the Secretary of State within the prescribed period. He must consider their objections and may decide to hold a local public inquiry or afford the objectors a private hearing. He may then approve the structure plan with or without modifications, and in so doing will aim to fit the various pieces of particular local authorities' policy into the jigsaw of a regional and national plan. If a local planning authority fails to prepare or review a structure plan the Secretary of State is equipped with default powers whereby he may appoint another body to undertake the task at the expense of the authority in default.

The control exercised by central government over local authorities is often of a more flexible and advisory nature. It takes the form of memoranda, design and planning bulletins, circulars, directives and notes. Between them these furnish a broad framework of policy which guides and controls the use and development of land. Obviously each particular area has its own problems and requires special attention, but once again to secure consistency and continuity the Secretary of State will lay down certain guidelines or principles which provide a common approach. The *development control policy notes*, for example, attempt to ensure that an informed and equitable judgement is made in respect of applications for planning permission over a range of possible land uses.

The Secretary of State also possesses extensive powers for

introducing delegated legislation. The *general development orders* enable him to remove a substantial amount of trivial matters from the normal planning procedures by automatically conferring planning permission upon them. The Town and Country Planning General Development Order 1973, as amended, authorizes the carrying out of twenty-three classes of specified development which are referred to under the general heading of 'permitted development'. The Use Classes Order 1973 specifies nineteen categories of use which assist both applicants and authorities in deciding whether or not a change of use is 'material' and thus constitutes an act of development requiring planning permission. It states that if a change of use takes place from one use to another within the same use class it is not 'material' and therefore does not require planning permission; it goes no further. Other orders relate to the control of advertisements, caravans, offices, factories, trees, inquiries and a host of other topics too many to list.

Another function connected with central government control of planning is where the Secretary of State acts in a quasi-judicial capacity in the hearing and determining of appeals. A person aggrieved by a planning decision may appeal to the Secretary of State, who is positioned at the apex of the planning pyramid. It can be argued that because of this position he is in conflict with one of the principal rules of natural justice that 'no man shall be a judge in his own cause'. It is perhaps fortunate that the Inspectorate, who actually sit in judgement at local public inquiries or receive the written representation, and either decide or make recommendations to the Secretary of State in respect of the appeal, is staffed by persons of such high professional repute and unquestioned integrity. A system in which the administrative and legislative powers are separated by the establishment of special courts, similar to the *droit administratif* under the Conseil d'Etat as exists in France, has much in theory to recommend it, but would be plagued with practical problems.

In the normal course of events, applications for planning permission will be dealt with by the local planning authorities. The Secretary of State may consider, however, that certain issues are of such outstanding importance that he would prefer to decide upon them himself at first instance. Such applications are then said to be 'called in'. This procedure is likely to be applied to development of a particularly controversial nature, or where the Department has not prepared a detailed policy towards a land use with singular characteristics but wishes to maintain balance and control, such as is currently the case with out-of-town shopping centres.

One of the more contentious problems that confronts the Department of the Environment is the issue of regional planning. It has proved difficult to administer in the past and will probably continue to be so in the future. Because it is so inextricably bound in with economic policy it was envisaged in the 1960s that the responsibility should lie with one of the ministries concerned with economic affairs. The Ministry of Housing and Local Government would merely attempt to translate the economic objectives into a physical plan. For a number of reasons this did not prove satisfactory and now the DoE has leading responsibility for regional policy. There remains, however, a large element of inter-departmental liaison and control, for industrial development is still very much the preserve of the Department of Trade and Industry. Moreover, Scotland, Wales and Northern Ireland retain a large measure of independence regarding regional development.

The Welsh Office, through the Secretary of State for Wales, has broadly the same range of executive responsibility in Wales as has the DoE in England, including town and country planning, housing, local government, environmental services, new towns, roads, national parks and historic buildings. Similarly, the Scottish Development Department, responsible to the Secretary of State for Scotland, is concerned with a number of services affecting the physical environment of Scotland, such as town and country planning, housing, roads and local transport planning, water supplies and sewerage, coast protection and flood prevention, building standards and the prevention of river and air pollution. The department is also generally responsible for local government organization and finance, but the Scottish Economic Planning Department has responsibilities for new towns, regional policies, and the formulation and implementation of plans for economic development in Scotland. The principal statute governing land use in Scotland is the Town and Country Planning (Scotland) Act 1972.

Local government

While the ultimate responsibility for the organization and management of planning rests with central government, who direct and administer the relevant legislation, it is the local planning authorities who implement the statutory provisions 'on the ground'.

Historically, local authority areas were conceived out of nineteenth-century expedience, principally to implement the succession of public health acts that emerged at that time. Industrial and commercial growth gradually outmoded the old boundaries and the organization of local authorities has been subject to prolonged and intensive scrutiny ever since the war. A Local Authority Boundary Commission was established in 1945, followed by the Local Government Commission in 1958, both of which spent a great deal of time and effort examining the demarcation of various areas and responsibilities. Although a few readjustments were made it was not until the reports in 1967 of the Committee on the Management of Local Government and the Committee on the Staffing of Local Government were received that a concerted and comprehensive attempt was made to rectify the deficiencies caused by a fragmented, outdated, poorly staffed, badly structured, ill-based and all too often hostile system of local government. A Royal Commission on Local Government in England was set up under the chairmanship of Lord Redcliffe-Maud and reported in June 1969. The members of the Commission were singularly united in their criticism of the existing structure. Its very boundaries were anachronistic; it did not accord with the changing social and economic patterns of an urbanized community; the proper planning of land use and development was not feasible with so great a piecemeal dissemination of authority and delegation of power, particularly as between county boroughs, counties, and districts; and finally, many local authorities were too small and lacking in both funds and expertise to carry out their work competently, which in turn led to excessive interference from central government.

Instead of the then 83 'all-purpose' county boroughs that were under an obligation to discharge all the functions of a local authority, and comprised most of the major towns and cities in the country, and the 58 administrative counties that were divided into urban and rural districts, with rural districts further subdivided into parishes, and local authority functions apportioned between the county and the various constituent districts largely according to their respective size, the majority of the Commission, and the then Labour Government, favoured a system of 'unitary authorities' based upon city regions apart from the four largest conurbations. The Conservative Government elected in 1970, and responsible for local government reform, came down, however, on the side of a two-tier system, and the Local Government Act 1972 introduced a structure of 6 metropolitan counties — Greater Manchester, Merseyside, South Yorkshire, Tyne and Wear, West Midlands and West Yorkshire containing 35 metropolitan districts, and another 39 county authorities comprising some 296 districts outside the metropolitan areas (Figure 21). Where there were already parish councils they continued; otherwise there are parish meetings, community meetings and community councils.

The new breed of county councils, both metropolitan and non-metropolitan, are responsible for strategic planning, including the preparation of structure plans, traffic, roads, education, social services (non-metropolitan only), refuse disposal, police, weights and measures, museums, playing fields and clean air. In other words, all those services that require considerable expenditure but not an inordinate amount of contact between the administrators and those administered. The district councils' function is to bring local government to the populace by administering the services that require greater direct contact, namely collection of refuse, housing, water supply, development control, town development and licences. The parish meetings and parish councils have very few specific responsibilities apart from looking after libraries, cemeteries and crematoria. As with the community councils, however, they act as an interest group representing the locality and exerting pressure upon district and county councils.

In Wales the number of local authorities has been reduced by local government reorganization from 181 to 45, made up of 8 counties and 37 districts, and with the division of responsibilities much the same as those in England. Parish councils have, however, been abolished and replaced by community councils, which have the right to be consulted on planning matters affecting their areas. In Scotland the previous arrangement of 4 city authorities, 21 large burghs, 176 small burghs, 33 counties and 196 districts has been superseded by a two-tier system of 9 regional councils and 53 district councils, in addition to which there are 3 island areas, Orkney, Shetland and the Western Islands that are 'most-purpose' authorities. Only 37 of the district councils, as well as all 9 of the regional councils, however, possess planning powers.

London, having singular metropolitan problems, possesses an exceptional administrative structure which was introduced by the London Government Act 1963 and became operational in 1965. Planning powers are shared between the Greater London Council (GLC) and the 32 Greater London boroughs plus the City of London. The GLC are responsible for strategic planning under the Greater

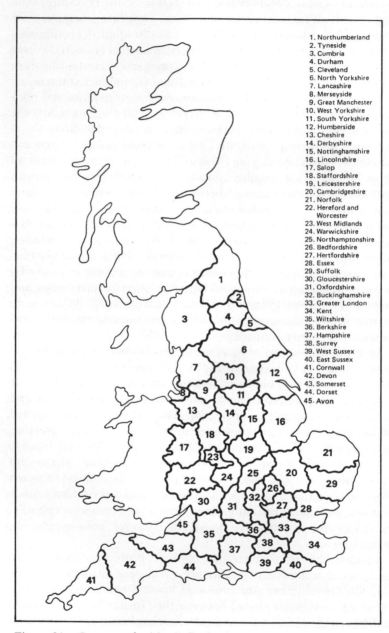

1. Northumberland
2. Tyneside
3. Cumbria
4. Durham
5. Cleveland
6. North Yorkshire
7. Lancashire
8. Merseyside
9. Great Manchester
10. West Yorkshire
11. South Yorkshire
12. Humberside
13. Cheshire
14. Derbyshire
15. Nottinghamshire
16. Lincolnshire
17. Salop
18. Staffordshire
19. Leicestershire
20. Cambridgeshire
21. Norfolk
22. Hereford and
    Worcester
23. West Midlands
24. Warwickshire
25. Northamptonshire
26. Bedfordshire
27. Hertfordshire
28. Essex
29. Suffolk
30. Gloucestershire
31. Oxfordshire
32. Buckinghamshire
33. Greater London
34. Kent
35. Wiltshire
36. Berkshire
37. Hampshire
38. Surrey
39. West Sussex
40. East Sussex
41. Cornwall
42. Devon
43. Somerset
44. Dorset
45. Avon

Figure 21   *County authorities in England*

London Development Plan (GLDP), and the London boroughs are responsible for preparing local plans within the context of the GLDP. The relationship between the GLC and the London boroughs is, however, different from that between counties and districts, because the boroughs are major local authorities in their own right for their own area, while the GLC, though retaining certain specific functions, such as education in inner London, is the authority for London as a whole.

Department organization in town planning

With the present structure of town planning in England and Wales, and the variety of local authorities that exist in terms of area, population, characteristics and problems, there is also a great disparity in the way individual town planning departments are administered. In many authorities planning does not even warrant a separate department but is a section of the engineer's, surveyor's, or architect's departments. For this reason it is difficult to generalize when attempting to describe the establishment structure of planning departments, because each authority will try to group its staff in the most efficient manner depending upon the work at hand. It can be said, however, that the most common division separates the functions of development plan and development control, with larger boroughs and counties increasingly opting for a research section as well. The *development plan section* will be responsible for the formulation of policy and the preparation of respective plans. It may be further subdivided with regard to research, central areas, urban design, conservation or implementation. The *development control section* is normally responsible for the detailed examination of all proposals and the consideration of applications for planning permission. In many authorities there will be separate development control officers for different parts of the borough or county. This section is also playing an increasing role in the implementation of planning proposals, the preparation of local plans, and the monitoring of plan performance.

Corporate planning

With the increasing complexity of urban, rural and environmental problems the machinery of local government is under increasing pressure to provide more and better services. Sophisticated techniques and professional expertise are required to provide viable solutions. There is often conflict between persons, agencies and departments in the allocation of resources to competing projects and policies. A growing relationship and interdependence across the gamut of local government services and facilities is seen to exist. The distribution of land between rival uses is not sufficient as a planning policy; there are social, aesthetic, administrative, economic and budgetary considerations to be taken into account. Thus there emerges the exigency to provide a new and more appropriate management system to meet these demands, a system that manages the affairs of a local authority as a whole. The case for overall authority policy planning was put far more cogently and succinctly by Professor J. D. Stewart in his paper to the Town and Country Summer School in 1969:

Local authority policy planning sets objectives for the authority in relation to the needs both of its area and of the individuals, families and organizations within that area. Local authority policy planning determines the strategies to be followed in pursuing these objectives. Local authority policy planning is concerned not with physical development alone, but also with social change: it is concerned not with capital expenditure alone, but also with revenue expenditure. It is planning not only land use, but also financial resources and manpower. It is planning the activities of the authority in relation to the needs and the problems it faces.

For far too long, local government has been undertaken by what is little more than a collection of semi-autonomous departments, reinforced by the custom-drawn boundaries of professional institutions, and providing essentially separate services. Reports over the last decade, such as the Buchanan report on traffic in towns, the Plowden report on education, and the Seebohm report on social services, have all pointed towards the need for integrated policy making and a unified management structure. The most popular description for this new approach to the management of local government is *corporate planning*. It involves bringing together the right expertise at the right time for the right problem, and thus implies a greater 'articulation' between professions as well as recognizing all the relevant constraints, be they financial, administrative, physical or political.

Other reports such as the Maud Committee on management in local government and the Mallaby Committee on staffing, both published in 1967, also stressed the need to break down departmental and professional boundaries. Many of their recommendations found expression in the Bains Committee report of 1972 on the management and structure of the new local authorities, which, among other reforms, called for a streamlining of committees, a management board of chief officers and a strong head of the management structure. During the late 1960s and early 1970s most major urban local authorities moved towards some form of corporate management approach, the aims of which are effectively summarized by one of the earliest councils to adopt such a system, Coventry, as follows:

to develop a management system that will assist the elected members to make policy decisions and to ensure the effective implementation of these decisions

to consider the resources, needs and problems of the authority as a totality with a view to formulating objectives and coherent plans to achieve those objectives

to break down barriers between committees and between departments by focusing attention on what the City Council seeks to achieve rather than by considering the development of individual services

to identify and evaluate alternative ways of meeting objectives with a view to making the optimum use of resources

to co-ordinate all the various plans of the authority, including the structure plan, and to ensure that these are integrated with a total management plan

to foster a corporate approach and spirit amongst elected members and officers to make the greatest use of their talents

thereby to ensure a planned and balanced development of the facilities available in the City to provide for its future prosperity and the well-being of the citizens.

To put this policy into practice, Coventry identified nine broad areas of concern, known as programme areas, such as education, housing and transportation, and established interdisciplinary teams of officers to staff them. Therefore, the programme area team concerned with the provision of housing, for example, had representatives from the City Engineer's, Estates, Treasurer's, Town Clerk's, Housing, Architecture and Planning, Public Health, Social Services and Education Departments. In this way the provision of housing did not become an end in itself but was seen in the context of the overall policy for the City.

Another common aspect of corporate planning is the appointment of a *chief executive officer,* sometimes called a *town manager,* who can co-ordinate the general management of departments. He in turn would be responsible to a small policy committee of the council who would direct broad strategy, identify objectives, and ensure a satisfactory balance of priorities and allocate resources accordingly.

The principal characteristics of corporate planning have been described by Professor Stewart as concerned with planning rather than administration, effectiveness rather than organizational knowledge, explicit rather than implicit policy, systematic policy review rather than *ad hoc* policy review, and corporate rather than separate services and resources, and it is fundamentally involved with management.[1]

One way in which corporate planning can be applied is by the introduction of the management technique of the *planning programming budgeting system* (PPBS), which concerns itself with the detailed running of the authority and the most efficient way of implementing and servicing the corporate plan. This method was first propounded in the United States by the Rand Corporation and subsequently adopted by the Pentagon to direct American defence policy and later by Mayor Lindsey in New York. It was introduced into this country in the mid-1960s and has been employed by a number of local authorities. PPBS attempts to bring budgetary policy and planning policy together in the decision-making process. It further aims to reconcile short-term financing with long-term planning. Moreover, it postulates that the name of a department and the number of staff employed within it are often irrelevant to the job in hand, hence the establishment of programme areas. Most important of all, it sifts and examines decisions at first instance, thereby forestalling the undertaking of abortive work and centralizing the decision-making.

Through time and experience a number of modifications have been made to theoretical corporate planning models to suit the particular needs and predilections of different authorities. Several common traits, however, can be identified in the practice of corporate planning,[2] such as the production of *position statements,* which attempt to give an up-to-date account of current activities, policies and commitments, and not only disseminate information widely but provide a reporting rigour for those responsible for individual programmes; the conducting of *policy or issue analysis,* which has been described as 'a systematic investigation of a particular policy area, probably executed by a small interdepartmental team of officers',[3] and often the selection of the issue of policy is at least as important as the implementation of the findings; the carrying out by a special subcommittee of a *performance review,* which, though recommended by the Bains Committee to be a watchdog body able to investigate any aspect of local government activity, has not proved as popular among authorities as most other proposals; and the adoption of *annual planning budgetary cycles* in order to improve the short-term nature of simple yearly accounting by producing a rolling programme linking estimated financial resources with planning objectives.

A certain amount of criticism has been levelled at corporate planning over the past few years, and can be concisely stated as:

1 The system has been described as mechanistic, has been too concerned with the structural change of local government administration and not sufficiently directed towards actual local needs, problems and political realities. In many authorities, for example, a Bains report blueprint was adopted as a management structure.

2 There is a danger of elitism among officers because much of corporate planning activity 'has been built at the centre of the authority by the centre. But there is much that cannot be learnt at the centre of an organization'.[4] Many informed professionals are excluded from decision making and many elected representatives feel relegated to the 'back benches' with all the ensuing resentment and lack of commitment.

3 While a greater degree of collaboration and co-operation has been achieved within a local government organization there remain problems of preparing a corporate plan where inevitably external agencies from both the public and private sector have to be involved. Truly effective corporate planning requires a fuller involvement of these other bodies at an early stage.

4 The vagaries and volatility of central government financing wreak havoc with most attempts to devise a proper fiscal framework for any length of time.

5 Corporate planning has frequently been said to conceal political values behind a management structure and provide a 'professional' cover for contriving political choice.

A more recent attempt to improve corporate procedures and relate the process of local government more closely to the community has been that of *area management*. Although definitions of area-based approaches vary, a preliminary one is given by Hambledon:

Area approaches involve gearing the planning and/or management of policies to the needs of particular geographical areas within the local authority and may involve delegating administrative and/or political responsibility for at least part of this work to the local level.[5]

Planning in this context is not limited to physical land use planning and, though inextricably linked, is also differentiated from management as a function, management being concerned with ensuring that the most efficient methods of overall present executive direction are employed to attain a given set of objectives, and planning being concerned with the formulation as well as the implementation of those objectives over a given time in the future. A number of separate local government services such as housing, development control, education and social services may have operated a partial area approach for many years, but area management is essentially the integration of all relevant services applicable to the solution of problems within a particular area, and is relatively recent. The first authority in this country to adopt an area approach was Stockport in 1971, where area subcommittees of the council were set up explicitly to tackle the comprehensive problems of given geographical areas. The idea quickly spread and, as mentioned in a later chapter, the government have established a series of six area management experiments in Dudley, Haringey, Kirklees, Liverpool, Newcastle and Stockport to test the effectiveness of the system. The aspirations held for area management are summed up by the DoE in a consultative paper[6] as

a means of adapting local government organizations so that it can respond more sensitively and effectively to the particular needs of areas. It is a means of identifying priorities and objectives at area level, seeing their relevance locally and putting them in their district-wide context.

Elsewhere, three factors in favour of an approach towards concentrating policy formulation and execution upon neighbourhoods have been advanced:[7]

First, they can promote new ways of learning about problems and opportunities in the city and the efficacy of current problems. They can cut across functional patterns of thinking. Second, they can bring important new perspectives to bear on the *combination* of processes which coalesce to give rise to our most serious problems of urban deprivation. Third, they can, by relating policies to areas which are meaningful to local residents, assist in the renovation of management *and* political processes at the local level.

5 The planning process

Planning and systems theory

Any community consists of a wide variety of geographic, social, political, economic and cultural patterns which both act and interact to form the nature and condition of society. The relationship between these various patterns is constantly changing, giving rise to new and different conditions, some beneficial to the community, some deleterious. It is the planner's function to comprehend this tangled web of relationships, and where necessary guide, control and change their composition. To achieve this, planning is concerned with prediction, not only of population size and land use in isolation, but also of human and other activities as well. It has been said that planners are now the prisoners of the discovery that in the city everything affects everything else.

Town and country planning, as we know it, is increasingly being subjected to a systems approach. The term 'systems' is defined in the *Oxford English Dictionary* as 'A complex whole, a set of connected things or parts, a department of knowledge or belief considered as a whole, a method or organization'. Town planning is certainly complex, comprising many separate but related elements such as transportation, employment, housing, recreation and education, which, being impossible to treat individually, have created an area of concern or department of knowledge that is viewed as a whole, both governmentally and professionally. The human environment itself can be seen as a system[1] within which a wide range of human activities take place – work, leisure, shopping and development, for example.

These activities are connected by channels of communication, such as rivers, roads, footpaths, pipelines and cables. These activities and their respective connections occur within 'space', not just on land, but between areas of land and also through time. The human environment is thus concerned with change; therefore the planning of it must be dynamic, not static, and it is a systems approach which helps to analyse dynamic conditions. Seen in this way the system is not actually the real world but merely a way of looking at it, supplying a greater insight into the forces and agencies that dictate its condition, providing a surer, more consistent and more sophisticated way of tackling problems. The advocates of the systems view would maintain that the approach represents a movement away from the entrenched 'physical determinism' so long associated with the planning profession, prepossessed as it was with standards of design and movement, neglecting the social decision-making aspects of the planning process, and being relegated to a position of 'land use accountancy'. The purpose of planning should be the attainment of a satisfactory state, health, prosperity and general well-being of the community, which is not always related to, or in accord with, what is often considered to be the most propitious spatial and physical organization of urban areas. A greater understanding of social circumstances as well as physical condition is called for. Again it is considered that the systems view can account for this.

The origins of the systems approach can be found in the natural sciences, a *general systems theory* being developed by von Bertallanfy, a biologist who besides proposing a systematic analysis of the interrelated parts of a problem also postulated that a set of rules or laws could be distinguished which applied to any system or problem.[2] The control or regulation of the system through the relationship and communication between its various constituent parts was first described in physiology and has since been developed as the study of *cybernetics*. Together general theory and cybernetics study form the *systems approach*, the one providing comprehension, the other permitting application. More recently the approach has been put into practice and further extended in the field of business management, equipped as it is with mathematical tools of expression and analysis. There exists, in fact, a very close relationship between cybernetics, operations research, modelling and systems analysis, for each discipline or technique gives a closer, more detailed, yet comprehensive appraisal of the results of a particular course of action. The application of this approach in the context of managing urban and rural resources inevitably differs, because planning, possessing so many imponderables, containing so many different elements each with their own criteria, lacks a universal measure of performance. It also requires vast amounts of accurate information that are rarely available, although the growth of a systems approach has been aided by the introduction of computers in planning studies.

In formulating policy in this direction the planner takes the city as an entity and examines the system that dictates its nature and form, a considerable task in itself as the very definition of what actually constitutes the system is arguable and arbitrary. Although he can rarely intervene directly, he attempts to establish a framework or set of procedures that regulate the activities 'at play'. In other words, he acts in a management capacity, planning, organizing, controlling, communicating and continually analysing the system. The management of the human and built environment that both concerns the social and physical sciences and depends upon decisions taken by elected representatives is, however, probably the most Herculean task of all. Moreover, planning is directed towards the future but again lacks sufficient techniques with which to assess future performance.

The city, town or other urban environment has this dynamic nature of varying components which requires an understanding of the guidance and control of change in terms of a system. Systems analysis can operate with changing circumstances in the relevant quantities, rates and quality concerned. In this way the development plan for an area can be made pertinent at all times, not just now, or at some remote date in the future. An entertaining example of the relationship of the structure of towns and the effect on human behaviour is to be found in the field of science fiction. Isaac Asimov's *Foundation* trilogy provides a superb account of systems and probability analyses and their application in a planning process.

Planning and decision theory

Allied with the emergence of the idea of a systems approach towards town planning there has occurred an examination of the way in which plans and policies are decided, and an investigation regarding the extent to which these decisions are rational. A rational decision is one where all the various alternative courses of action are considered, the consequences resulting from them are identified and compared, and the preferred alternatives selected in the light of the most valued ends. In addition, the various courses of action that present themselves should reflect the overall aims for the community. Too often in the past the profession has overlooked the need to begin planning exercises by defining the goals and objectives, assuming that they are known, agreed, and understood. In a dynamic situation such as the planning process the forces of rapid change are continually creating fresh problems and fluctuating circumstances. If a local planning authority can establish clearly stated and agreed objectives, the possible solutions are more readily discovered, for the definition of objectives almost invariably leads to the recognition of methods and measures of attainment and the methods themselves usually suggest alternative procedures for approaching the solution to the problem. Much inefficient and complacent town planning has occurred because there has been so little recognition of the nature of today that to envisage the shape of tomorrow has been impossible. It has been said that it is often more important to state the right problem than to solve it.

The process of reaching the best decision is known as *optimization*, but it must be remembered that the planning process takes place within a value-laden political context. The conflict between planning and politics is a critical one and can often result in the selection and adoption of plans that are not optimal. Planning, by its very nature and terms of reference, is concerned with the future, politics is all too often influenced by the present. The planner himself should seek to attain an unprejudiced attitude within the procedure of decision making; his task is principally restricted to producing technically feasible plans and submitting them for political consideration and decision. Greater accent has also been placed upon the mechanism of political decision making in recent years, and particularly upon the social implications that flow from it. It is possible to improve decision making in all fields by improving both the professional and political understanding and approach to the decision process, and also by improving the techniques for selecting specific decisions.

This development of techniques within the sphere of decision theory has continued to receive a growing emphasis. There has been an increasing reliance upon a mathematical approach incorporating the use of gaming, simulation, modelling and a host of other operational research techniques. Their application has grown to such an extent that there is a danger of them being regarded as a panacea for all problem solving and a prime determinant in the actual making of decisions. It is essential that policies should be chosen as the result of responsible thought processes and reasoning, and that such logical analyses should not be replaced by any therapeutic rag-bag of operational techniques.[3] Scientific method cannot guarantee a satisfactory solution or assure the planner of a correct decision. It can only assist him in working towards decisions which are reasoned and appear sensible depending upon the amount of information available in the first place. A good decision is a matter of thought but a good outcome is a matter of luck, and the best that any planner can hope for are decisions that appear to be satisfactory when viewed in retrospect.

Because planning is a continuous process, and therefore almost wholly future-oriented, an essential requirement in making the necessary and best decisions is the ability to forecast. In essence, forecasting is estimating, which involves understanding a process well enough to be able to describe its important relationships and to gauge the values of its variables. It is neither guesswork nor the slavish application of over-simple rules. As conditions change and circumstances vary each new decision requires fresh evaluation. The constituent variables that comprise the plan, which might be population, employment and communications for example, will require repeated analysis to check their performance and identify any departures from the original stategy. It cannot be emphasized enough that, because reality is immensely complicated, town planning is not a 'once and for all time' but a recurrent decision-making process requiring constant review and revision.

Planning as a process

The planner has been defined as 'an artist of rationality with reference to human activity'[4] which implies that the path he pursues and the manner in which he pursues it is reasoned and logical. This in turn suggests a hypothesis, argument or scheme which is formulated, tested and proved; thus following a chain of reasoning, or, put another way, a process. The process of planning the human environment requires the ability to analyse and comprehend the existing situation in the context of its social, economic and political, as well as it physical, circumstance; forecast any likely changes that are apparent from prevailing trends; understand the extent to which these changes will affect other aspects of the environment; judge their desirability; decide upon the best strategy and tactics to guide and control change; and assess the performance of the chosen strategy and tactics. The old 1947 Town and Country Planning Act style of approach was based on the simple adage of 'survey, analysis, plan', thus giving a process with both beginning and end, but which resulted in a static, inflexible 'once and for all time' master plan drawn up in the light of circumstances subsisting at one particular moment and designed for selected dates in the future. Although five-yearly reviews were allowed for, rather optimistically as it happened, it was a process incapable of adjustment to changing events. It could only be amended in fits and starts.

Because of its intricate nature, and the delicate balance that exists between the various related component parts, the process of planning should be continuative, it should not present a final definite panacea. It should be able to foresee, guide and influence change, taking a long-term perspective of short-term occurrences. It should be sufficiently adaptable to permit review, modification and revision. Planning is concerned with the future, but, as Sir Winston Churchill said, 'It is always wise to look ahead, but difficult to look farther than you can see'. The aim, therefore, should not be to specify in great detail the nature, size and condition of things to come, but rather to establish a procedure or framework that facilitates the manipulation of events in the desired direction. To achieve this it is always necessary to clarify at first instance the principal aims of the plan; in other words, specify what are the desired social, economic, political and physical directions. This will not only provide standards by which the performance of the plan can be judged, but also supply a method for selecting from alternative plans in the first place.

Owing to the need for continuity, adaptability, and revision, all geared towards the task of producing the best planning decision all the time, a procedure somewhat vulgarly called 'optimization', urban and regional planning has been described as a cyclic process. This can be demonstrated by setting out an example of the interrelated steps involved, one among many, for there exist various opinions regarding the exact nature of the process and number of steps.

Step 1. The first step is to appraise or *survey* the area, agencies, organizations, individuals and activities 'at play', and identify the way in which planning might function in the redress of any imbalance or anomaly that is present in the locality.

Step 2. Probably one of the most important, and previously one of the most neglected, aspects of the process is the formulation of broad community *goals*. Although they tend to be rather nebulous, often being framed as vague generalizations, they do have the effect of setting the stage. In essence they reflect the overall demands and desires of the community at large, testing the political temperature, and expressing the criteria by which the plan might be ultimately assessed. In practice, for example, they are couched in the following terms: 'to provide a better standard of housing throughout the local authority area' or 'to ensure that adequate open space is available withing reasonable walking distance of all residential areas'. From these broad strategies a host of tactical decisions can be made.

Step 3. This involves the identification of *objectives*, that is the more precise ways in which the goals might be achieved. In attaining the goal of a better standard of housing it might involve a policy of rehabilitating existing accommodation or undertaking widescale redevelopment, or perhaps a combination of both. This might be tackled by public- or private-sector development, or again by way of a joint venture. These, then, are the objectives. The drawing up of both goals and objectives will require extensive consultation and public participation to ensure that all community views and values are fully considered. Moreover, wherever possible they should be ranked according to the priorities placed upon them by the society that produced them. In this way the provision of more schools might gain precedence over the installation of a new sewerage system, or the case for a swimming bath might be advanced ahead of that for a car park.

Step 4. The possible alternative means of achieving these goals and objectives should be examined and compiled. There might be only one possible *course of action* or there might be many, but in virtually all cases they will be girded around by various constraints, financial, legal, social or political. The development in question might be too expensive, the policy might contravene the law of the land, the majority party on the council might not favour the release of land for private speculation, or the residents might not favour the construction of a ring road. All the thousands of component parts that constitute solutions to each objective, which in turn seek to fulfil a particular goal, must be analysed and tested; in this way a range of potential policies are formulated.

Step 5. All the complete courses of action are compared and measured. This *evaluation* stage is roughly akin to a sifting procedure. Some strategies will be immediately eliminated, being obviously unacceptable for one reason or another; the others might require the use of detailed and sophisticated techniques of selection to choose between them. This could include cost–benefit analysis, rigorous financial appraisal, or the construction of a goal achievement matrix. This last approach is a reminder that the evaluation should test and assess the performance of each respective policy against the goals and objectives already established.

Step 6. The chosen plan should be put into practice or *implemented.* This entails, on the one hand, positive action on behalf of the planning authority, not only in respect of public development but also in the stimulation of desired private-sector enterprise. On the other, it requires a large amount of control and regulation over development of a more negative or restrictive nature.

Step 7. Once the plan is operational there is a continuous need to scrutinize the way in which it is working. This *monitoring* stage reviews the performance of the policy regarding its effectiveness and efficiency. Where it has strayed from its course or where changing circumstances have overtaken it, adjustment might have to be made. The original plan might indicate, for example, that over the first five years an increase in the population of 10,000 is programmed. From this projected expansion any number of detailed planning decisions and other repercussions might have evolved, the provision of additional shops, schools, houses, hospital beds, jobs and so forth. If after the first two years growth falls far short of expectations, steps can be taken to rectify the situation if careful and continuous monitoring has been carried out. Additional planning permission for residential development or incentives to attract industry might provide the answer. Conversely, there could be a change of political power, either nationally or locally, and the very goals and objectives upon which the plan was devised might be questioned. These ever-changing factors thus produce an endless recycling of the process.

The planning process can thus be summarized as a perpetual series of steps as follows:

decision to adopt planning
formulation of goals
identification of objectives
preparation of alternative strategies
evaluation
implementation
monitoring and review

This description is by no means exhaustive or authoritative but it does serve to illustrate the departure from traditional land use planning. It should, however, be emphasized that no matter how sophisticated the process, and there is no merit in complexity, any plan or policy will only be as good as the data available and the people who prepare it.

Part Two
The components of planning

6 Survey preparation and techniques of analysis

In order to understand the society within which planning is to operate, to identify its problems and needs, to have a more complete comprehension of its varying and interacting elements and their effects upon each other, to formulate policies, to choose between them, to measure them in practice and to adjust them when necessary, the town planner must be suitably equipped with a variety of tools and techniques. Planning must be based upon knowledge, knowledge depends upon information, and information depends upon survey.

Because of the all-embracing nature of town planning and its comprehensive terms of reference, a wide and yet detailed survey of the many components that together form the built environment is required. In addition, the information yielded by such survey must be subjected to analysis to permit a full understanding of the conditions and relationships that exist between these various components. To this end, a range and variety of techniques that facilitate analysis, expedite comprehension and assist in forecasting are demanded. What then must the planner survey and appraise?

Physical characteristics

The nature, scale and form of the environment are the canvas upon which the plan is painted. A knowledge and record of the topography, geology, climate, minerals, areas of special interest, location of rich agricultural land and sources of pollution are prime requirements of the land use planner. With this information he is able to construct both land use maps and sieve maps which between them will indicate the extent of existing development and the potential direction of future development. It is important that these land use maps are kept up-to-date; the record of change greatly helps in understanding the nature of urban growth and the pattern of settlements.

Utilities

One aspect that is often neglected and much maligned, lacking as it does the charismatic appeal of so many other more topical elements of town planning, is the digestive process of urban areas. A map of existing sewerage, water, gas, refuse and electricity facilities should be maintained together with a note of their age, condition and capacity. It is surprising what influence the availability of utilities has in shaping planning policy and determining the scale of development.

Population

An appreciation of the size, density, characteristics and distribution of the population is nearly always the starting point in the preparation of all plans and policies. Without an idea of the existing and likely future needs of the community in terms of family size, age and structure, the planner is deprived of any premise.

Employment

The study of population leads naturally on to the need for jobs, demand for labour, and the consequent level of unemployment in a local, regional and national context. These must be fully appraised before the town planner can tackle the seemingly never-ending problem of attaining a true balance and stability within his area of concern. He must be able to forecast decline as well as growth, in order to achieve an optimum distribution of land between competing uses. He must also identify the different demands of basic employment and service employment.

Housing

From the location of employment springs the need for accommodation. The planner is occupied with the task of ascertaining the size, condition, age, tenure, distribution, density, rate of growth and occupancy rates of the existing stock of housing. From this he can again plot future needs and determine policy in respect of rehabilitation, redevelopment and overspill schemes.

Shopping

To ensure the most appropriate location for retail facilities the planner is obliged to assess the needs and potential of his local authority area. This entails establishing the regional hierarchy of centres, gauging any deficiencies in the existing pattern and catering for future proposals. It also involves an understanding of shopping habits and trends which might suggest a change in the hierarchy or a shift in emphasis.

Education

Although often separately dealt with in local authority management, the provision and location of educational facilities is largely dependent upon population survey, and an analysis of the trends, changes and implications in their social context.

Leisure and recreation

With the growth in available leisure hours and the upsurge in demand for recreation, this area has rapidly become accepted as a major part of the planning process. There exist many challenges in planning future facilities more carefully, making fuller use of existing facilities, preparing a more flexible approach towards the multi-use of school playing fields, initiating increased professional training for recreational management, propagating greater liaison between local authorities and ensuring fuller integration of research into recreation. Before this can be done a deeper knowledge of the forces that dictate demand and determine supply is required. This involves, yet again, the carrying out of extensive survey work and the creation of suitable techniques of analysis.

Movement

One of the principal factors contributing to the size and nature of urban development is accessibility, which in turn depends upon the degree of, and propensity for, movement. This includes the movement of both people and goods, and has given rise to an entirely new discipline, with its own language, which concerns itself with such tasks as origin and destination, pedestrian and desire line surveys. These in turn are employed in land use transportation studies in the assignment of traffic to networks, and in the testing of routes, capacities and standards.

Management

With the growing awareness of the need for better organization and administration, both in planning and in local government, there has recently been an explosion in the development and application of management techniques. Corporate planning, planning programming budgeting, linear programming, critical path analysis and network analysis have all been attempted in different forms and in varying circumstances.

Evaluation

Although it is rather unusual to single out one stage of the planning process and afford it separate attention, it is from this critical area of selection that several important techniques have emerged and been subsequently refined.

In the preparation of any survey or the construction of any technique it is essential to recognize that they themselves require planning. The cost must be estimated, the number of staff involved calculated, and the overall approach decided. Any bias or prejudice which can often creep in either surreptitiously or subconsciously must be avoided, for there is often a tendency in survey work and analysis to seek out desired information which substantiates preconceived plans.

Sources of information

With the introduction and application of increasingly sophisticated techniques in all fields of study, the researcher, and eventually the decision maker, is becoming ever conscious of the need for accurate, reliable and up-to-date information. Ideally the data required should be obtained first hand by way of surveys designed specifically for the particular problem at the precise time. Owing to the ever present constraints of time and money this of course is not always possible. The researcher, and certainly the student concerned with thesis or project work, is frequently forced to resort to existing sources, often poorly referenced, inadequately compiled, and rarely collated.

The vast majority of published information and statistics result from government inquiry, of which there is certainly no shortage. The cynic, indeed, might suggest that too much data can be every bit as misleading as too little. Owing to the sheer volume of official documentation there has been no publication post-war of the *Guide to Official Statistics* but Her Majesty's Stationery Office (HMSO) produces a series of *Guides to Official Sources* which relate to particular areas of study such as population, agricultural production and unemployment. Each year HMSO also issues *Government Publications* which lists and outlines every publication for which the government has been responsible over the past twelve months. In an attempt to introduce some order into the situation the Central Office of Information acts as the government's medium for the dissemination of facts and figures, especially in respect of the national press.

Each separate department and ministry is itself responsible for the production and propagation of a plethora of facts, figures and fancies. The Central Statistical Office issues, for example, an *Annual Abstract of Regional Statistics,* a *Monthly Digest of Statistics* and *Economic Trends,* as well as providing useful classifications for industrial and employment appraisal. The Registrar General, of course, compiles the decennial *Census of Population* and is also responsible for the more specific *Quarterly Returns* which detail certain aspects of population and housing more closely. A regional breakdown of housing statistics is provided in the two quarterly publications *Housing Statistics* and *Local Housing Statistics.* One further example of central government sources of information is given by the Department for Trade and Industry who, among their many studies, produce a journal, a *Census of Distribution* and a *Census of Production,* which between them greatly facilitate the examination of industrial and employment trends and problems.

Of paramount importance to the individual researcher is the intelligent use of library resources. It is here that he can inspect and review previous discussion relating to his particular field of study, examine the current situation, and formulate his own approach. In order to do this with any degree of success he must first be informed in respect of the system of classification employed. If a comprehensive analysis is called for then the British Museum receives a copy of all works published in this country, and the Bodleian Library in Oxford is almost as thorough. It must be remembered that most library catalogues do not reference periodical articles, and it is from this source that the most relevant information is often gleaned. Although most journals and periodicals prepare their own cumulative indexes they do not permit a wide-ranging investigation of all published material on a particular subject. It is for this reason that the Library Association produces an annual *Subject Index to Periodicals* and individual libraries in educational establishments sometimes attempt to compile their own periodical index. A number of other comprehensive bibliographies have been drawn up but almost as soon as they are published they are out of date.

On a narrower front it is an infinitely more manageable task to undertake a bibliography directed at a particular field of study or professional activity. To this end a variety of indexes, abstracts, reviews, and encyclopaedias have evolved. The production of packaged information is swiftly emerging as a major industry in its own right. The Department of the Environment produces an *Index to Periodical Articles*, originally for internal distribution but now readily available and much sought after. Professional institutions, such as the RICS Technical Information Service with its *Monthly and Weekly Briefing* and the RIBA with its *Annual Review of Periodical Articles* provide valuable information services for their members. The *British Humanities Index*, the *Building Science Abstracts*, the *Sociological Abstracts* and a host of other similar compilations scan and reference a wide array of sources and topics. Many practitioners in various disciplines would be foundering without their respective encyclopedias on housing, planning, taxation and compulsory purchase law. There exists a multitude of other sources such as newspapers, like the *Times Index*; research, like the Royal Town Planning Institute's *Register of Planning Research*; specific topics, like the *Economist Reports on the Regions 1965 to 1968* and the *Association of Planning Librarians Bibliographies*; they are, however, too numerous even to list, let alone describe. One largely untapped source that is worthy of mention is the growing collection of unpublished dissertations and theses that rest in college and unversity libraries throughout the country, the result of an army of researchers, innumerable man-hours, and no small anguish. Of inestimable worth in the sphere of planning is Brenda White's publication *Source Book of Planning Information*, a veritable cornucopia for the lonely researcher.

There are several problems associated with the information market. First, data often exist but are difficult to obtain or abstract. They might not fall within the scope of the more popular referencing or cataloguing systems, or they might be camouflaged by an erroneous title or classification. Second, although the information exists it might be of a confidential nature. There are many who can picture the Inland Revenue casting a covetous eye at the census returns, or who are familiar with the diffidence of government departments and private-sector concerns alike in the release of information. Third, information is often related to inconvenient or inappropriate areas. This has always been particularly true with housing, population and employment statistics, which have been based upon the custom-drawn boundaries of local government areas. This situation is likely to improve with the gridding of the country for statistical purposes. Fourth, it is sometimes the case that information relates to the wrong periods of time, is grouped inconveniently, or is slow in being published. Again the most notable example of this occurrence refers to census materials, which are geared to the decennial cycle; it takes as long as five years for all the collected information to be produced. Sample surveys during the intervening years and the application of computers will perhaps alleviate these problems. Finally, as has been previously intimated, information about information is not always available. A great deal of relevant unpublished material might lie gathering dust on the more remote library shelves for lack of adequate recognition and classification.

The great demand for facts and figures over recent years has given rise to an unparalleled growth in the establishment of *data banks.* As with many techniques whereby the means so often appear to justify the end, these banks have, of themselves, caused a vast information explosion. It is difficult to determine exactly how many exist, or where they are, or even what they refer to, for currently they are specialized and might be concerned with credit worthiness, criminal records and car ownership, as well as professional matters such as cost control, applications for planning permission and other related matters. They are largely computer-aided, their aim being to preserve past records and collate current information as well as promoting and facilitating interest in survey methods. They should act as a locus for national and international co-operation in research work, thus preventing any waste of energy while hopefully improving standards.

A final word of caution is perhaps appropriate for, no matter how diligent the compiler, no set of statistics, no source of information, and certainly no computer print-out, should ever be treated as perfect. Comprehension, manipulation and interpretation of data are every bit as important as collection.

7 Population

Demography, or population studies, represents the starting point for planning at all scales, providing guidelines for deciding total land requirements and a basis for allocating land between various competing uses. Most planning surveys and techniques require a substantial input of population information, and the nature of a community's population make-up and distribution dictates the policy for most urban needs including housing, shopping, employment, education and health services. A town planner's term of reference is principally directed towards people and their needs. He must therefore study the existing population structure, examine any inherent changes that are occurring, and equip himself to make future predictions.

The existing population

A knowledge of the present is necessary in order to plan the future. The following aspects of population must therefore be studied.

Size. If a particular local authority area is to be appraised the first prerequisite is to establish the current total population. This may appear to be a relatively simple task, but in practice it is complicated by several problems. At any point in time a resident indigenous population will be supplemented by visitors whose stay will be of varying duration. The inclusion of tourists, temporary visitors, and such things as army camps can distort the picture and hamper long-term planning.

Characteristics. Besides the overall total, it is essential to know the breakdown of the population in terms of age, sex and socio-economic group. In this way the specific needs of a community can be judged, and the provision of facilities can be linked with the respective demands. It is also possible to make a comparison between the local authority and regional, national and even international characteristics. This will indicate, for example, whether or not the authority suffers a particular problem in respect of an abnormally high incidence of low-income-group workers, old age pensioners or children of school age necessitating special attention or preferential treatment.

Distribution. Having established the size and characteristic of the population it is common practice to examine the distribution of all identified groups. This will assist, for instance, in the formulation of redevelopment programmes, but most especially in the more detailed land use location decisions – where best to place new schools, libraries, health centres and offices, for example.

The calculation of the size of the existing population is obtained from the Registrar General's *Census of Population*, undertaken every ten years in this country with a 10 per cent sample in the fifth intervening year. He also issues annual estimates and quarterly returns to facilitate planning policy. Owing to the obvious delay inherent in producing full and detailed census statistics, an approximation of current population figures is often required; this can be achieved by *censal ratio* methods whereby the last census is brought up to date by means of simple apportionment based upon previous statistics. Thus, if over the first ten of the last fifteen years the growth rate for a particular area had been 2 per cent per annum this is still assumed to be constant and a population of 100,000 at the last census five years previous is taken to be 110,410 now. Change in population takes place because of natural change, the difference between births and deaths, and migration, the difference between emigration and immigration from and to a particular area. Birth and death rates in measuring existing population are comparatively easy to assess, altering little over short periods of time. Migration is very much more complex to judge. The electoral role provides what is probably the most reliable source of information in this respect, although rating lists are sent by the Inland Revenue to the Registrar General giving some indication of new building and demolition. Lists of patients on doctors' panels can be of further assistance in tracing internal migration, that is migration within the country, and there exists a National Health Service register which correlates them for the United Kingdom. They are not, however, particularly accurate for planning purposes, as the process itself takes time and many people either delay registration immediately or do not register at all. In the United States they employ a technique in gauging migration which relates to the change in numbers of children enrolling at elementary schools, which is found to be in sufficiently reliable proportion to the overall population to give a rough indication. In some countries, such as Sweden, Holland and Japan, the situation is eased by obligatory notification of change of address which provides a virtually continuous census.

Some local planning authorities and regional boards have mounted sample surveys of their own, particularly in respect of detailed information regarding social conditions. This can be a most expensive operation, and the data, which are still generally on a sample basis, are not a substantial improvement on other 'desk' techniques for mere numerical population purposes. It does, however, supply a useful check and can be of inestimable worth in uncovering information not included in the official census.

The trends in existing population

Before being able to predict future population changes it is necessary to examine existing trends and consider their future relevance.

Size. It is important to know if there are any symptoms of change in the factors that govern population size, whether or not numbers are declining, stable or increasing. What are the respective birth, death, marriage and fertility rates, what is the level of migration, and what are the determining factors?

Characteristics. Any population analysis should ascertain certain characteristic trends. Planning policy will be affected by a tendency towards an ageing population, more women with a inclination to work, increasing levels of literacy, higher educational standards, earlier marriage, rising levels of household formation and a host of other factors.

Distribution. The town planner should be informed about alterations in the distribution of identified groups. The continual urban process whereby a particular class or community invades successive areas, placing social and economic pressures upon the town, requires investigation and monitoring. In this way policies can be drawn up to facilitate or rectify certain situations and circumstances depending upon the desired aims of the community.

The future population

By its very nature planning is future-oriented, and in order to assess probable needs in terms of schools, houses, shops, offices, factories and the like, over forthcoming periods of time, it is necessary to make predictions regarding the future population. Since the provision, location and nature of facilities depend upon the size, character and distribution of population, demographic expertise is critical to town and country planning.

Forecasting the level and nature of future population is a speculative enterprise. At their simplest, projections can be merely a continuation of the recent past into the future by extending a straight-line graph or adopting a formula which assumes that current trends will persist unchanged.

Graphical extrapolation of this kind can be classified into linear curves and non-linear curves. Linear curve extrapolation is a straight line which indicates absolute increments of growth over time, and can be performed by joining and extending two or more census points forward into time, or by drawing a line along the best fit provided by historical data. A non-linear curve extrapolation is used to reflect that a growing population tends to produce a continually longer natural increase, assuming no migration, and one such curve can be plotted to show a straight-line relationship on semi-logarithmic paper. Though possessing the merit of simplicity, graphic extrapolation very obviously has serious limitations and is only really of any use as a quick crude check or guide where past growth has been relatively stable. In similar vein, ever since an early application by Malthus, much has been made of the mathematical equation known as the exponential function, which recognizes the tendency for population to compound itself, and a number of refinements have been developed. One particular instance is the S-shaped logistic curve, one variety being known as the Gompertz curve, which is asymtotic at both ends and whose shape seems to describe more realistically the actual population growth frequently experienced. This is that growth proceeds through an initial period of relatively slow increase as the population becomes established, followed by a period of comparatively rapid growth, after which the rate of growth declines and the population becomes almost stable.

An important tool in the development of more accurate extrapolation techniques is regression analysis. This is based on an assumed relationship between population and such other factors as employment, income, density and costs of living, but again depends upon past relationships continuing into the future.

Another set of population forecasting techniques are those commonly grouped together under the title of socio-economic techniques and which assume some relationship between the study area and some other area exhibiting similar characteristics. One town might be compared with another, a city with a region or a region with a nation. Most methods make adjustments to allow for social and economic differences between the areas involved, but are still susceptible to the same errors as other graphical techniques.

The basis upon which the majorities of population forecasts are made in planning practice are demographic techniques. These concern themselves with the essential ingredients of population analysis, namely fertility, mortality and migration.

Birth and death rates are fairly simple to project, and as there is rarely more than a 5 per cent variance from year to year the short-term significance to an individual local planning authority is slight. The long-term total national population creates harder problems, for birth rate itself is dependent upon fertility and marriage rates. Fertility rates play a large part in determining the birth rate and have been steadily increasing, particularly in the younger age groups, since the war. The tendency towards younger marriage is likely to have a substantial effect on population growth, especially when fertility rates are higher at this age. It is difficult to forecast whether this trait of younger marriages and more children at an early age will eventually lead to larger families or is purely a matter of couples bringing their family forward.

Death rates have been continually falling throughout the world; in particular infant mortality has dropped from 30 per 1000 to around 6 per 1000 in this country alone over the last fifty years. Barring the outbreak of epidemics, or the onset of cataclysmic holocausts, it is likely that the downward trend in death rates will continue, but will become progressively smaller both overall and through the age range. One popular technique for forecasting population is the *cohort survival method*, which adjusts census figures forward by age and sex groups, year by year, to the date of the forecast, making separate adjustments for changes in birth, death, fertility and migration rates. In essence what it does is to trace a particular age group, for example 0–4 years, through their estimated life cycle making deductions for projected deaths based upon life tables, and amendments for net migration. The next 0–4 age group is calculated by reference to the fertility rate of the number of survivors remaining in preceding groups or cohorts. Special adjustments are made to allow for local trends, foreseen unique occurrences, and the death rate of migrants. Separate calculations are undertaken for male and female, high and low assessments being made for both.

In all population forecasts the most difficult factor to allow for is internal migration, relying as it does upon economic circumstance and social preference. Three principal characteristics can, however, be discerned. There continues to be a slight drift away from the northern parts of the country, rural depopulation persists unabated, and the most recent development is a movement away from the congested centres of large towns. Inter-regional migration has become a major planning problem and some success in arresting the drain of manpower from the North has been achieved. The seemingly inexorable growth of the South East has also been dampened down, switching instead to East Anglia and the South West.

If internal migration presents problems in assessment, then external migration is next to impossible. To a large extent it is subject to the vagaries of political change. In 1957, for example, 72,000 persons on balance left the country, whereas four years later, in 1961, there was a net influx, immigration over emigration, of 170,000 which dropped within a further two years to an intake of 10,000. Migration figures, both internal and external, illustrate the inherent difficulties of applying quantitative analysis to subjective variables. Even then, crude numerical forecasts are insufficient when a detailed breakdown of social characteristics is required, and it is part and parcel of the planning process to possess the ability of predicting both social and economic changes. Even changes in the age or sex structure of the population, which are the easiest to forecast, could be upset by medical advance; it might soon be possible to choose the sex of offspring, for example.

In recent years a great deal of research has been invested in setting up more sophisticated techniques to cope with population projection and forecasting. Mathematical models, such as EMCON, which was used in Ipswich and Sheffield, and the model developed jointly by the London School of Economics and the Greater London Council for use in predicting long-term metropolitan growth, have been introduced to assist the town planner in formulating policy.

Population policy

There is rarely any attempt at directly guiding the overall level of population, for government intervention in ordering such things as the birth rate is not thought to be a proper field for public action. This view is reinforced by the singular lack of success on the part of past population projections: all sixteen forecasts prepared by the 1949 Royal Commission have fallen well below actual current levels.

Influence, except for such incentives as family allowance, is normally exercised as an element in other planning policies such as housing, employment and communications. One recent development in the United States that might be suitably applied in this country, however, is an analysis of day-time population distribution as well as night-time or residential distribution. This information would greatly assist in establishing strategies to combat urban congestion and institute more advanced locational criteria. At the present time consideration of this aspect has been restricted to the current population but could be usefully extended to future appraisal.

Hazardous, complex and occasionally inaccurate as population studies are, it scarcely requires reiterating that without adequate data regarding the size, nature and distribution of population most other surveys would be rendered abortive and the whole spectrum of planning policy would be put in question.

8 Employment and industry

Two distinct approaches can be identified towards the location of industry, the theoretical and the behavioural. The theoretical sets out to refine further earlier classical studies relating to distance minimization theory, while the behavioural concentrates upon exploring the decision-making processes that take place within the firms and the planning agencies. A brief introduction is made in this chapter to the former, but the focus is placed more sharply upon the latter.

The level of employment is commonly used as a measure for assessing both economic performance and social condition. Because of this it has important political connotations and thus merits considerable attention throughout the planning process. The nature of employment opportunity, and the magnitude of potential growth or decline, dictates, to a large extent, the future size of population for a particular area, and is therefore essential information in calculating community requirements in terms of housing, shopping and other facilities. It is further necessary in estimating the actual space needs of industry and commerce themselves. In any study of employment three fundamental aspects can readily be identified, the worker, the employer and the area, and some of the basic techniques employed in appraising these components are briefly described. As a distinction must be drawn between employment planning and industrial development planning, the remainder of the chapter is devoted to the problems encountered and policies framed in planning for industry.

Industrial location theory

Both theoretical and behavioural approaches provide useful insights into the factors that determine industrial location and suggest means for controlling and guiding firms in order to gain an optimum use of land. The classical theories can really be divided into three categories, the least-cost approach, which attempts to explain location in terms of the minimization of factor costs; market area analysis, where more emphasis is placed upon the market demand side; and the profit-maximization approach, which is the rational combination of the other two.

The least-cost approach

Originally propounded by Alfred Weber in 1909, the essence of the theory centred around the principle that firms would locate themselves where their costs were least. In doing so he made a number of assumptions regarding a single isolated country, conditions of perfect competition, a given distribution of consumers, wide availability of some natural resources such as water, more limited access to mineral fuels and ores, and a fixed labour supply in restricted locations. Given these assumptions, Weber averred that three factors determined the location of industry, transport costs, labour costs and local conditions governing particular sites, and that a firm would position itself by substituting these factors in such a way as to minimize total cost. He also devised a material index which set out to show that a relationship between the respective weights of raw materials and final products could be devised, demonstrating if a firm was material-oriented or market-oriented. Much criticized for its remoteness from reality because of the assumptions relating to constant transport and production costs, and its disregard of institutional factors and varying conditions of market demand, several attempts have been made to improve the approach. The most notable is that put forward by Hoover[1] in 1948 who took a more sophisticated attitude towards transport costs by adjusting for length and direction of haul and the type of goods being carried. He also took account of institutional factors such as taxation, but his work remains essentially cost based.

Market area analysis

This attempts to rectify the neglect of market demand, and some of the earliest work in this direction was produced in 1940 by Lösch[2] who tried to incorporate the demand side into the theory by considering the optimum size of markets. In doing so, however, he made certain assumptions regarding the ready availability of raw materials, uniformity of population densities, constant preferences and no locational interdependence between firms. At its simplest, his theory adapted the ordinary demand curve to describe a market catchment area. The result is a similar disregard to the supply side of the market, and optimum location becomes a straightforward function of market demand.

Profit maximization

The natural concomitant to surmounting the deficiencies of the least-cost and market area approach is to consider variations in both demand and supply conditions. This has been attempted by a number of writers who have sought to take account of such factors as locational interdependence among both complementary and competing firms, and the difficulties of large modern corporations whose diversity of products and needs of management can affect locational decisions.

Because most of the classical theories ignore the realities of business decision-making, greater credibility has been placed over recent years upon behavioural theory, and some of the components which have affected the development of more empirically based analysis can be briefly listed as follows:

Satisficing. It has been suggested that many firms do not actually work towards a profit-maximizing location in a strictly rational manner, but rather they choose a position which most immediately appears to satisfy their basic requirements.

Personal preference. Many firms locate according to the predilection or predisposition of those in charge. Historical association, area of country and proximity of particular towns or cities all play a part.

Labour. Often thought of as the single most important factor, the availability of suitable labour does not just depend upon sheer numbers, but upon quality and attitude.

Transport and communication. Commonly regarded as a prime determinant of location, and apparently exercised as such from the evident pressure upon motorway sites, transport costs for many light industrial concerns are suggested by some research to form a comparatively low proportion of total production costs.

Site premises. Land costs are not usually thought to play as large a part as some might suggest in determining location decisions except at the extremes. As rental levels do not vary much within a broad area, the provision of a fully serviced industrial estate with advance factories and other facilities might be much more important.

Government aid. Although the range of inducements to locate in certain areas seems generous and alluring, it has again been suggested that financial support from government represents a relatively small saving to many firms. Local government assistance in facilitating the procedures of establishing an industrial operation might be more effective in attracting a firm to one location rather than another.

Environmental factors. The quality of life appears to be playing an increasing role in determining the location of certain industries, particularly the light industrial concerns associated with the electronics and communications industry. Climate, landscape, housing, education and leisure are all considerations of modern business.

The major problems of adopting a behavioural approach to industrial location are that it is even more demanding upon the availability of accurate and up-to-date information about firms, and that the more individual decisions are analysed the less in common they have, and the more difficult it is to construct any general theory. Any reliable theory, therefore, depends upon thorough survey and adequate information.

Survey and information

One way of looking at the range of survey and information required by planning agencies in the formulation of policy is to have separate regard for the worker, the employer and the area.

The worker

The town planner aims to match the need for employment with the availability of jobs, but in order to do this he must be able to predict change, and then be in a position to guide and control development. Certain elements warrant analysis in any employment study and can be said to constitute a rough procedure.

Definition of study area

Although this is often determined by local authority boundaries it is important to realize that any particular labour market can vary in size according to prevailing economic circumstances. In times of recession, or localized high unemployment, workers may well be prepared to travel exceptionally long distances to obtain employment. Distance is therefore critical, but so too are time and money. Cheap or subsidized fares could entice labour from a very wide area.

Activity rates
These indicate the total quantity of labour that is likely to be available at any particular time, and rely heavily upon an exhaustive study of population structure. The first step is to ascertain the total size of the population of working age. Next, because activity rates are sex, age and income specific, the overall working population should be subdivided into groups reflecting these characteristics. The activity rate itself is used to measure the total number of employed persons per hundred of the population, and is therefore expressed as a percentage. The average for an entire population of an area, for example, varies between 44 per cent and 50 per cent. When split into male and female workers on a basis of age and marital status, however, differing pictures emerge. Male activity rates, consistently above 90 per cent until retirement age, reach their highest level between the ages of 30 and 55 and then decline gradually for ten years with a significant drop to below 40 per cent after the age of 65 and around 10 per cent after 70. Unmarried females attain their highest activity rate of about 90 per cent between the ages of 25 and 30, after which there is a gradual decline until 60 years of age when the rate rapidly falls off to around 5 per cent after 65. Married females, on the other hand, reach their highest level of just over 40 per cent between 35 and 50 and fall away to around 8 per cent after the age of 60. While the make-up of the population and subsequent analysis of activity rates can thus be seen to exert considerable influence in assessing the supply of labour, other factors that determine the actual amount of time expended are the number of hours worked and the amount of annual holidays, which vary from industry to industry and are subject to change through time. Forecasting future levels of the availability of labour will have to take account of changes in the ages of marriage, school leaving and retirement, as well as changes in working hours, longevity and annual holidays. The same problems of prediction will exist in the study of employment as those discussed in population projection.

Earning capacity
This will play a prominent part in deciding the actual activity rates, particularly those of female labour. No definitive rules can be laid

down, however, because in some areas, where incomes are low and the risk of unemployment high, overall activity rates will be higher because families will be striving to secure an acceptable or adequate amount sufficient for their needs. In other areas, where incomes are higher and their incidence more secure, activity rates will also be higher because the more attractive terms will induce more women out to work. When appraising income opportunities and employment potential it is customary to review existing rates of unemployment which provide a crude indicator of untapped supply. Unemployment figures do, however, possess certain inherent drawbacks; some people, for one reason or another, are unemployable and others want to work but do not register. Other problems in measuring the supply of labour are encountered where an imbalance in the local structure of employment arises. This might occur where, for example, there are not sufficient jobs for women, or where few opportunities exist for better educated school leavers, or more commonly where there is one firm or one industry dominant, subject to severe economic fluctuations, in a certain locality.

Social attitudes
These can have a considerable effect upon the level of employment and the supply of labour. This factor is again particularly noticeable in respect of female workers. In the North East of England, where there is a long tradition of women going out to work, there are very high female activity rates, whereas in South Wales, where circumstances differ, they are extremely low. This naturally reflects the long-term lack of opportunity; nevertheless, social attitudes do vary from area to area. One aspect of this, of increasing importance, is the relationship between workplace and home. In the South East, for instance, the journey to work is significantly longer than elsewhere in the country, giving a greater mobility of labour. In traditional mining areas, however, great premium is placed upon proximity to work.

Labour reserves
As has been stated, the lack of opportunity can seriously lower activity rates, resulting in a pool of wasteful unemployed labour. L. C. Hunter pin-points the problem with great clarity:[3]

In an economy like ours, beset by labour shortages, it must be an aim of planned development that potential labour supplies are fully utilized. If labour reserves can be brought into action by providing more job openings, as we can reasonably assume, the future provision of jobs should be adequate not just to employ imported additions to the area labour force but also to take up the slack in the existing market situation.

The difficulty lies in distinguishing those areas where this problem occurs. This might be indicated by a high rate of unemployment or low activity rates, but without having regard to more detailed information relating to changes occurring within an industry and the gradual transition of workers from one job to another, or the influx of immigrant labour to areas of great potential opportunity, the picture can be misleading.

The employer

In general the entrepreneur is concerned with obtaining optimum access to raw materials, the market for his services or product, labour, utilities, communications and complementary services. The planner concentrates upon achieving a balanced industrial structure, alleviating urban congestion, and maximizing the allocation of land between competing uses. Naturally there is bound to be the occasional conflict of interest between them, but once again the town planner must comprehend the forces that dictate change in the demand for employment in order to formulate his policy satisfactorily in respect of the other components of urban structure with which it is associated.

Industrial structure

A knowledge and understanding of the current situation might highlight trends of production and employment that greatly influence the future pattern of development. It is necessary to examine the nature and scale of existing firms to detect signs of growth, decline or change. A relatively simple indicator is the *location quotient* which compares the number of workers in a particular local industry with the national average for the same industry. When figures for a number of years are available, signs of growth or decline, either locally or nationally, might emerge, thus providing some basis for analysis. If, for example, the local employment quotient is above one, with the national average setting the unitary base, it is likely that the employer will be seeking, by whatever means, to reduce his payroll unless exceptional circumstances prevail, bringing about a reduction in the area's total level of employment. A forewarning of this will enable steps to be taken regarding the provision of alternative jobs.

Similarly, employment might be based upon a declining industry such as shipbuilding, and the necessary action to stimulate a fresh demand for labour must be put in hand. This might take the form of retraining schemes, or preferential treatment such as cheap accommodation being afforded to prospective new employers. Areas that are themselves declining can often be discerned by examining the proportion of the working population that falls within a particular age range. In such an area there is often a significantly lower percentage of men falling within the 15 to 40 age range than exists nationally, in contrast to expanding areas where the opposite is the case.

Certain concerns possess specialized labour requirements or land needs, such as the pottery industry or glassblowing in the first instance, and the woollen industry and mineral extraction in the latter. Another aspect of location that affects the viability of production, and thus the demand for labour, is the importance of linkages. Many industries require to be in close physical proximity to certain subsidiary companies or complementary services; others act as positive generators of supplementary services and undertakings. Yet again it is incumbent upon the town planner to chart the relationships that exist between the diffuse factors that determine industrial growth and employment. J. N. Jackson suggests one way in which this can be achieved:[4]

One method might be for industrialists to rate predetermined industrial factors as an important advantage, or of little importance, or as a disadvantage of their existing location. . . . Replies can be tabulated by locality or by industry, and for the factors separately or in combination. In addition an 'advantage ratio' can be computed. This is simply the number of forms indicating that the factor is an advantage divided by the number that indicated it to be a disadvantage.

Technological change

This is perhaps the most difficult element determining the demand for labour to predict. More often than not such advances initially reduce the number of jobs directly available. In the long run, however, where the result is increased productivity, greater investment leading to an enhanced demand for workers might ensue. In addition the industry benefiting from innovation and displaying a healthy and efficient economic performance often acts as a stimulus for growth in other directions, with unrelated firms being attracted to the area by the sweet smell of success. The advent of the cybernetic revolution has lent an air of uncertainty to forecasting the future nature of employment. In Japan the competition for space, coupled with appalling commuting problems, has led to a radical change in office management whereby the employee remains at home to work, his only contact with colleagues and superiors by way of two-way closed-circuit television installed in his own house. Although not directly applicable to the whole range of employment opportunities, particularly industrial, it illustrates the devastating effect of technology upon locational decisions.

To assist in the procedure of forecasting demand, existing patterns of employment can be projected forward at prevailing average growth rates, in a way roughly similar to population forecasts. This kind of estimate tends to be rather crude and inaccurate unless certain trend factors regarding employment rates in particular industries and the growth or decline of these concerns are included. Information regarding future patterns can be abstracted from such sources as the ill-fated National Plan, published in 1965, which detailed projected growth, industry by industry, on a national basis; this can then be translated into a more appropriate context depending upon actual local circumstances. Growth rates are, however, somewhat problematic and a degree of uncertainty is bound to creep in.

The area

Having established the probable levels of demand for, and supply of, labour, the town planner must plot the course of action for his particular local authority area. He must decide to what extent development can be left to private-sector forces, exactly how much direct intervention is required, and of what kind. As labour markets are unlikely to coincide with local authority boundaries, liaison with neighbouring authorities is essential, for the repercussions of growth or decline are likely to spread out far beyond the area of immediate administrative concern. A need, therefore, emerges to define importing and exporting areas of workers in order to paint a more complete picture of the labour market. The nature of employment opportunity and the degree of industrial development exert a considerable influence upon the physical form and character of urban areas. Residential, retail, commercial and service distributions are derived from industrial location factors. Transportation both determines, and is likewise determined by, potential growth. Although the distribution of industry on a national basis is at present the prerogative of central government, its precise siting and detailed layout is the responsibility of the relevant local planning authority. Regard on their part must therefore be paid to accessibility, the provision of services and utilities, the disposal of refuse and industrial effluent, visual intrusion, noise, fumes, vibration, the prevailing wind, air currents and other similar factors. They should decide whether or not local industry and community needs would be best served by the establishment of a trading estate. Despite the fact that such estates take time to 'mature' because many entrepreneurs take up options in advance, they retain certain distinct advantages. A wide variety of undertaking can be catered for, thus providing a stable employment base; moreover, a range of sports, medical, canteen, rail and parking facilities can be provided communally. These estates, and for that matter any form of industrial development, can be expediently employed as a 'buffer' between motorways and other urban land uses, which is especially tempting if access to the motorway is furnished.

Sources of information

The principal sources of information are supplied by central government. A *Census of Production* is conducted every five years and the findings are published in the *Annual Abstract of Statistics* and the *Board of Trade Journal*. A similar *Census of Distribution* is carried out for wholesale and retail activities. Current statistics on manpower, unemployment, retraining schemes, wages, costs and industrial structure in general are issued in the *Department of Employment Gazette* which is published monthly. This is now supplemented by the annual *Year Book of Labour Statistics*. The various nationalized industries also produce annual reports that provide employment data. One of the most useful aids to industrial employment surveys is the Standard Industrial Classification compiled by the Central Statistical Office. This lays down convenient groupings of commercial and industrial enterprises. In the same vein is the Registrar General's publication which sets out a classification of occupations which can be used in handling information derived from the census of production.

Forecasting techniques

In the overall assessment of the various constituent components that affect and determine employment, several techniques are available to assist in prediction and planning. They are all at an early stage of development, and owing to the large number of components involved, their variable nature, and the long time scale, wide margins of error can often appear. Because of these inherent difficulties the techniques employed must be sufficiently flexible to adjust to changing circumstances. J. T. Hughes places great emphasis upon this aspect:[5]

Planners of all levels must be prepared to review the broad strategy and details of their proposals to take account of new trends. That is why it is important not to aim at a grand once-and-for-all-time projection but to set up machinery and techniques which will provide a continual revision of estimates in the light of new developments.

Economic base

This is a technique in regional planning and represents a slightly more sophisticated approach towards employment projection than that provided by the *location coefficient*, which merely compares the proportion of an industry's labour force within one area with the national proportion for that industry, thus indicating local specialization. The economic base of a region relates to that group of industries primarily engaged in the production of 'basic' or 'export' goods to other regions, employment in locally consumed 'non-basic' goods and services being dependent upon the level of production and employment in export or basic goods and services. A relationship expressed as a proportion or multiplier between export of basic employment and local or non-basic employment can, therefore, be derived from a fairly simple analysis. This can then be applied to the likely future trends in the respective industries within the area based upon national forecasts, thus indicating probable total future employment. It should be remembered, however, that the ratio or relationship could change over time due to such factors as technological advance. Problems are also encountered in distinguishing between basic and non-basic industries.

The technique is also used, in conjunction with a comparative cost analysis, in determining those industries that might be introduced into an area with the aim of creating an economic base for future growth 'points' or 'poles' which are locations ideally suited to the induction of new industries which would themselves generate further development.

Input–output analysis

This is another technique available for the study of employment and is again closely associated with the concept of relationships between both regions and industries and the calculation of ratios or multipliers to assist in forecasting. The analysis aims to discover how much input to a particular industry is obtained locally from the area under study, and similarly how much output is sold there and how much elsewhere. It is then possible to compare these results with other regions as well as with national figures and draw certain conclusions regarding future trends in the industry and its labour force. It might be, for example, that the input of labour in the industry was locally very much higher than the national average and likely to diminish proportionately with the introduction of automation. Another industry might prove to be heavily reliant upon sales to other regions and should be strategically placed in an optimum location for 'export', thus increasing productivity, growth and employment.

Input–output analysis detects and exposes the linkages and trans-actions that take place between industries and between areas. One major drawback is the lack of reliable information with which to construct the matrix that displays the relationships; it is both complex and costly to collect.

Technique for area planning (TAP)

To overcome the problems of data collection this approach has been developed, whereby the process of defining and examining linkages is considerably simplified. A distinction is made between major and minor industrial concerns and relationships are only identified for the major sectors where information is more readily available. H. Richardson describes TAP as

a mongrel technique, somewhere between an input–output model and an economic base study. It avoids the costliness of the former and the undue aggregation of the latter. Although it follows base analysis in giving exports primary consideration in the final demand sector, impact estimates from TAP were found to fall within 5 per cent of those resulting from comprehensive input–output studies. A TAP study may be used either for projection or for evaluating the impact of alternative policies (e.g. the choice between promoting the growth of an existing firm, a new firm related to existing local activities, and a firm in an industry new to a region) on local employment or income.[6]

Shift and share analysis

This is a technique for assessing the impact on manufacturing change of local differences in industrial structure. At its simplest it is a classification of manufacturing industry by performance according, for example, to whether they are considered to be fast growing, slow-growing or declining; then the proportionate share of each category for the area can be calculated and the tendencies to shift towards one category or another computed over time. Usually a more sophisticated approach is adopted in the analysis of regional structure, which is its most common field of application, whereby a region's growth performance, as indicated by some representative variable such as income, population or employment, is broken down into a number of components. The share component represents the amount by which regional employment would have grown if it had followed national growth rates for the period in question, and is, therefore, known as either the 'national share' or 'regional share', being the norm for the region from which deviations can be measured. The shift component represents any deviations in regional growth away from this national norm, and can be subdivided into the 'proportional shift' and the 'differential shift'. The proportional shift, also known as the compositional, structure or industrial mix component, measures the impact of industrial structure, and can be thought of as the additional amount by which regional industry grows as a result of the area's specialization in particular industries, so that this component would be positive in areas specializing in nationally fast-growing sectors and vice versa. The differential shift, also known as the regional, competitive or locational component, is what is left over after the national or regional share and proportional shift components have been calculated, and thereby measures the amount of net regional shift resulting from industrial sectors growing faster or slower in the region than nationally owing to internal location factors. In this way, a region with locational advantages would have a positive shift component and vice versa. Originally designed to analyse and explain the reasons for regional growth and predict future trends, it is now generally recognized as being only a partial and limited technique. While of doubtful worth as a growth theory, however, it is a useful tool for examining the relationship between industrial structure and regional economic performance.

Others

Income statistics can be used to gauge an approximate indication of future employment. Total figures of estimated future national income are subdivided into regional portions on the basis of how much each region can expect to share. Using forecasts of production and output per worker a projection of expected jobs can be obtained. Reliable information is once again the key to the success of this method, which is essentially a short-cut approach.

C. M. Law has described a means by which a similar approach to that employed in estimating future population levels can be applied to forecasting employment.[7] It is called *growth analysis* and is founded upon the assumption that jobs posses a kind of birth and death rate which can be measured by area over time.

Another technique described as *industrial complex analysis* gives attention to the interrelationships that exist between industries. The location and production of a motor car industry, for example, will affect the location and production of many other related concerns, all gaining external economies from enhanced accessibility. A modified form of input–output analysis is used to examine the ideal location for the 'set' or complex of related industries and measure potential growth or decline and therefore prospective employment.[8]

Planning for industry

As stated at the beginning of the chapter, it is important to distinguish between industrial development planning and employment planning, for while there is a considerable degree of overlap between the two, and the term employment planning is frequently used as a generic phrase, industrial development planning is more concerned with industrialists, factories and firms than with workers, unemployment and the supply of labour. This section is directed more towards planning for industry than planning for employment.

One of the most distinctive features of industrial planning over the past twenty-five years has been the marked lack of rapport between industrialists and planners. The position has recently begun to change, but until the mid- to late 1970s the most common cause for contact between the two parties arose on such occasions as relocation due to a proposed redevelopment or road scheme, problems resulting from non-conforming use designation, the need to obtain planning permission for alteration or expansion, or the need to establish new premises on a fresh site. Conflicting aims often led to dissension between the parties. The scene has to some extent changed, however, with a growing realization on the part of planning authorities as to the need to promote and support the development of industry. Before exploring the problems that beset individual local authorities and examining some of the policies they have framed in an attempt to overcome them, it is worth-while listing the various scales at which decisions are made regarding industrial development.

European Economic Community (EEC)

With entry into Europe it has been argued that the long-term advantages and disadvantages of mainland Europe relative to Britain, and of the South East of England relative to the rest of the country, will become more pronounced, and the strength of the 'golden triangle' defined by Birmingham, Paris and the Ruhr be reinforced. Conversely, incentives already provided by the British Government in pursuit of its regional policy have been supplemented by support for the peripheral and deprived industrial regions by grant aid from the European Regional Development Fund. It is too early to judge the full effects of EEC policy at the local scale.

Central government

No national plan now exists, but the various threads of industrial policy are woven by the Treasury in respect of overall economic policy, the Department of Employment and the Manpower Services Commission for employment policy, the Department of Industry for industrial strategy and inter-regional policy, and the Department of the Environment for intra-regional policy, structure planning and inner city policy. The Ministries are represented in the regions and co-operate with the relevant economic planning boards, which are themselves largely staffed by DoE personnel.

Regional councils and boards

The regional councils have suffered from lack of executive power and elective responsibility and their influence upon industrial development is minimal except for occasional lobbying of and by members. The boards are a useful source of information but the Whitehall view tends to prevail. Other regional agencies that affect industrial development are the various public utilities such as the gas, electricity and water boards. Most regions also have a standing conference of constituent local authorities to co-ordinate and monitor collective progress as far as possible.

Structure planning authorities

Structure plans are required to be consistent with an agreed regional strategy, and among the dozen aspects of society required to be covered in the written statement were 'employment and income' and 'industry and commerce', usually combined in practice as 'employment and industry'. Most structure plans remain complex, abstruse and not altogether helpful in guiding industrial development.

Local planning authorities

This is really where the action still takes place despite the overlying levels of government, and most of the decisions that are made which directly promote industrial development do so at the local level.

The problems of attracting industry to and retaining industry within a local authority area, coupled with the desire to encourage growth in some areas but not in others, are a familiar part of present day planning practice. Given the complexity of industrial legislation and administration, it is becoming increasingly necessary for the planner to have an overall awareness of the range of policy measures available and the departments of local and central government responsible for their administration. The major measures which can be taken by a local authority include the following.

Land availability. Land is of course the basic ingredient of industrial development. An authority cannot expect to attract industry without suitable and readily available sites, and while there is little evidence to suggest that development plans have not allocated sufficient land for industrial development, mere zoning is not enough if the land lacks proper access, services and facilities. A flexible attitude needs to be taken towards tenure, for while many industrialists might willingly accept leasehold terms, it makes funding more difficult and the length of the lease need to be acceptable.

Industrial estates. The step beyond simple land availability is the laying out of industrial estates, and it has been suggested[9] that the existence of trading estates owned by an authority with serviced sites is the main inducement to industrial firms. The local authority is also said to retain the initiative in such circumstances by having serviced sites available, with the additional advantage to an industrialist that he can negotiate directly with the local authority on all matters as a kind of package deal saving both time and expense.

Advance factories. A step further is the provision of readily disposable premises, and the latter part of the 1970s witnessed a steady growth in the construction of factory units by both central and local government. An advance factory is one built speculatively ahead of demand to varying degrees of finish but of sufficiently adaptable design to suit most light industrial operations. Now that industrial development certificates are less restrictive the facility to provide such premises should be even greater. Co-operation by way of partnership schemes with local authorities is increasingly employed as one means of bringing advance industrial accommodation onto the market, and some institutional investors have shown interest in proceeding with the funding of such ventures.

Transportation infrastructure. Whatever the contrary results of academic research, it is evident that the majority of industrialists place a very high priority upon good access, at national, regional and local level, and the provision of new roads circumventing congested areas or careful traffic management along existing routes will enhance the attractions for industry. Connections to other forms of transport, particularly freightliner terminals and airports, are becoming more important for light industrial operations

Development control. There are a number of aspects of the development control system which can materially affect the climate for industrial development. To begin with, the very speed at which applications for planning permission are processed by many authorities could be improved by a better understanding of the needs of firms, earlier and more positive discussions with the applicant, and a clearer idea of what would be acceptable and where, what would not and why. A more sensitive and less rigid attitude to land use zoning to allow a richer mix of industrial, commercial, civic, residential and other uses within neighbourhoods would often do little harm, and might prove of great help to existing firms wishing to expand. Sometimes environmental standards, while not abandoned, need at least to be moderated, and, at other times, there is a need to pursue very strict standards of control, coupled with other urban improvement policies, in order to upgrade a particularly poor area and attract further private-sector industrial investment. One further measure of development control used by local authorities to maintain employment is the restriction of warehousing and shopping superstores on industrial land, but employment ratios between sectors are not so divergent as they used to be.

Information and promotion. Many major local authorities are becoming aware of the need not only to provide information and advice about the availability of sites and premises, but also to adopt a much more aggressive attitude towards the marketing of them. The preparation of an industrial property register, the publication of statistics and information relating to industrial development, the production of development briefs for certain sites, the creation of an industrial development budget and the appointment of an industrial development officer are all measures adopted to promote industry.

Industrial improvement area. As part of the government's inner urban area policy it is possible for a local authority to designate an area as an industrial improvement area in order to upgrade and enhance the general amenity of inner city industrial neighbourhoods by stimulating better maintenance, adaptation, conversion and improvement.

Keyworker housing. It is fairly common for local authorities to provide council housing for keyworkers as well as encouraging private housebuilding for them. They can also assist in the setting up of housing associations and the provision of mortgage finance.

Financial assistance. Under certain circumstances local authorities may provide financial assistance to firms to help them expand, re-equip, or overcome particular difficulties. This may take the form of a rent or rate subsidy or occasionally it may even involve direct investment in a firm and subsequent shareholding.

Other. Many other measures exist to attract or retain industrial activity within a town or city. The reclamation of derelict land to provide additional land or merely improve the working environment; similarly, the renovation or clearance of obsolete buildings; the location of local authority business premises and placement of municipal contracts to favour disadvantaged areas and local firms; and the use of the job creation programme in industrial area improvement, are all examples. There is also a tendency for non-economic factors to be neglected in industrial promotion, and it has been suggested[10] that central and local government should provide for the social demands and personal ambitions of managers, especially in respect of the removal of eyesores, good public buildings, better schools, lidos, marinas and golf clubs.

Assessment of industrial development

The reverse side of the coin to industrial promotion is the need to assess the repercussions which might ensue from the siting of a major industrial development within a local authority area. The use and construction of environmental impact statements are discussed elsewhere, but it is in the field of industrial development that their value is highest. It is fair to say that the proposed preparation of such formal and detailed statements is reserved for major schemes whch which would have a large land take, be of a contentious nature, have a significant impact on the physical environment as well as on local employment structure and levels of service provision, be of national or regional significance, or be a major departure from approved development plans. Nevertheless, many of the principles established for appraising major developments equally apply to the likely impact of lesser projects in sensitive situations. Using the recommendations contained in the 1976 Department of the Environment publication *Assessment of Major Industrial Applications* as a basis, it is useful to set down the main factors a local authority might take into account in considering an application for planning permission for industrial development.

Physical characteristics

In examining the physical characteristics of the site and its surroundings it may be necessary to ascertain if the development involves significant excavation or earthmoving which may cause problems such as soil erosion, and if the general topography of the locality imposes constraints upon the design or siting of the proposed scheme. The drainage pattern of the area or flow of underground water might be affected, and in some areas there could be climatic factors constraining development, particularly in respect of noise and air pollution. With regard to landscape, the compatibility of surrounding land uses, the zone of visual influence, the need to protect any special trees or buildings, the suitability of building materials and the proposals for landscaping the site must all be taken into account.

Ecological characteristics

While little appreciation of ecological factors is had in the planning process, an awareness is dawning of the desirability to examine the compatibility of proposed development with existing habitats. Even if they are compatible, it will usually be necessary to devise conservation measures to protect habitats, and the means of ensuring their implementation. Where they are obviously not compatible the effect upon habitats from any probable changes in groundwater level, quality of standing or flowing water, silting pattern, air pollution, dust deposition and nutrient status of the soil, should at least be noted.

Human activity patterns

In simple demographic terms the likely level of population growth, any effect upon local migration flows, changes in age or sex structure, effects upon the lifestyles of existing residents and any influence upon tourist trade should be identified and acceptable levels determined. From the employment structure aspect, it is important to establish the effect any development might have upon the economic base of the area, what other industries could be affected, the degree and permanence of any reduction in unemployment or underemployment, and the possible influx and effect of non-local labour, and thereby generally assess the scale, rate and impact of projected employment growth in the local context. With regard to transport, it should be established to what extent the development might lead to an increase in the volume of public and private traffic in the area, whether the existing transport network is of a standard and capacity to cope, what additions or alterations to the network might be necessary, and whether there would be any environmental consequences.

Infrastructure services

It is necessary to know if the proposed development would lead to demands which exceed the planned level of provision of electricity, gas, water, sewerage, solid or liquid waste and by-product disposal. If additional off-site facilities could be required it must be decided by who, when and how, and what the financial effects might be. New supply lines could have an intrusive effect on the landscape and the extent of this incursion should be gauged and remedial measures appraised. It is also judicious to assess the likelihood of failure in the service systems, the consequences for local distribution and the need to insist upon the provision of emergency supply services. In respect of social infrastructure it will be necessary to calculate the increase in the demand for education and housing, and consider the ways in which this would have to be provided and how acceptable any changes in approved policy might be. Similarly, the effect upon social and community services such as health, fire and ambulance would have to be appraised.

Small firms and the inner city

Suddenly the emphasis over the past few years has swung towards policies aimed at the protection and fostering of small firms, with special reference to the problems of the inner city. The particular problems of the inner city and recommendations for action are described elsewhere, but suffice it to say that the economic structure of the inner areas has been subject to changes rooted deep in the basic structural problems of the economy. These structural problems, together with the world market recession, have resulted in the rationalization of plant and firms. Technological developments and increasing mechanization, mergers and the growing tendency towards concentration with fewer and larger firms, has led to the movement of industry out of the inner city areas; these areas have suffered in any event from the existence of old and obsolescent plant and premises leading to higher operating costs. The outward trend has been further exacerbated by regional and urban planning policies providing financial incentives to firms to move to assisted areas and new and expanded towns. At a local level, municipal redevelopment schemes, speculative pressures for offices, and locational disadvantages inherent in inner areas such as bad access, inadequate premises, insufficient room for expansion, and higher operating costs, have all conspired to reinforce the pace of closure. Larger firms have tended to move out and smaller ones to close. Small firms are rarely able to relocate themselves owing to lack of finance, lack of alternative premises, higher rents, loss of local linkages and markets, and a psychological barrier to moving. Moreover, the private sector has been slow to provide suitable accommodation for small businesses because of funding, management and construction difficulties. Thus, in the inner areas, firms have closed down or moved, often causing the out-migration of young skilled workers, and leaving behind pockets of unemployment, dereliction, blight and great uncertainty.[11]

It has become necessary, therefore, for the planner to understand the nature and role of small firms, the reasons for their decline, the case to be put in their favour, the problems they face, and the scope for local authority action. Much of this was considered by the Bolton Committee of Inquiry into Small Firms whose report was published in 1971.

The nature of small firms

The small-firm sector is extremely large and remarkably

Table 1   *URBED classification of small firms*

Number of employees	Typical workspace	Typical organization	Size classification
1–5	Work room Single room Office/studio	Personal/family co-operative/ partnership	Very small
6–25	Work shop Office suite	Specialization of functions	Very small
25–50	Factory/office	Divided management and employees	Intermediate
50–200	Office separate from factory	Possibly divided ownership and management	Substantial

Source: *Ensuring a Future for Small Enterprise in Covent Garden* (Urban and Economic Development Group 1976).

heterogeneous, with small firms accounting numerically for the vast majority of all business enterprises. They display a striking diversity within and between all sectors of industrial production, but share the one common feature that they are managed by the people who own them. The Bolton Committee included within the definition of a small firm all those with not more than 200 employees, while accepting that this was not always appropriate to all enterprises and all sectors. Subsequent studies have favoured a more refined definition such as that shown in Table 1 produced by the Urban and Economic Development Group in 1976. Investigation conducted as part of the Bolton Committee of Inquiry found that the common characteristics of small firms arose principally from five factors: their legal status, ownership and management; their financial structure; their role as employers; the motivations and social origins of their owners; and their role in the community. From an analysis of these characteristics it is possible to say that a small firm is one that has a small share of its market, is managed by its owners in a personalized way, and is independent of outside control. The inner area study of Birmingham identified the characteristics of the small firm as being under single, family or partnership ownership; employing up to 40 people; occupying not more than 700 m² of floorspace; and serving non-local needs, not being tied to the local economy. Naturally, all these characteristics vary and different forms of ownership, market orientation, size and independence are evidenced.

The role of small firms

The Bolton Committee attempted to classify the role of small firms according to the type of market they supply, being either satellites, specialists or marketeers. Satellites, occupying 6 per cent of the total, are firms heavily dependent upon one large customer. Specialists, estimated to be about 16 per cent of the total, are those firms carrying out activities that are only really feasible on a small scale. Marketeers, with around 78 per cent of the total, are those which compete in the same or similar markets as large firms. Even this classification can be misleading because, for example, it was found that in the manufacturing sector 35 per cent of all small firms are dependent on one customer for more than a quarter of their business. Numerically, their role in the economy is significant, for in 1971 there were approximately 820,000 small firms in industries covered by the Bolton Inquiry, accounting for 93 per cent of the total. They employed 4.4 million workers and contributed more than 20 per cent of total output in the industries concerned. A 1972 Census of Production for London revealed that over 40 per cent of all employment was in small firms.

The decline of small firms

The Bolton report showed clearly that the small-firm sector is in decline. The number of small manufacturing firms fell from 136,000 before the Second World War to around 60,000 in 1963 and it has been demonstrated that the trend has continued since,[12] with employment in small firms dropping from nearly 35 per cent in 1951 to under 30 per cent in 1968. It should be said that apart from Japan this trend has been experienced in all the advanced market economies, but the decline has been sharpest in Britain. This has been put down to high rates of taxation, precluding financial growth and discouraging entry; the structure and working of our capital market, which favours market concentration; the conservative attitude of the financial institutions towards small enterprises; the natural advantages enjoyed by large firms in their economies of scale in respect of technology, research and development, and marketing and management; the growth of public-sector industry by nationalization; and last, but by no means least, the phenomenal growth in legislation relating to such matters as public health, employment, safety at work, fire and building regulations, planning and taxation.

Concern has often been expressed about the threat to the free-enterprise system that is posed by growing market intervention. This concern relates to the role the small firm plays as a breeding ground for innovation and new industries, and the similar part it plays as a means by which fresh entrepreneurial talent can emerge and small firms grow into large industries. The private industrial sector is not static; some firms decline but others should grow, and it is interesting to note that many of the 1000 largest firms in the country have grown to their present size since the Second World War. Nevertheless, while some optimistic observers, including the Bolton Committee, consider that the decline of small firms was a temporary phenomenon caused by a one-off process of adjustment to modern technological and social developments, their decline appears to continue, particularly in the inner city. In this context, it has been argued that small firms do more than play an economic role, where they can more rapidly exploit opportunities which do not require large-scale investment, they play a social role within the community for small firms can be accommodated in inner city areas more easily than large firms.

Local problems affecting small firms

Most of the foregoing remarks refer to conditions prevailing in the general economy, but many of the closures and resultant loss of jobs can be attributed to local authority planned redevelopment schemes. In many towns and cities the wide-scale clearance of old slum housing has been responsible for the loss of many small firms because such old housing was often mixed up with small factories and workshops. Until about 1970, planning at both central and local levels viewed mixed land use zoning with disfavour, and small firms in residential areas were tagged with the dubious epithet of 'non-conforming' and encouraged or forced to move out. Even where new factory or workshop premises were contemplated or constructed following clearance, most local authorities felt obliged to charge a full economic rent, which might be twice or three times the previous level, and too high for firms to absorb. In any case, the provision of suitable industrial premises by local authorities has faced many financial difficulties, including the paradox whereby the costs of relocating a local business in new premises as a result of redevelopment had to be met from locally determined funds, whereas the compensation paid to those whose business was extinguished completely was a charge against key sector funds and did not prejudice other local spending. The *inner area studies* highlighted the fact that for the previous twenty or so years the balance of the inner city had been heavily weighted in favour of the residential needs of the community and against employment. Too much stress should not be placed upon the effects of past redevelopment upon small-business decline which should still be cast in the wider economic context of market concentration and recession. Notwithstanding, other local problems such as inadequate or outdated premises, lack of room for expansion, difficulties in obtaining finance, problems of labour supply and training, traffic and parking problems, access and loading difficulties and complex planning procedures have all been shown to affect the viability of small firms in inner areas.

A number of inner area local authorities have conducted surveys of demand for industrial premises and found that, in fact, there is a significant demand for suitable factory and workshop accommodation, but most of the demand is centred within the 100 m^2 to 500 m^2 bracket, with mainly expanding firms seeking accommodation of 200 m^2 to 500 m^2, and, generally speaking, for reasons of cost and management the private sector prefers to concentrate upon the provision of larger premises without multi-occupation. Even where refurbishment of existing premises might be a possibility the imposition of onerous and unrealistic conditions deters action and causes resentment. Moreover, the growing practice of placing existing or local user conditions on planning consents increases the task of rejuvenation and creates a dangerously static situation. Further aspects of planning aggravation include the pedantic approach taken by many authorities to the expansion or extension of small workplaces, particularly in residential areas, and the constraining effect of inflexible parking and loading regulations around small businesses.

Scope for local authority action

Despite the general pressures for dispersal and relocation away from the town or city centre, local authorities have an important role to play in stemming the decline of inner areas. A number of main priorities can be identified in this task — to maintain existing industry and employment opportunities, to encourage expansion and stimulate new initiatives, to avoid displacing acceptable small firms and to help them flourish, and to assist new small firms in starting and aid their growth. These priorities can be effectuated in three principal ways — by using planning controls effectively, by providing for the social and service infrastructure needs of industry, and by using its advocacy role in lobbying and acting as a catalyst for policy changes and action.

From a planning viewpoint, local authorities should do their utmost to allow existing small firms to remain undisturbed where redevelopment is proposed, and attemp to ensure continuity of production. Development plan zonings need to be reappraised to see if they are realisitic in their degree of separation of uses, or if there could be some mixed use reallocation. Within housing action areas and other residential areas, local authorities should relax controls over the expansion or introduction of small firms where the resultant levels of noise, fumes, vibration and traffic movement are not significantly higher. This more flexible approach could be facilitated if more emphasis were placed upon making local plans take the form of area community plans which reflected such key issues as employment as well as housing at a very local level. The identification and designation of industrial improvement areas should receive early and sympathetic attention. Policies aimed at protecting existing industrial buildings in areas where demand clearly persists or can be anticipated should be formulated, so that the loss of industrial floorspace within obvious 'work areas' can normally be resisted. The direct provision of industrial accommodation designed to suit the needs of small firms either by partnership, or out of locally determined funds or where an authority benefits from urban area aid, should be considered. Information and advice centres for small businesses could be established. Generally, therefore, local authorities should be seen to be pursuing a policy towards local industry of ensuring an adequate supply of small industrial units at rents that small firms can afford by a rolling programme of land acquisition and the development and rehabilitation of industrial premises. It is also imperative that both central and local government stimulate private-sector activity and foster co-operation between landowners and developers in the implementation of industrial regeneration programmes.

9 Housing

It is often said that housing is not one problem but many, and one immediate characteristic which readily identifies the housing market is its contentious and controversial nature, for housing gives shelter, security, privacy, investment and personal identity. The town planner, being concerned with housing need and provision, valiantly strives to marry the two, but is beset on all sides by administrative, statutory, financial, social and political constraints. These are exemplified by the hodge-podge miscellany of legislation that pertains to the problem, for since the Rent and Mortgage Restriction Act of 1915 there have been a dozen major housing acts and more than twenty-five other statutes relating to rent control and security of tenure. All that is possible in this chapter is an outline of the present position, policy and planning procedures.

The present position

Although reliable and up-to-date information is relatively difficult to obtain, the present picture of the housing market is probably clearer than at any time in the past. Nevertheless, significant changes are constantly occurring and in describing the current stock of housing accommodation, its size, quality and forms of tenure, some degree of estimation is inevitable. Most of the following information, however, is taken from the consultative document *Housing Policy (Cmnd 6851)* produced by the Department of the Environment in 1977 and represents the most comprehensive review of housing policy to have been undertaken in this country.

The housing stock

From about 1968 there has been no absolute national shortage of houses and in 1976 there were about 500,000 more houses than households, a figure which has probably grown since then. This apparent surplus of accommodation does not mean that all housing problems have been solved, for a vacancy rate of around 300,000 is likely to persist in any particular year owing to repairs, sales, purchases and second homes. The age of the housing stock is also an important factor in assessing policy, and while the number of homes in Britain increased by approximately 40 per cent to a total of 20 million during the 25 years to 1976, 5 million dwellings still date from before 1900.

Housing condition

Between 1951 and 1976 the number of households living in houses statutorily unfit for human habitation, in substandard houses lacking one or more basic amenities, in overcrowded conditions with a density of occupation exceeding 1.5 persons per room, or sharing a house with other households, in England and Wales has been reduced from 10 million to 7.7 million. Despite this striking improvement there remain about 900,000 unfit houses, of which 700,000 are occupied, 950,000 households in substandard dwellings, 150,000 households in overcrowded conditions and about a million households sharing accommodation. Moreover, these figures do not include all those houses which though neither technically unfit nor substandard are in serious disrepair. They also take no account of families living in housing of good standard but unsuitable to their needs. Nationwide figures further conceal great variations in local conditions, for while some local authorities have almost no shortage of decent housing others have serious and intense problems.

Housing tenure

There has been a marked change during the century in the structure of housing tenure. In 1914 about 90 per cent of the 8.5 million houses in Britain were privately rented, around 10 per cent were owner-occupied, and the number belonging to local authorities was insignificant. Now, in England and Wales, only 15 per cent are privately rented, 55 per cent are owner-occupied, and 30 per cent are in the public sector. The trend towards owner-occupation would seem likely to continue. Every year there is also a great deal of movement between these three broad categories of tenure. In 1971, for example, when a detailed study was made for the whole of Great Britain, it was estimated that within the owner-occupied sector

460,00 households entered, 410,000 moved within the sector, 70,000 left for another sector and 170,000 disappeared as a result of death, dissolution or emigration; within the public sector 325,000 households entered, 230,000 moved within the sector, 100,000 moved to other tenures, and 90,000 disappeared; and within the private rented sector 440,000 households entered, 300,000 moved from one tenancy to another, 390,000 moved to other tenures, and 185,000 disappeared. In all, after eliminating double counting, about 2.1 million households moved, or approximately one in nine throughout Great Britain.

Need and demand

In any consideration of housing policy it is necessary to distinguished between housing need and housing demand. Housing need relates to standards of accommodation deemed acceptable by society, whereas housing demand takes account of market conditions reflected in price and the ability to pay. In terms of housing need, it is difficult to measure precisely because the range and degree of need varies enormously, but it has been estimated that at least 1.8 million households in England and Wales, or over 10 per cent, are living in circumstances that would not normally be thought acceptable. In addition, it has been gauged that a further 50,000 to 70,000 houses become statutorily unfit every year and around 135,000 new households are formed annually, so that a substantial level of new housebuilding, rehabilitation, maintenance and repair is required to improve the housing situation.

Administration

It is appropriate at this juncture to set out briefly the principal agencies responsible for the framing and execution of housing policy (Table 2).

Central government

In England the administration of national housing policy, as established by Parliament, is the responsibility of the Department of the Environment, where, accountable to the Secretary of State, a Minister for Housing and Construction takes charge of all matters relating to housing programmes and finance, house improvement,

168   *The components of planning*

Table 2   *Annual housing starts and completions by sector (England and Wales) (percentages in brackets)*

	Private sector	Local authorities including new towns	Housing associations and government departments	Total
Housing starts				
1967	225,389 (56%)	167,208 (41%)	10,976 (3%)	403,573
1968	190,132 (54%)	148,549 (43%)	11,258 (3%)	349,939
1969	158,195 (52%)	134,074 (44%)	11,381 (4%)	303,650
1970	156,930 (56%)	114,778 (40%)	10,701 (4%)	282,409
1971	195,516 (63%)	101,600 (33%)	12,919 (4%)	310,035
1972	214,315 (67%)	90,855 (29%)	12,308 (4%)	317,478
1973	200,155 (68%)	83,871 (28%)	11,636 (4%)	295,662
1074	95,673 (43%)	111,397 (51%)	12,476 (6%)	219,546
1975	137,163 (47%)	134,302 (46%)	19,775 (7%)	291,240
1976	138,347 (47%)	126,509 (43%)	29,670 (10%)	294,526
Housing completions				
1967	192,940 (33%)	159,347 (44%)	10,611 (3%)	362,898
1968	213,273 (57%)	148,049 (40%)	10,404 (3%)	371,726
1969	173,377 (54%)	139,850 (43%)	10,938 (3%)	324,165
1970	162,084 (53%)	134,874 (44%)	10,308 (3%)	307,266
1971	179,998 (58%)	117,215 (38%)	12,563 (4%)	309,776
1972	184,622 (64%)	93,635 (33%)	9,037 (3%)	287,294
1973	174,413 (66%)	79,289 (30%)	10,345 (4%)	264,047
1974	129,626 (54%)	99,423 (41%)	12,124 (5%)	241,173
1975	140,381 (50%)	122,857 (44%)	15,456 (6%)	278,694
1976	138,477 (50%)	124,152 (45%)	16,031 (5%)	278,660

building regulations, new towns, relations with the building industry, building research and development, government accommodation, planning, development control and land. The respective central government departments for housing in Wales, Scotland and Northern Ireland are the Welsh Office, the Scottish Development Department and the Department of the Environment for Northern Ireland. The Ministry advises and guides the work of local authorities, imposes certain statutory standards, and maintains a firm control over broad financial matters, but as housing agencies the local authorities are autonomous for the administration and management of their own housing services. A housing services advisory group exists to provide support for the Ministry's professional advisory unit, which works under a housing adviser and aims to promote good professional practice within housing agencies. From time to time the Minister also appoints advisory and study groups to make recommendations on various aspects of housing policy.

Local authorities

In England since 1972 the district councils are the primary housing authorities, although the counties retain reserve powers, except in London, where the Greater London Council is a primary housing authority in its own right alongside the 32 London boroughs and the City of London. Similarly in Wales the 37 district councils are the primary housing authorities, as are the 49 district authorities in Scotland. The powers exercised by local authorities in respect of their housing function are extremely wide, and include the provision of municipal housing through new building, acquisition and conversion; the inspection of properties to ensure the maintenance of satisfactory standards; the exercise of powers and duties relating to clearance areas, unfit houses, overcrowded houses in multiple occupation, and the improvement of dwellings; the provision of temporary accommodation for the homeless; the exercise of powers regarding housing associations and the like; the provision of mortgage finance; and an array of duties in respect of the management of property, employment of direct labour, assessment and collection of rents, and provision of a housing advisory service. Most respectable local authorities now have a director of housing or housing manager in charge of a housing department to perform the above functions and ensure that a comprehensive approach is adopted towards all aspects of housing provision.

The all-embracing nature of housing policy means that a corporate attitude must be pursued within a local authority, solidly based upon research, continual reappraisal, sound management and effective training. An increasing emphasis is being placed upon tenant participation in the management of municipal housing, and alternative forms of tenure such as co-ownership and equity sharing are beginning to be more widely explored. With the growth in the stock of public-sector-provided housing in England and Wales from 2.2 million dwellings in 1951 to 5.5 million in 1976, the scale of resource expenditure demanded a more flexible yet more co-ordinated method for arranging local authority housing investment, and in 1976 the Minister announced the new system of *housing investment programmes*. These are a new form of housing plan, based upon a comprehensive assessment of the particular local housing situation, the main element of which is a reasoned capital budget covering the local authority's own capital spending plans and related to its broad housing strategy for a future period of four years. The programme covers all aspects of housing activity including clearance and demolition, renovation, conservation, home loans, improvement to private householders, and acquisition as well as new building. Once the allocations are settled, authorities are free to proceed with the minimum of central government intervention. These housing investment programmes are said to provide a means of controlling public expenditure while allowing resources to be allocated selectively in the light of varying local needs, conditions and preferences. They are also stated to give local authorities an incentive to devise a cost-effective mix of spending programmes, encourage them to take an overall view of housing provision, and afford some flexibility in spending within a financial year and from one year to another as circumstances change and needs arise.

New towns

The avowed aim of government to achieve a new balance between development within the cities and development outside means that for the forseeable future the role of new towns as housing authorities will be reduced. Nevertheless, it is worth recalling that the English and Welsh new towns have built some 220,000 houses since the Second World War and been responsible in recent years for a tenth of the public-sector rented programme. Pressure is also at present being applied to them to increase the level of owner-occupation by means of sale.

Housing associations

A dramatic growth in the activity of housing associations has been experienced since a new system of financial support was introduced by the 1974 Housing Act. The voluntary housing movement or 'third arm' of housing has, in fact, a long, varied and interesting history in providing rented and co-operatively owned housing accommodation of different kinds. Apart from a few cost-rent and co-ownership schemes, however, housing associations rely principally upon public funds and operate within the public sector. There are a number of

different types of housing association including general family, old
people's, industrial, self-build, cost-rent, co-ownership, co-operative,
special purpose and government sponsored housing associations. In
the strictest sense a housing association is defined as a society, body
of trustees or company established for the purpose of providing,
constructing, improving or managing the construction or
improvement of houses and who do not trade for profit. Under the
Housing Act 1974 the Housing Corporation was given much wider
powers in relation to the housing association movement, which
included the establishment and maintenance of a register of housing
associations and the supervision and regulation of those registered.
There are now well over 2000 so registered, and, with minor
exceptions, only registered housing associations are eligible to receive
loans from local authorities and the Housing Corporation. Their role
is likely to expand in the future, and their rate of construction and
conversion of dwellings already runs at around 30,000 to 40,000 units
a year. It is said that they have a particularly useful function to
perform in contributing variety and flexibility to the public sector,
being often better able to provide for more mobile households and
groups with special needs.

The private sector

Two distinct areas of activity in terms of supply can be distinguished
in the private housing market – the development of new houses for
sale and owner-occupation, and the letting of accommodation for
rent by private landlords. With regard to private housebuilding the
rate of new construction has been a source of much concern over
recent years. House prices have been particularly volatile during the
1970s with two sharp rises in 1972 and 1978. Demand is usually
affected by both economic and psychological factors. Economically,
the availability of building society finance and to a lesser extent the
cost of borrowing, and psychologically, the panic that follows
predicted, rumoured or achieved increases in house prices and winds
the inflationary spiral higher and tighter, are the main causes. Supply
is also affected by a number of factors including the problems of
maintaining a stable and efficient programme of work in the building
industry, the cost and availability of materials and labour, and the
release of adequate amounts of building land. The private rented
sector has been in decline thoughout the century but still accounts for
about 2 million private tenancies, not including the 700,000 that are

tied to employment or the 200,000 and more housing association tenancies. Most private tenancies comprise elderly people, single people, students, newly married couples, highly mobile persons or those with domestic problems, and while few fears need be had about the reduction in the number of private rented houses, many of the people in these groups would be seriously disadvantaged if the decline in the amount of some form of rented accommodation were to continue unabated. It has been argued, therefore, that action must be taken within the private rented sector to compensate for the loss of accommodation and to prevent further decay in the condition of rented property. Among the suggestions that have been made to make the provision of rented accommodation a more attractive proposition are the speeding up of the procedures by which a resident or returning landlord can regain possession, a relaxation from full security of tenure of accommodation normally let with a business, the creation of a publicly accountable letting agency in the private rented sector, and a thoroughgoing review of the Rent Acts.

Housing improvement

A major swing towards house improvement has taken place over the past ten years or so. Rehabilitation, renovation and improvement have never been seen as substitutes for redevelopment but as both complementary and supplementary to it. The most significant aspect of improvement policy during the 1970s has been the concept of area improvement, whereby the gradual improvement of a selected area of older houses, accompanied by careful action taken to improve their surroundings, can lead to the progressive renewal of a familiar neighbourhood. In this way, renovation policy can be seen to have twin aims — social as well as economic. The social aim is to enable those who live in poor-quality older housing to bring it up to a decent standard as soon as possible. The economic aim is to minimize the waste of resources resulting from the neglect and decay of houses which still have useful life in them if brought up to a reasonable level of amenity and repair.

A number of different measures and events which track the progress of housing improvement since the Second World War can be usefully identified as follows.

Discretionary grants

These were first introduced by the 1949 Housing Act, and, as the name implies, were made at the discretion of individual local authorities. They amounted to a subsidy of half the cost of approved work within prescribed limits. Although certain authorities proved somewhat reluctant to make them, some 160,000 discretionary grants were awarded between 1949 and 1958.

Standard grants

While the system of discretionary grants remained, the House Purchase and Housing Act of 1959 introduced a new facility of standard grants whereby an owner could claim financial support, as of right, for the installation of amenities so long as certain basic conditions were fulfilled. Home improvements blossomed as a result in the early years of the scheme. In the first year, for example, approximately 84,000 standard grants were made, but as the level of grant remained constant throughout the 1960s and building costs rose so their popularity fell.

Improvement areas

The 1964 Housing Act empowered local authorities to designate improvement areas where more than half of the dwellings within a chosen area lacked one of the five basic amenities that attracted grant aid. Area-based improvement was not a new concept, but the 1964 Act aimed to encourage local authorities in forcing owners to improve property. As there was little or no additional financial support made available the scheme was not a great success, and the process of designation was slow.

The Deeplish Study

Published by the Ministry in 1966, *The Deeplish Study: Improvement Possibilities in a District of Rochdale* was a study of an area of older housing which showed that if assistance was given towards environmental improvement outside the home for such things as traffic management, better paving, street lighting and planting, owners would be more prepared to invest in their own house improvement, aided again by grants.

The Housing Act 1969

Following the White Paper *Old Houses into New Homes (Cmnd 3602)* published the year before, the 1969 Act marked a significant step forward in house improvement. The levels of both discretionary and standard grants were raised; an extra kind of grant, a special grant, was introduced to assist owners and occupiers of property in multiple occupation but not self-contained; new limits were established for special areas such as London and special circumstances such as multiple-storied buildings; local authorities, new towns and housing associations became eligible for aid in actually acquiring premises for conversion and improvement; and the idea of *general improvement areas* (GIAs) was introduced. These GIAs were areas with a potential for upgrading, which had no positional disadvantages as residential areas, and included few buildings so far deteriorated as to make rescue impossible except by redevelopment. Reinforced by the 1971 Housing Act, which provided additional financial support in areas of high unemployment, general improvement area policy was largely successful and the number of approved grants rose from around 109,000 in 1969 to 198,000 in 1971, 368,000 in 1972 and 454,000 in 1973, until it fell to 300,000 in 1974 when the special help to areas of unemployment expired. A further trend was the eagerness on the part of many local authorities to avail themselves of improvement grants to renovate their own estates. Conversely, the system came under considerable criticism because of the degree of alleged exploitation that took place by owners and developers realizing their grant aid as profits from sale.

The Housing Act 1974

As a result of two white papers directed at formulating policy for areas of housing stress, *Widening the Choice: The Next Steps in Housing (Cmnd 5280)* and *Better Homes – The Next Priorities (Cmnd 5339)*, the Housing Act 1974 reached the statute book, despite a change of government and of party. The principal measure concerned with improvement work was the notion of rehabilitation, where areas of socially and physically unacceptable conditions could be identified, and major projects of wholesale reconstruction embarked upon, as opposed to the rationale of general improvement area policy which relied upon a significant proportion of easily retrievable properties. The main instruments for implementing this policy of rehabilitation were housing action area and priority neighbourhood designation, backed up by a more sensitive and co-ordinated system of grant aid.

Unlike GIAs, *housing action areas* (HAAs) are areas of poor housing and social stress which over a period of five years can be effectively treated so as to secure the improvement of the housing accommodation in the area as a whole, the well-being of the persons at the time residing there, and the proper and effective management and use of that accommodation. More favourable grants are available within HAAs and improvement may even be compulsory. Their designation may also be made as a holding operation pending future proposed clearance and redevelopment. It is still too early to judge their success, but though progress has been a little slower than was originally hoped, due to the multiplicity of problems encountered, they provide a useful weapon in the armoury of improvement work.

Priority neighbourhoods (PNs) can be designated in order to prevent housing deterioration in or around stress areas where other forms of immediate action are not possible, and to avoid stress conditions rippling out from areas, such as HAAs or GIAs, where action is being taken. The criteria for selection and the provisions for declaration and control are roughly similar to those for HAAs, but there is no requirement for an immediate five-year plan of action, and though PNs are declared for an initial period of five years they may subsequently be renewed for successive periods of five years upon review. Special powers for acquisition and use of land which apply to HAAs also apply to PNs, but no grants are available for environmental work and the more favourable levels of aid for house improvement do not apply. A PN must, however, surround or have a common boundary with an HAA or a GIA, and great emphasis is placed upon the significance of a high proportion of houses in the area being owned by private non-resident owners.

Grant aid towards renovation is the key to the implementation of housing improvement policy, and while grants are especially important to the treatment of GIAs, HAAs and to a lesser extent PNs, they are also available outside these areas. Grants for private owners are paid out by the local authority for the area, who in turn receive a subsidy from central government amounting to 90 per cent of the total in GIAs and HAAs and 75 per cent elsewhere. There are now four basic types of grant available under the 1974 Housing Act: improvement grants, for work of a high all-round standard to properties with a good life ahead of them; intermediate grants, formerly the standard grant, available as of right to provide certain basic amenities in particular circumstances; special grants, given at the discretion of the local authority for the provision of standard amenities in a house in multiple occupation; and repairs grants, introduced by the Act to enable a dwelling to be brought into a state of good repair, and only available within GIAs and HAAs at the local authorities' discretion where they are satisfied that the applicant could not otherwise afford to do the work. The percentage amount of grant an owner receives is usually 75 per cent in an HAA, 60 per cent in a GIA and 50 per cent elsewhere, but these rates can be varied in certain circumstances or by order.

Housing condition survey in England 1976

This survey showed that since the previous one in 1971 the number of unfit houses in England had fallen from 1,147,000 to 794,000 as a result of 440,000 dwellings being made fit and 260,000 being demolished but a further 350,000 becoming unfit. In the period 1971 to 1975 over 550,000 improvement grants had been made to home owners, but a significant factor was that the share of expenditure going to public improvement increased from about 30 per cent of the total to 40 per cent in a sector that had less than a sixth of the unsatisfactory stock by 1976. The survey also showed a dramatic increase of almost 50 per cent to almost one million in the number of houses requiring major repairs and a further 1.1 million dwellings which were in an unsatisfactory state of repair.

Housing Policy: A Consultative Document (Cmnd 6851) 1977

This publication, from which much of the information contained in this chapter has been drawn, is a major comprehensive review of housing policy originally directed towards the financial aspects of housing but subsequently widened to include a further consideration of the social aspects. Some seventy-four separate recommendations were made, too long to list in full here, but covering such matters as the need to undertake further surveys, prepare comprehensive local housing strategies, provide more financial assistance to those in need, ensure a steady supply of land for housebuilding, encourage the private rented sector, draw up housing investment programmes, establish more realistic cost controls and local authority allocation policies, and make a greater impact upon the inner city problems.

Special housing needs

There are a relatively large number of people who face special difficulties in obtaining suitable accommodation, and in framing their local housing policies it is becoming increasingly evident that local authorities must adopt a more flexible yet determined approach towards housing provision. The pressure upon those with special needs has, in many instances, been exacerbated by the dwindling stock and reduced mobility in the private rented sector, which means that a more sensitive and radical attitude to public-sector allocation procedures is needed to ensure an optimum use of public housing stock. Groups with individual housing needs include the following.

The elderly

Nearly 14 per cent of the population are over 65 and one of the most dramatic demographic trends we face is the inexorable future predicted rise in this figure coupled with a related growth in those over 70 and 80. Many elderly people live in substandard housing, and in 1971 it was estimated that a quarter of elderly households lacked at least one basic amenity, and the older they were the more amenities they lacked. Special consideration should, therefore, be given to the possibility of providing more easily managed accommodation, preferably on one level, easily and constantly heated, convenient to shops and community services, and integrated with, but not irritated by, local residents. Reassuringly, it should be noted that approximately 25 per cent of all new council houses are now especially designed for the elderly.

The handicapped

Around 3 million people in Britain are in some degree physically disabled, many of them being also elderly, and while special consideration must be afforded to them in terms of accommodation it is really a matter of internal functional design rather than planning provision and external layout. The 1970s have witnessed a commendable level of concern and action in this field, but, almost exclusively, the response has been from the public as opposed to private sector. The government accordingly have fostered a programme of new building directed to the needs of the physically disabled, and have assisted local authorities and housing associations through the subsidy system and design guidance.

Single people

There are now about 8.5 million people of working age in England and Wales of whom over 1.3 million live on their own. The major growth has been in young persons under 30 living alone, rising from 70,000 in 1961 to about 275,000 in 1976 and probably more by now. Young workers, trainees, nurses, apprentices, teachers, students and others form an important mobile section of society, but one for whom the housing market is ill-prepared. Until around 1970 there had been little special provision for young single households, apart from the private rented sector, but since then a certain amount of progress has been made in producing purpose-built accommodation in the form of flats and flatlets with certain shared facilities and at comparatively low cost, often along co-operative lines. Many local authorities have also begun to tackle the single householder problem.

Gypsies

Under the Caravan Sites Act 1968 local authorities were placed under certain obligations regarding the provision of sites for the use of gypsies and other nomadic people. Action has been slow, however, and a government publication *Accommodation for Gypsies* (1977) describes how difficult is their position with the growth and complexity of laws and regulations, and the nature of local reaction to them. It has been estimated that about 25,000 persons are without access to standard amenities, but with the financial constraints currently exercised upon local authority expenditure and the degree of public antipathy, many councils have sought exemption from the provisions of the 1968 Act on the grounds that suitable sites are not available or the demand for sites too small. Nevertheless, some of the sites that have been established are extremely successful, but it has been suggested that a further 300 or so are still required.

Others

There are a number of other categories commanding special attention in respect of housing provision, such as the 50,000 or so homeless households, the 620,000 one-parent families, and the whole thorny area of ethnic minorities, but most of the potential remedial policies lie way outside the domain of planning.

Land availability

One of the principal dichotomies that has divided the public-sector planning authorities from the private-sector housebuilding agencies over the past twenty years or so has been the constant debate about the availability of adequate land for residential development. Setting aside the Land Commission and the community land scheme, both of which have come and gone and are discussed elsewhere, the normal machinery of planning has been much criticized for its unsatisfactory response to the needs of the private new housing market.

Following earlier exhortations by the Minister to release more land for housing development, the Department of the Environment published a circular in 1972 called *Land Availability for Housing* (Circular 102/72) encouraging local authorities to explore ways of increasing the supply of residential land and requiring them to make a survey and report to this end. This was followed a year later by Circular 122/73, also entitled *Land Availability for Housing*, which for a couple of years became known as the 'developers' charter' because in the absence of approved structure plans it placed a presumption in favour of permitting planning permission for housing in areas of perceived population growth, and an onus upon local authorities to overcome obstacles such as inadequate infrastructure that might appear to prevent early release. As a result a considerable amount of land was released at appeal, but as new development plans were approved and the warnings of the DoE were heeded, so the effect of the circular declined. At about the same time, the government expressed their desire in a white paper to see more land owned by government departments, nationalized industries and public utilities released for development, but to little effect, for we still witness the unwarranted retention of potential development land by public authorities.

Yet another circular was published in 1975, *Statistics of Land with Outstanding Planning Permissions* (Circular 32/75), which sought to investigate the controversy between planning authorities who contended that sufficient land was available to meet the demands of housing development but developers tended to hoard land to maintain profit levels, and housebuilders, who complained that the planning process was obstructive, dilatory and unresponsive to the true needs of the private housing market. The circular requested a listing by local authorities of individual private-sector housing sites of over 0.4 hectare in metropolitan districts and 1 hectare in non-metropolitan districts which had an outstanding planning permission. The returns showed that for the whole of England the total stock of land with outstanding permission comprised some 27,720 ha on 7000 individual sites with a capacity for 623,400 dwellings. With smaller sites outside the scope of the survey it was estimated that the actual total stock of outstanding permissions in 1975 amounted to 37,860 ha providing for 852,200 dwellings. Of the potential 623,400 dwellings 53 per cent of the stock had only outline permission, 26 per cent detailed permission and 21 per cent were already under construction. In 1978 the DoE produced a report *Land Availability: A Study of Land with Residential Planning Permission* undertaken by the Economist Intelligence Unit based upon the returns made be local authorities to Circular 32/75, with the dual aims of assessing how accurate the stock of outstanding planning permissions is as a measure of the real availability of land for housebuilding, and determining what are the factors that hinder the implementation of planning permissions. The most important findings of the study were that work had started or even been completed on nearly 70 per cent of the sites but on some 26 per cent work had not even commenced. It was recognized that many of the sites contained in the 70 per cent starts would not have been problem free and might have taken a long time to come on stream. The study did, however, draw the conclusion that the stock of outstanding planning permissions in mid-1975 had proved to be about 70 per cent accurate as an indicator of real availability, on the assumption that real availability was taken to mean that a start can be made on a site within two years. The problem is, it can be argued, that much development land is potentially available which does not have planning permission and the study should surely have compared the amounts of land developed for housing that resulted, respectively, from successful appeals and from local authority allocation. Perhaps they looked at the wrong problem. Nevertheless, some of their findings relating to the non-implementation of planning permissions are of interest. The principal factors explaining non-implementation were classified as: physical, to do with site preparation difficulties and lack of suitable infrastructure, particularly sewerage; planning, to do with poor planning administration, disagreements between the applicant and the authority, and other planning policies external to the site; financial, involving problems of bankruptcy, and difficulties in raising funds; the market, because of poor overall demand conditions and changes in the pattern of demand; landholding, to do with owners deciding not to proceed with development, speculation by non-builders, a transfer of ownership and the creation of builders' land banks, and the phasing of schemes; ownership, relating to obstructive ownership, particularly in respect of access, and other problems such as multiple ownership, easements and covenants; and land use, regard possible transfer to the public sector or a change to essentially non-residential use. While not profound, these findings succinctly describe the known constraints that surround the act of private residential development and reaffirm the views of many housebuilders. The real problem of land availability, however, that of ensuring that sufficient residential development land is released to meet housing demand, remains.

Planning and housing

From the foregoing sections on housing policy it can be seen that it is a subject which crosses professional and policy boundaries. It is difficult to disentangle housing considerations from other social and economic aspects of society, and, therefore, the town planner cannot be said to embrace all questions of housing policy within his profession purview. Equally, it is not possible to isolate housing issues from other components such as employment, education, shopping, leisure and transport within the planning process. Certain basic tasks can, however, be identified that fall directly within the responsibility of the town planner, most of which are subsumed by the requirement to measure and forecast housing need, make the necessary land use allocations, and control the resultant physical form of the development or redevelopment.

The sort of questions which have to be asked by a local authority in preparing a housing policy for their area are:

How many dwellings are required to meet current needs?
Of what type should these be, in terms of tenure, cost, size and location?
How far does the current stock meet these needs?
To the extent that there is a deficiency, how far can this be met by new building in the public and private sectors and by conversion and improvements in the existing stock?
What future changes in needs are ascertainable?
What implications follow for housing policy?

The steps which have to be taken to do this can be summarized as follows:

survey of the existing population
forecast of future population
assessment of present condition and future requirements of the
 housing stock
allocation of land and designation of special areas accordingly.

The procedures of population prediction have already been dealt with, so the first major task to be considered here is the assessment of the existing stock, and a number of factors must be examined.

Density

The various means of expressing residential density and their relative merits are described elsewhere, but briefly it can be measured in terms of dwellings, habitable rooms, persons, or bedspaces per hectare. The purpose of surveying prevailing densities is to ascertain the degree of comfort that exists throughout the community, pin-point the areas of need, relate the size of population to provision of services, and permit the monitoring of a plan's performance.

Type of dwelling

It is important to know the range and variety of dwelling types within a particular area, for they all have different characteristics and requirements. Most surveys should therefore attempt to assess the housing mix in terms of small or large blocks of flats; detached, semi-detached, or terraced houses; bungalows. maisonettes, caravans, boats, down to institutional accommodation such as old people's homes. One important factor that should also be taken into account besides the mere number of dwellings is their relative size. This should not only be calculated in number of rooms but also expressed in persons per square metre, thus giving a clearer indication of crude accommodation capacity and use. It is common practice to obtain information regarding the age of dwellings within a particular area under study. Different bases are employed for this purposee but pre-1880, 1880–1919, 1919–44, and 1944 onwards are popular and easily applicable. It is interesting to note that due to early industrialization nearly one-half of the existing stock of houses was built before 1919, and that the average age of dwellings throughout the country is about fifty-six years.

Occupation

This is most generally gauged in terms of a household and the number of rooms available to it. One difficulty emerges in the very definition of a 'room', for different housing surveys have adopted varying measures. The Allen report of 1965,[1] for example, whose principal concern was with the impact of rates on households, included bathrooms and garages which are usually ignored. The *Rowntree Housing Study*, also in 1965, excluded attics unless specifically used as bedrooms, and the Office of Population Censuses and Surveys has now changed its policy in respect of kitchens to include them as a room for the purpose of the survey irrespective of their size of use. This variance can lead to anomalies because, as Cullingworth points out,

> households who are forced through lack of space to use attics as bedrooms may appear to have more rooms than smaller households in identical accommodation. Conversely, households small enough to eat in a kitchen may appear to have more rooms than larger households who eat in a living room.[2]

Once again the measures of persons per dwelling and persons per habitable room have been found inappropriate in assessing overcrowding. A more sophisticated approach is provided by the *social survey*, which views not only required capacity of accommodation but also takes account of sex and age separation. The statutory methods of judging overcrowding are very much more arbitrary and solely relate the number of rooms in a dwelling to the permitted number of persons, with some allowance for the size of the room. With the increasing rise in the standard of living, statutory measures fail to keep abreast with popular attitudes towards acceptable accommodation.

With the present housing problem, under-occupation has become as significant as overcrowding in assessing the overall allocation of accommodation. Whereas the 1960 housing survey of England and Wales indicated that only 0.6 per cent of households were statutorily overcrowded, 10 per cent of dwellings were found to be under-occupied.[3] Moreover, on the night of the 1961 census nearly 4 per cent of all dwellings were vacant, and with annual additions to the housing stock running at below 2 per cent this represents a significant factor in the housing crisis.

Another factor that should be considered when analysing the

nature and degree of occupation is the form of tenure, whether it is owner-occupied, rented, municipally owned, or tied to employment. Although it is often difficult to ascertain when conversion or a change of use has taken place within a dwelling, the consequence of such action has considerable repercussions upon planning policy in terms of the provision of services and facilities. In this context many authorities are experiencing great difficulty in forecasting future community requirements with the explosion in higher education and the demand for student lodgings.

Physical condition

Information regarding the condition of buildings is of consequence to the town planner in establishing his overall priorities, determining the nature and magnitude of the housing problem in his area, comparing it with the national picture, and enabling him to make decisions regarding alternative solutions. A detailed survey will require a set of objective criteria with which to assess standards of physical condition and permit comparison. J. N. Jackson in his book *Surveys for Town and Country Planning* cites the American Public Health Association manual as providing an excellent approach. This publication sets out a *housing condition index* whereby a very wide range of varying factors including heating, lighting, sanitation, access and overcrowding are awarded points based upon acceptable standards. In this way housing deficiency is measured and recorded. The National Institute of Economic and Social Research undertook a 3500 sample survey of the physical condition of dwellings in England and Wales using a ranking basis of good, fair, fair to poor, poor and very poor. Not surprisingly a direct correlation between age and condition of dwellings was discovered.

A more significant relationship is that between external and internal conditions recognized by Professor Parry Lewis at Manchester University. His researches have led to the formulation of a *survey for housing and environmental deficiency* (SHED), which is based upon the hypothesis that the internal condition of a property and its respective amenities are reflected in the external condition. The advantage of this method is that an inexpensive external survey is sufficient to determine housing deficiency, although where possible a brief internal inspection is advisable as a safeguard against inaccuracy. It is further possible to attach a figure for repairs and improvements based upon the 12-point housing standard advocated by central government and employed in SHED. From this the total figure can be obtained for bringing an authority's housing up to Housing Act standard, as well as figures for average improvement cost per house, per person, and per household adequately accommodated. The Department of the Environment now provides a similar housing condition index which relies, perhaps too heavily, upon the expertise of the individual inspector undertaking the survey who is required to estimate the cost of repair.

Several surveys following comparable procedures have recently been undertaken by local planning authorities. Besides the actual condition of the housing stock they have also paid regard to the condition of the environment, a notoriously difficult concept to measure objectively, the information being obtained from the census, particularly in respect of the provision of amenities, local authority housing returns, which provide details regarding the legal criteria of 'unfitness', and rateable values, which supply a measure of housing quality based upon tenure, condition and location, possessing a common basis. Notable amongst them are the *Teesside Study*, which adopted SHED as the basic model and applied to seventy-five environmental areas within its area, producing a programme of priorities for treatment; the *Leicestershire Study*, which instituted a field survey of dwellings, awarding penalty points related to the cost of rectifying deficiencies while attaching great weight to the environment; and the *Warwickshire Study*, which rejected a cost-based assessment in favour of 'an assessment based on socially desirable weightings defining a level of environment', which took into account such aspects as car parking, noise, proximity of shops, schools, open space and public transport.

With the increasing emphasis upon area-based housing renewal policies there has emerged the need to develop and improve methods of identifying and measuring degrees of housing stress, so that a more efficient and equitable means of allocating limited resources can be devised. While the construction and operation of these indicators, a number of which have been developed, is rather complex, typical objectives a local authority might have in employing them are to:

rank and order all the enumeration districts into which their
    authority area is divided according to housing stress
identify the concentration and severity of the worst of the housing
    stress according to prescribed cut-off points

describe the type of housing stress
relate the concentration and severity of the housing stress to current
   legislative options and identify the possible scale of housing action
verify wherever possible the applicability and suitability of previous
   housing action selection and designation.

Naturally such indicators can be used to measure degrees of housing stress between authorities as well as within a particular authority. It could almost be said that an early form of indicator was the Parker Morris standard for new public building established in 1964 for the purpose of indicating the appropriate amenities and services a local authority should provide. Similarly, the 'five'- and 'ten'-part standards have been introduced for improvement and rehabilitation work across all sectors of the housing market. Both these standards have been criticized for being exclusively concerned with physical condition and ignoring the income generating capacities, which influence the impact of the policies.

More sophisticated indicators have been devised which take account of a wider range of social and economic factors. In attempting to present a picture of the severity and distribution of urban deprivation in the country the *census indicators urban deprivation* (CIUD) reports were prepared by the Department of the Environment in 1974. In these, census material was classified into eight groups relating to housing, employment, education, assets, socio-economic groups, special needs, housing tenure and residential mobility, with all enumeration districts for all authorities being ranked against a minimum standard in each group. The worst areas picked out were Glasgow, Rutherglen, Paisley, Kensington and Chelsea, Islington, Kingston-upon-Hull, Salford and Bradford. A second procedure was employed to determine the geographical distribution of the worst areas on a combination of indicators, which were share or lack of hot water, share or lack of a bath, lack of an inside toilet, overcrowding, shared dwellings, lack of exclusive use of all basic amenities, male unemployment, female unemployment and households without a car. The number of enumeration districts displaying the worst conditions above a selected cut-off point, showed that Clydeside with more than 30 per cent of its enumeration districts selected, certain inner London boroughs with over 12 per cent, and Tyneside with 11.5 per cent were the most disadvantaged areas based upon the chosed indicators. The report then suggested that such analysis could be usefully adopted in the selection of housing action area designation. A similar exercise was undertaken as part of the Department of the Environment's publication in 1976 of a study entitled *Area Improvement Notes*, which showed that between two and four indicators were quite sufficient to select areas for treatment as housing action areas, priority neighbourhoods or general improvement areas.

The problem with almost any housing quality survey is deciding upon which particular factors merit attention, the way in which they should be measured, and the establishment of acceptable standards.

Future provision of housing

Any calculations regarding future housing needs are inextricably bound in with population studies and projections. Not only is it estimated that nationally there will be crude population growth, but increased household formation is also likely. Another factor that influences the demand for housing is the level and rate of change in incomes. Owing to the degree of government involvement in the housing market, and the limitations of economic models, it is difficult to be precise on whether or not housing demand is more or less responsive to changes in income than other goods and services. On balance, however, it is likely that rising incomes will cause an increase in total expenditure on housing. Thus, as incomes rise the demand for housing will also rise. F. Pennance, in the Hobart Paper *Housing Market Analysis and Policy*, suggested that the demand for housing is responsive to both price and income changes.

Another determining aspect that the town planner should consider in surveying future residential demand is migration, which has the effect of increasing household formation in particular localities and of exacerbating regional housing problems. Housing demand is further stimulated by urban renewal. More and more houses, however, might fall into the categories requiring replacement or improvement due to obsolescence, higher standards or comprehensive redevelopment. The town planner working at the local authority scale is required to translate these national traits into a local context.

Future provision is obviously not limited to the influence of the demand side of the market. The supply side is riddled with controversy, beset by political vascillation, stunted by lack of professional imagination, and constrained by a statutory straight-jacket. While, on the demand side, techniques of housing survey and analysis are becoming comparatively sophisticated and reliable, on the supply side, owing to the complex interplay of social, economic and political forces, they are virtually non-existent. The effects of rent control legislation, building standards such as those instituted by the Parker Morris report, subsidizing council tenants, density standards, public transport policy, credit availability, taxation, release of land, restriction on planning permission, and a whole host of other supply determinants, can only be guessed at. In the light of prevailing circumstances it becomes increasingly difficult to make a temperate statement on the subject.

The majority of those elements that exert authority over the housing market are determined as a result of political pressure or national economic policy and, as such, are outside the domain of the land use planner. There are aspects which are relevant to the local scale, warranting attention by a local planning authority, and deserving of more extensive survey. These can be summarized as follows:

Survey of existing stock. This is, as previously described, to ascertain its nature, range, location, environment, ownership, age, condition and occupancy in order to provide a' basis from which to formulate policy.

Estimate future need. This is done in terms of a programme linked to a time scale, taking into account migration, commercial, industrial and natural growth, household formation and urban decay. It might be necessary to decide, at a comparatively early stage, the most appropriate course of action for particular areas. Rehabilitation, with its inherent advantages of conservation of buildings of a special historic or architectural interest, preservation of existing densities, a minimum of disturbance to the indigenous population, no need to exercise compulsory purchase powers, the use of facilities already available and serviceable, and the distribution of the financial burden between the public and private sector, might be a more attractive proposition in certain circumstances to redevelopment, despite the advantages gained by planning afresh. It is also necessary to link the supply of house types with the demand for accommodation capacity. The 'three-bed semi-detached syndrome', supported by the entrenched bastion of financial reaction that supplies credit to the market, satisfies but part of the population who are forced to endure it.

Survey of land availability. Given the present housing shortage a review of land use allocation, often designated and zoned many years ago, is probably well overdue. A more positive approach to derelict land and land held off the market, and a change in the parsimonious attitude towards residential planning permission that prevails among all too many planning authorities, are urgently required.

Survey of existing densities and future potential. This might well indicate that minimum controls in peripheral urban areas are more expedient than maximum controls in central areas.

Survey of development agencies. Having decided the amount of future housing required, the desired location and the type, it is necessary to appraise the most suitable agency for building it. If private-sector participation is sought a successful way of stimulating its involvement is by the preparation of detailed 'planning briefs' which set out the local authority policy in respect of the particular site, detailing such things as the level of permitted density, necessary access, car parking, materials, height and use. This can often save a great deal of time and expense, and thereby renders the scheme more profitable to the developer, and the policy more viable to the authority.

It is always worth remembering that, in any survey or technique applied to housing, a large measure of value judgement is introduced. Whose opinion decides such criteria as fitness, overcrowding, environmental deficiency, building standards, space standards, high-rise development, high-density construction and priority regarding land release? These highly evocative and controversial topics can all too easily be subjected to sophisticated technical processing, and presented with a falsely accredited aura of objectivity.

10 Offices

As society becomes more economically mature so the proportion of tertiary or service employment and quarternary or exclusively office-oriented employment increases. Although total employment grew by 20 per cent between 1921 and 1951, office employment grew by 150 per cent over the same period, and since 1951, when 15 per cent of the working population were office-based, by 1971 28 per cent were so employed. The major growth took place during the 1950s, however, for while total employment grew by only 7 per cent during the decade, office employment rose by almost 40 per cent, accounting for almost three-quarters of the overall increase, most of which took place in such areas as management, marketing, government and insurance. The most recent trend has been for an expansion of professional rather than clerical employment, with a growth of 25 per cent as opposed to 5 per cent between 1966 and 1971, respectively. One of the main causes of such rapid growth has been the expansion of the public sector in order to manage and administer the successive bouts of intervention that have characterized so much of post-war government policy. The growth in employment has been accompanied by an acceleration in the rate of new office development and the demand for even more. It is probably fair to say, however, that the post-war pressures for office development have been met by an arbitrary and erratic set of policy measures, being the product of a scant and misconceived understanding of the office function. With the dearth of adequate techniques by which office employment policies could be framed and tested, all that is really possible is a brief chronicle of the attitudes and policies that have governed office location decisions over the past forty years. Straight away, however, it is important to recognize the overwhelming dominance of London and its environs, where over 40 per cent of the country's offices reside.

Historical background

The origins of the boom in office development can be attributed to the economic expansion of trade and industry in the nineteenth century. Apart from a slump in the 1930s, reflected by a sharp decline in rents and caused by an over-provision of accommodation and a general crisis of confidence, the demand for office space has continued unabated. A number of phases and events can be distinguished in the search for an effective means of controlling the distribution of office employment, the majority of which relate to London.

The Barlow report

Modern British regional employment policy rests heavily upon the recommendations enshrined in the Royal Commission on the Distribution of the Industrial Population, whose report was published in 1940. With the publication of this report, and its view of employment as being a national problem and not a series of local ones, and the main solution being some form of dispersion, the scene was set for the next thirty-five years. Although the report proposed the introduction of industrial development control it barely made any mention of office development and dispersal. Nevertheless, in advocating decentralization away from existing industrial conurbations because of their allegedly inherent strategic economic and social disadvantages, the Barlow report formed the basis of the philosophy which led to the various office control measures of the 1950s and 1960s.

The London Advisory Plans

Greatly influenced by the Barlow report were the 1943 County of London Plan and 1944 Greater London Plan produced by Sir Patrick Abercrombie and known collectively as the London Advisory Plans. These plans proposed the dispersal of over one million persons and a quarter of a million jobs away from the congested inner areas of the capital to destinations beyond the green belt. The surprising aspect of these proposals is that while they recognized the problems of commerce as well as industry within the congested central areas, they omitted to recommend any formal machinery for controlling office employment, confining themselves to the pious hope that the decentralization of certain commercial activities would take place, and, somewhat paradoxically, they both hoped and anticipated that the greatest pressure for development would come from commercial and trading concerns returning to London once the Second World War had finished. It is also worthy of note that in encouraging the relocation to new and expanded towns, the Greater London Plan centred around the notion that commensurate numbers of industrial jobs and people would move to factories and houses, with little mention of office employment, even though industry gave employment to only 28 per cent of the total working force of the County of London.

The Town and Country Planning Act 1947

The neglect of the office function and the possible need to control the allocation of commercial floorspace largely continued with the passage of the 1947 Act, apart from the general power conferred upon local authorities to grant or refuse planning permission for all acts of development. Under the provisions of the Act, the London County Council (LCC) prepared a development plan in the period 1948 to 1951, which, though not approved by the Minister until 1955, introduced for the first time the concept of plot ratio as a primary method of planning control over commercial development. At this time the supply of office accommodation was severely limited by the need to obtain a building licence from the Ministry, although the 1951 LCC plan actually extended the area zoned for offices and the Council pursued a generous attitude towards applications for the change of use of property from residential to offices.

The permissive years, 1953 to 1956

While planning permission for almost 2.2 million m² of new office space, and a further 600,000 m² for change of use to offices, had been granted between 1948 and 1954, the annual level of approvals had virtually doubled by 1954 and 1955. This was mainly due to the repeal of the development charge in 1953, the abolition of building licences in 1954, and the compensation provisions of the planning code which made local authorities liable to liberally compensate owners for the refusal of planning permission under certain circumstances, as well as a general upturn in the economy. The compensation provisions were enacted under the third schedule to the 1947 Act and were not repealed until 1963; they became notorious as the 'third-schedule loophole', whereby developers were allowed to replace certain buildings plus an extra 10 per cent of the original cubic capacity. Modern office construction and design, however, permitted considerably more than 10 per cent, and then up to 40 per cent, additional lettable floorspace to be achieved, and, owing to the extraordinary compensation provisions included within the Act, few applications, for what can only be described as excessive planning permission, were refused. It has been calculated, for example, that if the LCC had refused the Westminster Trust its 40,000 m² building, half of the density resulting from the loophole, they would have been liable to pay £7.5 million in compensation. Moreover, the third-schedule has been held directly accountable for the creation of 170,000 additional office jobs in central London.

Growing restriction

An awareness of the need to control office development had always rested in certain quarters of the planning profession, and even in the 1955 approval of the 1951 County of London Development Plan the Minister, Duncan Sandys, had made modifications so that some designated areas were converted from industrial and office zoning to residential. Following a decision in 1956 to reduce plot ratios for commercial development and to introduce bonuses for the provision of residential space in commercial schemes, the LCC published in 1957 a *Plan to Combat Congestion in Central London*, more colloquially known as 'the grey book', which recommended that the area zones for office building should be reduced by 23 per cent. This effort to limit the increase in office floor space should be seen against the continued operation of the third-schedule loophole, and was described shortly afterwards by the Town and Country Planning Association as a belated attempt to retrieve a situation almost irredeemably lost. A further slight reduction in density was effected in the first review of the LCC plan in 1960, which also began to place as much importance upon restraining office development in the centre of London as upon the restraint upon industry. Despite LCC pressure to introduce a system of certification, exhortation and persuasion remained the principal instruments of policy, exemplified by the creation of the Location of Offices Bureau in 1963, and private development continued unabated until 1964.

The Brown ban 1964

In the wake of the publication of the *South East Study* in 1964 which indicated that the rate of increase in employment in the London conurbation over the first few years of the 1960s had been about 63,000 a year, a white paper was introduced by George Brown, the Minister, that imposed a total restriction on office development within a radius of 40 miles of the centre of London. The provisions of the white paper were incorporated a year later in the Control of Office and Industrial Development Act 1965, which for the first time instituted a system of *office development permits* (ODPs). When initially imposed, ODP controls applied only to the London Metropolitan Region and the West Midland conurbation centred on Birmingham, but by 1966 the area was extended to include the rest of the South East and West Midlands as well as East Anglia and the East Midlands. To begin with, the limit for exemption from ODP control in London was 3000 square feet, being subsequently raised to 10,000 square feet in 1970, following a relaxation outside London in 1969. The evidence now suggests that the impact of ODP control between 1964 and 1968, when it was significantly relaxed, was not very great, owing to the backlog of outstanding planning permissions in the system. It may, however, have rebounded in that it reduced the mobility of existing firms to decentralize within the South East.

Boom and slump

Between 1969 and 1973 the office development market rose to unheralded heights only to plummet again between 1973 and 1977, and the economic vagaries of this market tended to affect the supply of office accommodation to a far greater extent than planning policy. During the middle 1970s, however, the Greater London Council has attempted to devise a more effective office location policy which is directed at three basic issues; the persistent over-concentration of office employment in the central area; the need to contain the decline in office employment opportunities in the inner boroughs; and the redistribution of employment to those more disadvantaged outer boroughs.

Greater London Development Plan

The aims described above have to be implemented within the two-tier structure of planning, and in London the concept of a comprehensive office policy for the metropolis is bedevilled by internecine disputes between constituent London boroughs and the GLC. To a greater or lesser extent this is mirrored across the country with county and district disagreements. The GLC had hoped to influence metropolitan office policy by identifying a number of preferred locations, by making strict floorspace allocations to sectors of London, and by insisting that all applications for office development over 279 m² are referred to them. They now appear to be moving towards a rather more flexible policy in interpreting individual cases which can show exceptional circumstances for being located in areas of strict control. Despite constant adjustments, however, a clear and operational office policy remains elusive and the system of control is still largely conducted on an *ad hoc* basis.[1] As something of a paradox in the evolution of London's restrictions on office growth, moreover, the GLC has now been forced to modify its attempts to decentralize office employment, declaring that they will no longer acquiesce in the planned movement of jobs, of whatever kind, out of the city.

Demand and supply

Assessment of the demand for and supply of office space has tended to rely upon hunch and intuition, but with the volatile nature of the commercial land market there is a growing need to make it a more specialized and sophisticated task.

With regard to demand, it has been suggested that there is a spatial structure followed by large organizations based upon hierarchy of urban areas, so that, for example, the headquarters would be sited in London, the district offices in major provincial cities and the local offices in small county towns. This is far too simple an explanation, however, even as a starting point, for many other factors such as tradition, staff availability, housing, prestige, proximity to markets, access to clients, sources of information, complementary activities, social facilities, and individual preference on the part of directors, and their wives, go to make up the complex ingredients of office demand. From another angle, demand can be said to originate for one of four reasons:

Growth: a demand for office services caused by a growth in population, wealth or production either within the country generally or specific to a particular areas. Trend extrapolation is normally used

Table 3   *Central London office costs*

Prime office accommodation in the city*

	Commer-cial rate	Rates per sq ft	Open market rent per sq ft	Rates as % of rent	Total rent and rates
		(£)	(£)	(%)	(£)
1970	65.83p	1.42	12.50	11.4	13.92
1971	78.00p	1.69	13.00	13.0	14.69
1972	88.50p	1.91	13.00	14.7	14.91
1973	29.63p	3.32	16.00	20.8	19.32
1974	41.45p	4.65	22.00	21.1	26.65
1975	65.52p	7.35	18.00	40.8	25.35
1976	73.48p	8.24	12.00	68.7	20.24
1977	78.33p	8.78	13.50	65.0	22.28
1978	78.29p	8.78	15.00	58.5	23.78

Cost per employee

	Rent (£)	Rates (£)	Rent and rates (£)
1970	1500	170	1670
1971	1560	203	1763
1972	1560	229	1789
1973	1920	398	2318
1974	2640	558	3198
1975	2160	882	3042
1976	1440	989	2429
1977	1620	1054	2674
1978	1800	1054	2854

*Based on an individual space requirement of 120 sq ft

to gauge this, but while trends are a good starting point they are unreliable indicators of future performance.

Replacement: a localized move to larger or more suitable premises caused by expansion or obsolescence. To some extent this can be ascertained by interview, survey and an inspection of the physical condition of existing stock.

Relocation: a complete move to a different area caused by a variety of reasons such as the expiry of a lease, rent revision, redevelopment,

Secondary office accommodation in the city†

	Commer- cial rate	Rates per sq ft	Open market rent per sq ft	Rates as % of rent	Total rent and rates
		(£)	(£)	(%)	(£)
1970	65.83p	0.50	4.50	11.1	5.00
1971	78.00p	0.60	5.00	12.0	5.60
1972	88.50p	0.68	5.50	12.4	6.18
1973	29.63p	1.42	8.00	17.8	9.42
1974	41.45p	1.98	8.50	23.3	10.48
1975	65.52p	3.14	7.50	41.9	10.64
1976	73.48p	3.52	5.00	70.4	8.52
1977	78.33p	3.75	5.00	75.0	8.75
1978	78.29p	3.75	6.00	62.5	9.75

Cost per employee

	Rent (£)	Rates (£)	Rent and rates (£)
1970	540	60	600
1971	600	72	672
1972	660	82	742
1973	960	170	1130
1974	1020	238	1258
1975	900	377	1277
1976	600	422	1022
1977	600	450	1050
1978	720	450	1170

†Based on an individual space requirement of 120 sq ft

the desire to expand at a reasonable cost, a limited local supply of larger premises, or the need to consolidate operations.

Fashion: a particular town or city can suddenly become especially popular. On the other side of the coin, a fall in the demand for office space can result from multinational takeovers, which might reduce provincial office growth because of an increasing headquarters function elsewhere; increased office efficiency; the rapid introduction of advanced technology into offices causing a reduction in the need for clerical staff; or a general decline in the national or local economy.

From a planning point of view, the supply side of office employment is even hazier and consists in the main of a reaction to market demand in the form of controls, discussed below. In theory it should not be too difficult for a local authority to devise a strategic policy with specific objectives relating to the reduction of aggregate travel distances or journeys to work; the complementarity to other commercial activities; and the recapture of community benefits through planning gain targets and the aesthetic and environmental impact of office development. These could then be realistically translated into site specific terms in the preparation of local plans, and while most planning authorities attempt this procedure the results are far from satisfactory.

In considering the appropriate supply of office accommodation for a particular area it is necessary for an authority to take account of the effects certain commercial activities might have upon their county or district. These effects might include such matters as the increased rateable value of the new offices, the number of employees who will be moving in with the firm, the likely demand for additional housing and education, the possible level of extra commuting, the number of local residents who might gain employment, the extent to which economies or diseconomies of scale might be effected upon local-authority-provided services, and the multiplier effects upon the local economy resulting from additional spending power and specialized services.

It is often said that rental levels are a good indicator of the degree to which demand and supply are matched, but total cost of rent and rates per employee is now becoming a more important criterion. Table 3 demonstrates the volatility of rents for central London during the 1970s and the growing importance of rates. The signs are that both rent and rates seem likely to increase throughout the 1980s.

Planning controls

Apart from the usual planning controls such as density, zoning, height, daylighting, design and car parking, several means of control either apply especially to offices or have a particular effect upon them.

Office development permits

The need to obtain an ODP that operated between 1965 and 1979 primarily acted as a licence to apply for planning permission and could also be used as a means of imposing conditions on individual development schemes. The permits were initially issued by the Board of Trade, but the powers were moved to the Ministry of Housing and Local Government in 1969 which was later incorporated within the Department of the Environment. The exemption limits for London, originally 3000 square feet, were raised to 10,000 square feet in 1969, 15,000 square feet in 1976 and 30,000 square feet in 1977, and no appeal against a refusal was provided. Although speculative ODPs could be granted, most applicants had usually to line up a prospective tenant before application could be made, and a condition would be attached that for the first five years from the date of occupation only the named tenant would be allowed to occupy the building.

The principal aims were to solve regional imbalance by attracting, or rather diverting, firms to development areas, ease congestion caused by office employment in Central London and increase the supply of houses by focusing the attention of the construction industry on residential building instead of commercial. The criteria for issuing an ODP in the selected areas for control were that no extra employment should be created and that the scheme should be in the public interest. Initially it was envisaged as a temporary measure, rather like income tax, until a more positive policy in respect of office location and decentralization could be formulated. The system has come in for a great deal of criticism, but it did provide a breathing space, although it probably contributed to the spiralling increase in rents that occurred between 1963 and 1973. In 1961 City of London office accommodation was letting at under £2 per square foot in prime positions, West End rents were under £1 and suburban and provincial levels were under 50p, whereas in 1971 the rents were about £15, £18 and £3, respectively. The introduction of permits has been vilified because it did not reduce congestion, demand increased unabated, firms made more intensive use of existing premises, there existed a continued pressure for prestige locations, and dispersal to the regions was not an acceptable alternative for many firms. In the period between 1964 and 1967, when an additional 35 million square feet of floorspace was constructed throughout the country, 56 per cent was in the South East, and the next 'blessed' region was the North East with 10 per cent.

Floorspace

The use of floorspace allocations as both a strategic and tactical instrument of planning control has been widely adopted throughout the country. Strategically it has been employed to guide commercial activities to preferred locations and restrict them in others. The Greater London Development Plan divided London into eight sectors and apportioned commercial floorspace among them by comparing the number and distribution of office jobs likely to be catered for by existing and approved floorspace with the total number of office jobs likely to be required by the 1981 resident population.[2] The Layfield Inquiry into the plan cast considerable doubts about the efficacy of floorspace allocations for controlling the distribution and growth of office jobs in London, but the GLC retained the view that floorspace controls were a necessary adjunct to other forms of planning control, suggesting further that 'the policy is best expressed verbally with the floorspace figures serving a supporting quantification of the Council's objectives'. Nevertheless, since the change of political control in 1977 the floorspace allocations have not played such a prominent part in policy and matters have been left much more to the thirty-three London boroughs. Moreover, as it is the number of employees commuting to work that causes urban congestion, and not the sheer bulk of office buildings, it should logically be the number of workers that is controlled and not the amount of floorspace. Worker density standards are themselves not ideal measures, however, because of varying conditions of employment and the inherent difficulties likely to be encountered in enforcement.

Local user conditions

Local planning authorities, particularly in the home counties of the South East, are increasingly attaching conditions to commercial planning permissions restricting occupancy of the offices to those organizations who already have connections with the local economy. Local user constraints are now being commonly coupled with conditions restricting the size of the occupied unit, and some even go so far as to prohibit adjoining premises from being occupied by the same users. Such conditions and restrictions are often very difficult to interpret and enforce and make it awkward for developers to raise funds.

Issues

Location theory for industry might be unsophisticated but for offices it is primitive. The policy underlying it is indiscriminate, inconsistent, tardy and heavily reliant upon trial and error. Too much emphasis is placed upon the existing stock and future supply without sufficient regard to the nature of demand. Virtually no attempt has been made to define which office functions are most appropriate to central metropolitan positions, which to peripheral positions and which to the provinces, and how a policy of decentralization, if considered expedient, might best be implemented. Moreover, there is a strong political reluctance to offer the necessary incentives to reinforce such a policy, in marked contrast to industrial relocation. A further major obstacle to the establishment of a consistent approach towards the problem is the conflict that persists at all levels and between all agencies involved in the execution of commercial development policy. National strategy is at odds with regional, regional vies with the dominance of the South East, particularly the Greater London Council, and the GLC possesses a dissident relationship with its constituent boroughs.

Apart from this, there are a number of other issues which must be faced over the next few years in the framing and execution of office employment policy. These include:

1 What kinds of office function are most suitable to central area locations and what kinds are most suitably sited in suburban areas? In considering suburban location there are certain advantages in that because employment is brought to the worker, commuting costs are avoided and the diseconomies of central area congestion reduced. From the local authority point of view there might be multiplier effects upon the local economy as well as increased rate revenue, but the costs of other forms of communication might rise, the existing social infrastructure might be insufficient, suburban congestion might be induced or heightened, and because less use is made of central area commuting services a greater degree of subsidy may be sought.

2 Should office development that is dispersed to the suburbs be scattered around all the suburbs or should it be grouped in strategic centres? The Greater London Development Plan, for example, selected six major strategic centres for significant growth and a further twenty-eight preferred locations for less intensive development.

3   What form will the pattern of office development take in provincial towns and cities? There has been a significant tendency for many major national and international companies to locate a large proportion of their office-based activities in other regions outside metropolitan London.

4   Should offices in central area, suburban and provincial locations be mixed with other land use activities such as hotels, shops, transport terminals or housing? The conventional approach to zoning whereby different uses are usually separated has been broken down over recent years, and in respect of small business premises could benefit from an even greater degree of departure.

5   To what extent should potential office development be seen as a mechanism for extracting community gains? Guidelines are provided by many authorities on the types of planning gain which are acceptable. Some are couched in very general terms, some are standardized and some very specific. Most potential gains relate to physical planning and no allowance is made by planning authorities for the more intangible gains such as the local multiplier effects on small businesses, increases in local activity rates, higher incomes or less arduous journeys to work. It is important, however, that a thoroughgoing knowledge of the local property market is retained by the authority so that a full measure of recoupment is attained and overexcessive demands are minimized.

6   What are the respective relationships between public and private transport services and optimum office location? Despite the stated aims of many structure and local plans it is still far from clear what exactly constitutes an effective level of transport services and good accessibility.

7   What will be the effect upon the size and distribution of office accommodation in the light of technological advances in communications and business equipment? There can be little doubt that the ubiquitous silicon chip and the advent of micro-processing will have far-reaching effects on every aspect of the way we live. The rate of application is likely to increase geometrically in the near future. Intensive office automation is already on the horizon, and with the real price of sophisticated office equipment falling at between 10 and 20 per cent a year the organization of business as we know it, the roles performed within it, the space it occupies and the location it demands could all be subject to drastic revision. Similarly, increased efficiency

through advanced technology might not only lead to a reduced demand for space, but it is quite conceivable that progressively more emphasis will be placed by office workers upon the quality of life, and relocation linked with improved business communication could be the order of the day.

8 To what degree will increased office space be provided as a result of refurbishment? With the advent of stronger conservation policies and a generally heightened awareness of the need to preserve buildings of architectural and historic interest, many local authorities might be well advised to adopt a more flexible attitude towards the change of use in older protected premises to commercial activities.

9 How good is local authority knowledge of the office market? With the growing uncertainties that beset the commercial sector it is increasingly incumbent upon local planning authorities to establish a closer working relationship with the private sector, agents, consultants, developers, institutions and occupiers, and pursue a more positive approach towards marketing their own portfolio of suitable development sites.

Owing to the tremendous conflict that pervades the area of commercial location policy, and the remarkable lack of continuity that exists, there is a pressing need to devise a more rational basis by which to assess the respective forces that dictate the demand for, and supply of, office employment and development. Even if this means the abandonment of comprehensive planning approaches to the problem because of the high degree of uncertainty that persists, the disparate nature of office employment, and the strong variations that exist in local office markets, at least a sensible, flexible and incremental approach could be designed, based upon a better understanding of office linkages and business requirements, which would facilitate a more effective management of commercial activity.

11 Shopping

Until recently the vast majority of shopping facilities in this country were unplanned; like Topsy they 'just grew', sometimes by historical accident and sometimes by way of convenience. Now great attention is being directed towards the provision of shopping, its location, size and character. This is scarcely surprising when retailing commands an annual expenditure of approximately one-third of the gross domestic product, employs over 2.6 million persons, or one in every twelve workers throughout the country, and exerts considerable magnetism over other land uses. Because of the important role it plays in the national economy, the location of shopping has become the concern not only of local but also of regional and central planning agencies, and increasingly exercises the minds of geographers, economists, surveyors, developers and town planners alike. Apart from these economic aspects shopping provides a social function, acting as a focus of the community, a meeting place, and generally contributing to the well-being of society. Over the last few years it has displayed a changing character; the corner shop is disappearing, and the old high street parades straddling the channel of greatest traffic congestion are giving way to the planned, covered, pedestrianized centres adequately supplied with car parking, children's crèches and a wide range of other services.

Central place theory

Being essentially, though not exclusively, a central area function, the assessment of shopping demand and the decisions regarding retail location have their roots firmly planted in central place theory. The origins of this theory are to be discovered in the writings of von Thünen, a nineteenth-century Prussian landlord, who propounded an 'isolated state' theory based on the concept of the economic rent to be gained from agricultural production. He constructed concentric rings of land use radiating out from the market place which were dependent upon, and determined by, labour and transport costs. The theory was developed and applied to retail service activity in the 1930s by two German academics, Walter Christaller, a geographer, and August Lösch, an economist. They extended the notion of centrality, defining and detailing the importance of central places with reference to a series of complementary regions, examining the trade areas or hinterlands for a range of different goods and services. From their analysis they ascertained that different types of business have different conditions of entry, which they described as thresholds, some requiring larger minimum trade areas, or support population, than others. Put another way, consumers spent varying amounts on different goods and services and purchased them at varying intervals. From this they postulated a clearly identifiable hierarchy of central places. In fact they approached the problem from opposite ends. Christaller constructed his hierarchy from the strongest or highest-order centre downwards, requiring all his lower order centres to take account of them in determining their own location. Lösch, however, built his hierarchy from the lowest-order goods and services upwards, allowing a certain degree of manipulation of the location of centres to obtain an optimum hierarchy taking account of every level.

In this country, a similar study, but this time employing more empirical information, was undertaken by Dickinson. He examined the existing patterns of centres in East Anglia, classifying them according to their function and establishing an index of the services they provide. Many other parallel studies have been tackled, not unnaturally, their principal finding being that time rather than distance is the major determining factor in location.

The shopping hierarchy

From these studies of urban hinterlands and the pattern of retailing that emerges from their analysis, a hierarchy of shopping centres can be distinguished. This hierarchy is liable to change over a period of time, and is currently undergoing considerable alteration owing to the following factors: less available shopping time through increased female employment, rising car ownership and therefore greater mobility, a growing proportion of families possessing deep freezers and thus an added incentive to bulk-buy, worsening central area congestion and increasing expenditure on luxury durable goods promoting the demand for comparison shopping.

Although different definitions of the hierarchy are to be found, the following is a widely accepted summation:

Regional centre. This generally supports a population in excess of 300,000 and contains many specialist services and a full range of department stores. The best examples are probably the major conurbations such as Bristol, Leeds and Newcastle. It is predicted that such centres are likely to experience a decline in trade owing to increased car ownership and worsening congestion, but that the severity of the decline will vary from centre to centre. Where the whole spectrum of alternative centres is available the regional centre receives approximately 15 per cent of total consumers' retail expenditure, most of which is spent on durable goods.

Sub-regional centre. This usually supports a population of between 100,000 and 300,000 and includes national department and variety stores such as Marks and Spencer, John Lewis and Littlewoods. There is still a strong element of specialization, but more limited than that of the regional centre. Examples of this level of centre include Warrington, Cheltenham and Portsmouth. Currently almost 40 per cent of expenditure passes to the sub-regional centre, and if current trends continue an increasing proportion of spending on durable goods will take place at this level.

District centres. These cater for a catchment area of about 50,000, sometimes less, and normally include a variety store such as Woolworths, a Boots, and supermarkets like Sainsbury or Tesco. There are few, if any, specialist services, and examples of this type of centre can either be isolated towns like Hertford and Colchester, or found in the suburbs of large cities like Cowley in Oxford or Leith in Edinburgh.

Neighbourhood centre. This is often indistinguishable from a district centre, but can contain as few as twelve shops serving a population of 10,000. The functions of the neighbourhood and district centre are tending to merge together, with the result that between them they account for about 25 per cent of total consumer expenditure and very much more if other levels are not present.

Local centre. This consists of a few shops supplying a population of up to 2000, but nevertheless accounts for up to 20 per cent of retail expenditure.

It must be stressed that this picture of the hierarchy represents a general description only. The exact nature of the pattern of retail expenditure can vary considerably from area to area, as can the

Table 4 *Trades' support populations*

Trade	Population
Grocer	750–1000
Butcher	2000–3000
Baker	4000–5000
Greengrocer	4000–5000
Off-licence	4000–5000
Chemist	4000–5000
Newsagent/tobacconist	4000–5000
Ironmonger/hardware	4000–5000
Fishmonger	5000–10,000
Delicatessen	5000–10,000
Clothing	5000–10,000
Supermarket	20,000

Source: R. K. Cox, *Retail Site Assessment* (Business Books 1968).

character and size of the centres. It often occurs that not all levels in the hierarchy are always represented within a region, in which case a regional centre might have to double as a sub-regional and even district centre. To illustrate the point, an alternative hierarchy was outlined by G. M. Lomas in his study of retail trading centres in the Midlands as follows:[1]

first order or metropolitan centre, namely London
second order or provincial centre, such as Birmingham
third order or regional centre, such as Shrewsbury
fourth order or local centre, such as Bromsgrove
fifth order or service villages.

The types of shop that are to be found in any particular centre depend upon the population required to support them profitably in business.

Table 4 gives some indication of the necessary support population for various trades.

Assessment of shopping catchment

Any analysis of the potential location for shopping facilities involves two basic assessments. First it is necessary to calculate the size, shape and extent of the catchment area. Secondly, consideration must be given to the degree of trade which any new development will capture or attract from competitors who depend upon the same catchment area, sometimes called the 'market penetration'.

The *catchment area* is that sphere of influence from which the vast majority of retail sales for a particular centre or development are derived. There are several techniques available to assist in its measurement, most of which mainly relate to 'generative' shopping locations, those which positively attract their own custom direct from residential areas, as opposed to 'suscipient' shopping locations which depend upon the impulsive or coincidental purchases by customers attracted by some other activity.[2] There are a number of underlying factors which affect the sphere of influence or catchment areas of any centre. These can be briefly listed as the size of the centre, the proximity of competing centres, the variety of trades provided, the general accessibility, the deficiency in other levels of the shopping hierarchy, the car parking facilities, and the availability of other services.[3]

The following techniques can be employed to calculate catchment areas:

Experience and observation

Although this scarcely qualifies as a technique, certain locations lend themselves to ready assessment. New housing estates, for example, will normally require a small local shopping centre, the catchment area of which is often all too obvious to see. The only problem remaining is deciding upon the correct number of shops.

Accessibility

Naturally, the nearer shopping facilities are to the customer the more attractive they will appear. Because of this it is possible to calculate the approximate boundaries of a catchment area for any particular centre by analysing the travel habits of the surrounding population. A map can be drawn from public transport time-tables showing the spheres of influence for the centre under consideration and for other competing centres. Because of the increasing importance of the motor car in determining shopping habits, the next step is to decide how much time people are prepared to spend in travelling to the centre by private car. This is called the *drive time* and is normally measured during off-peak traffic periods. The catchment area is calculated by constructing a series of zones devised by drawing a line connecting points of equal 'drive time'; these are called *isochrones* and are commonly established for 10, 15, 20 and 25 minutes. It is important that speed limits are strictly observed, that a standard family saloon is used, and that the calculation is done, as previously stated, in off-peak periods, that is between 10.00 a.m. and 3.30 p.m. A roughly similar procedure can be carried out for public transport, always remembering to take account of the pull or attraction of other centres. Having considered the degree of car ownership, and thus the likely division between private and public transport within the respective zones, the total potential population within the catchment area can be gauged by reference to the current census, or sample census of population, updated and corrected as necessary. Once the total population of the hinterland has been established, the next step is to assess what proportion of trade will be attracted to the new centre of proposed development. This is described later.

Reilly's Law of Retail Gravitation

This was propounded by Professor W. J. Reilly in 1929, and states that 'two cities attract trade from an intermediate town in the vicinity of the breaking point, approximately in direct proportion to the population of the two cities, and in inverse proportion to the squares of the distances to the intermediate towns'. This statement was expressed in the formula:

$$\text{number of miles from City A to the outer limits of its catchment area} = \frac{\text{mileage on road to adjacent town B}}{1 + \sqrt{\dfrac{\text{population of town B}}{\text{population of city A}}}}$$

The 'attraction factor' used by Professor Reilly was population and the 'deterrence function' distance. These have been found to be inappropriate in assessing both catchment area and turnover. This again is examined later when considering market penetration. Reilly's Law did, however, provide a basis from which a number of more sophisticated techniques have been developed.

Consumer survey

By employing shopping questionnaires and inquiring of customers their address, frequency of visit, purpose of visit, mode of travel, and general preference for particular centres, it is possible, by plotting their point of origin on a map, to establish in broad terms the extent of the catchment area. This technique is only suitable when assessing a new development within an existing centre; although similar market research techniques have been applied to proposed new centres they tend to be generally less reliable. To ensure a satisfactory degree of accuracy the survey sample should be comparatively large, at least 10 per cent, which can prove expensive.

Assessment of market penetration

Having calculated the total population within the sphere of influence of a particular centre it is necessary to discover how much trade is likely to be attracted there. Taking the total effective population, the overall retail expenditure can be gauged by multiplying this figure by the amount spent on shopping per head of population, available from the *Family Expenditure Survey* published in 1981. This provides information on regional variation, the proportion spent on food items, and can readily be updated to current price and volume levels by reference to the *Index of Retail Sales* issued by the Department of Trade and Industry. Based upon these calculations an assessment can be made in respect of the share which any proposed development might expect, depending once again upon such factors as accessibility, competition, car parking, complementary services, and size. Naturally, the farther away the prospective customers the less inclined they will be to travel. Experience, and the analysis of comparable developments in similar situations elsewhere, will indicate the proportion of population falling within the hinterland that will be prepared to travel to the proposed centre. The percentage in question, and the rate at which it 'shades off' with distance, varies according to individual circumstances. Other factors that must be taken into account are such things as unemployment, socio-economic groups, car ownership and future employment policy, which all determine the exact nature of retail expenditure within a locality.

Once total predicted expenditure has been obtained, the need arises to translate this demand into a physical context, in terms of how much floorspace, in how many shops, to assist in formulating a planning policy for retailing. This is achieved by the use of *conversion factors* which simply express turnover per square foot of gross floorspace. They can be related to turnover per square foot of selling space, but this is of greater moment to the developer in the management of his property than to the town planner concerned with the physical extent of building.

These factors display a regional variation, being highest in the South East, relatively high in the North and in the Midlands, but much lower in the South West, South Wales, East Anglia and Scotland. They also tend to be higher in newly constructed premises, areas with a highly developed shopping hierarchy, and in town centres as opposed to suburban locations.

Other changing aspects of shopping also play a part in the steady rise of conversion factors: longer shopping hours, the reduction of non-productive space, and an increased proportion of expenditure on durable goods. Although certain reservations have been expressed regarding the use of conversion factors they will provide a more reliable basis for trend projections than exists in forecasting employment, car ownership, population and housing.

The potential trade for a new centre can be calculated by employing what is variously described as the 'vacuum', 'residual' or 'remainder' method, whereby the total consumer expenditure going to other centres in the vicinity is assessed at first instance. The procedure briefly includes determining the prospective catchment area, gauging the total population by census district, calculating retail expenditure by goods and socio-economic groups, allocating expenditure to more accessible and convenient centres, allowing for local traders' share, and estimating the potential trade remaining, for where positive the turnover will be available to the new centre, where negative the area is already overshopped.[4]

Shopping models

Over the years there has been a rapid advance in the development of sophisticated techniques that aim to assist in the assessment of the retail hinterland, the measurement of market penetration, and provide some explanation for retail land use location. These techniques are grouped together as shopping models. They seek to represent a real world situation in simple enough terms to permit examination of past and present shopping patterns and the prediction of future trends. Three basic categories of shopping model can be identified. First, those based on *central place theory* which distinguish a hierarchy of centres derived from an appraisal of the purpose, frequency and length of shopping trips. These have been developed from Walter Christaller's original work in respect of the location, size and character of markets. Their main contribution is limited to supplying a general understanding of shopping habits. Second, those described as *spatial interaction* models, which analyse the collective movements of large numbers of shoppers. These have evolved from Reilly's Law of Gravitational Retailing, which merely established the 'breaking point' between two spheres of retail influence, useful enough in planning the provision of public transport services but inadequate when requiring a more accurate distribution of the trade area. Modifications have been devised providing more appropriate attraction factors such as floorspace instead of population, and a more reliable deterrence function, time in place of distance. Spatial interaction models have also been constructed to account for competition between more than two alternative centres. Third is the category collectively known as *rent models*, which seek to explain in terms of land values the relationship between land use, shopping demand and retail location.[5]

Probably the most popularly applied group are the spatial interaction models, all basically refinements of Reilly's Law and expressed as mathematical formulae. David Huff, for example, constructed a shopping model in 1963 that both took account of more than one centre, and, using floorspace and journey time, identified a series of 'breaking points' not only for different types of goods but also for varying frequencies of shopping trips. He thus introduced a more sensitive and detailed examination of the probability of certain activities occurring. One of the first gravity models to be applied in practice was devised in 1964 by T. R. Lakshmanan and W. G. Hansen to help in formulating a policy towards shopping centres in Baltimore. Using Huff's model as a basis it considered the overlapping of competition and distribution of retail expenditure between competing centres. Variations of this approach have been employed in this country. In the study of a proposed out-of-town shopping centre at Haydock a model was constructed to predict the future sale of durable goods at the new centre and indicate the effect it would have on existing centres. It demonstrated that if the new centre was built Liverpool and Manchester would eventually lose about 12 per cent of their trade, Warrington 46 per cent and Wigan 41 per cent. Permission was not granted. The same principle has been applied in the London Borough of Lewisham – a complex situation involving the analysis of the distribution of retail expenditure between ten centres within metropolitan London. Using the costs of travel as the deterrence function, and total retail sales as the attraction factor, it attempted to gauge whether or not existing development proposals would lead to an excessive supply of shopping space.

Shopping models, by their very nature, can only be as good as the information available to them. They remain as partial techniques, for they say little regarding the effect shopping habits have on other aspects of urban form.

Comparison within and between centres

The need to measure present and prospective performance within a particular shopping catchment area and between alternative shopping locations confronts both public planning and private development agencies. In addition to those techniques already described there are a number of other approaches which assist in deciding the most appropriate allocation of retail resources and monitoring the relative degree of success.

Turnover

The general approach towards the calculation of turnover was discussed under the assessment of market penetration, but in reality the actual levels of floorspace turnover vary enormously depending upon the precise location of a shop and its integral layout. Information on the turnover of individual premises is notoriously difficult to obtain and the way in which most operators jealously guard their figures is a principal factor behind the slow introduction of turnover rents in this country. Such statistics as are available tend to come through census or tax returns, the published information of retailing companies made on a countrywide basis and the occasional planning appeal documentation, and are most usefully applied in comparing between, not within, centres. In practice, therefore, turnover figures are used in establishing the hierarchy of centres and in assessing the impact of major new shopping centres, especially those proposed in unestablished retail locations, such as new district centres or hypermarkets.

Rental values

Similarly, reliable information on rents is also difficult to obtain, with both property owners and retailers being equally reluctant to disclose agreed rents once a deal has been struck. Details of individual transactions can be amassed from information released by estate agents anxious to announce their achievements. Various organizations also publish data on the general level of shop rents and the perceived trends. It should be appreciated that the use of rental values as a basis for comparison can be distorted by the time and frequency of rent reviews, and changes in the retailing strength of a centre, and certain positions within it, may not be reflected in the level and pattern of rents for some years. In the absence of reliable rental evidence the rateable value of retail premises has sometimes been used for purposes of comparison, but until the next rating revaluation, if there is one, little analysis can properly be performed.

Pedestrian flow

An analysis of the number and type of pedestrians passing certain points and along certain routes within a shopping centre can provide an indication of the absolute strength of the centre and the relative strengths of different retail positions within it. Moreover, it is a useful guide to determining the principal factors influencing the trading performance of the centre and an aid to planning possible improvements. To provide worth-while comparative information, pedestrian flow counts should be carried out for a number of different locations within centres over several weeks at varying times of the day and days of the week. This is a popular method because the information can be readily obtained and analysed by relatively unskilled staff, but great care must nevertheless be taken to allow for the effects of other non-retail influences upon pedestrian flow such as transport interchanges and short cuts to work. A pedestrian flow count is usually only an effective planning instrument when it is supported by a questionnaire survey.

Car park use

Any analysis of car park occupancy rates also needs to be carried out over a period of time before accurate comparisons can be made. Furthermore, the collected data should be adjusted to take account of such other factors as the level of parking charges, the use and availability of public transport, the existence of alternative parking facilities, and the level of non-retail parking facilities by office workers or commuters. It is not a common method of comparison because of the distortion caused by these other factors.

Occupancy levels

The number of empty properties within a shopping centre may reflect trading conditions but it may also be the result of a temporary or permanent over-provision of shops due to new development.

Kind of business

Different centres can be compared by an analysis of the composition of retailer and the kind of business they transact. The 1971 Census of Distribution classified shops into eight business categories. Three of the eight categories comprise the group known as convenience goods, which are shops that sell goods mainly in small quantities at regular and frequent intervals, and include all types of food shops, grocers, tobacconists and newsagents. Four of the other five categories form the group of shops known as durable goods shops and include clothing, footwear, household, electrical, furniture, books, chemist, toy and sports shops and department stores. The final category comprises service traders such as building societies, banks, estate agents, hairdressers and restaurants. Because of the nature of their trade many convenience goods shops are not located in town centres but in residential areas, whereas the majority of durable goods shops are located in town centres where they can draw upon a larger catchment area population making infrequent but comparison purchases. Conversely, the type of shopping mix will also determine the hinterland of a centre.

Shopping trends

The last three decades have witnessed enormous changes in the pattern of British shopping. Self-service, supermarkets, pedestrianized shopping streets, deep freezing, enclosed shopping centres, multi-storey car parks, out-of-town shopping, discount warehouses and hypermarkets are all phenomena of the post-war revolution in retailing. From a planning perspective it is possible to select a number of developments which have transformed the shopping scene.

Pedestrian segregation

With the redevelopment of many town centres occasioned by wartime bombing, and the opportunities to plan afresh afforded by new town development, came the concept of designing shopping centres so that traffic and the pedestrian were segregated from one another. Although there had been covered markets and shopping arcades that excluded the motor car before, the notion was nonetheless novel, and the practice of designing new pedestrianized shopping precincts has slowly spread so that the same treatment has been applied to existing shopping streets. Coventry can probably claim to be the first planned pedestrianized shopping precinct, and London Street, Norwich, the first traditional high street to restrict traffic, but few major towns are now without either. Some hostility was at first faced by local authorities seeking to impose traffic restraint and introduce pedestrianization, but as shopkeepers found that turnover went up as a result of street closure or constraint, and servicing problems could be overcome, so opposition has declined. The author's own professional offices are in South Molton Street off Oxford Street, where, since pedestrianization, rents have soared.

Planned in-town shopping centres

During the first half of the twentieth century little redevelopment of existing town centres took place, but as a result of war damage, population growth, structural decay, the emergence of the multiple trader and changing retail habits and requirements, more than two-thirds of the country's largest towns now have an in-town planned shopping centre, well over 100 of which have been constructed during the 1970s. Throughout the 1950s and early 1960s it was not considered necessary to protect shoppers from the weather, but in the wake of American experience, British designers and developers began to appreciate the potential of enclosed shopping centres. The prime innovator in the field was Sam Chippendale of the Arndale Property Trust, now a part of Town and City Properties, who was responsible for a number of the Arndale Centres such as those at Poole, Manchester, Leeds and Wandsworth. The early difficulties experienced at two notable centres, the Bull Ring, Birmingham, and the Elephant and Castle, London, was a cause of concern to some planning authorities, but gradually the success of open, covered and enclosed centres elsewhere soon led to a much greater acceptance of the large planned in-town shopping centre. Three categories of in-town centre have been identified.[7] First, the *regional shopping centre* of around 100,000 m^2 retail floorspace including department stores as their key tenants alongside a range of supermarket, specialist and high-quality fashion shops. They compete directly with traditional high streets, are often built in a partnership between local authority and developer and are exemplified by such schemes as the Victoria

Centre, Nottingham, and Eldon Square, Newcastle. Second, *core replacement schemes*, such as the Whitgift Centre, Croydon, Bond Street Centre, Leeds, and Market Square, Sunderland, which are variable in type, smaller in size, frequently replace obsolescent retail space, are focused upon variety stores complemented by a wide range of durable goods and fashion stores, and tend to provide an extension to the high street rather than an alternative. And third, *peripheral accretions*, containing a miscellaneous assortment of development schemes, constructed alongside the central area away from the main axis of trade, are generally smaller in size – for example, the Merrion Centre, Leeds, the Butts Centre, Reading, or the Westgate Centre, Oxford – and often provide a greater range of convenience outlets. These classifications are somewhat crude, but a number of planning problems common to most of them have been identified. Being relatively successful they must inevitably threaten the economic viability of surrounding retail premises; where over-provision has occurred the trade of the traditional high street has been seriously weakened; little provision is normally made for future expansion; larger towns with planned centres benefit to the detriment of smaller ones without; traffic congestion invariably worsens; the accent is said to be too commercial as opposed to social and cultural; the gravity of the business sector can move dramatically within a town centre, with unforeseen repercussions upon urban design and communications; and many schemes present a dead frontage and can be out of scale with surrounding buildings. One of the most notable features of central area shopping development is the marked contrast between

Table 5 *Major new shopping developments: total of new shopping developments of over 50,000 sq ft gross opened each year*

1965 to 1967 inclusive	2,800,000
1968	2,450,000
1969	2,650,000
1970	3,150,000
1971	4,200,000
1972	3,900,000
1973	5,350,000
1974	4,150,000
1975	6,650,000
1976	7,550,000

Source: Hillier Parker May and Rowden (1977).

London and the rest of the country, for whereas only one-third of London shopping centres have planned schemes the figure is two-thirds elsewhere. Another feature is that despite the overall reduction in the amount of retail floorspace nationally, the level of development of new planned shopping centres continues unabated as can be seen from Table 5.

Out-of-town shopping

The development of hypermarkets or superstores in out-of-town locations represents about the single most controversial issue of retail planning in Britain today (Table 6). Definitions vary, but probably the most all-embracing is that a superstore is a single-level, self-service store, offering a wide range of food and non-food merchandise, with at least 2500 m^2 of sales area, and is supported by car parking. Those superstores of over 5000 m^2 are commonly referred to as hypermarkets. It is difficult to be precise but there are probably around 200 such superstores in out-of-town locations throughout the country in 1980. The most important characteristics of superstores in respect of retail planning are that they have a large single-level sales and storage area; they generate a large volume of retail sales and hence need a big catchment area with at least 50,000 people within a ten-minute drive time of the store; because of their large size and turnover they can operate with bulk deliveries direct from the manufacturer; they generate a large volume of shopping trips, particularly car trips, and hence need good road access; a large number of free car parking spaces are normally provided, about 500 spaces for smaller stores and in excess of 1000 spaces for stores of 500 m^2 sales space and above; and because of the large store size and number of car parking spaces required, the minimum land requirement is approximately 2 hectares for a small store, rising to about 4 hectares for every 500 m^2 of sales space above that.[8] Geographically there is a preponderance of superstores in the North and in the Midlands, and while all stores share the aim of providing for 'one-stop shopping' the mix of goods supplied varies enormously with some being convenience-based stores and others durable-based stores. The trading policies also differ among superstore groups, but most are geared towards low overheads, high turnover and discount prices. The effects of superstores and hypermarkets have been summarized as:[9] they attract a wide cross-section of the population, but with the accent upon young middle social category family groups;

Table 6 *Growth in the number of UK hypermarkets and superstores and other large food stores, 1967–78*

Year	Hyper-markets (over 5000 m² net)	Superstores (2500–4999 m² net)	Other large food stores	Total
1967	2	1	—	3
1969	4	6	2	12
1971	6	16	7	29
1973	10	35	18	63
1975	19	55	29	103
1977	29	90	43	162
1978	36	117	50	203
Planned or under construction, November 1978	9	59	9	77

Source: P. Jones, 'Retail planning: recent trends', *Estates Gazette*, 9 June 1979.

shoppers come from a wide catchment area, typically 25 per cent drive for 20 minutes or more, and convenience-based stores have a wider hinterland than durable-based stores; 90 to 95 per cent of shoppers travel by car, although some obtain a lift; a regular weekly or fortnightly pattern of shopping is common to convenience-based stores, and a more infrequent irregular one to durable-based stores; locally the opening of a superstore will affect some small neighbourhood shops but the major trading consequences are for small- and medium-sized supermarkets; and prices have been shown to be on average some 5 to 10 per cent below other neighbouring in-town stores.

The principal arguments advanced on behalf of superstores are that lower prices are achieved by more efficient buying, handling, distribution and storage of stock; increased shopping comfort is attained by easier and more convenient parking, sheltered shopping and a single point of financial settlement; employment factors of over 75 per hectare have been achieved despite criticisms about unsatisfactory employment levels compared with industry; and traffic congestion in established town centres is reduced. On the other hand, out-of-town superstores have been criticized on grounds of the debilitating effect they have on existing shopping centres, the traffic problems they cause at the point of access and on the surrounding road network, the visual intrusion they create, the inefficient use of open land, their prejudice in favour of the car-owning shopper, and the general effect they have upon local amenity.

The polarized arguments for and against out-of-town superstores is bound to continue, and like most contentious planning debates there is really no right or wrong; each case must be judged on its merit. In order to assist planning authorities identify suitable locations and determine applications for such stores, the Department of the Environment published Development Control Policy Note 13 in 1977 entitled *Large New Stores*. Some of the recommendations are mentioned elsewhere, but one of the interesting guidelines set down by the DoE is the statement that 'it is not the function of land use planning to prevent competition between retailers, or between methods of retailing, nor to preserve existing commercial interests as such', thereby ruling out of court many of the arguments advanced by local authorities in rejecting large out-of-town or edge-of-town developments.

Decline of the local shop

Although independent traders still account for more than 80 per cent of all shops in Britain some parts of the small-shop sector have experienced a difficult time over the past twenty years. The main period of decline took place during the early 1960s when there was a fall of 7 per cent in the total number of shops from 542,000 to 504,000, but between 1966 and 1971 the fall was only a further 4 per cent to 485,000, and the lower rate of contraction seems to have continued since. The main casualties have been the food trade – grocers, greengrocers, fruiterers, butchers and confectioners – all of whom fell in numbers by over 20 per cent. An expansion during the 1970s of the voluntary trading groups slowed down the pace of closure among food shops, but their future seems less assured now. Several specialized durable good shops, especially in the hardware and electrical goods area, have also recovered to a significant extent, and though the independent clothing and footwear trade has not fared well, certain fields such as the fashion boutiques blossomed in the 1970s. Decline has by no means been consistent throughout the country, but where it has occurred the causes have comprised competition from larger stores, obsolescent premises, poor delivery services, statutory price controls, tax problems, high rents and loss of trade resulting from a movement of population away from inner city areas to the suburbs, and planning policies aimed at concentrating retail development opportunities in selected centres. Planning can, therefore, only bear a part of the responsibility for any decline in the number of small local shops, and can equally provide only a few of the possible remedies in the form of more sensitive land use allocation and more flexible development control. It has also been suggested that tighter control of changes of use within retailing by amending the Use Classes Order might protect essential local shopping facilities. Perhaps the only long-term solution to preserving certain non-viable local shops is to view them as a social service and allocate appropriate funds accordingly, even to the extent of establishing local authority trading outlets.

Local authority participation

Ever since the post-War reconstruction of town centres, local authorities have shared in the responsibility for certain shopping development schemes and the rewards from them. The power to assemble sites using compulsory purchase powers available in comprehensive development areas, and now action areas, coupled with the control exercised over communications infrastructure, has enabled many councils to benefit from partnership arrangements with private development companies. In the early days the developers took a simple long lease on a ground rent from the local authority, but through time the basis of partnership has become progressively sophisticated, so that most local authorities now derive a greater share of the equity.

Branch offices

The expansion of branch offices of certain service businesses such as banks, building societies, estate agents and betting offices has provoked considerable concern on the part of planning authorities fearful for the future of their shopping streets. Table 7 shows the growth in service business centres between 1965 and 1976, and many councils believe that these offices cause a dead frontage on the high street, and further, that the tendency for estate agents and building societies to group together in otherwise prime retail locations undermines the attraction of a shopping centre and its trading potential. It

Table 7   *Service businesses in town centres 1965–76*

Businesses	1965	1976
	(% of total occupied outlets)	
Banks	3.8	3.6
Estate agents	1.6	2.2
Building societies	0.6	2.1
Betting offices	0.4	1.0
Other services	13.5	14.5
Total services	19.9	23.4
Retail outlets	80.1	76.7
Total occupied outlets	100.0	100.0

Source: Unit for Retail Planning Information. P. Jones, 'Retail planning: recent trends', *Estates Gazette*, 9 June 1979.

is debatable at what level of incursion this might occur, and uncertain to what extent such service businesses attract passing trade. Some authorities seek to control service business by allocating selected secondary positions to them, thereby creating a kind of service business ghetto. Others establish a quota system by which controlled integration of these business premises into high street locations is allowed up to a predetermined number and in chosen positions. By and large the quota system would seem to be most acceptable on commercial as well as planning grounds. Although the pressure to expand some types of branch office appears likely to continue in the short run it is possible that in the long run the rationalization of many businesses may lead to a reduction in the number of outlets.

Discount warehouses

A less startling and more insidious trend is the process by which existing storage and industrial buildings are adapted to retailing operations in the non-food sector. The principal areas are do-it-yourself superstores, furniture warehouses and electrical goods warehouses. Planning authorities appear to be extremely cautious about granting permission for these operations because of their possible effect upon existing centres, the traffic they generate and the alleged industrial employment loss. Consumer demand, however, is high, and in an expanding market their competitive impact is small.

12 Transportation

The need for transport is an integral facet of everyday life. There is no escape from it; everybody is concerned and to some degree everybody is affected. It plays a dominant role in determining the scale, nature and form of our towns and cities. Its efficiency contributes largely to the level of productivity, economic growth and thus the standard of living. Its character greatly impinges upon the solitude of life, and yet its presence provides the life-blood of the community.

Motoring gives great pleasure to large sections of the population, and contributes enormous sums to the Treasury by way of taxation. In a country where over 80 per cent of the inhabitants live in towns and where there are 2.5 miles of road for every square mile, the highest proportion in the world, the continued and growing presence of the private motor car is rapidly becoming incompatible with urban life. With an increasing population, expanding urban areas, rising car ownership, greater demand for space by every method of transport, sharper and sharper traffic peaks and growing competition for land from every quarter, the situation continues to worsen.

The problems inherent in any urban transport system, be it car, train or bus, are therefore pitched into the tumult of public controversy and subject to the vagaries of political, economic and social expediency. These impediments severely limit any truly objective analysis or comprehensive solution capable of immediate implementation.

The evolution of transportation planning

It has been suggested that the framework within which planning policy towards transportation has been formulated since the Second World War can be divided into three phases,[1] to which I would hesitantly add a fourth.

Phase one, 1947–57

Beginning with the 1947 Town and Country Planning Act, the first decade saw few developments in transportation planning and little government expenditure upon it. Local development plans began to propose short-, medium- and long-term improvements on a limited scale and central government adopted a restricted programme of interurban highway improvements and started to conceive a network of intercity motorways.

Phase two, 1958–67

Although the motorway programme was enlarged and accelerated during this period, attention was primarily focused upon the problems of traffic in urban areas. The impending impact of the private motor vehicle, and the likely repercussions upon towns and cities were clearly identified by Professor Colin Buchanan in the report *Traffic in Towns* published in 1963. The committee of inquiry explored the conflicts between the demands of the motor car and the nature of the built environment. Certain solutions were suggested based on design standards which included the separation of conflicting traffic, pedestrians and cyclists, as well as the division of the city into environmental precincts linked by high-capacity roads.[2] Comprehensive urban road redevelopment schemes became the order of the day during the late 1950s and early 1960s, forming an integral part of most development plan reviews and attracting relatively little criticism. Towards the end of this phase, however, the accent changed towards a policy of greater restraint, and by 1967 the government was openly promoting the notions of road pricing, parking restrictions and other methods of traffic control. It was also proposed in the White Paper *Public Transport and Traffic* that public transport should be subsidized, that public transport authorities be set up in major conurbations and that all transport facilities should be co-ordinated.

Phase three, 1968–74

The white paper proposals were implemented by the Transport Act 1968, which has been described as a watershed in British transport history.[3] Capital grants for public transport infrastructure were introduced as were fuel subsidies, and authorities were permitted to subsidize local services. At the same time a growing awareness of the scale and effects or urban transportation planning was taking place. The techniques of traffic planning were subject to increasing criticism, and powerful amenity groups emerged. Community participation and local resistance to road schemes grew as the blight which they spread was recognized.

Phase four, 1974–80

The 1973 fuel crisis and the more recent energy debate of the late 1970s and early 1980s have focused even greater attention upon the problems of personal mobility and the inadequacies in both public and private transport systems. This realization has been coupled with an increasing restraint upon public expenditure, and the 1977 White Paper on transport policy reflected a much greater sense of financial realism by placing more emphasis upon solving present-day problems with the current level of resources. It also proposed a larger measure of devolution to the counties, accepted the need for local variance in transport policy, expressed concern over the problems of employment in public-sector transport industries, gave support for rural transport, advanced the case for a better use of private cars, recognized the disparity between public and private energy consumption, and intimated that further road construction and maintenance cuts were likely.

Traffic management

This approach is very much the domain of the transportation and physical land use planner, and although traffic management in its many forms has been employed for years there still exist areas for improvement. Some of the most important aspects can be described as follows.

Banning of cars

This is probably the most difficult, politically, though not administratively, to implement. Having placed a total restriction upon the entry of private motor vehicles into central areas, problems arise in deciding whether or not there should be exemptions, and if so for whom; doctors, midwives and the police spring immediately to mind as worthy causes, but what about builders, plumbers, window cleaners and milkmen? The line would be extremely hard to draw, and the repercussions hotly debated. A mounting pressure exists, however, to rehabilitate cities for pedestrian use and to permit them to return to fulfilling their proper function as civic and cultural centres. An alternative to the rather drastic solution of total prohibition would be partial restriction during certain hours, and in this context it should not be forgotten that congestion is not just a twentieth-century problem, for even in first-century Rome wheeled traffic was restricted to the hours of darkness to combat this menace.

New road construction

Although travel times can sometimes be shortened, and average speed increased, building new roads as a solution to urban congestion and environmental degradation is rather like printing more money as a cure to rising inflation. More roads tend to generate more trips and thus exacerbate the situation. Aldous[4] highlights one paradoxical contribution that major urban road construction has made towards the battle for the environment. It concerns the outcry that accompanied the development of Westway in London where public interest was focused upon the real social cost imposed on the neighbouring communities by such a scheme. He suggests that society owes a great debt to the engineers and politicians who pushed through the proposals, unconsciously awakening unparalleled public concern regarding the future of towns and their traffic.

Park and ride

This is a description of what might provide one of the easiest, most attractive and least expensive answers to the problem of congestion. It involves the construction of multi-storey car parks unobtrusively, yet conveniently, sited at major transport termini or route intersections on the periphery of towns or central city areas where land is relatively cheap. From these points a fast regular public transport service would convey the erstwhile motorist to his destination in town, relieved of the frustration and cost of central area parking.

Experiments introduced in Leeds, Oxford and Nottingham have met with mixed success and the growing habit of 'railheading' in London is being positively discouraged in certain circumstances, as evidenced by the closure of the Finchley Road car park for that purpose.

Parking control

The number of cars entering nearly every conurbation in the country continues to increase, and at a much faster rate than the provision of parking space. The chances of a motorist finding a meter within a reasonable time in London are now placed at seven to one against. The supply of more spaces would assuredly lead to the generation of more traffic. While one answer is to increase charges, another is to introduce selective control whereby the commuter, who is the prime culprit of the diurnal chaos, is actively discouraged from indulging in his long-term parking. Several local planning authorities are operating a system of 'shoppers only' car parks which remain closed until 10.00 a.m. and shut again at 4.00 p.m., thus denying access to the car-borne office worker.

Separation of traffic

This involves the provision of separate lanes for public and private motor vehicles. Athough it has operated abroad for many years the scheme was first fully introduced in this country in Reading. A one-way traffic management scheme was put into practice with the buses running in their own lanes against the flow of other vehicles. A measure of its success is demonstrated by the fact that journey times have been reduced by around 40 per cent, accident rates are down, and the number of passengers carried is up. Certain inherent difficulties would be encountered if this approach were comprehensively applied in all towns; street widths, numerous intersections, and complicated route patterns all detract from its viability. Bus priority lanes have, however, become relatively common and seem to work well.

Better management of existing roads

The present transport network is capable of carrying a greater capacity with improved and more flexible planning. The designation of 'tidal flow' lanes, carrying traffic one way in the morning and the other way in the evening, can facilitate movement. Similarly certain routes can be restricted to one-way traffic for part of the day only. During the various railway strikes, London-bound commuters were pleasantly surprised by the efficacy of one-way radial routes at rush hours. Another method of improving the capacity of the existing road system has been developed with the installation of computer-controlled traffic lights which take account of actual, and often unpredictable, traffic flows, and adjust the timing and sequence of lights accordingly. Experimental schemes pioneered in Glasgow and Kensington improved the flow of traffic by 16 per cent and 9 per cent, respectively.

Improved public transport system

The alleviation of congestion caused by private motor vehicles is the improvement most sought after by public transport operators. Meanwhile, certain other steps can be taken to ensure a more efficient and satisfying service. The introduction of yearly, quarterly and monthly season tickets together with the sale of 'rover' tickets on buses has been extremely successful on the Continent, particularly in Sweden. Early fears regarding a loss of revenue proved groundless, for takings actually increased. Moreover, the changeover to one-man buses is made a great deal easier with fewer people requiring change and causing delays. Other suggestions for improving the public transport system include the use of two-way radio sets in buses in order to identify and sometimes avoid hold-ups, moving pavements to connect transport interchanges, a separate elevated reserved track system that would accept and automatically control both private and public vehicles, monorails which can be designed to economize on valuable urban space and computer-controlled dial-and-ride taxi services which can be operated on a very flexible basis to meet the demands of passengers.

Changing working conditions

As previously indicated it is the work-bound commuter and the consequent rush-hour congestion that lie at the heart of the urban transportation problem. Many social scientists firmly predict a radical change in the nature, scale and location of future employment, a kind of second industrial revolution. The first signs can already be discerned. In Japan several large companies, thwarted by congestion and the detrimental environment of city centres, have reversed the normal patterns of work, installing two-way television in employees' homes; any essential personal contact is arranged from home. The results have been increased productivity and enhanced leisure time. Another interesting innovation over the last decade is the voluntary and flexible staggering of working hours under a system known as 'flexi'- or 'sliding time', whereby workers are permitted to arrive and leave at times of their own choosing within two-hourly limits at the beginning and end of the day, being paid according to the number of hours worked. This method of spreading the impact of peak hour travel represents a useful contribution to the overall problem.

Economic charging

In any economic appraisal of the provision of transport services it is immediately apparent that there is a serious imbalance between demand and supply. Not only is there a general excess demand and limited supply of services and stock, but it is also exacerbated at certain times and in certain places.

The result of this disequilibrium is congestion, associated with a loss in efficiency through reduced accessibility and, more often than not, a deterioration in the quality of the urban environment. Thus we are presented with a 'Buchanan's Law' situation whereby the degree of accessibility, the quality of the environment, and the cost of providing transport services are all interrelated. For instance, if the environmental standards are held constant then the degree of accessibility depends upon the amount of money spent on transport services; if the degree of accessibility is held constant then the environmental standard again depends upon the amount of money spent upon the transport services. This may appear to be a statement of the blindingly obvious, but it lies at the kernel of any appreciation of the urban transport problem, that is, the question is as much one of deciding priorities in the overall distribution of national resources as well as how effectively they should be spent once the decision is made.

An underlying cause of the problem is the fact that urban transport is a rising cost industry but, unlike other rising cost industries, prices have not risen selectively to choke off demand, particularly when one considers peak hour, and peak location, travel demands. The result is, of course, the commuting chaos of which we are all only too aware, owing to the fact that supply cannot meet demand. The 'market solution' would be flexible discriminatory pricing, as for example with telephone services, where, after a basic charge, consumers are levied according to their individual use.

Transport policies and programmes

In order to link and integrate transport planning policy more closely with the financial budgets of local authorities, a system of *transport policies and programmes* (TPPs) was introduced in 1974 in the wake of local government reorganization. The TPP system is designed to promote the development of comprehensive transport plans by county councils, eliminating any particular bias towards either capital or current expenditure, avoiding any emphasis upon specific projects, and allowing individual authorities, as far as possible, to satisfy the needs of their own areas. Before this, such matters as highway improvement, public transport revenue support, public transport infrastructure provision, and car parking, were treated as almost separate items. The TPP is not, however, a statutory document, its formal purpose is merely to enable the government to distribute each year its *transport supplementary grant* as well as providing a basis by which key sector loan sanction is allocated. It is thus a bid for grant and loan sanction, and how it will be affected by the proposed changes in central government control over local authority expenditure published at the time of writing in 1979 is not yet clear.

An initial over-bid by county councils of around 50 per cent of the amount actually set aside in the first year of operation led the Department of the Environment to issue expenditure guidelines for each county regarding the TPP submissions for 1977, asking for five-year base expenditure programmes in respect of lower and upper guidelines. While reducing the degree of flexibility afforded to counties this has introduced a greater measure of financial reality. The basic concept remains the same, namely, that county councils are encouraged to develop comprehensive transport plans within a financial framework that ensures their implementation.

The transportation planning process

The greater the degree of specialization, development and growth in society the greater the degree of dependence among urban activities and the greater the extent of movement between them. This movement or transportation has therefore assumed a paramount role in determining the location of activities and thus the use of land. Because of its impact and importance the measurement, guidance and control of the demand for movement and accessibility has become one of the major areas of concern for the physical land use planner. So much so, in fact, that a separate breed of transportation planner has emerged, equipped with its own theories, tools of analysis and techniques. The provision and management of transport facilities are among the most expensive of all urban services to cater for. They can only be properly designed if the present situation is fully understood and future requirements can be adequately predicted. Because of their complex and sophisticated nature, however, the treatment of this aspect of town planning is even more partial than many others dealt with in this book, providing little more than a glossary.

The essential format of the transportation planning process is based upon two fundamental assumptions. Firstly, that demands for movement are directly related to the various land use activities that are pursued at both the origin and destination of journeys. Secondly, that a relationship inevitably emerges from these movement demands which can not only be readily quantified but also remains constant in the future. In this way, if the transportation planner can establish consistent quantifiable relationships between present-day demands for movement and can also predict future land use activities, their nature, intensity and distribution, then by adroit application of current travel and land use equations he can further gauge future movement from land use activity forecasts.

A number of separate stages can be identified in the transportation planning process, and while different authorities cite varying approaches the following is a convenient summation: surveys, forecasts, goal formulation, network design and testing, evaluation and implementation. Although it is but one stage in the overall process, attention is primarily focused in this section upon certain inventories and the collection of data that are contained in the survey stage. Apart from making brief references in order to provide a general context the other stages are largely ignored, but can be followed up by consulting the list for further recommended reading on pages 483–7.

Surveys

As with any other planning process a clear understanding of the present is a vital prerequisite to a forecast of the future and the pre-paration of appropriate policy.

The first step in any survey is to carefully define the area of study, draw a suitable boundary around the significant catchment or hinterland of the area concerned, and divide it into apposite zones. Although some external zones will be described outside the boundary to account for commuting or through traffic, they will be, comparatively, much larger than the zones drawn internally within the boundary. All zones should be drawn up to coincide as closely as possible with *enumeration districts* so that demographic data can be related to transportation. The internal zones are further subdivided according to different urban activities such as residential, commercial or industrial so as to assess more accurately the varying transport demands of alternative land uses. The actual number of zones employed depends upon the degree of accuracy required and the budgetary constraints imposed.

Two main types of survey can be distinguished, those relating to land use activities and those relating to the pattern of movement between them. Although a host of major surveys relating to land use such as employment, commercial floor area and population, as well as those relating to the characteristics of movement such as the speed, volume and density of traffic, are undertaken, the principal inventory which frequently includes, or is classified according to these other elements, revolves around the *origin and destination survey*. The purpose of this is to obtain information on traffic (a) that passes through the area, with both origin and destination outside, (b) that travels to the area, with its origin outside and destination inside, (c) that travels away from the area, with its origin inside and destination outside and (d) that travels within the area, with both origin and destination inside. In this way the pattern of transport for the particular town or city can be identified, and the needs and priorities for alternative strategies can be established. Depending upon the type of traffic movement involved a range of survey techniques are available which can roughly be divided into home interview surveys and cordon surveys.

Home interview surveys on a representative sample of the population can be carried out on either a personal basis or by means of a carefully prepared questionnaire. Besides collecting mere statistical information on the travelling habits of the local inhabitants they also provide an insight into the general characteristics and behaviour of households, enabling conclusions to be drawn which can be incorporated into a transportation model at a later stage in the process. This technique provides very detailed information and is singularly successful in appraising the journey patterns to particular establishments such as factories, army camps or universities. It cannot be used, however, for collecting information regarding trips having origins outside the study area, which can exceed 30 per cent of total trips; its reliability depends heavily upon the expertise of the interviewer, a large proportion of non-work trips are all too often forgotten, and it is relatively expensive to mount.

Cordon surveys, sometimes called screenline surveys, are conducted on traffic routes at specially selected points, permitting easy and comprehensive measurement. Cordons or screenlines should be so situated as to record interurban and intraurban trips. Once again an interview approach is normally employed, either at the roadside or by issuing prepaid postcards. With the full roadside interview all motorists, or, more usually, a predetermined proportion of them, are stopped at selected points on the various cordon lines and questioned about the origin, destination and purpose of their journey. Because of the inevitable delays involved, the consequent shortage of time for questioning, and the reluctance and avoidance on the part of drivers, the results are not always reliable. The cost of mounting the surveys is also extremely high. The postcard questionnaire, however, provides a fairly cheap form of survey. The cards are handed out at check points along the cordon lines and filled in by the recipients at a later time, thus reducing delay to a minimum. The response rates vary but are generally around 30 per cent, which is an adequate base upon which to conduct an analysis. Data regarding the travel habits of persons using public transport can also be obtained from direct interview while they commute, or from questionnaires that they are asked to fill in either during or after their journey. In both cases response rates are likely to be very much lower than those from private motorists. The volume and length of journeys in the public sector is, however, comparatively simple to calculate from observation and ticket sales, but the actual origins, final destinations, and therefore real desire lines, are very much more difficult to compute. Detailed information relating to commercial traffic movements can be obtained from office interviews with firms based in the locality, and a similar procedure can be adopted for taxi-cab operators.

Cruder survey methods by way of simple traffic counts or the recording of vehicle registration numbers are available but rarely advisable except as checks and monitoring devices. *Traffic counts*, for example, which can be undertaken manually using Ministry enumerator forms or by employing continuous meters known as tally counters, record the overall direction and volume of traffic but only provide information regarding road capacity at a particular point. They say little about the beginnings or ends of journeys and are therefore irrelevant in constructing *desire lines*, that is what the travel lines would be if straight line routes were provided, which are essential in plotting general policy.

Because the scale and location of car parking facilities can exercise a marked influence on the level and flow of traffic within an urban area, and the availability of parking space can itself be a generator of movement, the management and control of parking becomes an important aspect of overall local planning authority transportation policy, and to ensure an informed approach a number of surveys are crucial.

To be in a position to plan for future provision a detailed record of existing facilities is essential. Plotted on a map, it should include private as well as public, temporary as well as permanent, and 'on' as well as 'off' street car parks. The road network should also be examined to make sure that no parking bays cause undue obstruction to the traffic flow. The information obtained from the transportation survey regarding the trip destinations give a useful indication of the locational demand for car parks, and the distance motorists have to travel from their cars, once parked, can be gauged by use of questionnaire.

Once the planner knows how many parking spaces are available, and where they are, it is vital for him to ascertain the intensity of their use, and the length of time they are used for individual cars. The intensity of use should not only be measured at different times of the day to allow for commuting, shopping or entertainment peaks, but also on different days of the week to allow for local markets, early closing and weekend trippers. The duration of stay is calculated to identify the relative proportions of short-term and long-term parkers.

From an appraisal of the parking demand of different land uses, how many employees require long-term facilities, how many clients require convenient short-term, and what degree of service traffic requiring access is likely, for example, an overall picture emerges. From this information a set of standards can be devised which apply to offices, shops, restaurants, theatres, hospitals and all other urban activities that generate traffic and demand parking space. Apart from describing the existing space available and the extent to which it is used, the survey results will also reveal any deficiency or surplus in the system. One further aspect of conducting a survey regarding planning for parking provision is the location of car parks in respect of transport routes. The sudden uncontrolled disgorgement of large numbers of long-term parkers at peak hours onto important inter-sections can have disastrous repercussions on the performance of the road network.

Forecasts

Once an outline of the existing situation has been established, fore-casts are required to estimate what the transportation system for a particular area will have to cater for in the future.

In order to estimate future provisions of transport services, it is imperative to know the likely trends in population for the area under study. Not only does demand increase in absolute terms as population grows, but the number and length of trips made per head of population also increase. The techniques for predicting population growth have already been outlined, but suffice it to say that they are subject to uncertainty.

Having conducted population projections it is possible to relate these to the other forms of human activity that constitute urban life and which require both land use provision and communication. This involves forecasting the future patterns of retailing, employment, leisure and education to provide some indication of the number of trips that will be created based upon an analysis of existing travel habits and prevailing trends. Once again the larger and more dispersed the urban structure becomes the greater the number and length of trips.

Apart from these general population and land use considerations it is essential that social and economic factors are taken into account to ensure effective forecasting. Even a change in the pattern of house-hold formation can affect the demand for transport services, for as households increase so too do car ownership and total trips. In this country the change is now so gradual that it exerts little influence. Of some relevance, however, is the fact that richer residential areas, having a higher degree of car ownership, produce more traffic per head of population than do poorer residential areas. It is therefore advisable to take the socio-economic distribution of the population of a town into account when planning the provision of roads. Furthermore, the proportion of employed persons in a community can have a similar effect, particularly at peak hours, at which time the transport system has to cater for its greatest capacity. It is therefore necessary to study the nature and characteristics of existing and possible future activity rates. In the same context it is worth giving some consideration to the length and pattern of the working day. Reduction in the number of working days, staggering of hours, introduction of shift work, shortened lunch hours and longer holidays all contribute to the overall level of demand for services, particularly public transport.

Another important economic aspect that determines transportation demand is the general level of prosperity. When a high level of economic activity is experienced a greater pressure is placed upon existing road space, and if the prevailing rises in the standard of living are maintained both car ownership and mileage are likely to increase.

Goal formulation

The clear and rigorous statement of goals and objectives is a vital part of any planning process. They are the criteria by which any scheme is framed and tested. In transportation studies they may take the form of relatively quantifiable aims such as achieving a certain benefit/ cost ratio, minimizing residential demolition, attaining certain capacities, removing through traffic from central and environmental areas, or even minimizing the loss of human life from traffic accidents. Alternatively they may be related to the overall development plan in a more subjective manner such as revitalizing public transport, minimizing the disruption to the general environment, or maximizing convenience and comfort. Whatever transportation plan is selected it must be shown to be the best in terms of the stated goals.

Network design and testing

Perhaps the most intricate and involved stage in the transportation planning process is the construction and simulation of possible networks or systems which meet future movement forecasts within the broad objectives of the development plan. To assist in the design of these networks a large number of computer-aided transport models have been developed. In essence a transport model simply attempts to describe the travel patterns of large numbers of people. In the light of existing information regarding land use activities, the movement between them, and projected trends within the study area, the model examines the reasoning behind individuals' decisions to make journeys (trip generation), the probable destination of those journeys (trip distribution), the route they will take (traffic assignment), and the means of transport that will be used (modal split). Significant improvements have been made of late in the development of comprehensive land use prediction models which seek to describe the location decisions of households, firms and other types of urban activity based upon the principle that such decisions are to a large extent dictated by the costs of overcoming distances which separate inter-related and interacting activities. The transport model, which is itself composed of the many sub-models relating to the generation, distribution, assignment and mode of movement, is therefore seen to be part of an integrated process of urban spatial interaction.

Evaluation and implementation

Such technical advances as those outlined above have permitted the transportation planner to create increasingly more realistic working representations of urban areas and to test various alternative plans by computer simulation, assessing their performance against prescribed objectives. It has been suggested that there are four ways in which transportation plans should be evaluated; numerical, checking the computational validity of forecasts; operational, assessing the potential stresses and failures that might occur in the system; environmental, gauging the aesthetic impact of any proposed transport plan; and economic, measuring the respective cash flows and financial repercussions that result from particular plans.

Plans are of little value unless they are put into practice and yet the stage of implementation is possibly the most neglected of all in any planning process. Essentially it involves the co-ordination and management of public or internal agencies involved in the execution of the transport plan, the stimulation of private or external agencies, the control of resulting development, and the careful scrutiny or monitoring of the way in which the plan performs.

Although transportation planning has assumed a major role in determining the nature and function of urban development, it is essential that such studies are not seen in isolation, set apart from the other stages and components of the planning process. Being a comparatively complex discipline, possessing a range of seemingly sophisticated techniques, and achieving further deification by some owing to the extensive use of computers, there is a danger that the policies and programmes for transport might dominate those of other land use developments. Fortunately, there has been increasing co-ordination of late between the various aspects of urban planning, and the knowledge, propagated perhaps by a systems approach, that everything affects everything else, ensures that the execution of the broad strategy and the relationship of the constituent parts receives continuous review and revision.

The bicycle

One of the most neglected forms of urban transport has been the bicycle, but the recent period of austerity has brought an upsurge in the popularity of cycling. The advantages of the bicycle are said to be that it is a simple and inexpensive machine to build, buy, ride and maintain. It is a fast means of urban transport, with most journeys to work being within the range of the average cyclist, and, where the trip is under four miles, cycling is faster than travel by car, taxi, train, tube or bus. Small demands are made by it upon valuable urban space in respect of both travel and parking. The bicycle is virtually silent in operation and causes no pollution. It is also said to be a healthy form of travel by promoting regular exercise. The main disadvantages of cycling are usually associated with the vagaries of the British climate, the restrictions of hilly terrain, and the dangers of competing with other forms of urban transport.

The principle problem is really the conflict that takes place between the bicycle and motorized vehicles in a transport system almost exclusively designed for the latter. It has been argued that cycling could be made very much safer without having recourse to the complete segregation of bicycles from motorized transport. Back streets could be made available only to cyclists and pedestrians, except for vehicular access. These backstreets, coupled with foot-paths, combined bus and cycle lanes, and routes through parks and open land, could then be the basis for the creation of a network of city cycle routes.[5]

Some local authorities have already adopted a positive approach to bicycle planning. Stevenage, for example, has one of the most comprehensive systems of bicycle routes in the world, with about 23 miles of segregated cycleways and around 90 subways, and boasts an enviable safety record with accident rates of approximately one-third the national average. Peterborough has incorporated the provision of cycle routes in its master plan, an important feature of the planned network being that it runs directly from home to shops, schools and workplaces, avoiding major roads wherever possible. Swindon has steadily introduced bicycle facilities into a number of areas of the town over recent years. Two major lengths of combined bicycle–pedestrian routes have been established, road closures have been made which exclude all vehicles except buses and cycles, short sections of footpath and cycle track have been built to create convenient short cuts, special bicycle parking spaces have been set up in the city centre, and a major cycle route is planned as part of a comprehensive transport plan.[6] Not all experiments in the field of cycle planning have been successful, but the prime lesson to be learnt is that provisions for cyclists should not be random but form part of an integrated approach to urban transportation.

The pedestrian

Perhaps even more neglected than the cyclist as a separate interest group in transportation planning is the pedestrian. It can be argued that in preparing any comprehensive plan for an urban area the needs and desires of the walking public should be taken into greater account. Such matters as the points of conflict between pedestrian and vehicular traffic, the main generators and attractors of pedestrian flow, the principal desire lines of pedestrians, the areas of special delay or congestion, and the causes of interruption in pedestrian flow should be identified. It has been suggested that the existing quality and potential improvement of pedestrian routes should be examined under the headings of continuity, safety, comfort, convenience and delight. In doing so a number of individual problems can be recognized, including:

Vehicle-reliant premises. Petrol filling stations, garages, warehousing and showrooms, for example, require careful siting and special consideration regarding access. Deliveries to shops should be examined for the possibility of alternative servicing or restricted times of delivery.

Noise. Surveys should be initiated to establish the volume and composition of passing traffic, the conditions of speed and flow, the type of road surface and the effect of building layout. Where unacceptable levels of noise pertain, alternative routes should be examined and existing enforcement procedures checked.

Vandalism and violence. In many parts of the city it is necessary to ensure that walkway systems are under a reasonable level of surveillance, both formal and informal. In laying out new areas, and determining urban design criteria for redevelopment within existing ones, sight lines, blind corners, dead ground, sudden changes in level and direction, lighting standards and general configuration should all be examined from the viewpoint of security.

Space standards. Little thought is given to the non-leisure standards of the walking environment, and in the same way that trip generation, desire lines, delays, peak times, accident spots and linkages are ascertained for vehicular traffic and related to a given transportation network, so should a roughly similar procedure be carried out for pedestrian movement. Path widths, walking speeds, flow density, effective capacity, tailbacks and congestion levels can all be calculated and employed in achieving a better performance of pathways.

Others. A number of matters such as air pollution, litter, dogs, subways, small spaces, seating, shrubs, wind, sunlight, surfaces, school crossings, wheelchairs and footbridges must all be considered suitable aspects in consideration of the walking environment.

13 Leisure and recreation

In common with most other Western European and North American countries, Great Britain is having to cater for ever-increasing demands for recreational and leisure facilities. The process and its impact are described by Michael Dower in his book *Fourth Wave, the Challenge of Leisure*.[1]

Three great waves have broken across the face of Britain since 1800. First, the sudden growth of dark industrial towns. Second, the thrusting movement along far-flung railways. Third, the sprawl of a car-based suburbs. Now we see, under the guise of a modest word, the surge of a fourth wave which could be far more powerful than all the others. The modest word of leisure.

Though often used in the same context, the terms leisure and recreation are not synonymous. 'Leisure is essentially the time one has free from income earning responsibilities and from personal and family housekeeping activities. . . . Recreation, in any socially accepted sense, involves constructive activities for the individual and the community'.[2]

Alternatively, a widely quoted definition adopted by a number of government agencies is that

Leisure is the time available to the individual when the disciplines of work, sleep and other basic needs have been met. . . . Recreation is any pursuit engaged upon during leisure time, other than pursuits to which people are normally committed.[3]

Demand

A number of basic factors determine the demand for recreation.

Population. The population of the United Kingdom in 1951 was 50.3 million; by 1971 it had reached 55.6 million, and it stood at 55.9 million in 1976. Post-war growth, however, has gradually given way to decline over the period 1974–8 and it requires a carefully polished crystal ball to predict future population change.

Changing work patterns. Though figures vary the working week is now, on average, under 40 hours long whereas in 1950 it was 45 hours long, and it is expected to decline by at least a further 25 per cent by the end of the century owing to increasing automation, the advent of microprocessors and a different attitude towards work. Paid holidays are becoming longer and more common, for whereas only 1 per cent of the working population received more than three weeks annual leave in 1951, and 4 per cent in 1966, well over 75 per cent are now in receipt of such benefits. The retirement age might also be lowered, but in any event there will be 33 per cent more pensioners by the year 2000. Work sharing is also a possibility.

Income. It has been found that there is a higher degree of participation in recreational activities by those in higher-income groups, and while future income levels are again difficult to forecast, it is still likely that real income will grow. Moreover, where previously leisure was the prerogative of the few, economic circumstances have dictated a change in the leisure and recreation patterns throughout all income groups. This view is reinforced by changes in occupation, because the percentage of the population engaged in professional and managerial jobs has grown from 16 per cent in 1951 to a present level of almost 25 per cent, and similarly those employed in semi-skilled and unskilled jobs have fallen from 33 per cent to about 25 per cent in the same period.

Education. The group of people that indulge most in outdoor recreation are those pursuing a course of education, and the proportion of the population staying on at school after 16 years of age has risen from 28 per cent in 1951 to almost 40 per cent today, and is expected to reach 100 per cent by the year 2000.

Car ownership. Increased mobility means increased accessibility to recreation facilities, and driving is itself considered by many to be a leisure pursuit. Car ownership, which stood at 2 million in 1949, is now at about 14 million, and is predicted to reach 20 million by 2000; and the number of households owning a car is almost 60 per cent.

Demand studies have been said to fall into three broad categories as follows:[4]

The first examines the whole pattern of demand of the total population over the full range of leisure activities, a necessary preliminary to any realistic assessment of priorities. Overall studies of demand, however, have the inherent disadvantage that many minority activities are represented by only a tiny proportion of the total population, and in a general survey such small sub-samples may lack statistical significance. In consequence, a second approach seeks to isolate the population pursuing a particular activity and thus to examine its characteristics in far more detail than would otherwise be possible. The third category changes the focus from participant to place and concentrates attention on the site where a specific type of recreation is undertaken.

The methodology for the measurement of demand for recreational facilities was pioneered in the United States and the leading proponent has been Marion Clawson. This technique of assessment is essentially based upon using the cost of gaining access to recreation, including the costs of travel and entry, as the price variable, and the participation rate calculated per 1000 population in distance zones, as the quantity variable, so as to arrive at an estimate of the demand function for the 'whole recreational experience' which is said to include the journey to and from the site. From this function the overall response of potential consumers to hypothetical changes in entry charges is used to construct a demand curve for the particular facility in question, which in turn can be used to show either consumer surplus or maximum revenue obtainable. This technique has been applied to a number of recreation planning studies in this country including a major recreation appraisal of the Lake District and another of state-owned forests. It has been suggested that there are six principal ways of collecting the necessary information for measuring recreational demand.[5]

1 *Interview survey.* This is a flexible approach and can be conducted along standardized or non-standardized lines, and by household or on site. It is probably the most popular way of collecting data, particularly by household interview, but has the problem of identifying and obtaining an adequate sample of respondents and of ensuring compatibility between different surveys.
2 *Self-administered survey.* This usually entails a postal survey and requires the respondent to complete a questionnaire without an interviewer. The main drawback is ensuring a sufficient response rate to avoid bias, and it is more commonly employed in determining the supply of recreational facilities.
3 *Observation.* This is principally employed to monitor small-scale

and localized activities of an essentially behavioural character, such as how many people leave the paths and tracks in the country areas or how children react to different forms of equipment in adventure playgrounds. It is naturally subject to the vagaries of the observers' views and the effect of the observers' presence.

4   *Documentary.* These can be of either a continuous kind, such as census data, club membership lists and ticket receipts, or a discontinuous type, which takes the form of diary or record completed by participants in the recreation process. Continuous documentary evidence is normally used in conjunction with other information and as a supplement to it, and while it is relatively cheap and easy to sample it is somewhat selectively available. Discontinuous documents are increasingly employed in recreation studies and provide the basis for constructing a 'time-budget diary' which has been found to be extremely valuable in determining real demand for recreational facilities.

5   *Physical evidence.* This includes, for example, the wearing down of rock on favourite climbs, the erosion of paths and trails, or the deposit of litter. In this context aerial photography has been usefully employed in some recreation studies.

6   *Mechanical and electronic devices.* These are used to monitor attendance and incidence, such as a traffic counter on the road or a turnstile at a sporting event. Cameras and microphones have also been used, but their use can raise problems of privacy. Again such instruments are usually employed to supply additional or supportive data.

The underlying factors behind the demand for a particular recreational facility have been usefully summarized as:[6]

Factors relating to the potential recreation users as individuals:
   their total number in the surrounding tributary area
   their geographic distribution within this tributary area
   their socio-economic characteristics (age, sex, occupation, family
      size and composition, educational status and race)
   their average incomes and the distribution of incomes among
      individuals
   their average leisure, and the time distribution of that leisure
   their specific education, their past experiences and present know-
      ledge relating to outdoor recreation
   their taste for outdoor recreation.

Table 8   *Recreation demand*

% of trips	Professional and managerial	Clerical	Skilled and unskilled	Total
Coast	69	72	78	75
Urban	18	17	15	16
Mountains & moors	21	10	8	11
Lakes and rivers	10	7	6	7
Other inland	12	9	8	9

Source: British Tourist Authority.

Factors relating to the recreation area itself:
    its innate attractiveness, as judged by the average user
    the intensity and character of its management as a recreation area
    the availability of alternative recreation sites, and the degree to
        which they are substitutes for the area under study
    the capacity of the area to accommodate recreationists
    climatic and weather characteristics of the area.
Relationships between potential users and the recreation area:
    the time required to travel from home to the area, and return
    the comfort or discomfort of the travel
    the monetary costs involved in a recreation visit to the area
    the extent to which demand has been stimulated by advertising.

It should be recognized, however, that in any assessment of
recreation demand, at whatever scale, rural recreation only forms a
very small proportion of the total, and that increasing the supply of
rural facilities will probably have little effect on aggregate demand.
Table 8 demonstrates the point, and suggests that more attention
should perhaps be paid to planning recreation on the coast.

Supply

Most analyses of the supply of recreational facilities relate to the
problem of capacity. A great deal of research has been undertaken
recently in respect of the concept of *recreational capacity* which has
been defined as 'the level of recreation use an area can sustain without
an unacceptable degree of deterioration of the character and quality
of the resource or of the recreation experience'. In many ways it is

similar to Professor Colin Buchanan's notion of environmental capacity for residential areas. Three main elements can be discerned that together constitute the overall concept. First, ecological, because the intense use of an area for recreational purposes can cause damage in the form of erosion and compaction of the soil which in turn can have far-reaching effects on the local plants and animals. Second, physical, for the sheer weight of numbers can produce the most horrific visual impact, as anyone who has watched the cancerous growth of caravans along our coastline will substantiate. Third, economic, because other aspects of society regulate use and fix capacity by application of market forces.

The planning profession is required to predict change and distinguish between fads and fancies currently in vogue and the establishment of any long-term trends. In order to assess the recreational capacity of an area or a particular facility the following steps have been suggested:

compilation of an inventory of recreation resources and facilities
estimation of present levels of use of each site and facility
assignment of capacities to each site and facility
comparisons of the levels of use and the assigned capacities to reveal
   over- and under-usage
estimation of alternative methods, costs and management techniques
   for bringing use and capacity into better balance.

Recreation, by its very nature, however, lends itself to a variety of interpretations. To some it represents the immediate environment around their homes where they can while away their leisure hours. There seems little doubt, however, that current residential design is not geared towards providing adequate space for solitude or for hobbies. To others it means an escape to the countryside for any one of a range of activities, and, as already mentioned, the availability of land and facilities is gradually being whittled away.

It can, therefore, be seen that a need exists to plan urban open space with greater attention paid towards recreational demand. It has been suggested that such provision falls into two basic categories. One is the local park, where children can play, mothers meet and the older generation relax; this must necessarily be close to the home. The other is the park, less local in character, still accessible, which supplies facilities for the whole community, such as golf, sailing and swimming. A more positive approach towards the green belt could assist in catering for the latter, together with the further development of 'green fingers' or 'wedges' of land penetrating to the heart of built-up areas. The Lee Valley scheme is an admirable pioneer attempt in this direction. A further accomplishment in the context of urban recreation would be the formation of a network of interconnecting footpaths linking open spaces, community centres and residential areas, and the improvement in canal towpaths and riverside walks.

Increasing pressures are being placed upon the countryside from both agriculture and rural recreation demands. The two forces are not, however, unreconcilable; they merely require careful planning. One approach put forward refers to the special development of recreational areas in addition to the use of farmland, whereby the poorer-quality agricultural land could be transferred to leisure uses, being ideally suited because of its varied topography with trees, water, and varied flora and fauna. Furthermore, camping and caravan sites could be provided, picnic spots selected, sporting facilities made available, all fitting within an existing agricultural economy. These measures in poorer areas should strengthen rather than weaken the rural heritage.

To promote a greater degree of consistency and continuity in the assessment of recreation demand a classification of constituent elements is extremely valuable. Although none has been applied in this country, an example is provided by the *Report of the Outdoor Recreation Resources Review Commission* published in the United States. This sets out six basic recreation area groups:

1 High-density recreation areas suitable for weekend leisure, managed for recreation and sited close to major conurbations.
2 General outdoor recreation areas designed for less intensive use, with a great variety of activities in a natural setting.
3 Natural environment areas with natural surroundings and basic facilities.
4 Unique natural areas with natural phenomena that can be studied without harm.
5 Wild areas managed to maintain their wildness, with no facilities.
6 Historic sites, protected from overuse and managed to encourage proper use without spoiling.

A more detailed classification has recently been devised by Max Nicholson and appears in his book *The Environmental Revolution*. Here in the form of a chart of human impacts on the countryside the whole range of recreation pursuits are listed under the activity concerned, the area or type of land affected, the nature of effects arising and their incidence.

Work of this nature provides a foundation for recreation planning. What is really required, however, is a national plan that would take account of all the various interacting aspects of recreation planning: the calculation of demand, the problem of supply; the protection of footpaths, green belt and coastline; the conservation of wilderness areas for peace and solitude; the development of disused railway land for leisure pursuits; the creation of farm trails as well as nature trails for educational as well as recreational purposes; the promotion of urban open space and linked footpath systems, and a whole host of other considerations. It virtually amounts to a national scandal that no land use classification for leisure and recreation exists, and whereas this country possesses the most sophisticated control over urban areas, no similar decisions regarding priorities and associated regulation in the form of zoning or density restrictions are provided for rural areas.

14 Evaluation

Once the broad goals and objectives for a particular planning problem have been established, and alternative courses of action have been prepared, the next step is to test these alternative strategies, comparing their respective advantages and disadvantages. This testing process is described as 'evaluation' and is intended to assist the decision maker in selecting his final choice. As evaluation entails more than just a description of alternatives, the various constituent elements of the plan must be identified and subsequently measured. In conducting this measurement the town planner will need to be equipped with techniques that assist him in the task. Lichfield[1] suggests a distinction between testing and evaluation, stating that tests of various kinds are continuously undertaken throughout the planning process appraising such aspects as conformity to density standards, adherence to green belt policy, feasibility, consistency, and ability to solve the planning problems posed. The evaluation of alternative plans takes place after testing, and the technique employed should take account of the fact that a town or city is a complex organism with many, often divergent, interests. To cater for this, Lichfield[2] sets out ten criteria which an appropriate technique should satisfy. It should:

1 Have regard to the stated or implied objective of the decision makers (which may or may not be the objectives of those for whom they are planning)
2 Cover all systems of urban and regional facilities which are encompassed in the plan
3 Cover all sectors of the community which are affected, that is those which should be included within the decision maker's concern
4 Subdivide the sectors into producers/operators of the plan output and its consumers so that all the 'transactions' implicit in the plan are considered
5 Take account of all costs to all sectors, including externalities
6 Take account of all benefits to sectors, including externalities

7   Measure all the costs and benefits in money terms
8   Facilitate the adoption of a satisfactory criterion for choice
9   Show the incidence of the costs and benefits on all sectors of the community
10 Be usable as an optimizing tool with a view to ensuring the best solution.

It is impossible to describe the entire range of techniques that present themselves for adoption. The principal methods of evaluation have been selected for consideration, most other approaches being derivatives of some form.

Cost–benefit analysis

The technique of cost–benefit analysis (CBA) has largely developed in response to requests for a more effective way of choosing between alternative policies in the public sector. It provides a practical way of assessing the desirability of projects and in doing so takes account of all the relevant and foreseeable consequences of a particular decision. It places particular emphasis upon the consideration and measurement of social costs and benefits as well as private costs and benefits, taking both a long and wide view.[3] In making a decision, for example, the individual entrepreneur considers only his own private costs and benefits, but in pursuing a particular course of action which to him appears attractive he might impose a whole range of costs upon others not directly concerned. Conversely, there are certain services and facilities of a non-profit-making nature that both confer benefits upon large numbers of persons in the public sector as well as render other profit-making uses of land more profitable. CBA is a means by which a longer and wider view of the full implications of respective strategies can be judged. It attempts to ensure the optimum allocation of available resources so as to maximize the welfare of the whole community.

It has a relatively long history, emanating in France in the mid-nineteenth century in the writings of Dupuit, and later in this country with Pigou, who were both largely concerned with the utility of public works. It came into prominence in the USA at the turn of the century and gained considerable currency in the 1930s when it was applied to investment in the vast water resource projects undertaken as part of the 'new deal'.

Prime consideration was given, however, to 'internal' cost and benefits, that is those directly concerned with the implementation of the particular project. The application of cost–benefit analysis was broadened by the end of the Second World War when operating agencies included more and more 'secondary' costs and benefits, or, put another way, those repercussions external to the project under consideration. Greater attention was also given to the problem of assessing 'intangible' costs and benefits – those which defy ready quantification in a numerical form such as aesthetic or environmental factors.

Through time the major limitations are becoming increasingly evident. Above all the political or social character of many decisions distorts the true value of CBA, as does the very scale at which this technique is employed, for the greater the magnitude of investment the less accurate the analysis.

Five basic stages to undertaking a cost–benefit analysis can be identified:

project definition
identification and enumeration of costs and benefits
evaluation of costs and benefits
discounting
presentation of results.

Project definition

Probably one of the most critical decisions to make is what exactly is the scope and purpose of the evaluation. Many analyses neglect to include a 'do-nothing' alternative, for example, while others encounter the problem of *joint products* where the scheme in question, such as a proposed bridge, is complementary or dependent upon other projects, such as a motorway programme. It is also necessary at this stage to question the suitability of CBA as opposed to other analytical techniques.

In tackling a cost–benefit analysis it is vital to recognize the various constraints that surround project evaluation. They can be conveniently grouped as follows:

Physical: one or more of the inputs might be in inelastic supply.
Legal: there could be many problems associated with rights to access, easements, restrictive covenants, acquisition, and delays due to legislative procedure.
Administrative: two or more conflicting authorities or agencies might be involved, or the method of implementation might be too costly or complex, as in certain proposed road pricing schemes.

Distributional: the effect on personal incomes by their reallocation might be contentious or unwise. It might affect regional policy, or other pricing policies.

Budgeting: as always!

Political: perhaps above all! It is, however, a factor that is hard to account for in an objective manner in conducting such an evaluation.

Identification and enumeration

The respective costs and benefits entailed in the various alternatives can be divided into *internal* or *primary*, and *external* or *secondary*. The identification and inclusion of primary costs and benefits is comparatively straightforward, but in accounting for the external effects of their actions undertakers of public investment projects should only consider those aspects that alter the physical production potentiality of other producers. They should not take into account any side effects that merely reflect in price changes of products or factors. The closure of a local bus service might reduce the catchment area for a regional shopping centre and cause a decline in retailing, thus imposing an external cost which should be included, but the fall in the shop rentals and the drop in the price of land for retailing should be excluded. If not it would amount to 'double counting'.[4]

One of the major difficulties encountered whilst conducting such an analysis is in defining the 'cut-off point', for proposals involving large-scale public investment tend to have a ripple effect spreading out from the centre and becoming increasingly more diffuse and difficult to identify.

Valuation

Once identified, the various costs and benefits must be valued. This should be done in terms of money value wherever possible, with annual sums being discounted back to a present capital value. Some components with a record of open-market transactions easily lend themselves to valuation, for example rents, loans and construction costs. Others, where no market exists, require a system of substitute or 'shadow' prices to permit financial appraisal. This system of 'shadow pricing' is popularly employed in the evaluation of time saving, particularly in respect of leisure time.

The problem is that shadow prices represent a valuation on the margin, and while attempts have been made to construct a sophisticated range of demand curves it is very difficult to measure consumer surplus.

Grave problems occur when investment projects are themselves large enough to affect prevailing prices and values; further market imperfections such as the monopolistic control over certain factors may influence the prices for particular goods and services, thus hindering the calculation. Taxes and controls can also affect the valuation of respective costs and benefits. It has, for example, been decided in many schemes to exclude the tax element in the estimation of fuel saving from road improvements. The tax foregone, however, must be recouped from another source – but with what effect!

Another aspect of the evaluation procedure relates to what are often described as the 'distributional' consequences. The schemes under consideration will often reallocate resources from one sector to another; some might gain, some might lose. The result might well have social, economic or political undertones. This redistribution of wealth involves other questions regarding the marginal utility of money; £1 in London is not necessarily worth the same in Sunderland. Similarly, £1 to a rich man cannot be equated with £1 to a poor man.

Because the varying marginal utility of money can modify results it has been argued that CBA is really an application of welfare economics. In this context, a concept called the Pareto Principle stated that only schemes where at least somebody is better off and nobody worse off should be allowed, whereas Pigou had contended that if the gainers from a scheme could more than compensate the losers the scheme was acceptable. From this, conventional economic thinking applied to CBA only requires that the gainer could, in theory, more than compensate the losers for the scheme to be acceptable, but it should be recognized that this implies an equitable distribution of income, a unitary marginal utility of money, and an initial equilibrium to produce proper rankings between schemes. The need for some form of equity criterion as well as economic is, therefore, advanced to achieve a satisfactory ranking procedure.

Perhaps the most vexed and thorny aspect of valuation is in respect of those elements that defy financial quantification, the 'intangibles'. It has become fairly common practice to set these factors aside and consider them separately, either by merely listing or noting them, or by applying some form of crude weighting or ordinal ranking. This is very much the preserve of the politician or decision-maker.

Discounting

In conducting a CBA there is invariably a need to reduce future cash flows to a common comparable base. Two problems emerge in this procedure – choosing the most suitable method of discounting and selecting the most appropriate rate of discount. With regard to methodology, five alternative approaches present themselves:

net present value
internal rate of return
benefit–cost ratio
payback period
first-year rate of return.

The net present value method and the internal rate of return method are briefly defined later in the section dealing with financial appraisal. In essence the *net present value* (NPV) is simpler to calculate, and compares the flow of discounted costs and benefits either as a ratio of present-value benefits over present-value costs, as a cash sum of present-value benefit less present-value costs, or as a ratio of this net present value (benefit minus cost) over the present value of costs, and is generally accepted as the most appropriate method. The *internal rate of return* (IRR) method effectively indicates the rate of return on a project but suffers from certain disadvantages: it is more difficult to compute iterative solutions; projects must be similar in kind; the use of NPV and IRR can lead to conflicting ranking of schemes; where the cash flows involve significant negative elements there may be no positive real solution or more than one; and acceptability might have to be determined by an exogenously decided rate of interest. It does, however, avoid the selection of an arbitrary rate.

The *benefit–cost ratio* method, which simply gives the total sum of benefits as a proportion of the total sum of costs, is a useful guideline but frequently clouds monetary issues. The *payback period* method, which compares alternative schemes according to the time it takes to recoup the initial investment, is misleading and rarely used, and the *first-year rate of return* was popular with transport economists but is now largely discredited.

The selection of an appropriate discount rate is one of the main problems in CBA but remains fundamental to the technique and four approaches are possible:

opportunity cost rate   government determined rate
government lending rate   social time preference rate

The *opportunity cost* is that rate of interest that could be gained if the project were not undertaken and the capital were invested elsewhere. It is market-oriented and has certain advantages but in reflecting private-sector investment decisions it makes no allowance for social criteria, community perspectives or less risky circumstances. The *government lending rate* is easily applicable but has been so volatile over recent years as to be inaccurate and unreliable. A *government determined rate* of say 8 or 10 per cent is often used but has been criticized for not being set at levels which truly reflect the opportunity cost of public-sector capital. A *social time preference rate* is sometimes adopted because it is thought that the very nature of public investment is to attach greater weight to the needs of the future by way of long-term planning than would the private individual, who prefers to discount far-off costs and benefits at a much higher rate of interest. In other words, individuals are often short-sighted about the future and government intervention is justified to 'give adequate weight to the welfare of unborn generations'. The social time preference rate is, therefore, established at a lower level such as 2, 4 or 6 per cent depending upon prevailing market rates.

As most of the factors taken into account in a CBA will be subject to degrees of risk and uncertainty it is advisable to explore the outcomes possible due to changing circumstances. Such factors as time, cost and rate of interest can be varied according to their likely probability of change, and a series of different possible results established. This procedure of testing for risk and uncertainty is known as *sensitivity analysis* and is a crucial component of CBA, where a single precise best solution is unlikely.

Presentation

Where no intangibles exist the presentation of results is a relatively simple task consisting of a rank order of alternative schemes according to their respective net present values, internal rate of return, benefit/cost ratio or whatever indicator of performance is used. More usually there will be an appraisal of intangibles, which should be presented separately from the tangible components, each with a suitable explanatory statement as to the way they have been adjudged. A full explanation of all assumptions that have been made at all stages of analysis should be included in the final presentation, and although a close contact between the analyst and the eventual decision maker should have been maintained throughout the process, it is especially important at the presentation stage. Essentially, the analyst is faced with the problem of either trying to produce a comprehensive picture which is inevitably complex, or of presenting a single indicator that the decision-maker can easily grasp but which can gloss over many unresolved dilemmas of policy. Simple solutions should, therefore, be rare, and the technique of CBA remains an aid to, and not a substitute for, decision-making.

Some applications of cost–benefit analysis

One of the earliest CBAs undertaken in this country was the Motorway 1 study carried out jointly by the Road Research Laboratory and Birmingham University. It was largely experimental in nature and being retrospective it merely sought to investigate the problems inherent in the technique, attempting to establish some form of approach to deal with such contentious items as accident costs and social time preference.

In 1963 Foster and Beesley conducted a CBA of the Victoria Line underground extension. This was considered necessary because if a conventional 'internal' balance sheet were drawn up the proposed line would have made a loss at existing 'subsidized' fare levels. When 'external' costs and benefits, such as time and cost saving, together with greater convenience and comfort on that and other routes, were included, however, the construction was justified.

Another early example of CBA was the study produced by the Barnsbury Association as a reaction to proposals made by the Ministry of Housing and Local Government in 1968 for that part of London. The district was a conservation area comprising 8300 dwellings, of which one-half were constructed before 1876, 700 were unfit for human habitation, and only 3775 were classed as in either good or fair condition. The aim of the study was to evaluate the respective costs and benefits of rehabilitation as opposed to redevelopment from the three standpoints of the local authority, the residents and society at large. It is interesting to record the differing results according to the various standpoints as follows:

	Rehabilitation	*Redevelopment*
Local authority	−4,144,000	+2,106,000
Residents	+3,949,000	−4,992,000
General	+ 394,000	−14,629,000

Probably the most notorious of all CBAs undertaken in this country was that undertaken by the Roskill Commission in their search for a third London airport. The commentaries and criticisms evoked by this study are numerous and contradictory, and the controversy continues, but the search procedure adopted by the Commission is interesting. Five discernible cycles emerged in arriving at a preferred solution. To begin with, seventy-eight alternative sites were identified and subsequently reduced to twenty-nine, fifteen, then four that were the subject of the final inquiry, of which one, Cublington, was then submitted by the Commission as its recommendation to the Government, who chose Foulness. Whatever the criticisms levelled at the Commission the study remains a thorough, logical and consistent example of CBA, dealing not only with the most obvious issues of passenger, construction, noise, and displacement costs, amenity losses, defence and surface access, but also with the more intractable problem of attempting to trace the full welfare consequences of alternative proposals. Perhaps the only question that was omitted was – do we need a third London airport at all?

The value of cost-benefit analysis

Whatever its shortcomings, the value of CBA lies in the fact that it declares the hand of the planner and the decision-maker, laying bare his objectives, criteria and costing. It acts as a checklist for the professional, and at the same time sets the stage for public participation and criticism. There is, however, the grave danger of a valuable and essentially simple device becoming over-sophisticated and the means of evaluation becoming more important than the end.

Some of the criticisms that have been made of the technique, however, can be usefully summarized as follows:

Problem definition. There is a need for greater clarity of objectives; joint products need to be recognized and included in the evaluation; and real alternative plans should be produced, not simply alternative approaches to the same problem.

Enumeration. The study boundary is usually too narrow; more externalities should be considered; the treatment of taxation as a transfer payment requires standardization; the elimination of transfer payments and double counting should not conceal the incidence of costs and benefits within the proposals; equity considerations should be given more weight; and intangibles should be given more attention.

Quantification. Shadow pricing should give more consideration to
   allow for opportunity costs, local variations and the perceived
   values of users and others; alternative assumptions to the unity of
   the marginal utility of money and their impact in terms of equity
   should be considered; the quantification and ranking of intangibles
   should reflect the decision-maker's and not the analyst's values;
   and much greater attention should be paid to the proper forecasting of costs and benefits through time, rather than at a
   particular point in time.
Discounting. A range of discount rates should always be used; the
   DoE should reject single-year rates of return as indicators of
   economic benefit and encourage proper discounted cash flow
   techniques; and far more use of sensitivity analysis should be made.
Others. More thought should be given to presentation; greater interaction between analyst and decision-maker should take place; and
   economic evaluation should be more prominent throughout the
   decision-making process.

The planning balance sheet

This technique is closely associated with cost–benefit analysis but was
first put forward in 1956 by Professor Nathaniel Lichfield as a
practical way of applying CBA in town planning and development.
The planning balance sheet sets out by identifying two broad
categories of individuals or groups within the community – the
producers responsible for introducing and operating the particular
project, and the consumers who will be the recipients of its effects.
Having determined the respective membership of these two sectors,
the costs and benefits that accrue to them are compared and valued.
Those that are capable of being assessed in money terms are entered
into the *balance sheet of social accounts*, which is divided into annual
and capital, costs and benefits. In that form, those that are considered
to be intangible and defy monetary quantification are entered as *I* if
capital items and *i* if annual, and similarly those that are measurable
but because of time, expense or lack of data are not measured are
entered as *M* or *m*. If an increase over the existing 'do-nothing'
situation is envisaged then a positive (+) sign is employed; conversely,
if a decrease is predicted a negative (–) sign is used. Some attempt is
also made to gauge the degree of change between alternative plans by
comparing the various elements one against another and arriving at
either net advantage to one plan, or, where several alternatives exist,

an order of preference. In more recent studies[5] a further sophistication has been introduced by attempting to rank or weight the various elements such as the relief of congestion or the displacement of population, and the affected agencies such as private and public vehicles or owner–occupiers and council tenants. This practice of weighting or ranking involves a considerable amount of value judgement and political interference being injected into the evaluation, but if properly conducted can lead to far more realistic estimates.

Another problem that continually crops up in nearly all cost-benefit analyses is that of double counting, but the *planning balance sheet* approach aims to eliminate not only double counting but also transfer payments and common items of cost and benefit at what is described as the reduction stage. The sheet used for reduction subtracts all items entered more than once, which are marked with an *E*, and all items of equal worth in each alternative; the remaining items are summed algebraically and reduced to a common form, either annual or capital.

As with other evaluation techniques, the planning balance sheet encounters difficulty in valuing those items which possess no market price, the inevitable intangibles, and further encounters the problem outlined previously in the appraisal of cost–benefit analysis regarding the selection of an appropriate rate of return for discounting public-sector investment. The balance sheet does not, however, set out to provide a result for proposed schemes in terms of a rate of return or net present value, its inherent value lies in

exposing the implications of each set of proposals to the whole community and to the various groups within that community, and also in indicating how the alternatives might be improved or amalgamated to produce a better result. The purpose of the approach is the selection of a plan which, on the information available, is likely to serve best the total interest of the community.[6]

Goal achievement

This technique seeks to establish the extent to which a plan meets the original objectives set by the politicians. The most notable approach is that put forward in 1968 by Morris Hill in the evaluation of alternative transportation plans.[7] Hill's technique evolved from criticism of the planning balance sheet for its tendency to classify all the costs and benefits of alternative strategies with no regard to the politics of a particular situation. He suggests that the goals and objectives of a scheme should be made explicit and that the alternative strategies be measured in terms of the extent to which they achieve them. The constituent elements of the plan, such as housing, employment and open space, are pre-weighted to indicate the political preference or priority attached to them. The various agencies or groups that will be affected by the plan are also weighted to reflect the political pressure they exert. In this way a matrix, or table, showing the relative performance of the weighted objectives and agencies is constructed. Subsequently, social accounts are drawn up in much the same way as in the planning balance sheet.

The most controversial aspect of this technique is the assessment of weights. Probably the most effective way of establishing these and incorporating them into the evaluation is by public participation and the use of questionnaires. His approach was adopted in the preparation of the South Hampshire Structure Plan when the goals and objectives devised by the professional planners and the political representatives were tested and in fact confirmed by a random sample survey of 3000 local residents. The results of this survey were used extensively in the evaluation of four major alternative strategies.

Although conceptually pleasing, goal achievement is very difficult to apply fully in practice, and its viability relies very heavily upon the validity of the weighting procedure.

Partial evaluation techniques

Because it is impossible to include all the repercussions of any particular planning proposal it can be said that to some extent all evaluation techniques are partial. In certain circumstances, however, owing to a shortage of funds, the restriction of time, or the nature of the investigation, it may not be possible to attempt a full cost–benefit analysis and resort has to be taken to a more limited approach.

Urban threshold analysis

This technique was first propounded by Professor Boleslaw Malisz in 1963 to establish certain boundaries for calculating economic growth in relation to long-range physical land use planning.[8] It was originally formulated, tested and applied in Poland and subsequently in Russia and Italy. In this country it has been successfully incorporated by the Planning Research Unit of Edinburgh University into a number of planning studies in Scotland, notably the *Grangemouth–Falkirk*

Regional Survey and Plan,[9] and the *Central Borders Study*,[10] both published in 1968.

The theory upon which the technique has been devised is concerned with the initial investment costs required to overcome successive limitations in the urban development of a village, town or even region. While not providing a comprehensive approach to planning it is intended to assist in the selection of alternatives and provide a firmer foundation for decision-making. Basically the theory suggests that towns encounter certain physical limitations to their growth. These limitations are called *thresholds*, and while not insuperable can only be overcome by exceptionally high injections of capital investment. Once this additional investment is made the average costs of development decline until the next threshold is encountered. In this way threshold costs can be described as variable costs, over and above the normal investment costs associated with urban development.

Three basic categories of threshold can be identified. First, *physical* thresholds such as marshland, steep slopes or a river which restrict urban expansion. Second, *quantitative* thresholds imposed by the maximum potential capacity of public utilities such as sewage plant, drainage, water supply or a road system. Third, *structural* thresholds created by the internal structure of a town; for example, an increase in population might require an expansion in the existing shopping facilities where in fact no extra space is available, necessitating considerable expenditure to achieve a satisfactory solution such as multi-decking or expensive redevelopment of the surrounding area.

Although some degree of overlap is inevitable, these various thresholds come in different sizes and at different times in a town's expansion. The programming of the application of threshold theory and analysis to long-range town planning presents certain problems, but in general certain advantages of using this technique have been distinguished.[11] It assists in defining growth potential and in assessing the most efficient alternative approaches towards future development by indicating, if various thresholds have to be crossed, the least-cost alternative. It aids in establishing the programme and priorities of public investment. It shortens the process of reviewing and revising development plans. Moreover, it can be used in the selection of regional growth points. Thus it provides, albeit in a more sophisticated cost-oriented manner, a technique that is not entirely dissimilar to the 'old-fashioned' sieve maps which showed land physically difficult to develop, areas of high landscape value and agricultural worth, commercial woodland and water catchment grounds, as well as that land that could only be supplied with sewerage, drainage of water with great difficulty and expense, and those areas that were relatively inaccessible.

Despite the inherent advantages of threshold analysis in identifying the most suitable direction for future urban expansion certain reservations regarding its application have been expressed. It has been criticized for placing too much attention upon cost and not enough upon benefit, for stressing capital costs and playing down recurrent ones, and for ignoring some costs, such as accident and congestion costs, altogether. Further, there are a number of thresholds, particularly quantitative, that are extremely difficult to measure. Also costs may change over time relative to one another, development on flooded or steep land becoming suddenly much cheaper owing to technological advance. Lastly, it has been said that many thresholds exist, all interacting and virtually indistinguishable.

It is clear, however, that threshold analysis can plan an important role in the evaluation of alternative planning policies, particularly as part of a wider cost–benefit analysis, and in respect of focusing attention upon the suitability and availability of land for urban development.

Financial appraisal

Evaluation involves the choice between alternatives, and each alternative will possess a range and variety of respective costs and benefits, some of which will be quantifiable in money terms and other 'intangibles' which will defy such quantification. In any planning proposal there is likely to be a large element that can be costed. It is, perhaps, unfashionable to direct great attention to this aspect of town planning, but with an ever-increasing proportion of investment in connection with the 'built environment' being undertaken by public agencies, it is critical to be as precise as possible in respect of public moneys.

There has, in the past, been a distinct lack of harmony between the financial analyst and the physical planner. The former is an accountant, valuer, quantity surveyor or economist, concerned, in essence, with judging the relative 'cash flows' or prospective developments, how much revenue they will bring in, for what expenditure, at what time and at what risk. The latter is an architect, planner, sociologist or engineer associated with design, aesthetic, social and environmental factors. These diverse disciplines, grouped for convenience into their two categories, often appear to be pulling in different directions. This is caused by their ill-conceived and poorly timed integration within the planning process. Financial appraisal is frequently introduced all too late in evaluation, being neglected in the preliminary investigation stage where it could save a great deal of otherwise abortive work. Moreover, it is the dilatory nature of its exercise that precludes it as a device for improving plan preparation and selection, and relegates it to the rather stigmatized position it has occupied. It is, however, capable of assisting in the working up and improvement of proposed plans by indicating a more propitious development or funding programme. It can also expose, at an early stage, those elements that warrant greater consideration or alteration. It might, for example, be advisable to change existing public transport services to enlarge the potential catchment area of a new shopping precinct prior to development in order to render it commercially viable. An adjustment in the phasing of a town centre redevelopment to allow for early completion of shops and offices rather than civic buildings might so transform the cash flows of the scheme as to make a seemingly redundant proposal acceptable, or a delay in landscaping by two or three years might elevate one alternative above another.

In tackling the financial appraisal, conventional valuation methods are being replaced by *discounted cash flow* (DCF) analysis which differs only in being more sophisticated, more detailed, more time and risk conscious, and yet more flexible in operation. There are two basic methods of conducting a DCF analysis. First, the *net present value* method which calculates profitability by subtracting the present value of all expenditures *when they occur* from the present value of all revenues *when they occur*, employing an 'opportunity cost' rate of discount, that is the rate of return that could be earned by investing in the next best alternative. Any project that has a positive present value is basically viable, and the one displaying the highest net present value is, in purely financial terms, the most profitable. Second, the *internal rate of return* (IRR) or *yield* method which employs the present value concept but seeks to provide an evaluation procedure that avoids the arbitrary choice of a rate of interest. Instead it sets out, by trial and error, to establish a rate of interest that makes the present value of all expenditure incurred in a project equal to the present value of all revenue gained. When calculated this interest rate is known as the yield of the investment. Having calculated the IRR or yield for each alternative they should then be compared with the cost of borrowing the capital. Any project or alternative having a return higher than the cost of borrowing is fundamentally viable, and the highest return is naturally the most financially attractive.

The evaluation of plans, projects or development of any kind requires the actual tangible measurement of the constituent factors forming the scheme, together with an estimation of their future performance. Such estimates of future events depend largely upon an interpretation of what has happened in the past, and since experience shows that the pattern of past events is never exactly repeated, future predictions can be at best imprecise approximations. To be as accurate as possible, however, it is advisable to introduce a sensitivity analysis combined with a probability distribution which will explore, list and examine the possible range of likely outcomes. Despite an entrenched reluctance in certain spheres to apply this approach, it does provide a significant improvement over conventional techniques. Furthermore, financial appraisal readily lends itself to adoption within the wider framework of cost–benefit analysis. Perhaps the most interesting example of a slightly different form of financial appraisal was the analysis of the performance, in terms of costs and revenues, of six English new towns undertaken in the late sixties by Nathaniel Lichfield and Paul Wendt.[12]

15 Associated planning techniques

It can be argued that planning as a profession has suffered over the years from a positive plague of techniques. The bewildering array of techniques employed throughout the planning process at such stages as survey, systems analysis, forecasting, plan generation, evaluation, participation, decision taking, budgeting, implementation and monitoring have not always been applied with a full understanding of their limitations. Nevertheless, though the value and reliability of many techniques introduced into planning procedures during the heyday of the techniques approach, say from 1965 to 1975, have been seriously brought into question, the need remains in planning to make a conscious effort to employ logical methods, to observe and display internal consistency, and to minimize the area of final decisions based upon personal opinion. With a desire not to omit at least a mention of some useful techniques used in planning practice not included elsewhere in the text, this chapter is an attempt to remedy that possible defect, recognizing that it inevitably becomes something of a rag-bag in the process.

Gaming

With the development of a systems approach towards town planning, which attempts to distinguish the various activities that determine the nature of the human environment and understand their relationship, a range of associated techniques has been devised to assist in analysis and experimentation. The most notable of these is the construction of mathematical models to represent the real world in abstract but manageable conditions. One of their major drawbacks, however, is that they preclude the study of decision-making in situations of personal conflict. Most planning decisions are influenced in one way or another by political, social, economic or professional human attitudes and behaviour. To permit the introduction of individuals, agencies and ideas into controlled and experimental conditions a number of 'games' have been conceived. These games are models or simulations of possible real-life circumstances which allow for interaction between individuals, thus portraying the politics of a situation. The history of gaming has its roots in military training. This can be traced as far back as 3000 BC in China where the great military thinker and general Sun-Tzu simulated and played out his battle plans in a game called Wei-Hai, known today under the Japanese name of Go. The French constructed games in the eighteenth century to familiarize cadets with basic military strategy, and the Prussians characteristically introduced a certain element of scientific method and rigour into their Kriegsspiel which was extensively played throughout the nineteenth century.

Having found further service in the field of business management, it was not until the late 1950s that gaming was introduced into urban planning, and only in the late 1960s did it really establish itself. It fulfils several basic functions; it is a method of self-teaching, it is widely used in training of all kinds, it can be employed in research, and it can be used for evaluation where numerical or quantitative techniques are inappropriate. It is therefore suitable on any occasion where it is necessary to replace the complexity of the urban scene with a simulation which allows certain representative features to be understood and recognized or where the study of phenomena by any other means might be dangerous, expensive or impossible.

One of the first urban planning games to be developed was the Cornell Land Use Game (CLUG), which is still widely used, principally for educational purposes, and has provided the basis for many other games. Originally concerned with the study of land economics and location theory it has been expanded to include the effects of town planning, taxation, legislation and politics. Another, more sophisticated, game is Metro, which, based on a typical medium-sized American metropolitan area, relies heavily upon the use of a computer, setting out to examine not only the economic but also the political systems and pressures influencing various sections of the community. The players adopt the roles of the politicians, professional planners, administrators, pressure groups and land developers. A number of mathematical models are built into the game and serviced by a computer which supplies information and projections regarding population, industrial growth, household distribution, voters' response to changing circumstances, crime rates and development. These models also make allowances for the actions of the players during the game in their respective roles. A roughly similar, though slightly less complex, game is available in this country, called the PTRC game, which traces the growth of a medium-sized country town, taking account of British town practice and procedures.

Apart from its educational function this approach readily lends itself to establishing and testing organizational and administrative structures by recreating real-life situations in a practical manner. It has been used by local government in this country to test the introduction of corporate planning into an authority by speeding up the processes involved. One year's possible events were played out in a matter of days in order to search out any inconsistencies in departmental policy and structure and to identify the factors, agencies, personalities and pressures concerned.

As with so many other new techniques there is always a danger of too much importance being placed upon the method and performance of gaming, but it can provide a useful way of examining and understanding human behaviour and political decision-making and their effect upon town planning.

Models

A model is merely a simple reconstruction of reality that reduces the apparent complexity of the real world to something that the planner can adequately comprehend and cope with. It describes a system, and the relationship of the various activities or factors associated with that system. It is used in town planning to understand the forces that determine the size and nature of urban areas and the location of land uses therein. The planner uses the model to examine, and subsequently make statements about, the real world that will assist him in controlling and changing events in the real world. As models may be used to estimate unknown values of one variable, given a range of known values of other variables, it is essential in planning, if indeed the model is to assist in foreseeing and guiding change, to select variables which can themselves be controlled. In a shopping model, for example, floorspace is eminently suitable, future provision being dictated by planning permission. Some of the variables may not be directly measurable, such as the attractiveness of a shopping centre. These variables are called parameters and can be adjusted to simulate a particular circumstance by assuming, for example, that while the attractiveness of a shopping centre is not directly proportional to its size, the larger a centre is the more attractive it becomes because of the wider range of goods offered. Although the precise value of the parameter is not known, trial calculations are undertaken and the results compared with actual figures. The procedure is continued until there is agreement and a satisfactory fit is obtained. This process of introducing and adjusting parameters is known as calibration and testing. It is inevitable that the simplification implicit in model building involves some loss of aspects of real life.

The development and application of the model building approach evolved because of a changing attitude towards the theory of urban structure. The traditional view of town and country planning is being subjected to considerable challenge, 'the merely morphological perception of the city that ruled the early literature on planning, whose signal features were size, shape and density, having fallen to pieces'.[1] The advent of systems theory and its introduction into the planning process demands a more thorough analysis of the aspects, activities and agencies at play in society, and a greater understanding of their relationships and interdependence. Modelling introduces a greater degree of rigour into planning practice; despite the fact that it can still be highly subjective, it does permit a more precise examination, expose certain thought processes, require values to be placed upon items, declare the hand of the planner or decision-maker, aid communication, and facilitate comparison between alternatives.

Models divide themselves into different categories, depending upon their sophistication or purpose. First, they can either be partial, relating to only one form of activity or land use, or general, where more than one form of activity or land use are considered and their respective relationships simulated. Second, they can be classified as being descriptive, showing the existing situation; predictive, forecasting future trends; or prescriptive, examining alternative policies and deciding between them.

As with so many other 'technological advances', the construction of land use models was initially developed during the late 1950s and early 1960s in the United States of America, and was primarily concerned with the study of transportation. Although Reilly's Law of Gravitational Retailing, put forward in 1929, is essentially a simple model, the first land use models were developed and applied during the 1960s. Probably the most comprehensive general model is that devised by Ira Lowry for Pittsburgh.[2] This is really a set of models closely associated with economic base theory which assumes that the location of basic employment is independent of the location patterns of other activities such as non-basic employment and population, but that these other activities are locationally dependent upon basic employment Therefore, the model assumes that population and non-basic employment can be uniquely derived from basic employment.[3]

In this way it distributes households to suggested residential areas, having taken into account where they must work, shop, and obtain other services. This model has been further developed by a number of social scientists – notably in 1966 by R. A. Garin,[4] who brought the technique even closer to economic base theory, the derived result being commonly referred to as the Garin–Lowry model.

In this country, similar land use models have been constructed for the last five years. As Batty pointed out, the Garin–Lowry model readily lent itself to adoption in British planning practice.[5] It was a most comprehensive approach, and singularly well suited to the structure planning process established by the 1968 Town and Country Planning Act. Models have been devised at both sub-regional and urban scales. The former have been applied for Central Lancashire in appraising the designated site for a new town,[6] for Bedfordshire to evaluate alternative strategies, and for Nottingham-shire–Derbyshire,[7] Severnside and Merseyside. The latter have all been developed at the Centre for Land Use and Built-Form Studies, Cambridge University, and relate to Reading, Cambridge, Stevenage and Milton Keynes. All are derivatives of the Garin–Lowry model.[8]

The various inherent qualities of a land use model permit it to be used at several stages in the planning process. First, at the analysis stage, where it helps in setting down and clarifying the problems that present themselves in a manner that facilitates discussion. Second, in formulating a policy and designing the plan. Third, in providing a most useful basis for comparing or evaluating alternative strategies. Fourth, and perhaps more tenuously, in monitoring the plan's performance.

The vast growth in the development and application of land use models has been greatly aided by the advent of the high-speed computer. Nevertheless a model is only as good as the information with which it is supplied. They tend, moreover, to possess a voracious appetite for data. A comparatively simple shopping model will require, for example, the following:

boundary data
population statistics

existing retail expenditure in various categories of goods
socio-economic structure of population
total income of population
future income of population
definition of retail hierarchy
car ownership rates, present and future
proximity of competing centres
travel distance, speed and cost
trends in conversion factors
existing sales
existing floorspace

It is not intended to explain in any detail the mathematical working of a model, but to illustrate their nature a modified version of Reilly's Law, which attempts to establish the 'breaking point' between two retail spheres of influence, is described:

$$D_{01} = \frac{D_{12}}{1 + \sqrt{\dfrac{A_2}{A_1}}}$$

where D_{01} is the deterrence function expressed in distance, time or cost between town 1 and the breaking point, D_{12} is a similar measure between towns 1 and 2, and A_1, A_2 are the attraction factors expressed in sales, floorspace or population of towns 1 and 2.

Although many problems exist regarding the construction and handling of land use models, F. Stuart Chapin concludes his book *Urban Land Use Planning* with this statement on their role:

In larger urban areas and certainly in the major metropolitan areas, planning agencies cannot hope to cope with the demands on their time and provide the kind of staff work for policy formulation that will be increasingly their responsibility to provide unless they avail themselves of these tools of analysis.[9]

Linear programming

This operational research technique assists in selecting the best way of employing valuable resources in order to reach a desired state of affairs. This desired state of affairs or result is known as the *objective function* and the degree of availability of the various constituent resources that are required to produce the result are called the *constraints.* The overall process is described as being one of *optimization.* This approach lends itself to short-run problems when resources are comparatively scarce and fixed in supply and when the respective constraints can be easily identified. The result is obtained algebraically or, where the problem is extremely simple, graphically, and the technique is particularly well suited to computerization when many hundreds of possible solutions consequent upon many thousands of resources can be examined in a matter of seconds.

This method of analysis, widely used in business management, has been employed in tackling regional planning problems where development has been restricted by the scarcity of one or more resource. Linear programming indicates the best way of applying all the available resources in such a way as to achieve the maximum return. One of the areas in which it has proved of considerable value is transportation planning, where it is often necessary to minimize either the cost of travel or the time of journeys.

It has been further developed in Israel as a means of finding optimal solutions to overall planning problems. As such it has been applied to the preparation and evaluation of alternative plans, whereby one variable element of the plan at a time is allowed to change, all other variables are held constant, and a variety of combinations are tested in order to produce the best solutions.[10]

In most planning studies, however, the number of constraints that have to be incorporated in the analysis is likely to be very high; moreover, they are rarely in a quantitative form appropriate to linear programming methods. In a similar way the objective function, or desired result, is itself frequently hard to define and operational research techniques of this kind cannot adequately handle non-quantifiable or intangible variables.

Scenario writing

This is a technique designed to aid forward planning and forecasting by which a number of alternative futures are described for a particular planning area or problem and the sequence of events that determine their evolution identified. Different sets of circumstances are established and the likely repercussions that flow from them are traced ahead in time. These varying circumstances might relate to a possible range of available resources or to foreseeable changes in political complexion. The process of scenario writing can be pursued both ways. A desired solution could be drawn up and, by working backwards, all the necessary decisions, activities and inputs that lead to its realization distinguished, and a probable timescale defined. Conversely, existing conditions could be projected forwards, making various assumptions as to the social, economic or political decisions that might be made at different stages, so that scenarios could be constructed at almost any point in time. While it lacks the quantitative rigour of some techniques, it is an extremely useful way of exercising the minds of those responsible for decision-making and revealing the dependent relationship between different events.

Environmental impact analysis

Since 1970 all major projects in the United States of America which would have a significant effect upon the human environment must be preceded by an environmental impact statement (EIS). Environmental analysis or assessment has already been formally introduced in France, Canada, Japan and Australia, many other countries are preparing legislation, and as early as 1974 the European Parliament advocated the worldwide application of the need to produce an EIS in the project appraisal of such developments as power plants, industrial plants of a certain dimension or handling hazardous substances, motorways, airfields, railways, harbours and other significant urban schemes. The Windscale Inquiry into the siting of a nuclear power station focused attention upon the desirability of introducing such planning instruments in this country, although the Dobry report on development control had proposed the preparation of impact studies by developers for certain major applications.

It has been suggested that a good environmental impact analysis has five objectives:[11]

First, it should forecast clearly the likely consequences of a development so that decision makers decide not whether the forecast is accurate, but whether those consequences are in the interests of those they represent. Second, its execution should provide a flexible framework for the thoughts of the man who advises the decision-makers. Third, it should provide the documentation to inform and reassure the public that everything relevant has been considered and that while the resulting decisions may not suit everyone they are at least well considered. Debate is thus confined to the significant. Fourth, it will give a baseline of the existing situation against which to measure the effects of the development, if it proceeds. Finally, it should suggest how the impacts identified can be modified to maximize the beneficial and minimize the injurious.

Although an environmental impact analysis may be conducted in a variety of ways it has been put forward that essentially it comprises nine activities, namely:[12]

1 Examine the existing environment.
2 Forecast the future of the environment if the development does not proceed.
3 Examine the proposed development.
4 Forecast the future of the environment if the development does proceed.
5 Identify, in quantitative and qualitative terms, the differences between (2) and (4).
6 Propose amelioration measures, where possible, to reduce adverse impacts.
7 Analyse the impacts, and where alternative locations are possible, compare.
8 Present results of analysis.
9 Make decision.

Measurement of individual components of a scheme and objective comparison between alternative schemes present the same problems as those encountered in cost–benefit analysis. The use of social and economic indicators, thorough consultation with interested parties, the adoption of ranking procedures, and the commissioning of attitude surveys can all be employed to refine the analysis, but inevitably a high degree of subjective judgement will occur.

The Department of the Environment sponsored two studies on the application of environmental impact assessment, and the DoE research report 13 published in 1976 reported favourably on the technique. It should be stressed though, that only about twenty-five to forty major development projects a year are thought likely to demand the preparation of an EIA if they were formally to be introduced.

Indicators

In order to improve decision-making in all sectors of the economy a number of economic, social, technological, scientific and environmental indicators have been developed over the years which identify and measure rates and levels of performance or condition. One of the first was the use of *gross national product* to classify the economic performance of different countries, even though it has been criticized for excluding many important attributes of a particular country and is prone to external influences which affect its value.

For an index to be useful it has been argued that it must have certain general and specific properties. Generally it must be: *reliable*, demonstrating a consistency over a number of replications; *valid*, relating to the definition and criteria used in the construction of the index, thereby measuring what it purports to measure; and *reproduce-able*, showing qualities of rigour when tested at accepted levels of statistical confidence. Specifically, it must have: *independence*, being mutually exclusive of all other components of the index, and, while data is rarely that homogeneous or independent, correlation and multiple regression tests can be used to check degrees of association between the various components of the index; *linearity*, so that scaling intervals can represent the equivalent increase or decrease at whatever point they appear on the index, thus ensuring a straight and direct relationship exists between what is being measured and the scale; and *comparability*, so that it can be assessed against prescribed norms and allow the index to classify the items being measured into specific groups for potential policy action. Furthermore it has been asserted that indicators can only effectively be used to measure aspects of a social system if they are applied regularly so as to derive time series data, and be aggregated for studies on a lower level such as individuals, households or localities. Four types of indicator have been described:

Informative, depicting parts of a system which change spatially over time as in the case of housing, education and health.

Predictive, which form an integral part of theoretical formulation and assessment of past and present trends.

Problem-oriented, which provide information for the analyst to observe particular localized problem areas and guide policy makers to possible policy and programme solutions, as instanced in educational priority areas and housing renewal areas.

Programme evaluation, which allow the analyst to assess the efficiency of an on-going policy and provide further target levels, and be able to decide whether to change or continue with the present policies.

Some examples of the use of indicators in planning are included in the chapter on housing where they have been employed in identifying and measuring housing stress as part of housing renewal policy.

Part Three

Some aspects of town planning

16   Rural planning

Rural planning has for long remained a much neglected aspect of the overall planning process, for, given a post-war preoccupation with urban problems, attention has largely been directed at urban containment and countryside protection. The distinction between urban and rural, however, is often unclear, as most urban policies have a rural dimension and certain common problems can be discerned in town and country. Nevertheless, the situation that confronts the rural poor in respect of housing, employment, transport and the provision of other services and facilities is often very different from that in the cities, and similarly demands a set of comprehensive and cohesive planning policies to meet the particular circumstances prevailing. Another characteristic feature of rural planning is the limited amount of study that has been paid to it and of published material about it.[1] With the likely distinction between town and country in mind a notable study was undertaken by Hampshire County Council in 1966, intended to provide a research basis upon which a rural settlement policy could be devised, and which found, somewhat surprisingly, that setting aside cities there were certainly more similarities than differences between towns and villages. The proportion of indigenous population in both was around 20 per cent, the employment characteristics were alike, as were the travel patterns to work, the distances travelled, the reasons for immigration and the attitudes towards the facilities available.

Demographic change

One of the difficulties in appraising rural change over time, especially demographic change, is that the census base is inappropriate for analysis. A number of readily identifiable traits emerge, however, such as the rapid increase in population of areas within easy commuting distance of major cities and their social transformation; the maintenance of a relatively stable population in small market towns; and a continuing drift of population away from the more isolated areas of the country. The population decline experienced by these last isolated or remoter areas can largely be attributed to the falling demand for agricultural labour, the lack of social and community services, the failure to introduce small-scale industrial enterprises, the scarcity of employment opportunities for women and the sheer psychological effects of isolation upon such communities. Although poor housing conditions have often been cited as a reason for decline this is probably a less important consideration, the lack of suitable employment being almost certainly the paramount factor. The majority of migration away from remoter areas is by the young, and, coupled with a certain amount of in-migration by older groups this naturally further deteriorates the age structure of the population. A concentration of craft industries in local towns has also led to a serious rundown of public transport facilities in these areas. In this context a correlation between population decline and village size has been identified. Villages with less than 120 persons have experienced a rapid decline, those between 120 persons and 160 persons a steady decline coupled with an aging population, those between 160 and 180 persons have generally proved resilient, those between 180 and 450 persons have demonstrated an erratic performance, but those of over 450 persons have invariably grown.[2]

Planning policy in many countries over the past twenty years or so has been aimed at rationalization, so that resources can be directed at safeguarding and promoting the stronger village communities, often at the cost of the weaker. This has frequently been described as a 'key village' policy, and one of the earliest and most extreme programmes was designed by Durham County Council, who defined four categories of rural settlement in their County Development Plan classified according to their anticipated population change. One category of village, category D, was expected to continue losing population, and a policy was formulated whereby approximately one-third of these villages would be run down and eventually cleared, and the rest would not be allowed to develop further. The planned decline approach by Durham is exceptional, but the 'key village' concept of directing growth to chosen settlements is actively pursued throughout the country. It has yet to be proved completely successful in stemming the population loss of remoter areas, and requires a sensitive and flexible application according to the peculiar needs and circumstances of individual areas. Great care must be taken in determining such matters as minimum size and operating a policy of redistribution.

At the other end of the scale there are those rural or semi-rural settlements closely linked to large urban areas. Commuting to work has become very much more common, with city workers being prepared to travel longer and longer distances; second home ownership has generally been on the increase since the war; and retirement to the countryside has become more popular. Disadvantages can occur to the host population in the way of inflated land and property values combined with a distortion in the housing market; consequent recreational pursuits can cause congestion and abuse; and, as the majority of immigrants are middle class, there is usually a slow process of social assimilation and integration. Some villages virtually act as dormitories for nearby towns, and the constituent village society can become extremely polarized. Conversely, many such hybrid villages have achieved a harmonious and successfully integrated community. Paradoxically, of course, it is often the newcomers who are most opposed to suggestions of further expansion and related development. Rural planning in these urban linked settlements is characterized by the absence of an overall strategy and most of the prevailing policies are adopted piecemeal or as stereotypes from elsewhere, the problem being especially severe in the rural–urban fringe. In terms of population a threshold size of over 2000 persons is normally accepted as being a reasonable minimum for the supply of a basic range of communal services, and understandably the process of village expansion encourages the provision of further facilities which in turn makes the place even more attractive and so the pressures for growth accumulate. The desultory demographic reaction of town and country planning to these pressures has been criticized as follows:

Planning and other statutory controls are rudimentary or non-existent in respect of population problems, and such policies as do exist (notably in relating to development control in green belts and areas of attractive landscape) serve only to redistribute urban pressures in an intensified form in other rural areas.[3]

Rural services

While the village and small county town are invariably depicted as well-endowed and stable communities, the rate of change, not merely in terms of population but in respect of social condition, has been appreciable over the past two or three decades. The means and degree of mobility have altered, educational facilities and availability have changed, health and community services have been reordered, the housing market has been transformed and employment opportunities completely recast.

The access to *transport* and consequent mobility is the way in which the inefficiencies of rural life, particularly small-village life, are surmounted, and, perhaps not unexpectedly, the level of car ownership at between 65 per cent and 75 per cent is generally much higher than the national average of 53 per cent. Because a high proportion of travel to work takes place by car, however, the remainder of the household is left to varying degrees immobile during the working day. Moreover, the aged, the sick and the lowest income groups have poor access to a car, and, with a predominantly middle class influence exercised over local government decisions resulting in a preoccupation with other policies ahead of public transport, the social implications of immobility in rural areas is often ignored. This deficiency is to some extent reflected by the level of subsidy for rural bus services, which in very many county areas stands at less than 10 per cent of the highway budget, and, despite government avowals of greater support in the White Paper on transport policy of June 1977, the method of grant allocation to county councils and the mere hope of persuading bus operators to direct more of their subsidy to rural services paints a pessimistic picture for the future. Possibly what is required is a more flexible and better co-ordinated approach to the problem, and while the idea of 'postal buses' seemed initially attractive, and is working well in some areas of mid-Wales and Scotland, their routes, direction and frequency are not always suited to rural public transport needs. Perhaps a more fruitful field of innovation lies in the development of a 'social car service' manned by volunteer car-owning drivers and supported financially on a limited basis by the county council. An early experiment along these lines was conducted in Lindsey, part of Lincolnshire, and has since been taken up elsewhere in the county with notable success.

With *education*, the principal policy has been the rationalization of existing schools and their consolidation into fewer and larger ones serving wide rural hinterlands. Primary schools have suffered most, declining in number by almost 40 per cent since the war. The days of the small village school are fast disappearing, and though conflicting views are expressed regarding the absolute minimum acceptable size, it would seem that those with less than 40 pupils are distinctly threatened with closure and those with less than 60 subject to scrutiny. Arguments both for and against small rural schools can be advanced. Those for include the confidence and security engendered by small village schools; the rapport that is built up between pupils, the village community and the teacher; the lack of discipline problems; a low pupil–staff ratio and low staff turnover; and the value of teaching students in vertically integrated age groups. Those against include the constrained curriculum that can be offered; the waste of dissipated resources; and the possibility of an entire school suffering from the dominance of one bad teacher. A proposed compromise is now operated by some county education authorities whereby primary schools remain small and village-based, a middle school is established for the over-9s to serve a group of villages, and a high school set up for the over-13s on a much wider catchment area basis. One of the most important aspects of the school in rural communities, however, is the opportunity it provides for accommodating alternative educational and community activities in out-of-school hours. Though obviously not unique to the country, the lack of other community facilities places a high premium upon this potential use and again reinforces the need for a flexible planning approach to rural problems.

As with education, *health and other community services* have been subject to consolidation over recent years. Large specialist medical centres are traditionally located in major urban areas, but even the cottage hospital is becoming a thing of the past with the advent of massive regional hospitals. There has been a reaction to this trend, however, and these major centres are fast being supplemented by smaller community hospitals. One of the more novel developments has been the proposal for creating mobile 'plug-in' clinics, taking the specialist to the patient, which could support local general practitioners and cover wide country areas undertaking the more straightforward or routine clinical tasks. Libraries have long employed a similar practice and are still evolving even more innovative procedures to service remote areas. Arguably, one of the most serious elements of rural decline is that of the village shop. Increasingly, local village shopkeepers find themselves at a marked price disadvantage in comparison with their urban counterpart, and with the growing mobility of the majority who can thus shop around, they, and their dependent immobile customers, are caught in an escalating poverty trap of lower sales and higher prices. There has been a certain amount of banding together by small shopkeepers to form co-operatives or to participate in one of the existing voluntary wholesale groups, but the prospects for the village shop are again dim.[4]

The question of *rural housing* is essentially one of the relative deprivation of particular groups and the unequal competition persisting between them. Local indigenous working-class villagers in search of their first home are forced to compete in a market frequently filled with relatively affluent middle-class executives seeking some form of bucolic retreat. Urban and rural housing markets display very different characteristics. Though at 75,000 dwellings they represent a small proportion of the whole, the anachronism of tied cottages remains; tenanted accommodation, at about 20 per cent, is comparatively high; and, while not often recognized as a special rural symptom, council housing in the country is particularly divisive in its form, location and social standing.

It has been estimated that there are approximately 4 million to 5 million people in Great Britain whose livelihood virtually requires them to live in rural areas, of whom around 600,000 are farmers or farmworkers.[5] Another 4 million to 5 million persons comprise the total rural population, and collectively they have been classified into eight groups which assist in identifying competing housing needs[6] – large property owners, salaried immigrants with some capital, 'spiralists' (highly mobile young executives), those with limited income and little capital, the retired, council house tenants, tied cottagers and other tenants, and local tradesmen and owners of small businesses. Housing pressure caused by the competition between these groups for a restricted supply of property, particularly between those associated with the land in one way or another and those who have been described as 'marauding urbanites',[7] is not confined, as is commonly thought, to the commuting hinterlands of London and a few other major cities, but is widespread throughout the country. The decrease in housing opportunities for local young people is probably the most disturbing feature of the rural housing market. This situation is exacerbated by the growth in second-home ownership, which has been variously placed at 200,000 and 370,000; the increase in most county areas of the council house waiting lists; the shortage of building land within village envelopes for public housing; the high costs of rural housing with expensive service provision and the diseconomies of small-scale development; and, with planning control usually being restricted to matters of design, the great proportion of private-sector residential development is for higher-income groups given the current pattern of demand for rural housing.

Because a great deal of rural activity is now centred in urban areas the numbers involved in *rural employment* have dwindled to about only 5 per cent of the total labour force, and those concerned directly in farming to less than 2 per cent. In many ways it is becoming difficult to distinguish clearly between urban and rural activities with the growing industrial or 'big-business' attitude that has to be taken towards modern agriculture. As has already been mentioned, the employment structure is particularly unbalanced in remote country areas, where there is a low activity rate, few opportunities for women and a poor infrastructure. Although the growth of tourism has slightly eased the situation, the rapid reduction in the number of farms from around 400,000 in the 1960s to approximately 250,000 in the 1970s has meant a further rationalization of farm labour. Forestry and mineral extraction are productive and present employment opportunities, but are often considered despoiling. While forestry, for example, is not as productive as agriculture, it is more labour intensive and a large employer of secondary trades. Ironically, the potentially most economic locations for mineral extraction invariably seem to be in areas of high landscape value, and the volatility of world markets can lead to sudden and unexpected changes in the margin which affect viability, as the exploitation of potash on the North Yorkshire moors exemplifies. There are also costly conservation conditions attached to most permissions for mineral excavation. One interesting development over the past few years, however, is the emergence of fish farming as a rural industry and employer. Traditionally manufacturing industry has provided little employment in rural areas. Where it accounts for approximately 40 per cent of all employment across the country as a whole, it falls to around 25 per cent in rural areas, and as low as 10 per cent in the more isolated parts. Apart from the historical reasons associated with access to coal power, one of the prime causes of the continued scarcity of manufacturing industry in rural areas is the lack of an entrepreneurial base, such as the ready availability of finance, premises and skilled labour.[8] Poor industrial linkage, therefore, limits the chances of promoting successful rural industry in both scale and type, and probably the most suitable activities are those related to craft and design. Service employment is high in virtually all rural areas, being on average about 10 per cent above the national norm of 50 per cent. Not surprisingly, rural locations are attractive for office purposes, and a considerable number of educational and research organizations have moved to the country, providing more jobs themselves and also acting as a generator of even more service employment. Until fairly recently most employment policy was aimed at alleviating the congestion of some large industrial conurbations and underpinning the employment base of others. Little attention was given to rural employment, and until the Local Employment Act 1960 only one rural area was accorded development area status. After 1960 the new development districts included a considerable number of rural troublespots, but were again inappropriate in that they were identified by reasons of past failure rather than future potential. The Industrial Development Act 1966 saw a return to regionally based policies on wider areas than districts; nevertheless the emphasis remained on ameliorating the problems of urban employment. In the context of rural employment there exists the Development Commission, established as long ago as 1910, whose primary objective is to co-ordinate local action by providing a nationwide service of advice, intelligence, instruction and limited credit for small rural manufacturing and service industries; the development of factory premises where increased or more diversified employment is needed to check or prevent rural depopulation; the support of experimental or pioneering schemes until they either become self-sustaining or incapable of further support; the encouragement of voluntary bodies which enrich social and intellectual life for rural people; the promotion of miscellaneous marketing or co-operative schemes designed to strengthen agricultural or fishing communities; and the carrying out of surveys or research into the rural economy.[9] The Commission is also responsible for two other agencies, the Council for Small Industries in Rural Areas (COSIRA) covering England and Wales, and a similar body, the Small Industrial Council for the Rural Areas of Scotland (SICRAS) who both aim to implement the bulk of the work of the Commission in their respective countries. Another aspect of their work is the designation of *special investment areas,* which are those parts of the country with a consistent record of population decline, and whose work has been described as follows:[10]

In these areas, since 1965, the Commission has employed an experimental policy of concentrating investment in a limited number of 'trigger areas' centred around growth points where a nucleus of small industries might be developed. The idea behind the policy is to retain the population in the area as a whole by providing more varied employment, but in fewer locations.

Although the funds are limited the principal method of assistance is financial aid towards the construction of industrial estates. Outside the special investment areas priority is given to firms providing increased opportunities for employment, firms likely to benefit the balance of payments, firms providing a service to the agricultural industry, and firms holding the promise of significant development.

One aspect of rural planning that is difficult to treat in anything approaching an objective way is the question of *rural landscape*. As a result of the immense impact man has made upon his surroundings, few landscapes can be described as entirely natural. The cumulative effect of changes such as those brought about by motorways, power stations, communication masts, electricity grids and reservoirs, has increasingly, however, become a cause for concern; because while a continually evolving landscape is inevitable, the need for protection, as opposed to preservation, is ever more immediate. In order to formulate a pertinent planning policy it is first necessary to appraise or evaluate landscape, and the planner wittingly but warily enters the realms of subjective opinion and aesthetic taste. Despite the aptness of the adage that beauty lies in the eye of the beholder, a number of attempts have been made to evaluate the general visual quality of landscape. Basically they fall into two categories, those based upon subjective judgement in the field, and those based upon the measurement of defined physical components of landscape from maps and aerial photographs.[11] One of the major problems is the way in which different people view landscape, and a report published in 1976 by Manchester University distinguished ten separate concepts of landscape. Landscape, it stated, could be seen as a total regional environment, as countryside, as land use, as topography or land form, as an ecosystem, as scenery, as heritage or historical artifact, as a composite of physical components, as an art form or as a resource or utility feature.[12] While a classification of this kind is quite feasible, it remains debatable, however, whether it is a subject that permits rational evaluation. Legislatively and administratively the problem is simpler and the performance more heartening. Notwithstanding the decline of mixed farming, the terrible onset and spread of Dutch elm disease, and the clearance of hedges to create larger fields, the establishment of national parks, areas of outstanding natural beauty, a more sensitive afforestation policy, the protection afforded by green belt zoning, the designation of areas of great landscape value in development plans, the creation of national forest parks and national nature reserves, and the mounting of the heritage coast protection plan have reflected a greater awareness of the need to conserve our landscape and contribute to a significant improvement in its quality.

Planning and farming

The seeds of countryside planning were sown in the report of the Committee on Land Utilization in Rural Areas 1942, otherwise known as the Scott report, among whose terms of reference were

To consider the conditions which should govern building and other constructional development in country areas consistently with the maintenance of agriculture, and in particular the factors affecting the location of industry having regard to economic operation, part-time and seasonal employment, the well-being of rural communities and the preservation of rural amenities....

A planning strategy was proposed for rural areas leaning heavily towards the protection of the countryside for the benefit of the countryside's inhabitants, predominantly agricultural, as advanced by the Council for the Preservation of Rural England; this was in opposition to those arguments forwarded by the Town and Country Planning Association who stressed the importance of decentralizing the urban population into planned new towns.[13] Emphasis was also placed upon the need to provide general access to rural facilities to all, and the Committee recommended the establishment of national parks and green belts. In supporting the protection of the countryside, and particularly agricultural land, as a valuable national resource in itself, the Committee has been criticized for ignoring the complex relationships between agricultural land and output, for increasing agricultural production may well be associated with a diminishing supply of land, as indeed has been the case. Even in respect of the protective aspect of their recommendations the report wrongly assumed that farmers were, and would remain, the most appropriate and diligent conservators of the rural heritage. The report was followed in 1945 by the Dower report on national parks in England and Wales, which in turn saw the implementation of many of its recommendations in the 1949 National Parks and Access to the Countryside Act as a result of yet another report by the Hobhouse Committee.

The antecedents of most planning controls relating to urban areas can be traced back to these various reports, and the outstanding feature of rural planning is that, as a consequence, the degree of control over farming is very limited. Housing development, transportation routes and mineral extraction are subject, for example, to strict planning control, but farming and forestry are largely left free. Even the erection of farm buildings and farm workers' dwellings have been treated as special cases, and the only significant planning control over farming operations and land use to have been introduced is the provision contained in the 1968 Countryside Act which empowers the Secretary of State for the Environment to make orders covering areas of national parks, so that any person intending to plough up moor or heath land in the area covered by that order must first notify the National Park Authority who may then secure an agreement with the farmer, or exercise compulsory acquisition, in order to preserve the quality of the land. To date only two such orders covering together a total of 109 hectares of Exmoor have been made. The only other major attempt to control rural land use is the indication in development plans of those areas which are to remain in agricultural use. As a result, not only has the landscape quality been destroyed, but also the quality of the soil and the flora and fauna has been lost. Such controls as exist, have, therefore, been properly described as either cosmetic or negative. The lack of a positive planning approach towards farming land has led to a number of problems which have been identified by the Centre for Agricultural Strategy in their report *Land for Agriculture* as being:[14]

Insufficient consideration of the consequences of land use changes in the context of national policies for agricultural and urban activities

Lack of clear cut, definitive agricultural development policies within planning policies

Lack of recognition of agriculture as the principal activity in the countryside

The planning process is inadequate for making local planning decisions in relation to national consideration of agricultural development policies

No effective containment of urban sprawl and the unnecessary encroachment on agricultural land with consequent permanent loss of productive areas of land

Involvement in the planning process of those concerned with agriculture is often inadequate

Lack of thorough consultation and co-operation, through the dispersal of responsibilities to separate bodies.

There is obviously a need to design a more coherent approach towards integrating the farming industry with the planning machine so as to maintain and promote agricultural efficiency while simultaneously strengthening protective measures for the countryside. The basic aims behind any recommendation for an improved relationship between farming and planning must be to seek to reduce agricultural land loss, control development in the countryside and allow continued amenity use of the countryside. More specific proposals include:

The division of a proper comprehensive land use strategy for the entire country, covering both urban and rural activities and reconciling competing claims on an orderly basis.

The introduction of landscape planning techniques so as to identify those areas most suitable for change and determine acceptable levels of environmental and ecological change.

An extension of the notification and management agreement system empowering local planning authorities to enter into arrangements to restrict or regulate the use, or change of use of land within prescribed areas.

The establishment of consultative bodies to foster a closer relationship between existing countryside bodies and involve both farmers and planners.

All agricultural land to be subject to special planning permission procedures along the lines of protected buildings, and a greater emphasis to be given to retention of grade 3 agricultural land.

The introduction of far more stringent design controls for agricultural buildings, particularly in sensitive landscape areas.

The formulation of management schemes to promote a better multi-use of land, whereby productive agricultural land is maintained but more attention is paid to the careful integration of amenity and recreational pursuits alongside farming activities. This might involve the planning of areas, such as urban fringe land and marginal land, where agriculture may cease to be the primary land use, so that productive and unproductive areas are linked into a framework of uses.

Most of these recommendations, however, presume an understanding on the part of the planner of the farming industry and an acceptance by the farming community of some kind of social responsibility towards the provision of public access to their property. Both presumptions may be questioned.

Derelict land

While not exclusively a rural planning problem most dereliction occurs as the result of mineral working, and predominantly this takes place in the countryside or on the rural–urban fringe.

The avaricious exploitation that befell the country's natural resources as a consequence of nineteenth-century industrialization has left us with a legacy of dereliction accumulated over years of past neglect. The landscape is pockmarked with spoil heaps and wasteland as a result of coalmining, iron working, quarrying and chemical extraction. The gravity of the situation has prompted the government into action. Since 1964 every local authority has been required to make and return an annual assessment regarding the amount of derelict land in its area. This is defined as 'Land so damaged by industrial or other development that it is incapable of beneficial use without treatment, but not land which has become derelict from natural causes, such as marsh land'. Also excluded are certain classes of man-made dereliction.

In 1964 there were estimated to be 34,358 hectares of derelict land which grew to 39,292 hectares in 1971 and 43,273 hectares in 1974, but much of the increase can be accounted for by more sensitive identification owing to changing attitudes and a stricter assessment. The North has the worst problem, particularly in those counties where coal mining predominates, although the National Coal Board (NCB), albeit in the shadow of Aberfan and atoning for past misdemeanours, is attempting to remedy the situation. Even in the South there is no escape from the despoliation of modern industrial needs, as witnessed by the cavernous holes gouged out of the Thames Valley in the lustful search for gravel. Although the South East, for example, contains only 5 per cent of the nation's derelict land it has over 12 per cent of the derelict mineral excavations, and the highest concentration of abandoned workings where restoration conditions have not been enforced.

Coal mining is almost a separate problem from the surface pit working of such minerals as sand, gravel, chalk and brick clay, and, as a nationalized industry, the NCB is covered by special legislation. Similarly the question of spoil heaps is essentially an urban problem associated with industrial processes.

The impact of surface mineral working upon the landscape depends upon the depth of deposits, the geological formation, the surrounding topography, the water table and the method of extraction. In this way, abandoned workings can be classified in two basic ways – shallow or deep, and wet or dry. Shallow workings above the water table rarely present any long-term problems, and the land can usually be restored quite easily by replacing topsoil and 'overburden', that is covering layers left over after extraction, or by filling with refuse and other waste. Deep workings above the water table can also be relatively easy to restore if there is a high proportion of overburden to extracted material, for by replacing the overburden, often as work progresses, the only effect is a lowering of the land surface which can be filled in a straightforward manner. Deep workings with a low proportion of overburden tend naturally to create large pits with little filling material left over for replacement. Smaller pits may be filled with refuse and rubble, but the sheer volume of material and need for compaction over time makes filling a prohibitive operation in larger pits. Some quarries have, therefore, been left and used as concealment for other non-conforming uses such as storage, caravan sites, industry and even playing fields, but it is important to grade the dangerous quarry edges. Workings below the water table, such as most land taken for sand and gravel extraction, usually become water-logged and there are certain risks attached to the filling of such workings. The major risk is that of pollution to the water supply which can be overcome by commencing the filling operation with an inert material to above water level, or if it is known that there is an existing impervious substrata. The most popular form of reclamation for such pits, however, has been for water recreation.

Refuse is generally a difficult material to use in land reclamation owing to the risks from smells, flies, rats, birds and pollution, although a system known as controlled tipping is used, where the pit is dry, in which refuse is deposited in layers of up to 2 m and each layer covered by 20 cm of overburden. Moreover, to prevent nuisance from smells and disease, only about 10 m² of land should be uncovered at any one time and no refuse should remain uncovered for more than 72 hours. Glass and metal containers should be smashed or flattened and placed at the base of each layer, and each layer should be consolidated by use of vehicles. Once filled the land is usually topped with about 30 cm of topsoil or other composted material. After a fallow period of grass, the land can then be used for agriculture or forestry, but if it is to be built on it must be allowed to settle for at least ten years. With wet workings some experimentation has taken place to develop methods of depositing refuse without creating nuisance or risk, but it is rarely used, being expensive and hazardous.

One of the best methods for minimizing the impact of mineral workings is the use of phased extraction and filling so that at any particular time the size of actual pit is limited. This approach also

Table 9 *Grants for the restoration of derelict land*

Area		
Development areas	100% ⎫	Local Employment Act
Intermediate areas	100% ⎬	1972 and Industry Act
Derelict land clearance areas	100% ⎭	1972
National parks	75% ⎫	National Parks and Access
Areas of outstanding natural beauty	75% ⎭	to the Countryside Act 1949
Elsewhere	50%	Local Government Act 1966

Source: Department of the Environment Explanatory Memorandum PRM3/802/81 (HMSO 1976).

ensures that restoration is performed throughout the period of working and cuts down the possibility and degree of eventual dereliction. Perhaps the most notable example of such a process is that at Dunbar where Blue Circle have installed special machines which remove layers of rock and replace that not required in the pit from where it was extracted. This system retains the geological sequence and allows the land to be contoured to lower levels, the topsoil replaced and the land returned to agriculture.[15]

A major stumbling block in reclaiming or restoring derelict land is cost. Reclamation for alternative commercial uses averages out at anything between £3000 and £9000 per hectare, with even a simple cosmetic treatment of planting, screening and generally tidying up on land already owned costing about £2000 per hectare at 1979 prices. There is, as such, no obligation upon local authorities regarding the restoration of derelict land, but it is a course of action strongly urged by ministerial circulars, and to sponsor initiatives there are a number of sources from which grants may be obtained as outlined in Table 9.

All these grants represent a maximum and are discretionary, the grant being a percentage of approved costs including site acquisition, preparation of plans and all rehabilitation works, but not restoration works such as the laying of roads or drains for specific after-use. The total expenditure on land reclamation forecast for 1978–9 and 1979–80 was estimated to be just over £18 million in each year, and generally speaking preference has consistently been given to areas of wide-scale dereliction such as those to be found in the West Midlands, the North and North West, with comparatively little being allocated to the South. There are a few other minor sources of public funds available to assist reclamation, but the principal financial impediment is the procedure known as 'after-value' whereby the value of the intended use of the land, after it has been reclaimed, is deducted from any grant that is actually given. This, however, does not apply where the land is to be used for amenity purposes, nor, of course, is the question of grant aid relevant where mineral extraction and subsequent restoration is undertaken by private commerical firms and subject to a planning agreement. A backlog of dereliction persists, but the rate of reclamation has improved from around 600 to 800 hectares per year during the 1960s, reaching 1013 ha in 1969, to a situation in the middle 1970s where it is over 2000 hectares per year, indicating perhaps that generous grants and better planning control have had some effect. The position is still a serious one given the identification of greater areas of dereliction and further refinements to the planning system are sought.

A number of recommendations have been made regarding the way dereliction through mineral extraction could be improved within the planning system, and these can be usefully summarized as follows:

1   Structure plans largely leave the detailed implementation of a mineral workings policy to local plans, and it is held to be important that these plans should indicate the preferred after-use of mineral working areas before permission to extract is given. This is a prerequisite of effective restoration schemes as it determines the suitable form of restoration, infilling, surface treatment and contouring to be adopted,[16] and also gives a necessary degree of certainty to the operator and a guideline for integration with other future land use policies to the planning authority.

2   While general guidance on the wording of planning conditions[17] and specific directions for the control of mineral working have been provided,[18] most local authorities with a significant experience of handling such applications have designed their own standard conditions over the years. The Stevens Committee looking into Planning Control over Mineral Working in 1976 suggested that in addition to the usual requirements constituting a legal condition in a planning permission, conditions should be practicable so that they are technically and economically feasible for the operator to comply with, and soundly conceived for the long term to take account of future possible changes. It also suggested that because of the unenforceability of conditions requiring a continued liability, such as the replacement of dead

trees, new planning powers should be introduced whereby local authorities could impose conditions for up to five years 'aftercare' to bring land back into productive agricultural use. With regard to conditions, the Stevens Committee also encouraged the wider use of phased planning permissions with commencement of a fresh phase of extraction being dependent upon satisfactory completion of previous restoration programmes. As a general statement the Committee recommended, as have many others before and since, that the law should be changed to permit positive covenants to run with the land and thus obviate the need to have recourse to section 52 agreements under the 1971 Town and Country Planning Act which bind only the two parties to the contract.

3　There should be introduced a levy on all mineral extraction, to be devoted towards restoration. A limited levy, the Ironstone Restoration Fund, is already operated on the working of ironstone, which has proved comparatively successful. Problems of predicting costs, making exceptions, exemptions and allowances, and calculating and collecting the levy across a diverse range of operator and circumstance probably preclude it as a viable scheme. Alternatively, the idea of a reclamation bond has been floated, whereby a bond is deposited in respect of each working, or stage of working, as a precondition to the grant of planning permission, and though under existing legislation such a condition is *ultra vires* several authorities are known to operate these transactions by way of planning agreements at common law. The strength of this proposal is that it can be tailored for each individual case, thus avoiding possible inequities of flat rate levies,[19] but there are also problems of calculation and forward funding by the operator.

4　A realistic penalty system for non-compliance with restoration conditions should be enforced.

5　A simplification in the legal procedures and site valuation in respect of the compulsory acquisition of derelict land.

6　The introduction of 'cessation notices', suggested by the Stevens Committee, to be served by a local authority upon an apparently recalcitrant operator who has stopped excavating, possibly as a result of market fluctuations, and may hope to resume some time in the future, stating that working has ceased and restoration must commence.

7   A central agency responsible for managing and co-ordinating the problem of derelict land and its reclamation and reuse should be set up.

As a concluding remark upon the problem of dereliction it is reminiscent of many other areas of planning practice where commercial interest is at odds with environmental control; a reconciliation of both positions requires a greater understanding one of the other.

17 Conservation

With the unprecedented economic expansion, population explosion, and speed of technological advance of recent times, there are ever-increasing demands placed upon land for competing uses. These pressures often promote change, and change can imply the destruction of existing things and their replacement by new. This process is not always a welcome one for it may include the loss of features treasured by the community at large but in the hands of private individuals. It is therefore desirable to foresee, guide, and, where necessary, control the forces of change.

Urban conservation

Increasing attention is being paid to the significance and supervision of our historic and architectural heritage, for although change is implicit in urban life, economic forces are not always selective in their innovation and transformation of towns. The need to conserve that which is cherished is wide-ranging and applies to individual buildings or parts of buildings, areas, landmarks and the atmosphere.

In this way, the cause of conservation has gained enormous ground over the last decade and, with half the present built environment having been constructed since the last war, mostly of an undistinguished character, a strong emphasis upon the protection of townscape as well as individual buildings is justly warranted given the rapid rate of demolition and redevelopment that has occurred in old town centres.

Politically there now appears to be a wide measure of popular consensus on the need for conservation, but this does not preclude criticism. On the one hand it is said to inhibit progress and natural change, while on the other it has occasionally been attacked on the grounds of social justice, with conservation and gentrification being seen as synonymous. Redevelopment, it is argued, benefits the poor, whereas rehabilitation benefits the wealthy. The apparent artificiality of some conservation policies has also been criticized, and a more extreme vilification advanced along the lines that

our society is dominated by conservationists of one kind and another...what society suffers from are the extraordinary tastes of that small group of people who constitute the Historic Buildings Council. It is these people who dictate what is good and beautiful according to aesthetic standards known only to themselves, but which are supposed to have absolute value.[1]

A somewhat extreme view in itself. It must also be mentioned, however, that conservation control creates many professional problems of building design and performance. Nevertheless, adaptation, rehabilitation or renovation are, on the whole, still cheaper than comprehensive redevelopment, and most old buildings are remarkably adaptable. The Georgian terrace, for example, has survived not so much because of its inherent aesthetic value but of its extreme flexibility, and a study undertaken by the Royal Institution of Chartered Surveyors in 1975 into the cost of conservation concluded that 'it can often make better economic sense to restore and modernize an old building rather than to tear it down and build a new one'.[2] This does not imply that a rigid protectionist approach should be adopted towards historic buildings in all circumstances, however, for changing social, economic and technological frameworks determine that different demands are made upon urban space through time. As pressure for space increases, therefore, land inevitably becomes more valuable, and the need to replace old buildings by modern structures capable of new and more intensive uses is strengthened. The conflict between conservation and change is a matter of balance and degree and must be resolved in a reasoned, responsible and informed way.

The legislative framework

Nearly a century has passed since the first piece of conservation legislation was enacted, the Ancient Monuments Act of 1882, but the main achievements have taken place over the last thirty years or so, and more particularly over the past decade. The principal means of legal protection are the listing of buildings, the designation of conservation areas, and the removal of deemed planning permission rights conferred by general development orders.

Although the Royal Commission on Historical Monuments set up in 1908 is still compiling a detailed and scholarly inventory of all monuments and buildings of importance erected before 1855, at the present rate of progress, with less than a fifth of the country covered, the completed work could take several hundred years to produce. To compensate for this dilatoriness a procedure for identifying, selecting and listing buildings of special architectural or historic interest was first introduced by the Town and Country Planning Act 1944 and remains enshrined in the 1971 Town and Country Planning Act. A list of selected buildings is published by the Historic Buildings Bureau of the Department of the Environment and is based upon the recommendation of DoE investigators from within the Historic Buildings Division who are also responsible for checking local authority development control decisions in respect of listed buildings. The first list was completed in 1968 and comprised some 170,000 buildings; ten years later this has increased to around 230,000. Since 1970 there have been only three grades of listed buildings, grade I, grade II* and grade II, a previous grade III having been largely absorbed into grade II. To be included in a list a building must satisfy certain criteria which include being a work of art, a curiosity or freak, representative of a particular achitectural style, having 'group value' as part of an outstanding composition, being an example of technological development or being associated with great people or events. Only just over 2 per cent of listed buildings are included in grade I and the vast majority are contained in grade II. In practice most pre-1700 buildings are listed but comparatively few post-1918.

In addition to listing through the normal DoE survey procedures a building can be 'spot listed' by the DoE as a result of public representation, or a local planning authority may issue a *building preservation notice* where they consider an unlisted building, but one worthy of inclusion, is under threat of demolition or alteration. In both cases the effect is to protect the building for a period of six months during which time the Secretary of State may consider inclusion in the statutory list. Central to the concept of listing is the provision that all protected buildings are subject to the need to obtain listed buildings consent where any proposed change to them would affect their character as a building of special architectural or historic interest. Special advertising and consultative procedures are involved in the process of obtaining listed building consent, and despite the existence of DoE guidelines a certain amount of adverse criticism has been attracted owing to the vagueness of definition of such matters as 'character' and 'alteration', and the widely varying interpretation of policy between local authorities to whom application is initially made and who have certain powers of determination. It is also contended that little advice is given to owners of listed buildings as to their rights and responsibilities.

While an owner may take steps for reasons of health, safety or preservation, a listed building enforcement notice procedure exists to control offending works, and errant owners unlawfully altering protected buildings may be fined or imprisoned. Local authorities are also empowered to serve a repairs notice in situations of neglect requiring work to be done which is 'reasonably necessary for the proper preservation of the building'. Where the neglect can be shown to be wilful, moreover, and the building has been allowed to fall into disrepair in order to justify demolition, powers of compulsory purchase with minimum payment of compensation are available. The service of such repair notices is comparatively rare, however, because of the difficulty of proving wilful neglect and the fear of receiving a purchase notice in reply. Nevertheless, some authorities have entered into agreements with local building preservation trusts so that the trust would acquire and restore a building following enforcement proceedings. Such a threatened course of action can often be used as an effective bluff against recalcitrant owners. The Town and Country Amenities Act 1974 has extended the powers of local authorities so that they can now enter not only unoccupied listed buildings to effect urgent works of repair but also, with ministerial sanction, those unoccupied buildings in conservation areas for similar purposes. It is always open for local authorities to use their powers under the Public Health Act 1961 to require an owner of premises which are in a ruinous or dilapidated condition to repair or demolish them, and since demolition of a listed buidling itself requires consent the pressure would be to repair. Again, however, enforcement is difficult and the likelihood would be that a purchase notice on the authority would result.

Generally listing has been criticized as being insufficient protection, for omission from a list ought not to condemn a building as without historic or architectural interest, though inevitably in practice it does. Further, that listing is too specific, too individual and not positive enough, particularly in terms of combating obsolescence.

Conservation areas

A more comprehensive approach towards urban conservation is

provided under the Civic Amenities Act 1967 whereby local authorities are encouraged to define and declare areas with special character and quality as conservation areas. This no longer restricts attention to individual buildings but includes an appreciation of the character and appearance which deserves preserving or enhancing. This might relate to notable views or to buildings or groups of buildings, which, though unexceptional in themselves, add to the general quality of the area; equally it might apply to park railings as well as to trees and shrubs, the principal aim being to prevent excessive intrusion by out of scale redevelopment. To date over 4000 such conservation areas have been designated. Perhaps in some areas it could be said that too many have been identified and greater discretion might have ensured a greater degree of success. In certain towns virtually the whole urban area has been included whereas only parts justify special treatment and there is a danger that the powers conferred by the Civic Amenities Act could be diluted.

The 1967 Civic Amenities Act was essentially permissive in nature and together with the subsequent Circular 53/67 only encouraged local authorities to designate conservation areas. Until the introduction of the Town and Country Planning (Amendment) Act 1972 gave them statutory meaning they remained merely optional lines on maps with no special protective or financial provisions. The 1972 Act now enables local authorities to control the demolition of unlisted buildings in a conservation area and the Secretary of State, on the advice of the Historic Buildings Council, to make available conservation grants or loans in 'outstanding' conservation areas, and nearly 300 areas have so far been conferred with outstanding status in respect of grant aid. In this context, the advent of European Architectural Heritage Year in 1975 evoked considerable interest in the designation of conservation areas and the implementation of policy. Conservation area legislation has been further strengthened by the Town and Country Amenities Act 1974, together with subsequent circulars, whereby demolition control is simplified, the Secretary of State can himself designate conservation areas and direct local authorities to produce 'schemes of enhancement' for particular conservation areas, special notices must be given for proposed tree surgery, and new provisions are made in respect of advertisement control within conservation areas.

Cases may obviously arise when the visual impact of a listed building or premises within a conservation area is affected by works falling outside the controls described above, such as external decoration or the erection of a low fence or wall. Additional control is, however, provided by making a direction under article 4 of the General Development Order 1973 which limits the classes of development otherwise permitted without the need to obtain planning permission. Such a direction requires approval from the Secretary of State who must be convinced of a special need, even in a conservation area, and the qualifications and procedures involved often militate against authorities making full use of it.

In order 'to examine how conservation policies might be sensibly implemented' four historic towns of outstanding worth were chosen as subjects for pilot studies, Bath, Chester, Chichester and York, and for a short time a Preservation Policy Group was set up within the Ministry of Housing and Local Government to co-ordinate their efforts. Many of their recommendations are incorporated in the Civic Amenities Act and the Town and Country Planning Act 1971. Between them the resultant reports highlighted the major aspects of planning for conservation, but have been criticized because the selected towns were not a typical basis upon which to frame conservation policy. Nevertheless, they did focus attention upon some of the principal issues confronting historic areas, namely, economic pressures, difficulties in providing appropriate uses, decay and grant assistance to inhibit it, and traffic and design difficulties in adaptation. To these can be added the more recently perceived problems of gentrification and tourism.

Traffic

The terrifying impact of the motor car upon the character and environment of urban areas, and especially upon our historic towns, presents one of the most intractable aspects of conservation. It is a problem that begs innumerable questions and anything approaching adequate discussion is well beyond the scope of this restricted text. The visual intrusion alone, apart from the congestion and pollution caused by traffic in towns, detracts greatly from a satisfactory urban environment. Suffice it to say that in formulating a conservation policy there are certain factors that deserve special attention and this will inevitably involve:

Identifying environmental areas. The policy must be selective, and a balance struck between those areas which merit treatment and the demands for an efficient transportation network within the town.

Exclusion of through traffic. If the motor vehicle is to remain as the mainstay of any urban transport system it is important to channel the longer movements from town to town and from one locality to another, on to effective and well-designed distributor roads. Some environmental areas will attract considerably more traffic than others but the aim is to secure a suitable 'environmental capacity' above which danger, noise, fumes, vibration and intrusion would be unacceptable. This level is likely to be considerably lower than the areas sheer capacity to pass vehicles.

Provision of a pedestrian network. In association with the gradual removal of vehicles, and the provision of alternative car parking facilities elsewhere, it is essential to ensure that there are adequate pedestrian ways to, from and around chosen areas.

Provision of vehicular accessiblity. Some forms of traffic will 'belong' to the area, such as commercial vehicles required for servicing the buildings and the buses and cars of persons either employed in or visiting the area. The easier their access, the shorter period of time they will be present, and the less detriment they will cause. This facility will have to be measured against the danger of attracting extraneous traffic.

Provision of adequate off-street parking. The ease of parking may have a direct bearing on the prosperity of the area under consideration; therefore, priority must be given to the use most essential to economic viability. Whether this is the long-term officer worker, the short-term shopper or the resident will vary according to circumstances.

Provision of attractive public transport. Peripheral town car parks linked to a fast, frequent and efficient public transport system are likely to prove essential to the future functioning of concentrated urban areas. Leeds and Oxford have operated a 'park-and-ride' policy and more towns will surely follow.

The ultimate solution to the worsening problem of urban transportation probably lies in the adoption of a long-term, far-reaching and more radical scheme such as flexible discriminatory road pricing at realistic marginal cost levels, or even the final sanction of banning the private motor car altogether.

Finance

Even the most stringent legal framework and assiduous conservation area policy can achieve little without proper financial support, and it would be foolish to pretend that present public expenditure is anything but woefully inadequate.

Central government grants towards the repair and maintenance of individual buildings and for the enhancement of conservation areas are allocated according to recommendations made by the respective Historic Buildings Councils for England, Wales and Scotland. The budget for distribution in England over the past few years has been:

1974–5	£2.5 million
1975–6	£3.5 million
1976–7	£4.2 million
1977–8	£4.6 million

Both listed buildings and conservation areas have to be of outstanding quality to attract grant aid, and taking all Grade I buildings and, say, the top third of GradeII*, this means that with 13,000 buildings less than 5 per cent of listed buildings and less than 8 per cent of conservation areas are eligible for assistance. The increase in available funds between 1976–7 and 1977–8 did not even keep pace with the rise in building costs and thus reflected a reduction in real terms. The grant also covers a number of town schemes which are designed to deal with the repair of groups of buildings, important as a whole but not individually special or outstanding. There are currently about sixty-five town schemes in operation, the most heavily financed being those in Chester, Bath and York. The cost of repairs, which have to be approved by DoE architects, are divided half by the owner and half by the DoE and the local authority in equal proportion.

Under the Local Authorities (Historic Buildings) Act 1962, local authorities can make grants or loans for the repair and maintenance of historic buildings. The total sum made available throughout the country, however, is negligible, amounting, for example, to under £350,000 in 1972, and varying enormously from one authority to another. Not including expenditure on their own property, Oxfordshire, for instance, have been known to spend nothing some years, and Surrey managed only £17,000 out of a total budget of £163 million in 1976–7 despite having 3750 listed buildings, 98 conservation areas and 2 town schemes in operation. Another picture is portrayed by Chester, however, who by levying a special conservation rate, have achieved a level of spending of around £100,000 in most years. Various grants made under the Housing Acts can also be applied in the pursuit of conservation policy, and in general improvement areas, for example, allowances of up to £200 per dwelling are available to local authorities from central government for the environmental improvement of land in private ownership. In recognition of the importance of independent organizations in the field of conservation, the government makes an annual grant to the six national organizations described below who advise on proposals to demolish listed buildings. A National Heritage Fund was established in 1975, administered by the Civic Trust, to provide financial assistance in the way of short-term loans to what was hoped to be a countryside network of around 200 building preservation trusts, but only about 30 or 40 were ever founded, of which perhaps 20 are truly active, and, while private sources raised nearly £500,000, an amount matched by the government, the application of this money has been slow and restricted.

One of the keys to successful conservation must be the extent to which private-sector investment takes place in the refurbishment of old buildings, and while the rehabilitation of certain residential estates within the inner city has proved extremely effective, many more are in a very serious state of dereliction. A significant improvement has also been witnessed in the restoration of commercial premises, and though the greatest steps have been taken in the office sector, the first small signs of optimism can be expressed regarding industrial premises in privileged locations. Nevertheless, a great deal more needs to be done to encourage further significant restoration of listed buildings and enhancement of conservation areas in economically marginal positions, and a reform of the tax laws is one obvious way in which this could be effected. There are other financial aspects of a more practical nature, such as the importance of the tourist industry, to be considered in any study of the economics of conservation. It is also becoming increasingly evident that employers and employees are demonstrating a preference for a more amenable industrial and commercial location, and it has been argued that areas or towns of environmental distinction are likely to progressively be placed at an economic advantage in respect of future investment.[3] It is possible, therefore, that while those authorities who adopt a strong conservation policy will find themselves under financial pressure in the short term, they might benefit from economic growth and activity in the long term if they keep their nerve.[4] Concomitantly it may also mean that the forces of change, and the problems of implementing a programme of conservation, will be greater.

Nathaniel Lichfield in *Economics of Conservation* has applied the balance sheet approach to conservation areas, and proposes a form of betterment charge to be levied on those uses such as hotels, restaurants and tourists that benefit from the improvement or enhancement of the area. In whatever way it is provided the conservation of the country's architectural and historic heritage cannot possibly be effected unless there are sufficient funds available; legislation alone is not enough.

European Architectural Heritage Year

It is perhaps right that separate mention should be made of European Architectural Heritage Year (EAHY) which was so designated in 1975 by the Council of Europe with the aim of halting the erosion of character in historic European towns and the loss of irreplaceable monuments and launched under the slogan of 'A future for the past'. A series of conferences led up to EAHY throughout the continent, and in this country during 1972–3, as a pipe-opener, 'operation eysore' pumped £36.5 million mainly into the reclamation and reinstatement of derelict industrial land in special areas. The principal objectives of EAHY in the United Kingdom were to promote co-operation and initiatives from local authorities and other interested groups in the enhancement of conservation areas; to inaugurate a campaign for environmental education with schools, the professions, property owners and public authorities; and to establish the aforementioned National Architectural Heritage Fund to support an eventually self-generating renovation fund. Heritage Year grants amounting to a measly £180,000 were provided by the government; a succession of conferences, symposia and seminars were held; a number of Civic Trust 'non-competitive' Heritage Year awards were made for a diverse array of conservation projects; and Exeter participated with thirteen other European towns in a special study of the 'social and cultural animation of towns'. Though the tangible and lasting results of EAHY are debatable it did at least focus attention, however transistory, upon the need for watchfulness in the care of our historic towns.

Interest groups

Amenity societies and interest groups of all kinds have a significant role to play in the field of conservation, and have been immensely stimulated by the formulation and example of the Civic Trust. The trust was founded in 1957 by Duncan Sandys when only about 200 amenity societies were in existence; now, largely as a result of their efforts, there are over 1250. Among the range of activities in which these societies engage are the drawing up of conservation area proposals, representation on local authority committees, concern with improvement schemes such as tree planting, riverside walks and removal of eyesores, recommendations regarding the listing of buildings and consultation when listed buildings are to be demolished. They can even assist financially. One of the Civic Trust's first ventures was the 'facelift' of Magdalen Street, Norwich, where what was previously a rather shabby shopping street was carefully and sympathetically refurbished. All the clutter of unsightly wires and sordid signs were removed, and the shop fronts were repainted using a harmonious colour scheme at a cost little more than would, in any case, have been expended by individual traders. The scheme, although only a skin-deep cosmetic treatment, was demonstrably a success and showed that a large number of separate interests can be unified in a common purpose if the right management approach is applied. A further example of the Civic Trust participation in planning for conservation was the memorandum submitted in February 1970 to the then Minister of Transport urging closer appraisal of the proposal for extra heavy lorries on existing roads. In conjunction with the other local amenity societies, the Trust itself carried out a survey, and a year later put forward a report containing thirty specific recommendations relating to the legislation concerning the use of these monster vehicles. The report and recommendations were instrumental in the Department of the Environment's decision not to sanction their use at that time.

In the context of conservation control the most influential national interest groups are those mentioned alongside the Civic Trust in the DoE circular regarding notification by local planning authorities of listed building consent applications for demolition. These are the Ancient Monuments Society, founded in 1924 to promote the conservation and knowledge of places of historic interest, ancient monuments, historic buildings and 'fine old craftsmanship' throughout the country; the Council for British Archaeology founded in 1944 to promote the care and study of archaeological sites and the protection of ancient monuments and historic buildings, which has had a considerable effect in making councils aware of the importance of below-ground archaeological remains in redevelopment areas; the

Society for the Protection of Ancient Buildings, founded in 1877 by William Morris, and the oldest of such bodies, being concerned with all aspects of the preservation of ancient buildings; the Georgian Group, founded by Lord Derwent in 1937, in an endeavour to awaken public opinion to the need to protect Georgian buildings; and the Victorian Society, founded in 1958 with the objective of gaining greater recognition for undocumented Victorian buildings, and who are compiling a list of all important buildings erected between 1830 and 1914. Several familiar organizations such as the Royal Fine Art Commission (1924), the National Trust (1895), the Landmark Trust (1965), the Pilgrim Trust (1930) and the Council for the Protection of Rural England (1928) play a notable role in conservation matters as do innumerable other independent campaigning bodies at both national and local level. As already mentioned, the Civic Trust register of local amenity societies, now unpublished, stood at over 1250 in 1975 when last produced, and Circular 61/68 introduced the notion of conservation area advisory committees to advise local authorities on applications for planning permission affecting conservation areas. Inevitably the creation, constituency and effectiveness of these committees varies enormously throughout the country.

Conclusions

Despite the criticisms – of superficial treatments (commonly called 'facadism'), a lack of economic reality by both central and local government, a paucity of financial support, the sheer number of listed buildings and conservation areas which, it is averred, debases the conservation currency, suggestions that the 'outstanding' league of buildings and areas should be more exclusive, the dangers of standardization, and the generally poor standard of new design – a number of other, more positive, recommendations have been made. These include the cessation of exemption from control of Crown property and the extension of full control to statutory undertakers and ecclesiastical bodies; a strengthening of the powers relating to repairs notices, combined with more regular inspection of grade I and grade II* buildings; the adoption of the recommendation in the Dobry report on development control that all demolition should be made subject to the need to obtain planning permission; the procedures regarding the listing of buildings should more clearly acquaint property owners with their rights and responsibilities and those relating to the issue of article 4 directions should be made simpler to perform; more attention should be paid to the production of relevant design guides and planning briefs for conservation areas, and the training and sharing of specialist planning staff among authorities; and relief from taxation allowed on private expenditure on approved conservation work.

A comprehensive policy for conserving the urban environment cannot consider buildings and areas of architectural and historic interest in isolation, but must have regard to all the forces of change, and recognize the priorities for action and be competent to implement them. Conservation must therefore form part of the overall planning process and lay claim to its rightful place in the structure plan. A lesson can be taken from France where Malraux's Law of 1962, which combines national, regional and local agencies in providing for the comprehensive restoration of every historic urban site in the country, is paying handsome dividends. Despite certain financial problems the French appear to have mastered the art of integrating the past with the present while maintaining an eye to the future. They tackle the problems of rehabilitation, redevelopment, traffic congestion, pedestrianization, local industry and the social infrastructure in relation to conservation as a totality. Our own policy in this country is perhaps too negative in character and we could well remember that positive forward planning is the surest way of avoiding conflict.

Rural conservation

Over the centuries the face of the English countryside has undergone drastic changes owing to increasing areas of land being put to agriculture, the advent of widescale sheep grazing, the development of Great Britain as a naval power, and the onset of enclosure. The first discernible movement to preserve the countryside developed in the nineteenth century, probably as a reaction against the urban squalor consequent upon the industrial revolution. The Commons, Footpaths and Open Space Society was established in 1865 and was eventually responsible for securing the Rights of Way Act 1932. The Royal Society for the Protection of Birds was founded in 1889 and again initiated the pressure that finally accomplished the setting up of sanctuaries under the Protection of Birds Act of 1954.

The National Trust, founded in 1895 and conferred with unalienable rights of land ownership in 1907, was formed to promote the cause of conservation and empowered to receive and manage land and estates in the interests of our national heritage. It is now the third largest landowner in Britain, owning about 153,000 hectares in England, Wales and Northern Ireland, and having accepted protective covenants in respect of a further 25,000 hectares. A National Trust for Scotland was separately constituted in 1931. As much of the Trust's land is farmed, the Trust has special landlord's responsibility for 1000 agricultural tenancies over the layout, design and maintenance of farm buildings and the planting and felling of trees as well as the historic buildings placed in its care. With approximately 4 million visitors a year to its various properties the Trust is experiencing serious pressure upon certain particularly popular houses and is having to adopt a policy of limitation and restraint.

An organization that exerts considerable political pressure on rural conservation matters is the Council for the Preservation (now Protection) of Rural England which was founded in 1926. In 1970, European Conservation Year, the CPRE set up a number of working parties to look at various aspects of the rural environment. One of them, for example, looked at the vexed problem of transmission cables and power lines and recommended that the electricity generating boards should be made to take professional landscaping advice, set aside a fixed portion of their annual budget for visual treatment, adhere to amenity clauses in their articles of establishment, consult with local authorities whose areas might be affected, place more power lines underground, and spend larger sums of money on the design of equipment. How much influence they have in determining national policy is hard to say, but anyone who has experienced their advocacy or attracted their wrath, particularly at local public inquiries, will vouch for their efficacy as a watchdog of private interest.

The largest landowners in the country are the Forestry Commission who hold 1.2 million hectares of land and were set up in 1919 to rectify the appalling rape of the forests that had occurred during the First World War, and to build up a stock of timber for the future. This they have done, although it is inconceivable that we shall ever provide for our own timber requirements, and thankfully the Commission have time at last to consider the quality of the countryside as well as the quantity of wood, and are tempering their policy of covering our hillsides with a chequerboard of green.

The Nature Conservancy Council was established as a separate body in 1973 having had its origins as the Nature Conservancy since foundation in 1949. It is responsible to the Secretary of State for the Environment and has three statutory committees to advise it on the exercise of its functions in England, Scotland and Wales. These are the establishment, maintenance and management of nature reserves in Great Britain; the provision of advice for Ministers on the development and implementation of policies for, or affecting, nature conservation in Great Britain; and the provision of advice and dissemination of knowledge about nature conservation together with the commissioning or support of relevant research. The term 'nature conservation' in this context means the protection of flora, fauna, geological or physiographical features, and in discharging their functions the Council must take account of actual and possible ecological changes. The Council also has power to provide grant aid to various agencies towards the cost of nature conservation projects. The Council owns about 27 per cent of the *national nature reserves,* holds a further 13 per cent under lease, and has entered into agreements in respect of the management of the remaining 60 per cent. In all the reserves the accent is firmly placed upon conservation and any recreational facility is entirely incidental, although, wherever possible, access is provided for visitors. More recently the Nature Conservancy has shown an increasing interest in developing the educational side of its work.

National parks

A growing concern and interest for the countryside and for leisure pursuits between the wars gave rise to the National Parks and Access to the Countryside Act 1949. The aims of this act were conceived in the work of the Wildlife Conservation Special Committee in 1945, which recommended greater research in conservation and advised in favour of the acquisition and management of special areas of scientific importance, together with the Dower report on national parks in England and Wales (1945), and the Hobhouse report of the National Parks Committee (1947). The act aimed at:

1   The preservation and enhancement of natural beauty in England and Wales and particularly in the areas designated as national parks or areas of outstanding natural beauty, and

2   encouraging the provision or improvements, for purposes resorting to national parks, of facilities for the enjoyment of them and for the enjoyment of open-air recreation and the study of nature.

A National Parks Commission set up under the 1949 Act was succeeded in 1968 by the Countryside Commission as a result of the 1968 Countryside Act, and the Commission's terms of reference were extended to

review, encourage, assist, concert or promote the provision and improvement of facilities for the enjoyment of the countryside generally, and to conserve and enhance the natural beauty and amenity of the countryside and to secure public access for the purpose of open-air recreation .

They also aim to liaise with a number of other agencies in the field of rural conservation, for the purpose of research and the formulation of a common policy. The Countryside Commission is further empowered to give grants towards the creation of country parks.

There are currently ten national parks in the country (Table 10), although a further proposal for a Cambrian Mountains Park was rejected in 1972 by the Secretary of State for Wales as not being in accord with local interests and needs. It should be appreciated that the Commission does not of itself own land, and its powers are mainly advisory and not executive, although the access to government afforded to it is of great benefit in encouraging the co-operation of other bodies. A number of problems face the Commission in attempting to produce a cohesive management plan for the parks. These include:

Table 10   *Summary of statutorily protected land, England and Wales, 31 December 1969*

	Square miles	Square kilometres	Percentage
Total land area	58,349	157,124	100.00
10 national parks	5,258	13,618	9.02
25 areas of outstanding natural beauty	4,291	11,114	7.35
19 green belts	5,709	14,786	9.78
66 national nature reserves	129	334	0.23
	15,387	39,852	26.38
Less areas in more than one category	522	1,353	0.89
Total	14,865	38,499	25.49

1 The complex geological nature of the national parks has made them a valuable source of raw materials for industry. Limestone, fluorspar, potash and many other minerals are to be found in relative abundance, but their extraction is unsightly and the frequent need to locate industry close by incursive.

2 The extent of military land within the parks has proved a continuing source of conflict, because it denies public access to large areas of land and the debris left behind by service activity is both unattractive and sometimes dangerous.

3 The parks all tend to lie in the wetter regions of the country and the demands by water authorities for more reservoir facilities on what are ideal gathering grounds are compelling. Problems of access, however, are again occasional as many waters authorities restrict public entry on health and safety grounds.

4 With the development of telecommunications and radar the high ground of the national parks is under great pressure by civil and military authorities alike for installations.

5 In efforts to improve yields, hill farmers have combined fields and converted additional moorland into pasture. In places the effect upon traditional park landscape has been dramatic, and because of the difficulties of sustaining soil fertility not even agriculturally efficient. Moreover, such land is often replaced by private afforestation with even greater consequences for the landscape.

6 The increase in car ownership and the general mobility of car owners has led to severe traffic problems in national parks. This is not only caused by recreation traffic and locally generated traffic but also by the growth in heavy vehicle traffic using the trunk routes that run through most parks.

7 Apart from the increase in road traffic, the boom in recreation throughout the 1960s and 1970s has had an inevitable impact upon the countryside. The passage of people through the parks has led to erosion, damage and visual deterioration.

8 Fragmented local control of national parks up to local government reorganization proved a major drawback in the development of the parks. Few co-ordinated plans were produced, non-conforming development was rife, and little expenditure was allowed.

With the benefit of hindsight it is easy to find fault with the national park system as it existed between 1949 and 1972, but what emerged was national in name only. It was not nationally administered, it had no nationally enforceable policy, and it was not nationally owned. Nevertheless, it did increase the level of public awareness towards the countryside, improve access to it, and control the worst excesses of development. Since the announcement of local government reorganization in 1972 the Countryside Commission has been able to work within a different structure. The problems of divided responsibility that affected Snowdonia, the Yorkshire Dales, Exmoor and the Brecon Beacons have been removed as these parks all now have a majority of their area within one county. The two largest and most heavily used parks, the Peak District and the Lake District, have their own planning board and the eight other parks are all administered through county council executive committees. In addition, all national parks now have their own staff under a chief officer to co-ordinate policy and liaise with other planning agencies.

Prior to 1974, and because of the special problems involved, only the Peak Park had its own management plan, but an important element of policy since 1974 is that every national park is required to produce its own management plan. The objectives of the management plan are to negotiate agreements between the various rural interests on park policy, to permit public participation in the development of the parks, to produce projects of management that solve problems in a practical way, and generally to design comprehensive management agreements for the parks. By 1978 all the parks had published their plans and the Countryside Commission view the potential impact of them with some optimism, hoping that as they already cover approximately 9 per cent of England and Wales their successful implementation could lead to a similar planning approach being applied to all rural areas, thereby providing a comprehensive rural management policy for the first time. Their success, however, will largely depend upon the extent to which county councils will allow the parks to operate.

At a more informal level the Countryside Commission is also involved in the Chairmen's Policy Group and the Countryside Recreation Research Advisory Group (CRRAG). The former has as its members the chairmen of the British Tourist Authority, the British Waterways Board, the Countryside Commission, the Countryside Commission for Scotland, the Development Commission, the English Tourist Board, the Forestry Commission, the Nature Conservancy Council, the Scottish Tourist Board and the Water Space Amenity Commission, and discusses matters of mutual interest and importance. The latter was set up by the Countryside

Commission in 1968 to avoid duplication of work by the above agencies and to promote joint research, but it has evolved over time into a much more positive and influential body in the whole field of related research.

A further function of the Countryside Commission is the designation of *areas of outstanding natural beauty* which attract special powers of control and endow the Commission with the right of consultation by local planning authorities in the preparation of development plans. The Commission also promotes the establishment of long-distance routes throughout the countryside and meets the whole of the cost of creating and maintaining them. They are also developing the range of their work in connection with other footpaths and bridleways.

18 Resource planning and pollution

It it hardly possible to read a paper or switch on the television these days without being regaled about the latest chapter in the sorry saga of man's despoliation of his own environment. The frightening explosion in population growth, the pillage of the earth's natural resources, the contamination of the air, the creation of agricultural wasteland and infertile dustbowls, the poisoning of the waters and the gradual extermination of much of the world's flora and fauna are but a few of the chilling episodes in man's lustful drive for growth and productivity, a growth that appears to place greater emphasis upon quantity than quality. Many of these modern tragedies do not directly fall within the sphere of responsibility of the physical land use planner; many, however, do, if not wholly then in part. The very development, management and maintenance of the built environment claims a large proportion of the effort and output of the nation's manpower and resources. The extent of these claims from construction industries alone has been estimated at approximately one-eighth of the gross national product.[1]

Population

The demand for resources is determined by the size and distribution of population and the nature of human activities. It can fairly be stated that we now face a situation of pollution by over-population. The world total population which, it has been estimated, stood at approximately 5 million in 6000 BC, 500 million in AD 1650, 1000 million in AD 1850, 2000 million in AD 1930, and now stands at around 4000 million,[2] is beginning to demonstrate those Malthusian properties that were scorned for so long. The time in which it takes to double is now down to about 35 years but in underdeveloped countries, where 40 per cent of the population are under 15 years old and a phenomenal decline in the death rate is being experienced, it is as low as 20 years, compared with that in developed countries where it falls to between 50 and 200 years. Although the situation is less severe in the United Kingdom it is nevertheless predicted that the population will double about 140 years hence.[3] The birth rate might have declined since the extraordinary immediate post-war levels, but it is still running at a relatively high rate, which, when coupled with the longer life expectancy in England and Wales of 69 for men and 79 for women, produces statistics for growth that defy complacency.

The general level of population and the factors that determine it are thankfully not considered suitable areas for the town planner to exercise judgement. Probably the only effective controls that exist in this country are tax concessions or family allowances. Experience in France, albeit in the opposite direction, has shown how powerful these measures can be. There exists, however, a great political reluctance to employ them to any great extent in combating the menace of over-population. As opposed to influencing growth the planner is concerned with comprehending, predicting and catering for it. The surveys and techniques available in this task have already been described; suffice it to say they are not faultless. In 1946 the population for the United Kingdom at the turn of the century was forecast to reach between 28 and 44 million, in 1964 it was calculated to reach about 73 million, and it is now thought that it will reach 64 million, being currently 56 million (Figure 22).

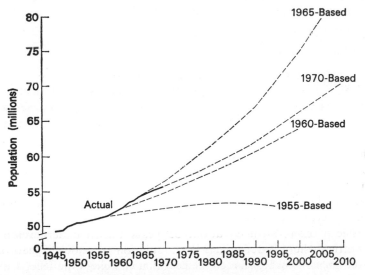

Figure 22 *Actual and projected total population of the United Kingdom*
Source: *Population projections 1970–2010* (HMSO 1971).

The changing distribution of the population is also an important factor in the management of the country's resources, particularly when over 80 per cent of the inhabitants live in towns, 37 per cent residing in the seven major conurbations, and the process of urbanization places increasing demands upon these resources. It is the imbalance and distributional inequality of Britain's resources, both real and financial, that are inextricably bound up with the emergence of regional planning. As the continued high standard of living depends upon increased productivity and increased productivity requires the use of additional resources, the taxing and stretching of the nation's assets behoves the town planner to devise more and better ways of understanding and predicting population growth, and thus aggregate demand.

The problem of population growth is essentially a universal one for there is a direct and necessary corollary between population growth and the use of resources. It has been suggested that

the increase in human numbers has caused a totally disproportionate impact upon the environment because, for example, the provision of minerals and fossil fuels for an expanding population even at fixed levels of consumption requires that as the nearest and richest ores are worked out, then the use of lower-grade ores, deeper drilling and extended supply networks all increase the per capita use of energy and hence the per capita impact on the environment.[4]

Agriculture and forestry

A recent and drastic transformation, whose scale and intensity virtually amounts to a revolution, has overtaken British agriculture. In a country where there is only just over one acre of agricultural land for every head of population, land is quite naturally considered a scarce resource and great premium is placed upon its efficient use. Over three-quarters of the land is given over to farming, which, with an annual output amounting to £5500 million in 1975, supplying half the population's food requirements, remains the nation's largest industry, even though it now employs only 2 per cent of the labour force.

The advent of mechanization and the introduction of industrial methods, stimulated by economic pressures and supported by government subsidy, has led to a sudden change in the face of the countryside. Farms have got fewer and larger, and fields have become more expansive, particularly in the Eastern Counties where arable farming predominates. A more efficient and scientific approach has led to increased densities of stocking, higher yields of produce, and better conversion factors of foodstuffs. Production has more than doubled since the 1930s and the present rate of productivity, running at approximately 1.3 per cent per annum, is more than sufficient to keep pace with the 50,000 acres lost every year to urban encroachment.[5]

Improvements continue, so that present-day agriculture is still an advancing industry, and current policy is geared towards making use of this advance to maintain the proportion of home produced food, on a decreasing land acreage and with a diminishing labour force. Such progress is dependent, however, upon even larger inputs of energy, chemical fertilizers and mechanization, and the cheering performances in agricultural production are but the harbingers of accelerating problems in rural resource management, themselves associated with the technical advance and intensification of farming. The increasing use of antibiotics in the development of factory farming could eventually endanger human health. The extensive application of artificial fertilizer and pesticides could cause untold repercussions. For instance, a satisfactory level of organic matter in the soil is considered to be about 8 per cent; it has now declined to around 3 per cent, which necessitates further artificial treatment, thus perpetuating the decline, and closing the vicious circle tighter and tighter. Resistant strains develop and residues appear in the final product. The delicately balanced stability in the natural order of things, *or eco-system*, is tragically disturbed, often with unforeseen and irreparable results. Heavy applications of fertilizer ultimately find their way into lakes and water courses, inducing weed growth to such an extent that they become choked and stultified. This process is known as *eutrophication*.[6] In addition the tearing up of hedgerows, destruction of thickets, and felling of trees, all to promote efficiency, can deprive a variety of wildlife of their natural habitat. The effect of removing hedgerows, currently at a rate of 5000 miles a year, is succinctly described by Allaby:[7]

Hedges and trees play a crucial role in the water economy and their removal may affect drainage. They provide shelter for the soil and crops, as well as for animals. Wind speed is reduced to zero on the lee side of a hedge for a distance equal to twice the height; for a distance equal to twelve times the height of the hedge, wind speed is halved. In this sheltered area moisture is conserved in the upper layers of the soil and the soil temperature is higher.

They also act as invaluable windbreaks, preventing the erosion of topsoil, which is already a serious problem in the East Midlands and East Anglia.

Despite conflicting views as to the rate and impact of agricultural land loss, the basic resource of land must be husbanded with care, and one method of assessing priority is the *agricultural land classification*, which groups land into five grades according to the degree that its physical characteristics impose long-term limitations on agricultural use.

Grade I. Land with very minor or no physical limitations to agricultural use. The soils are deep, well drained and lying on level sites or gentle slopes that are easily cultivated, and no climatic factor restricts their agricultural use to any major extent.

Grade II. Land with some minor limitations excluding it from grade I usually connected with the texture, depth or drainage of the soil, but a wide range of crops may be grown.

Grade III. Land of average quality, with limitations due to the soil, relief or climate, or some combination of these factors which restrict the choice of crops, timing of cultivation, or level of yield.

Grade IV. Land with severe limitations due to adverse soil, relief or climate and generally only suitable for low output enterprises.

Grade V. Land of little agricultural value with very severe limitations due to adverse soil, relief or climate and generally to be found under grass or rough grazing (Table 11).

Table 11 *Proportions of different grades of agricultural land in England and Wales*

Grade	Total land area (%)	Total agricultural area (%)
I	2.3	2.8
II	11.8	14.6
III	39.6	48.9
IV	16.0	19.7
V	11.3	14.0
Urban	8.5	—
Other	10.5	—

Source: Ministry of Agriculture, Fisheries and Food, *Agricultural Land Classification of England and Wales* (HMSO June 1974).

Another aspect of the countryside meriting attention is that portion given over to forestry. Currently this amounts to 1.9 million hectares, representing approximately 8 per cent of the total land surface, consisting of 53 per cent coniferous high forest and 20 per cent broad-leaved high forest with the rest being largely scrub, and only three-quarters of which is managed. The figure of 8 per cent coverage falls well below that of other members of the Common Market who average out at around 22 per cent each, and home production understandably accounts for only a small proportion of total timber production. Despite planned increases in production the proportion of home produced timber is still estimated to reach only 13 per cent of total demand by the end of the century. Being one of the few renewable resources, as well as permitting pulping and recycling, the production of timber would appear to warrant encouragement, especially in the light of the exhaustion of many other mineral resources. To this end the Forestry Commission, established in 1919 and owning just under 40 per cent of the total area of woodland, aims to plant and replant 22,000 hectares a year of which about 4000 hectares is replanting. Thankfully, the dull conformity of the unnatural chequerboard layout, and the monotonous planting of a single species so diligently pursued by the Commission in the immediate post-war period, have given way to a more imaginative and aesthetically pleasing policy. This is reinforced by the 1967 and 1968 Countryside Acts which lay a special duty upon the Commission to have regard to amenity in their forestry operations, and subsequently there has been a rapid increase in the provision of recreational facilities in state forests and a social consideration for the creation and maintenance of employment opportunities in upland areas.[8] Private planting has also been encouraged under what are known as *dedication schemes* whereby a private landowner may receive grant aid on approved land and where he can show acceptable management objectives in respect of forestry practice, amenity, agriculture, nature conservation, public access, recreation and general planning considerations. Once dedicated these woodlands cannot be made the subject of a tree preservation order and the felling of timber does not require a licence from the Forestry Commission which, with certain exceptions, would otherwise be required. Nevertheless, concern as to future possible tax impositions have led to a sharp fall in private forestry planting rates.

A report made in 1972 to the Secretary of State for the Environment on the management of natural resources made several recommendations in respect of agriculture and forestry. These included the discontinuance of cosmetic pest control, that is the saturation of crops with pesticides to make them appear more attractive, the abandonment of hedgerow removal grants coupled with incentives for tree planting, the expansion of forestry, and perhaps above all the inauguration and development of research programmes into the long-term effects of modern agricultural methods.[9]

The atmosphere

Probably one of the most apparent aspects of pollution is the desecration of the air we breathe. As a predominantly urban and industrialized society the problem is one of long standing. London has suffered from choking smogs since the twelfth century, and this despite the existence of more drastic measures of control, for it is recorded that an inhabitant was executed in the fourteenth century for burning coal and making too much smoke.[10] The period since the introduction of the 1956 Clean Air Act has seen the amount of smoke disgorged into the atmosphere fall from 2 million tons per annum then to 800,000 tons now. The chief culprit, where smoke is concerned, remains the domestic chimney, which is directly responsible for 85 per cent of the total. The situation, which varies throughout the country – being worse in the North and in South Wales – continues to improve with the switch from coal to other forms of central heating.

Another contributory source of atmospheric pollution is industrial production. Apart from the emission of smoke, 5 million tons of sulphur gases and 1 million tons of grit, dust and ash are pumped into the air every year. As well as the power to designate smokeless zones conferred under the 1956 Act, local authorities are now responsible under the Clean Air Act 1968 for preparing a policy to combat the continuing problem of air pollution. This includes the control of the emission of dark smoke from industrial premises. Furthermore, certain industries with a propensity for such emission are required to register under the Alkali Acts, whose regulations and standards are enforced by an inspectorate charged with the duty of ensuring that these concerns adopt the 'best practicable means' of preventing or minimizing pollution, a stipulation that lends itself to wide interpretation. The costs imposed upon society by atmospheric pollution were calculated to be in the region of £350 million every year in 1973, but the position regarding industrial air-borne waste does, however, appear to be improving (Figure 23).

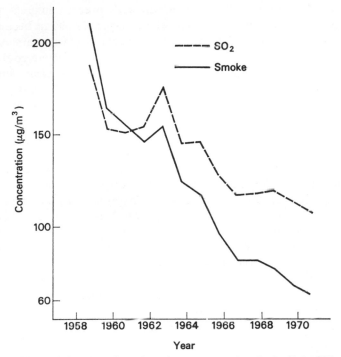

Figure 23   *Sulphur dioxide and smoke concentrations in the United Kingdom*
1958–1971

A very different picture emerges when considering the degree of
pollution caused by the motor vehicle. Although the actual level is
still comparatively small in comparison with industrial processes, the
motor vehicle, which manifests itself as millions of separate mobile
chimneys murderously close to the ground and perilously proximate
to pedestrians, presents a major pollution problem, as anyone
unfortunate enough to be caught in an Oxford Street traffic jam will
surely testify. Every year a horrifying 6 million tons of carbon
monoxide gas containing 3000 tons of lead are discharged into the
atmosphere, a large percentage of which must occur in centres of
population. Although measures are being taken to reduce the lead
content of petrol, the estimated 22 million cars currently on the road
is expected to rise to 32 million by the end of the century – what then?

Although town atmospheres have a considerable capacity for self-
cleansing through thermal circulation this process is sometimes

obstructed by layers of static air which settle over urban areas and trap polluted air. This takes place when a layer of cold air becomes sandwiched between the ground and a higher layer of warm air and is called *inversion*. It is usually experienced in valleys, where cool air flows down the slopes and becomes trapped, or in clear winter conditions, where rapid heat loss occurs close to the ground.

For all these reasons there emerges a need to formulate a comprehensive policy towards the planning of space as a complete entity. The physical land use planner is well accustomed to allocating land to competing uses, zoning activities to their most appropriate location, and controlling movement between them. It seems a logical progression to take account of the environmental forces above, as well as on, and below, the ground. This idea would involve an understanding of prevailing air currents and 'air sheds', which are defined as 'areas where air currents come together and flow in such a way as to create a zone of distinct character'.[11] This form of survey would then permit 'air-zoning' as a complement to land use zoning. A further remedial course of action would be the imposition of fines, levies and charges upon the perpetrators of noxious substances, pitched at a level that would not discourage economic activity, the proceeds of which could be devoted to research on the development of cleaner processes.

Water

As with so many other natural resources the demand for water continues to grow, the current annual rate of increase being about 3 per cent. The figures relating to future predictions vary enormously but it does appear possible that demand will have doubled by the end of the century. A government publication places current consumption at 55 gallons per head per day, half of which is used for domestic purposes and half for industrial.[12] Although this country appears richly endowed with rainfall, sometimes too much so, the supply is seasonal and unevenly distributed – where water is plentiful population is sparse. Nevertheless with an average daily downpour of 40,000 million gallons and a total demand of 25,000 the situation has obviously not reached crisis point. The United Kingdom, however, possesses fewer untapped sources of supply than almost any other European country and with increased demand, as well as the regional and seasonal variations, the proper management of water resources merits considerable attention.

The increase in supply is likely to be achieved in a number of ways –

the tapping of new sources beneath the ground, increased reservoir construction and capacity, an extended network of pipelines, the reuse of water through the purification of sewage and effluent, the cleansing of river water, and the introduction of vast barrages across estuaries such as the Dee, Wash, Solway Firth and Morecambe Bay, coupled with desalination techniques. It is envisaged that the latter developments could carry toll roads across them to assist in defraying their cost. It also appears probable that eventually domestic water will be metered and a charge made according to the amount consumed, in the same way as now occurs for industrial and irrigation supplies. It is worth noting, however, that with an advance in purification systems, recycling procedures, and coastal location of industry requiring water facilities, there are the first signs that the demand for water could well slacken over the next twenty-five years.

The responsibility for the administration of the nation's water resources has recently been transferred to ten specially created all-purpose *regional water authorities*. For the first time all hydrological processes, water supply, sewerage, rivers and canals will be considered together. This should greatly enhance the supervision of recalcitrant local authorities regarding the disposal of untreated sewage in rivers.

The most urgent and critical problem that commands attention is the appalling condition of the rivers. The pollution from animal manure slurry, pesticides and fertilizer, as well as domestic sewage and industrial waste, has reached alarming proportions – some rivers consist of 75 per cent effluent, being little more than open sewers. Admittedly, since the 1951 and 1961 River Acts came into force the total mileage of grossly polluted rivers has decreased by 25 per cent but there are still approximately 5000 miles that are in an unsatisfactory condition. The Acts introduced legislation whereby any discharge of effluent directly into rivers must be authorized and is subject to controls in respect of its volume, temperature and composition. Investment by industry in installing equipment for treating waste has substantially increased but at only £25 million per annum it is still far from being adequate. Over three-quarters of domestic sewage now also receives some form of treatment, demonstrating that modern technology can cope; the situation is not irreversible, but the necessary finance, legislation and enforcement must be forthcoming. Moreover, to check the effectiveness of these measures a continuous monitoring system is required. Regard should not only be paid to the rivers but also to the seas and oceans of the world, which are themselves in danger of being turned into vast cesspits, having already been denuded of large areas of underwater forest, the habitat of marine life and possible future source of nutriment.

Energy

One of the principal issues that confronts mankind is that of energy, for the transformation of human societies from agricultural to industrial communities has depended mainly on the use of fossil fuel to drive machines, and the need for fuel has grown as more and more tasks are undertaken by machines rather than by people. Indeed, the hallmarks of an industrialized society are said to be energy and communication, and even communication requires energy. The consumption of power can also be used to compare relative levels of economic activity; the United States, for example uses the equivalent of 9.4 tons of coal per person every year, whereas in Western Europe the figure is 3.1 tons, in Eastern Europe 1.5 tons and in the rest of the world 0.5 tons.

Estimates of future energy demand are notoriously difficult to make, being so heavily dependent upon forecasts of population and economic activity. World energy consumption during the 1970s, however, rose by about 5 per cent a year, and if this rate continues it is cleat that the oil and gas reserves will quickly become exhausted. Uncertainty also persists on the supply side, but extractable resources of all kinds are predicted to be depleted within the next 200 years. More significant perhaps, because of its physical and technological flexibility as well as its comparative ease of exploitation, is the probable future supply of oil. Estimates vary from a pessimistic 20 years[13] to a sanguine 120 years[14] and more, but whatever the actuality the supply is finite and relatively immediate. The United Kingdom has been granted a temporary respite from the energy crisis by the discovery and exploitation of North Sea oil, but given a 2 per cent annual increase in demand for energy it is unlikely that at currently envisaged rates of extraction reserves will last far into the next century. The energy resource that fuelled the industrial revolution in this country was coal and, while actual production continues to expand at an annual growth rate of around 3.5 per cent, coal has consistently accounted for a smaller and smaller share of energy consumption since the 1930s. Other alternative sources of power include nuclear, solar, geothermal, wind, water, natural gas and waste. Probably the greatest unknown factor in the energy equation is that of nuclear power, for still only less than 1 per cent of the world's energy needs are met by the electricity produced by the process of nuclear fission. The advent of the fast breeder reactor would appear to solve many of the efficiency problems previously posed, but it also correspondingly increases the environmental problems of disposing of the vast amounts of hot water used in cooling, the potential hazards resulting from accident or sabotage, and the difficulties encountered in the treatment and disposal of radioactive waste. The prospects presented by the exploitation of solar energy are held by many to be among the most promising of all future sources of energy. The main problem with solar energy, however, is that it is least available when it is most required and the costs of conducting and storing it remain high. Nevertheless, at the limited level of domestic water heating by way of flat-plate collectors the initial results are good, and it has been suggested that up to two-thirds of domestic heat and hot water in the United Kingdom could be provided in this way.[15] A rarely used form of energy is that emanating from the heat of the earth's interior, for to date such geothermal energy is only used in those areas where underground hot water reservoirs are most readily available. It would, however, be possible in this country to drill several miles down, preferably through granite, to reach usefully hot rocks, so that water could be pumped down, heated and returned, but the costs are high.

As the United Kingdom is one of the windiest parts of the world the notion of harnessing wind power is appealing, but in a heavily urban and industrialized country the potential is strictly limited and can really only provide a minor supplementary form of energy. Moreover, the physical impact of a significant system of wind power generation and storage would have profound environmental repercussions. Water can be employed in the generation of energy by exploiting wave, tide and gravitational power. It has been estimated, for example, that the total mechanical energy of the waves impinging on the shores of the United Kingdom is more than twice that of the present installed electrical power systems of the country, and peak production from anchored booms during stormy winter months would coincide with peak demand. Potentially less expensive is the use of tidal power in favoured locations such as the Bristol Channel where the second highest tides in the world are experienced. A barrage across the channel would trap the high tidal water and gradually release it through turbines, and while the possible environmental consequences upon coastal waters would have to be carefully monitored it is suggested that up to 10 per cent of the country's electricity could be generated from tidal schemes.

It has further been estimated that hydroelectric power could provide approximately half of the world's power currently supplied by fossil fuels, but, as in this country, the best sites are those most removed from centres of population and industry and lengthy transmission is very costly. The emergence of natural gas as a major source of energy in Britain over the past decade or so has had a number of environmental benefits in respect of underground storage and transmission, alleviation of road and rail traffic, and improved atmospheric conditions. One way of reducing the demand for raw energy is the utilization of otherwise wasted energy sources such as by-products and refuse, and an early experiment was conducted in Westminster where the Pimlico district heating scheme was opened in 1965 to serve approximately 3600 dwellings with heat provided by the surplus steam from Battersea power station.

In a similar way, the incineration of domestic refuse has been used to provide heat for schemes such as those in parts of Nottingham.

The link between power resources and other aspects of town and country planning has for long been a tenuous one, but with the recognition of a possible energy crisis and the awareness of the need to promote policies of energy conservation, the relationships between power and planning are becoming more obvious. The way in which local authority planning decisions affect energy consumption can depend upon a number of variable factors. The demand for energy varies not only between different land uses but also within the same use. Alternative forms of housing development, for example, will demonstrate contrasting energy characteristics, with high-rise flats requiring facilities for powered movements and high-pressure services and consuming more energy in their construction than more conventional residential accommodation. Conversely, low-rise housing may be more costly to insulate and heat as well as impose higher vehicular and power infrastructure costs as a result of wider spatial dispersal. The imposition of various design, space and performance standards also has a major influence upon energy consumption as do policies aimed at improvement or expansion. Furthermore, transportation is a field with very obvious energy consequences. Most planning decisions can, therefore, be seen to have energy implications, and a compelling case can be made for the inclusion of some kind of energy budget in the framing of overall planning policy.

As a reaction to the allegedly profligate use of energy resources throughout the century there has emerged a school of planning thought advocating the promotion of low-growth planning based upon a low-energy society. The adoption of this change of strategy implies a reordering of priorities and aspirations in the community combined with a new role for planning, which will be required to produce positive policies with less rather than more available resources.

Minerals

Not including coal mining, the extraction of minerals can be divided into two convenient categories. First, *sedimentary*, the working of lime, chalk, limestone, clay, sand and gravel used extensively in the construction industry and therefore in part responsible for the employment of 1.3 million men and an annual turnover of over £1000 million. Secondly, *metalliferous*, including the winning of iron, tin and lead, forming a small proportion of the whole, but greatly encouraged in an attempt to reduce the heavy dependence upon imported metals. Together, the extraction of these minerals accounts for a gross annual turnover of over £600 million per annum.

The degree of control exercised over the winning and working of minerals by town and country planning is very much greater than that over any other natural resource. The very nature of the extractive process, with a predominance of open-cast workings, the tremendous generation of traffic, the scars left by finished operations, and the unsightly deposit of waste products, commends it to supervision within the sphere of environmental planning. Despite a certain amount of criticism to the contrary, a great deal has been achieved in regulating the way in which the working of minerals is pursued and the extent of landscape deterioration that is involved. As the industry falls exclusively within the private sector of the economy, unlike other resources, the principal control is the need to obtain planning permission. Within the planning permission can be incorporated a number of conditions relating to road access, screening, level of production and, perhaps most important of all, restoration. Many worked-out sand and gravel pits are easily adapted to alternative uses; for example, the filling in with waste and refuse followed eventually by residential development. A popular, and commercially attractive, after-use in some river valleys has been the flooding of exhausted pits and the introduction of recreational pursuits such as angling, water skiing and sailing. Other sites, particularly metalliferous, can be returned to agriculture or forestry, or developed as wildlife sanctuaries. Some exciting and imaginative adventure playgrounds and recreational complexes have been established on what were previously mineral workings and slag heaps.

The wider problems of land dereliction are more fully discussed elsewhere, but there still exist problems regarding the use of an ever-diminishing supply of mineral wealth. In this context certain recommendations have been put forward in an attempt to formulate a national policy. These include the need for further research into the development of alternative materials and processes, particularly in respect of the construction industry, more extensive recycling of metals, increased offshore mining, even further planning control and enforcement over mineral working, and the setting up of a Derelict Land Agency to supervise the task of reclamation.

Noise

The solitude of life is increasingly disturbed by an unseen, and largely intangible, atmospheric pollutant – noise. The aural invasion produced by motor vehicles, aircraft, industry and other human activities is fast becoming more than a nuisance and begins to assume the proportions of a major health hazard, both physical and mental.

Probably the most intrusive is that produced by motor traffic, which, when one considers that the amount of horsepower on the roads has doubled over the last seven years, is scarcely surprising (Figure 24). Following the report of the 1963 Wilson Committee on noise and subsequent Road Traffic Acts, fairly strict standards regarding permitted noise levels of individual vehicles have been laid down. The standards have been made even more stringent in respect of vehicles produced since 1973. It is not always possible, however, to ensure that this legislation is fully enforced; the equipment is expensive and the task time-consuming. Moreover, these regulations and standards do not apply to streams of traffic, and the incessant drone produced by the sheer volume carried on urban motorways is a far more serious problem than the occasional individual miscreant.

The basic unit for measuring sound pressure variations is internationally known as the 'pascal', but for everyday planning purposes this scale is too unwieldy and is replaced by the decibel (dB) scale, which provides a more manageable series of numbers over the audible range. The scale is a logarithmic one, so that an increase of 10 dB roughly corresponds to a doubling of loudness and a noise of

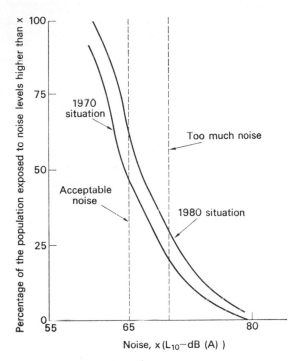

Figure 24   *Traffic noise exposure of the urban population in 1970 and 1980*

70 dB is therefore twice as loud as a noise of 60 dB. Table 12 gives some typical examples of noise levels, and the matter is also discussed later under development control standards. Because road traffic noise is generated exclusively at ground level, special interest attaches to the capacity of obstacles, screens and barriers blocking the transmission of sound, and a measure reflecting the general frequency and intensity of noise peaks is required, as opposed to a measure of individual vehicles. The unit most commonly employed is the $L_{10}(18$ h) index, which is an average of the noise level exceeded for 10 per cent of the time during each hour from 6 a.m. to midnight on a normal working day. The readings are made on a noise meter with the scale weighted electronically to compensate for the response of the ear, the *A scale*, and are thus expressed in 'A-weighted' decibels of dBA. Current recommendations can vary between authorities, but typically noise levels outside a house should not exceed 68 dBA and those inside not more than 50 dBA for a house alongside a busy

Table 12   *Examples of noise levels*

Decibels (dB)	Sound pressure, pascals (Pa)	Examples
120	20	Jet aircraft at 150 m
		Inside boiler-making factory
110		'Pop' music group
		Motor horn at 5 m
100	2	Inside tube train
		Busy street
90		Workshop
		Small car at 7.5 m
80	0.2	Noisy office
		Inside small car
70		Large shop
		Radio set — normal volume
60	0.02	Normal conversation at 1 m
50		Urban house
		Quiet office
		Rural house
40	0.002	Public library
		Quiet conversation
30		Rustle of paper
		Whisper
20	0.0002	Quiet church
		Still night in the country
10		Sound-proof room
0	0.00002	Threshold of hearing

urban street and 45 dBA for a suburban house away from main traffic routes. So far as planning is concerned, however, the task is not only to ensure that new housing and new road schemes meet the required standard but that existing conditions within areas of unacceptable noise levels are improved. Naturally, an immediate solution would appear to be the reduction of traffic flow, particularly heavy lorries, but paradoxically at some traffic levels a reduction of flow will actually increase the degree of annoyance because the useful masking effect of background noise has been diminished. As the L_{10} scale takes little account of background noise, other measures such as the *traffic noise index* (TNI) and the *noise pollution level* (NPL) have been devised, which do. The simplest methods of reducing noise disturbance are either to increase the distance from the source to the recipient or to erect barriers between them. On a level site, for instance, at distances of over 15 m noise levels fall by 4 dBA each time the distance from the carriageway is doubled, and the effectiveness of barriers can be readily assessed using routine calculations produced by the Department of the Environment.[16]

Another major contributor to the disquiet of modern society is aircraft noise. Excluded from control under the Noise Abatement Act 1960, the advent of supersonic flight further threatens public privacy. The Air Navigation (Noise Certification) Order of 1970 has introduced standards for future types of aircraft to ensure that the noise from supersonic jet flights will be about half the level of that produced by present machines. Although these measures again ignore the problem caused by the volume of traffic, it is difficult to see how the desire for tranquillity and the need for transportation can be reconciled.

Around any airport it is possible to draw a noise contour map using units of measurement designed to reflect the degree of annoyance likely to be felt by people living within different noise zones. Surveys have shown that annoyance is created by two essential factors, the total number of aircraft heard during the day and the average peak noise level as each aircraft approaches and recedes. These two factors have been combined into a single function known as the *noise and number index* (NNI), from which contour maps can be constructed. Many countries accept that all areas within the 55 NNI contour are unsuitable for residential use, and that existing housing in the 45 to 55 NNI zone should have special protection against noise. Moreover, it is felt that the more stringent 45 NNI standard should be applied to new housing schemes.

To assist in tackling the problem of noise and to maintain a watching brief over the agencies involved, a Noise Advisory Council was set up in 1970. An independent body consisting of members of the public as well as accredited experts in the field, but chaired by the Secretary of State for the Environment, it has already made important recommendations, which are likely to be adopted, regarding acceptable levels of noise borne by residents unfortunate enough to front on to motorways.

There are two basic ways of solving the contentious issue of noise – by eliminating it at source by better design, and by separating the noise from the people affected. The latter approach falls very much within the province of the planning profession, which can reduce the impact by improved techniques of location and layout in respect of roads, airports, industry, schools and housing. The setting of standards, the use of noise protractors, the zoning of land use activities with an appreciation of noise, and possibly the introduction of noise control areas similar to those relating to smoke control, could all assist in ameliorating the situation.

Town planning and resource planning

The ability to strike a balance between economic efficiency and environmental amenity is the art and science of modern town planning. The planner is not just a conservationist or 'land accountant' but also an arbitrator of conflicting pressures and demands upon land and other resources. He is concerned with establishing and working towards long-term objectives, ensuring continued growth with progressive improvement. It is, therefore, encumbent upon him, in the preparation of a development plan, to undertake a survey and compile a record of such existing resources as coal, iron, water and power and also to promote an understanding of their availability, future demand, priorities for use and expected life. Moreover, he must be in a position to exercise control over their employment, condition and impact upon society.

Because any change in the use of land is potentially a source of disruption and most land use activities have resource and pollution connotations, it is the task of every planner at all scales to supervise the rearrangement of these activities so that any disharmony they cause is reduced to a minimum. Furthermore, in reviewing the relationship persisting between different operations on land the planner should not only be attuned to the preferences of public opinion but must know when to take the advice of a wide variety of specialists including geologists, sociologists and ecologists, as well as the more traditional professions associated with the built environment.

In order to achieve this, the nature and training of the physical land use planner must change. He must have regard for space and time as well as form. He must cultivate a knowledge of the human and economic, as well as built, environment. In other words, he must adopt and develop a more comprehensive approach towards the environment, perhaps not individually but certainly as a profession. To implement his plans and policies, and to ensure their full perspective, a greater degree of co-ordination and co-operation is required at all levels of government and between all agencies active in society. Pollution, for example, is no respecter of boundaries. To be effective, therefore, the planning process needs to be more flexible and better conditioned to respond to ever-changing social, economic and political circumstances. In addition, to eliminate contradictions and anomalies in a policy a more closely integrated approach between local authority departments and their constituent professional staff is called for.

19 The inner city

An awareness of growing social, economic and physical problems occurring in those zones of old residential and industrial development lying between city centres and nearer suburbs has been dawning over the past ten or more years. It is only within the last few years, however, that a concerted government effort, supported by the injection of financial resources and enactment of remedial legislative measures, has been launched to combat the malaise of urban deprivation.

The problem is a complex one but is neatly summarized as

The general outcome of the process of change to which these areas have been subjected has been progressive decay of the physical fabric, rising economic insecurity (manifested principally in terms of discontinuity of local industrial employment) and a tendency towards greater social instability and breakdown of the structure of community life.[1]

The nature of the problem, however, varies enormously from city to city and from area to area. London, for example, is characterized by severe housing stress, Clydeside by extreme poverty and other English cities by low levels of skill. Common to most deprived parts of the inner city are increasing levels of poverty, crime and unemployment linked with a decline in services and facilities, particularly in education and public transport. The major conurbations of London, Glasgow, Tyne and Wear, West Yorkshire, Manchester, Merseyside and West Midlands suffer predominantly, having collectively a population of about 4 million in their inner areas, representing approximately 7 per cent of the country's total population but around 12.5 per cent of the unskilled workforce, some 20 per cent of whom are in a degree of housing stress.

Despite the recent limelight, the problems of the city are not new. The very origins of the town planning movement were deeply rooted in a reaction to the combined forces of squalor, congestion, disease, poverty and physical decay manifested by the large industrial cities of the nineteenth century. As has already been described, earlier measures of social reform initiated through public health, housing, local government and planning legislation, together with the campaigns and enterprises of the philanthropists and pioneers, have provided a partial abatement, but never a solution.

Concern for the plight of those deprived in the inner city has grown gradually over the past decade, and is reflected in the succession of reports that have emerged, such as the Milner-Holland report in 1965, which mainly investigated housing conditions in the twilight areas of London; the Plowden report in 1967 on primary education, which contended that deprivation in certain inner city areas resulted in various forms of family and educational instability, and recommended that schools in these areas should be given priority in the allocation of educational resources; and the Seebohm report in 1968, inquiring into the provision of social services and advising that the then separate welfare committees and departments of local authorities should be amalgamated into a single administrative structure so as to deal more comprehensively with the social problems of inner urban areas. In the wake of these and other reports, a series of government sponsored projects were instituted. Some, such as housing action area and general improvement area policies, were conspicuously orthodox in their physical environmental approach to the problem. Others have been of a much more experimental nature, and include the *urban aid programme*, designed to provide additional financial resources through local authorities for agencies operating in areas of deprivation; the *educational priority area* programme, set up in 1968 to implement the recommendations of Plowden and encourage local authorities to designate areas of special educational need where additional resources could again be made available; the *Six Towns Study*, commissioned in 1973 and divided into distinct phases – the *urban guidelines programme* where consultants studied Rotherham, Oldham and Sunderland with a view to making recommendations for the improvement of urban government and the better management of local government resources, and the *inner area studies* where consultants were again instructed to explore the problems, structure and possible solutions in respect of the inner city areas of Liverpool, Birmingham and Lambeth; and the *community development project* established in 1969, consisting of twelve local projects co-ordinated by the Home Office and aimed at investigating new ways of meeting the needs of people living in areas of high deprivation, principally through the co-ordination of social services by the special project team and exploiting community and individual self-help. There have also been a number of other smaller projects undertaken by either the Home Office or the Department of the Environment, variously concerned with the co-ordination and management of urban area policy, such as the two *neighbourhood schemes* in Liverpool and Teesside in 1971, the *quality of life studies* in 1973, the *comprehensive community programme* in 1974, two *deprived area projects* and four *area management trials* also both in 1974. Arguably, the two most important studies were the community development project and the inner area studies, which were commonly commissioned in an attempt to comprehend the dynamics and structure of urban deprivation. From a town planning viewpoint the inner area studies merit close scrutiny and have been reviewed as follows: 'I do not think we shall ever again discuss urban environment except in the terms of these three studies. . . . This mass of new evidence supersedes what has been done on the inner city before, and no one has yet begun to evaluate the riches that are found in this mountain of material.'[2]

The inner area studies[3]

The picture of exceptional concentrations of poverty and deprivation in the inner urban areas of the large cities is well drawn by the Liverpool study, where a most striking impression of physical decay was described. The study reported a situation in the inner city where 10 per cent of the land in the central city was vacant, the population had fallen from 750,000 in 1921 to 300,000 in 1971, 80,000 jobs had been lost between 1961 and 1971, an unemployment rate of 11 per cent persisted and was steadily growing although job opportunities existed on the periphery of the city, and the remaining workforce was overwhelmingly working class with the departure of the skilled and professional classes.

In addition, housing dissatisfaction was widespread, with predominantly old housing or poorly maintained council estates, and the incidence of vandalism and racial discrimination was deplorably high. An alienation between the inner city residents and authority in general was apparent, with government conveying an unfortunate impression of being an uncaring bureaucracy, and private-sector investment was extremely scarce.

The consultants concerned proposed four basic programmes for regeneration, as follows:

1 The promotion of economic development, by preparing and ensuring continuous up-dating of a co-ordinated economic plan; the promotion of industrial prospects to potential investors; an increase in the supply of serviced land; the construction of advance factories; the conducting of feasibility studies in areas of disused dockland and railway land; the general improvement of the industrial environment; the encouragement of smaller and emergent firms; the development of new business opportunities; and the need to attract firms to relocate inwards towards the city centre.

2 The provision of expanded opportunities for training by undertaking regular assessments of manpower and training needs, ensuring that corresponding adjustments are made to agencies involved in employment, the creation of more retraining schemes, the provision of youth training programmes linked to capabilities and not to jobs, and an improvement in the operation of transfer schemes so that some unskilled workers could actually move away.

3 The improvement of access to housing for disadvantaged groups by undertaking the further conversion and better management of council property, providing furnished flats and sheltered accommodation, generally giving better advice on housing matters, supplying mortgages for low-income earners, devising a new definition of social needs priority, and facilitating the operation of being able to transfer elsewhere.

4 The channelling of resources to areas of greatest social need by establishing more local housing advice offices, increasing the level of tenant participation, allowing a greater degree of local control over the use of funds, providing better schools, improving the take-up of welfare support, and the allocation of more resources to the voluntary sector.

Overall the consultants recommended the need to take a total approach to the problem, by all parties at all levels of government, and not only were additional resources required from central government, but there was an absolute call for the adoption of a policy of positive discrimination in favour of the deprived areas. They also considered the most appropriate form of local government administration for the inner city, and while conceiving of a new inner urban area administrative body as an alternative, possibly along the lines of a development corporation, it was rejected on the grounds that it could actually lead to greater confusion and bureaucracy. The best approach, they concluded, was still to make the city council fully responsible but to create better area management, attempt to introduce improved decision-making procedures, contrive more local involvement in and decentralization of policy, and consider the advisability of setting up a committee for the inner area.

In similar vein, the Birmingham study observed that their selected area of Small Heath, some two miles from the city centre, also demonstrated a poor physical fabric costly to maintain, a loss of population, an increasing concentration of lower skilled workers, very low income levels, a high proportion of immigrants, a declining economic and industrial base, and little public or private investment over a long period of time. Their recommendations largely mirrored those of the Liverpool study and included such suggestions as the subsidizing of jobs in the manufacturing sector, the development of modern industrial estates, a re-think on the treatment of non-conforming uses, the provision of grants for the rehabilitation of industrial premises, the creation of an industrial task force, the setting up of day-care services for working mothers, a raising of the levels of child benefit, more acquisition of tenanted property by the council, greater assistance to mortgagors, the establishment of informal area committees, the encouragement of more organization within local communities, an added emphasis on the role of local planning, the spelling out of financial implications, the achieving of a greater flexibility in local authority staff employment, the acceptance by central government of responsibility for the supply of strategic resources, the attainment of a more efficient use of existing resources and the furnishing of extra incentives for stimulating self-reliance and self-help. Above all they echoed the cry for a policy of positive discrimination to nourish the inner city.

Many of the findings and recommendations of the Lambeth report were roughly analogous, but a number of additional suggestions were made, including the abolition of industrial development certificates, the relaxation of office development permits in certain areas, a similar relaxation of control over non-conforming uses, a guarantee of continuity of work in the construction industry, a major expansion of training opportunities, the encouragement of an outward movement by some of the lower-paid workers, a significant improvement in housing management, an amendment of the housing cost yardstick standards, and a re-alignment of welfare services.

Town planning and the inner city

By now it will be apparent that many of the central issues and the prospective paths for remedial action either lie outside, or are at least peripheral to, conventional town planning practice. The advent of corporate and area management has, however, led to a greater integration of the town planning function into a wider context of policy planning. This integration has not necessarily led to proposals for traditional planning activities and professional town planners playing a fuller part in the process at the local scale. The Lambeth report, for example, posed the question

What scope is there for local planning in areas like Stockwell where the basic structure of land uses is unlikely to change over the forseeable future?

and stated further that

We can see the need for local plans in expansion areas on the edges of towns or cities, or in urban districts likely to experience major redevelopment. But there is little point in devoting scarce staff resources to such activities in places where there in no likelihood of new houses, parks, roads, shops or other major developments.[4]

Because the problem of the inner city is essentially a strategic one, translating a range of national policies into a balanced set of local initiatives, there is clearly a need for some form of strategic plan relating such components as population change, housing need, employment opportunities, social services, transportation and education to a coherent policy framework. The accent, however, will be firmly placed upon management and the efficient allocation of existing resources to meet realistic objectives. While the conventional expertise of the town planner enters into this process, the final 'plan' is much more an instrument to be designed and operated at officer level by those versed in management science and public administration. The effective implementation of this strategic plan would seem to depend upon the satisfaction of certain fundamental criteria, and a report by the Institute of Local Government Studies[5] identifies these criteria as:

political and administrative commitment
identification of the problems and their causes
the ability to amend current policies and initiate new ones
the capacity to change patterns of resource allocation
the ability of the local authority to implement the strategy

a reviewing mechanism
a co-ordinated approach, both interdepartmental and interagency
community involvement and influence.

Supplementing this strategic dimension there would be a need for
fine-scale proposals and detailed plans for the few major developments that might occur. Moreover, a policy for promoting and
controlling small-scale change would have to be framed, and again
one of the inner area studies advocated that 'Inside the inner city,
selected schemes of local environmental improvement should be
mounted in areas where physical and social conditions are bad, and
where a rapid change can be effected'.[6] Action projects should,
therefore, be launched which are designed to have an immediate
effect in deprived areas, and which should also test new forms of local
authority initiative involving several departments. Another one of
the studies recommended that the most appropriate vehicle for taking
action should be an *area community plan*, which would provide a
policy link between local action area plans and strategic planning
documents.[7] These area community plans would be produced for
localities of a similar size to their study area, namely a population of
around 30,000, and should provide a programme for physical, institutional, economic and social development and for private investment based upon available resources, and a realistic time-table
enabling all agencies to co-operate in the realization of the plan. They
should also be undertaken in collaboration with representative local
groups from the outset.[8] Cogently, the criteria to which local
authorities should be working in the preparation of all kinds of plan
for inner city areas have been usefully summarized as:[9]

the plan should be problem-oriented
the plan should be corporate
emphasis should be placed on monitoring and amendment of policies
    and not end-state planning
implementation should be carried out speedily and efficiently
emphasis should be given to community involvement
emphasis should be given to resource and the private-sector's role in
    implementing the plan.

As a concluding note on the inner city, an unorthodox and somewhat
dissident view is that the growth and decline of different parts of the
city at different times is an inevitable feature of urban society; further,
that such cycles of change are healthy and to be welcomed in that they

foster innovation and provide the necessary conditions for economic resurgence and prosperity. Naturally, the state of social deprivation that is often left in the wake of switching urban fortune is a matter of concern and proper field for subvention to the disadvantaged. Nevertheless, it can be argued that massive financial support aimed at pinning up a deteriorated physical fabric, regulatory legislation designed to deflect investment to deprived areas, and positive inducements intended to attract industry to locate there, are a profligate and foolish way of allocating the nation's resources. Some areas, the argument continues, should be allowed to die and the investment made elsewhere at a significantly higher opportunity cost.

Vacant urban land

For different reasons, land in urban areas lies vacant for varying periods, from a few months to several decades. This land represents an eyesore, a health and safety hazard, a sanctuary for vermin, a mecca for illegal users, a wasted resource and a monument to bad planning.

The problem

The problem of vacant urban land is essentially different to that of derelict land, for statutory derelict land forms only a small proportion of vacant land. Although there is a wide variation in definition, and a relative dearth of reliable information, it has been estimated that probably 5 per cent of land in metropolitan areas lies vacant, rising to an average of over 6 per cent in the major cities. The inner areas of certain cities suffering from particular dereliction can produce even higher vacancy rates; Liverpool, for example, has over 10 per cent, and Glasgow 12 per cent rising to around 20 per cent in the worst inner city areas. Boroughs in the East End of London also show high vacancy rates, and generally there is marked tendency for a high concentration of vacant land to be found around principal corridors of communication (Tables 13, 14).

Three broad types of vacant land can be identified by appearance – land derelict and spoiled by its former use, neglected undeveloped land, and demolition sites. The ownership of vacant land can roughly be divided equally between public and private sectors, and one of the more significant aspects of ownership is the high proportion which is in the hands of statutory undertakers. An average of one-third of

Table 13   *Vacant land in the metropolitan counties*

	Officially derelict 1974 (ha)	Total vacant (ha)	% of county area
Greater London	324	7727	4.89
West Midlands	1535	4296	4.80
Greater Manchester	3405	n.a.	(2.6)
West Yorkshire	2857	n.a.	(1.4)
Merseyside	529	3789	5.80
South Yorkshire	1565	9084	5.79
Tyne and Wear	1314	n.a.	(2.4)
Strathclyde Region	n.a.	9250	0.70

Table 14   *Vacant land (v.l.) in four major cities*

City totals	Total v.l. (ha)	% of city land	Number of sites	Average site size	% of city v.l.
Birmingham	834	3.07	823	1.01	100
Glasgow	1562	7.70	1054	1.48	100
Liverpool	648	5.59	544	1.19	100
London	7727	4.89	n.a.	n.a.	100
Inner areas					
Birmingham	262	7.26	512	0.51	31.4
Glasgow	418	11.93	494	0.85	26.7
Liverpool	359	10.26	426	0.85	55.5
London	1885	5.58	n.a.	n.a.	24.3

Inner areas defined here as the most central 35 km² of Liverpool, Glasgow and Birmingham and 338 km² in the case of London.

Source: J. Burrows, 'Vacant urban land', *Planner*, January 1978.

vacant land in urban areas is zoned for public open space, but more by default than by design, and much of it is unlikely to be developed in the immediate future. In the vast majority of cases, however, it is not the physical condition of the land that prevents development, for this can nearly always be overcome, but the question of land ownership and land use zoning in the statutory plan that is more important. A multitude of causes can be cited for the presence of vacant land, including the scarcity of public money to promote development, the lack of interest by private-sector financial institutions in investment, the general decline of the inner city, the existence of high historic land values, the continuing sanguine expectations of landowners, the change in locational preference away from central areas by both commercial and residential sectors, a basic unwillingness to bring land onto the market, procedural delay for both public and privately owned land, the uncertainties surrounding the operational land of statutory undertakers, and the inappropriate size, shape, structure and servicing of some sites. An edifying feature of the vacant land problem is that many local authorities are not always fully aware of the extent of their own land ownership, and even where they are, different committees within an authority, such as housing and education, will own land independently and either guard jealously their proprietary rights or be unaware of other opportunities for alternative municipal development.

Transfer of land, even within an authority, however, can be a lengthy business, as can the negotiation of planning permission by external agencies. Other procedural aspects affecting the incidence and degree of land vacancy include the relative failure of comprehensive redevelopment plans, the over-ambitious nature of other statutory plans, the out-of-date condition of many zoning proposals, the scant development control available over demolition, and the lack of any planning control at all over the cessation of use.

The consequences of leaving land vacant for long periods are many and troubling; some of them are the general promotion of environmental degradation, a debilitating effect on local residents, an increase in vandalism, the spread of poor management and deteriorating conditions to surrounding areas, the fostering of further out-migration, the discouragement of investment, a high opportunity cost of developments forgone, a consequent loss of rate income, expensive holding costs, and frequently incurred external costs on adjacent land.

Policies

In common with so many other issues in planning there is no single and simple solution to the problem of vacant land. Different approaches will inevitably suit different circumstances, but among the possible palliatives which have been proposed at one time or another are the following:

1   The creation of a more flexible planning base, so that policies can more readily be attuned to the particular exigencies of an individual area. The advent of more pertinent local plans should assist in achieving this objective, as should the introduction of a corporate management approach and the policy of establishing area-based teams currently being pursued by many authorities. Alongside these organizational reforms there also needs to be a fundamental change in zoning practice, away from the traditional wide-area, single-function form and towards a more diversified and sensitive system.

2   The new political initiatives that are being taken in respect of inner urban areas is bound to exercise a beneficial effect upon certain vacant inner city sites. Moreover, it is possible that the positive fiscal inducements proffered to inner city regeneration could be accompanied, for better or worse, by restrictions upon development elsewhere.

3   The trend towards the renewal and rehabilitation of existing buildings, as opposed to wholesale redevelopment, is likely to ameliorate the problems of vacant urban land.

4   The preparation of land policy statements similar to those proposed under the community land scheme, and a more aggressive application of the acquisition and disposal powers, might expedite the release of land from recalcitrant private landowners and statutory undertakers. More scrutiny and control of the true operational needs of the latter is certainly required.

5   The compiling of a public register of vacant land, and the production of an annual position statement, reviewing and monitoring the prevailing condition of vacant land, reporting the progress over the previous year, and indicating possible opportunties for the forthcoming twelve months.

6   A strengthening of demolition control, together with a more realistic attitude towards the allocation and management of public open space.

7   The production of relevant and detailed planning and development briefs aimed at encouraging and guiding private-sector investment. Linked with the issue of these documents should be a positive programme for areas adjacent to vacant land so as to overcome the uncertainties of blight and dereliction.

8   Among a number of legislative amendments that have been promulgated are the presumption of abandonment by private owners of land after a certain period of vacancy, the void rating of

vacant and developable land, and a revised code of valuation for the compulsory purchase of vacant land.

9 A more enterprising approach towards the search for, and support of, temporary uses of vacant land which, it is argued, should be appreciated and husbanded as a valuable short-term asset. Amid those projects already implemented on vacant sites are such activities as mobile housing, Portakabin offices, adventure playgrounds, car parking, advertising, allotments, garden centres, community gardens, landscaped open space, temporary advice centres, open markets and city farms. One of the most interesting ventures, Inter Action's Fun Art Farm in London's Kentish Town now boasts ten separate uses on what was previously a vacant site – a group garden for the elderly, a family kitchen garden, a picnic area, animal pens, compost and manure plot, chicken run, stables, indoor riding school, motor repair workshop and a household repair workshop and meeting room.

The problems of vacant land have been put succinctly into overall perspective as follows:[10]

Vacant urban land is already a political issue and an issue about which the public, the politicians and the press might reasonably expect planners to be well informed and active in solving. As our cities stand today, however, one is forced to question the current priorities of a system of planning which spends so much time and energy exercising strict control over the extensions of individual houses and minor changes of use, while allowing whole areas to be demolished and laid to waste for years, even decades, at the heart of the most populous cities in the country.

20 Planning and public participation

Public or citizen participation has become an 'idea in good currency' and provides a watchword to both professionals and politicians involved in the planning process. A basic lack of communication exists between the planner and the planned, one that is exacerbated by an ever-increasing technical sophistication and the persistent use of professional jargon. Incomprehensible American articles on the very subject of participation amply portray the problem. By its very nature, planning affects every member of the community, albeit to varying degrees. In allocating the use of land and promoting future change, it determines the value of land, creating, apportioning and redistributing wealth. Because of this a veil of secrecy is often drawn over the preparation of plans and the choice between alternative strategies, until all is suddenly revealed in the final decision. The planning process in general, and the preparation of development plans in particular, has always appeared remote to the individual citizen, that is until he suffers an adverse decision in respect of his own property, or receives a notice to treat prior to compulsory acquisition, or finds an urban motorway spawning outside his window. Planning, therefore, is frequently stigmatized by its aspects of control, regulation and intervention, bearing the brunt of personal and political attacks caused by poor communication and understandable self-interest.

Background

The 1947 Town and Country Planning Act displayed supreme indifference to the need for discussion and consultation within the constituent community during the period of plan preparation. Its only gesture to participation was the limited quasi-judicial procedure of consideration of objections and representations before submission of the plan to the Minister and its publication as a *fait accompli* following approval. Thereafter, the legal right of dissent was restricted to certain persons who suffered an adverse planning decision or proposal.

The Planning Advisory Group, set up in 1964 to review the future of development plans, had as one of its main objectives 'to ensure that the planning system serves its purpose satisfactorily both as an instrument of planning policy and as a means of public participation in the planning process'. In their report they stated that a better public understanding of both the general aims of planning policy and the way in which it affected the individual was required. They also pointed out that because of the esoteric nature and technical detail of statutory plans this amounted to a major public relations task, calling for a great deal of careful thought and preparation, together with skill in presentation.

The 1968 Town and Country Planning Act, now re-enacted in the 1971 Town and Country Planning Act, attempted to incorporate these laudable objectives. A conflict, however, presented itself, for on the one hand there was the desire for greater consultation between the public and the planning agencies, while on the other there was the need for quicker decisions in the planning process. The government of the day endeavoured to reconcile these twin aims without seriously detracting from either by:

the devolution of responsibility in certain areas from central to local government, from local government to its appointed officers, and from the Secretary of State for the Environment to his Inspectors

providing that a local authority in drawing up a structure plan, and consequent local plans, give 'adequate publicity' to their survey, report and policy, and 'adequate opportunity' for public representations, which should be taken into consideration in preparing the plan

depositing the plan for public inspection prior to submission and adoption

requiring the Secretary of State to be satisfied that the necessary steps to ensure full consultation have been taken

In general terms the marked increase in government intervention had not been matched by an equal growth in participatory procedures. Although planning remained a high-status profession during the 1950s and early 1960s, public anxiety and uncertainty regarding the planning process grew. Public opinion tended to follow plan production, and gradually a growing realization of the ineffectiveness of planning began to take place. Appeals against planning decisions trebled between 1953 and 1961, and the system of appeal was seen to be excessively legalistic and inadequate to properly redress grievances. A number of movements concerned with challenging and debating planning issues developed and the Civic Trust register of such groups grew from 200 to over 1200 in a matter of 18 years.

The Skeffington report

As a corollary to the 1968 Act the government commissioned a report concerning people and planning (the Skeffington report, 1969) from a committee headed by the late Arthur Skeffington. Its terms of reference were to 'consult and report on the best methods including publicity, of securing the participation of the public at the formative stage in the making of development plans for their area'.

Many of its recommendations were couched in the most general of terms, which reflects the controversial yet universal nature of the subject, and the implicit difficulties in establishing an acceptable procedure for citizen participation. It referred, for example, to the fact that 'people should be kept informed throughout the preparation of a structure or local plan for their area' and that they 'should be encouraged to participate in the preparation of plans by helping with surveys and other activities as well as by making comments'. It did not examine in any great depth the methods by which this could be achieved.

At a more practical level it did, however, propose the appointment of *community development officers* who would assist in securing a greater degree of involvement from all sections of the community, and also the introduction of *community forums* to provide an opportunity for local organizations, agencies and inhabitants to discuss local problems. It envisaged these forums and officers positively stimulating interest and concern to such an extent that formation of neighbourhood groups would result.

The report acknowledged that increased participation would probably mean increased planning blight. The 1968 Act itself, by way of 'strategic' structure planning, could with its 'broad brush' daub blight over a far wider area than did previous legislation, even though it might be a thinner coat. This might be acceptable if our laws in respect of compensation for injurious effects were adequate and equitable. The exposure of the decision-making process throughout all its stages could well extend the range of blight by the very consideration, through participation, of various alternatives. The uncertainty that goes hand in hand with the flexibility generated by structure plans could be aggravated by any delay in the preparation, and particularly publication, of local plans – a serious temptation to local authorities unwilling to determine and define the exact area and degree of blight.

While attempting to lay down the ground rules for participation and provide advice on how to interest and involve people in the process of planning, the Report has been criticized severely since publication. It is argued that the recommendations were firmly set within the existing framework of representative democracy, which left the power with the local authority who could still largely decide when, how, where and who participated. Further, that it failed to confront the central issues of political power and control in planning and also omitted to describe how the actual effectiveness of participation could be tested. Many viewed it as promoting participation as a public relations exercise, aimed at reducing opposition to planning proposals by raising the level of consent and thus absorbing those sections of society interested in planning into what has been termed as an 'internal validation process', with the community still regarded as some form of aggregate representing all constituent individuals and groups. Criticisms also related to certain specific proposals, such as the notion of community forums, which were thought to be mere talking shops, devoid of any executive function and a potential focus for extreme political activism; and the community development officer, who was seen to fall between the two stools of being neither one of 'them' nor one of 'us'. Probably the greatest single mistake made by Skeffington was in identifying the final stage of the plan formulation process, that where a statement of preferred alternatives is produced, instead of the preceding stage, where available choices are identified, as the principal point of participation. It has been suggested that instead of trying to graft public participation onto existing decision-making machinery, Skeffington should have tackled the basic problem of how local government operates and sought remedies relating to a new relationship between councillors, officers and the public.

Although the government accepted the findings of the Skeffington Committee they only found limited statutory recognition in those parts of the 1969 Housing Act concerned with general improvement areas, and administrative presence in a number of advisory circulars produced by the DoE. The idea of establishing community forums was quickly dropped and that of appointing community development officers discarded in 1973.

Nevertheless, some communities set up their own forms of

independent local representation, but many, such as the renowned Golborne Neighbourhood Council, foundered because they were unable to influence key issues such as housing and planning, had limited finance for community initiated schemes, and lacked any statutory power in respect of local issues, and the forging of close links with local authorities frequently led to an alienation of the majority of residents.

An appraisal

The act of participation embraces a wide range of occasions and varies according to both type and scale of activity, from protest about a proposed third London airport, for example, to that surrounding a single property issue. Some critics of participation maintain that it has slowed down the planning system, has weakened the position of planning within government, reflects particular disillusionment with local authority administration, and is equally unrepresentative and partial in its own way by invariably favouring a vociferous and articulate minority. Conversely, advocates of adopting participatory procedures argue that properly applied it improves the image of planning held by the public, produces better decisions, facilitates the implementation of proposals, and not only represents the spirit of true democracy but actually provides a healthy and educational activity for the participants.

Apart from other strictures regarding the preoccupation by many authorities with the techniques and procedures of participation, and a neglect of monitoring the eventual effectiveness of public consultation, the debate about the respective merits and demerits of formal participation within a statutory or administrative process devolves around the divergent concepts of conflict theory and consensus theory. On the one hand, it can be said that society changes and develops as a consequence of conflict, with the degree and effectiveness of change being dependent upon the issues at stake and the relative power of the parties involved; whereas on the other, the avowed object of participation, implicitly or explicitly, is to achieve agreement. Statutory procedures thereby aim at consensus while local interest groups usually represent a conflict approach towards participation.

Looking at the statutory development planning process, both structure plans and local plans have been the subject of criticism.

Structure plans, whose participatory exercises are supervised by the DoE, have attracted disapproval because of their alleged vagueness and ambiguity, the complexity of the issues presented, the lengthy approval period, the remoteness of their application, the partiality demonstrated towards certain organized middle-class groups, the late stage at which consultation has taken place, the limited and un-imaginative dissemination of relevant information, the selective and inquisitorial nature of examinations in public, and the bureaucratic presentation of case at public meetings. Too much criticism is perhaps unfair, for structure plans are not instruments ideally suited to participation at an individual or neighbourhood level and a great deal of constructive consultation has taken place in the preparation of structure plans between organized groups from trade, commerce, the professions, the conservation lobby and like areas of vested interest. Among recommendations for improvement, however, are that better use of the media could be made, exhibitions could be mounted at more attractive and convenient locations, meetings could be arranged in a clearly discernible sequence and not at isolated inter-vals, greater efforts should be made to ensure that a representative cross-section of the community is involved, the idea of neighbour-hood group meetings might be more successful than larger community forums, consultation and report should not end with the conclusion of a meeting, and the atmosphere at examinations in public should be less formal. Sensibly it would seem that a more significant approach towards participation and the fuller involve-ment of individual viewpoints can take place at the local level of planning, and, to this end, it is thought more appropriate to assess the criteria by which effective participation can be judged at that scale, than simply list the criticism which has been passed.

Criteria for effective participation

Certain circumstances have been shown to be especially conducive to the process of participation, such as the existence of a particular issue or policy affecting a local group, a readily identifiable physical area, the presence of a professional element in the community, a sympathetic and not defensive attitude by the local authority, and a good local community organization. Given these circumstances a number of criteria can also be established from experience of participation with community groups over the past few years upon which the likelihood and degree of success can be judged:

What is the proportion of the total population belonging to the local group being consulted? Naturally the larger it is the more effective is the involvement.

What is the degree of cross-sectional representation? It is necessary to ensure that the full range of local views are heard.

What is the number and quality of the suggestions made by the group? This is largely a function of the time and effort expended. Also, how many suggestions are reasonable and relevant and intended to be helpful?

How many demands made by the community are actually met by the authority? Participation is discredited if reasonable responses are not acted upon.

How adequately are proposed plans and policies explained to the community? Good communication has frequently been the missing link in participatory exercises.

How do councillors and officers respectively respond? Many elected representatives and professional planners feel threatened by involvement with community groups, sense that their authority might be undermined or resent changing established procedures.

How much feedback is provided? Again, participation quickly loses credibility if no results from consultation are seen, and no reports on action taken, or not taken, received.

What level of mutual understanding is achieved? Participation is essentially a two-way process designed to be jointly instructive to the needs and problems of each party.

Was the local group automatically consulted? Participation has usually proved far less successful when the community group was not initially approached and was left to take their own initiative.

Is participation seen to be on-going? Where an authority are obviously pursuing a one-off involvement community groups are justly sceptical and reluctant to co-operate fully. Continuity tends, therefore, to make the contributions of the community more positive and helpful.

Public participation is all too often synonymous with the mounting of exhibitions, the display of colourful maps and magnificent models, the delivery of professional talks, the showing of informative films, the holding of public meetings, and the carrying out of questionnaires. These techniques, valuable in their own way, provide but a partial approach to the problem. Citizen involvement needs to be more closely associated with the identification of interest groups and the actual making of decisions that affect the local community, as well as consultation, education and information. It is perhaps worthy of note that the most vociferous and active citizens, those who tend to involve themselves in participation, are normally quite capable of representing themselves in any case. The problem is to stimulate concern amongst the 'silent', unrepresented, majority.

Planning aid

The complexity of the planning process, together with the technical nature of many planning decisions and the highly legalistic procedures by which adverse planning decisions are challenged, has given rise to the concept of planning aid during the 1970s. Following the lead given by the legal profession, it is a means whereby members of the public may obtain expert information and advice about planning matters which personally impinge upon them, and sometimes obtain professional representation on their behalf at inquiry or appeal. As implied there are a number of different aspects to planning aid; it may consist of general advice about proper procedures or prevailing policies, specific advice about a particular planning problem, formal consultancy involving a technical service, or advocacy on behalf of an individual or client group to a local authority or public inquiry. Although many professional planning officers have frequently assisted local people or groups on a personal basis, it is only since the early 1970s that any formal provision of planning aid services have been available. Perhaps the best known agency has been the Town and Country Planning Association's Planning Aid Service, which was founded in 1973 and has handled several thousand cases over the intervening years. Some of these cases have been full-scale policy campaigns such as the Association's own representation at the notorious Windscale Inquiry. They have aimed to shift their emphasis away from giving official technical representation towards supplying an educational programme that will help people to help themselves in planning procedures, thus avoiding recourse to expensive professional advisers.[1] But in circumstances where technical expertise is required they concentrate on advising people how to make the most effective use of their advisers, especially by explaining to them how to instruct and how to agree fees. Several 'planning shops' have successfully operated along similar lines in Scotland for some years, and a number of planning aid centres have been opened in this country, often as a supplementary service to a citizens advice bureau. Although it is perfectly possible to obtain legal aid to acquire technical advice for representation at inquiry, the procedure is tortuous and the means test constraints severe. There has been pressure to make more public funds available to assist individuals and voluntary groups in the hire of expert advice, and one suggestion towards finding the additional finance has been the levying of a charge on applications for planning permission. A cynical note must be struck, however, for with all the mention of 'expert advice' it is usually detailed assistance on matters of planning law, compensation, valuation and the physical condition of buildings that is required; while many might be eager, it is possible to ask, how many planners are suitably versed in such questions?

Community action

Society, however 'democratic', is clearly not equal, nor could it realistically aspire to be, but the hints and promises of participation, involvement and consultation lead many to expect a greater role in the decision-making process. When this does not happen in the way it was designed to, the reaction on the part of those who are in authority and are formulating the participatory processes is to put the lack of enthusiasm and involvement down to apathy, averring that the democratic channels are open but not being used. Over the past decade or so there has been a swelling tide of political opinion holding that in reality these avowed channels are not effectively open to all, nor do they properly provide culverts that lead to any reservoir or power or decision-taking. There has, therefore, been an upsurge in what has become known as 'community action', which, while linked with participation, could rightly be described as an alternative to it – and relating back to the aforementioned concepts of consensus and conflict theory, provides a conflict antithesis to participation's consensus.

Community action has also been called 'grass roots radicalism', whose essential ingredients are social conflict, some kind of geographical or spatial definition, an entirely non-institutional ethos, and a vituperative attitude towards local government. Alternatively, it has been defined as 'the field of public activity wherein citizens utilize all methods of overt protest available to them in order to register their own interests with those in power by inducing conflict with bureaucratic domination'.[2] Many might detect more than a smack of Marxist philosophy. In its widest form, however, it is not restricted to what is loosely called 'working-class' activism, for it also extends well into the community-related activities of the middle-class, where many of its most notable successes have been witnessed. Nevertheless, the expression has attracted a limited currency in planning circles by becoming virtually synonymous with some form of urban class struggle. In a field riddled with political polemic, and where conjectured theory is so often at odds with known practice, a refreshingly succinct, if somewhat prosaic, summary of the aims of community action has been coined: ' It is about attempting to redraw the rules of the power game to the advantage of those who have hitherto been the losers'.[3] It is thus an ambition to alter the distribution of power based upon an equal assumption that those in ascendant authority will attempt to preserve the advantages of their partial position and safeguard their own vested interest – the natural game of life.

The examples of community action in operation are becoming more and more numerous; some are transient and relate to a particular passing issue, others are represented by the formation of continuing groups. Among the most familiar movements are the various organized housing squatter groups throughout the country;[4] other notables include the Notting Hill Community Workshop, the Gairbraid Housing Committee in Glasgow, and, at the time of writing, the Moncrieff Community Association. One of the features of community action is the emergence of what can almost be described as a new profession – that of the community worker. Momentarily it is sometimes interesting to contemplate how some of the young intellectuals, students and radicals helping to organize communities are viewed by the community on whose behalf they act.

Few would deny the benefits of community action, however, for undoubtedly it serves to ameliorate the conditions of the dis-advantaged, promotes a wider distribution and exercise of power, elicits information from those frequently diffident in communicating, assists in educating the community as to their rights and responsibilities and, perhaps above all, makes those in power and authority more accountable and aware. A modest purpose neatly summarized by the view that

It will not build the houses, end the poverty, or whatever, but the effort may have justification elsewhere in providing a challenge to national and local policy makers and a bid for public opinion in a world where those who cannot make their voices heard or their muscles felt are very liable to neglect.[5]

21 Planning and land values

In a society of ever-accelerating social, economic and technological change, a complex and sophisticated urban pattern is bound to evolve. Inherent within this structure are the cross-currents of conflicting personal, political and philosophical pressures. Perhaps the principal area where these opposing forces collide is that concerning land. The disputatious elements of tenure, proprietary interest, speculation and social need have entangled to produce a monstrous legislative morass, riddled with anachronism, befuddled by anomaly, and founded upon obscure theory.

Private and public land uses, though related and interdependent, vie for dominance, and though the value of one is inextricably bound up in the fate of the other, they lie in uneasy harmony, even in the planner's presumed dispassionate design.

Land value

The initial study of the concept and development of the theory of land value originally dealt almost exclusively with North America. The problems implicit in managing the wealth that accrues from land, and the implementation of a social and economic system that administers the equities of land ownership, and reconciles the public and private interest, are very much more related to our own experience and circumstance in the United Kingdom.

Concern with land and its associated value dates back to the eighteenth century and has its origins in David Ricardo's theory of agricultural rent. Ricardo, himself a man of considerable property, pointed out that land as a factor of production has two unique characteristics. First, it is limited in quantity, and second, its existence is fortuitous, being a free gift of nature and owing nothing to man's enterprise. The monetary return to the owner was due, therefore, to demand and not to his individual labours. The different values on varying plots of land was caused by an intrinsic qualitative advantage, for in his view the 'corn was not high because rents were high, but rents were high because corn was high'.

Von Thünen, a German economist and incidentally another wealthy landowner, echoed Ricardo's analysis and developed it a stage further by demonstrating that the yield from land was not simply a function of fertility or fortune but was also dependent upon the distance and transport costs to the market. Land in close proximity to markets would be used intensively and in connection with those products having high transport costs and demanding centrality. Von Thünen thus showed that rent more usually arose out of a locational, rather than an intrinsic, quality of the land and this advantage with regard to a market only exists because someone has created the market.

This is even more clearly demonstrated when one examines the relationship in terms of urban land, for where Von Thünen and Ricardo were principally concerned with agricultural land, all plots in a given urban area are of approximately the same quality, their function being basically that of support. Probably the earliest, and still one of the most succinct, analysis of the determination of urban land values was that set forth at the turn of the century by R. M. Hurd who asserted that 'since value depends upon economic rent, and rent on location, and location on convenience, and convenience on nearness, we may eliminate the intermediate steps and say that value depends on nearness'. Thus the pattern of urban structure is largely a result of a continuous struggle to maximize proximity or accessibility and minimize friction or transportation. In combination these forces aim to minimize cost, thus producing a situation where all urban activities compete for sites where costs are lowest. This process of competition, and resultant 'bidding' that takes place in such a climate, leads, in an unrestricted market, to the activity which can most successfully exploit the locational attributes of a particular site, obtaining and occupying it. In effect these activities are 'bidding' away their economic rent, and it is the level of economic rent that determines the level of land values.

The very purpose of town planning, however, is to ensure that the welfare, efficiency and productivity of the community as a whole is maximized, not just the return to a particular activity on a particular site. The regulation, intervention and guidance exercised on behalf of the community through its planning power establishes the nature and degree of accessibility and the location and strength of markets. This is especially true in this country where land is a scarce commodity, suitable and available undeveloped land is virtually non-existent, and the majority of urban growth takes place within the city through the process of redevelopment. In such circumstances, therefore, where the economic rent accruing from land is largely publicly controlled some will gain while others lose.

Betterment/worsenment

It is first advisable to explain the terms *betterment* and *worsenment*, and clarify the relationship between them. Betterment is the increase in the value of land which accrues to the owner of that land as a result of the action of others, often public authorities. Where a decrease in the value of land due to the action of others occurs it is described as worsenment, and on those occasions when payment is made to mitigate the hardship of this loss it is described as *compensation.* The philosophy that underlies the contentious concept of the collection of betterment stems from the notion that being a community-created value it is fortuitous or unearned; moreover, large portions of it must be rendered up to ensure adequate measures of compensation are made available to alleviate the incidence of worsenment. The philosophical and political arguments are lengthy, tortuous, and beyond the scope of this text. They are, however, cogently summarized by Palgrave in his *Dictionary of Political Economy*; he defends the recovery of betterment as follows:

. . . that persons benefited by public expenditure should contribute to such expenditure to the extent of the increased value of their property, and this not only if the improvement effected by the local authority was carried out for the purpose of conferring a benefit on such property, but also if the resulting benefit was purely accidental, the expenditure having been undertaken for a totally different purpose.

Although certain individual and locally applied attempts to collect betterment were made in the murkier undocumented depths of the Middle Ages, and again in 1662 by Charles II, who attempted to recover a portion of what was then described as 'melioration' regarding the increase in value due to London street-widenig schemes, the recent legislative history can be traced back to the advent of the rail-building boom of the last century.

   With the widespread application of compulsory purchase powers, and the general incorporation with acquisition of a standard code for compensation embodied with a common practice of awarding an extra 10 per cent or more above normal purchase price to account for the 'forced sale', there came a realization of the increases in land values elsewhere as a result of public undertakings and a pressure for collection. It was not until 1895, however, and the Tower Bridge Southern Approach Act of that year, that any betterment provisions were enacted. The scheme was very limited and merely allowed the London County Council to make a levy on the annual increase in value of properties immediately benefiting from the authority's road improvement works. It was also unsuccessful.

There were several other similar Acts which found their way on to the statute book around the turn of the century, while at the same time there was a strong current of feeling in favour of the introduction of some form of site value rating which failed to find sufficient parliamentary support. In 1909, however, the first comprehensive attempt to tackle the vexed question was included in the Housing, Town Planning etc. Act which permitted local authorities to impose a 50 per cent betterment levy on properties that had benefited as a result of one of their planning schemes. The following year saw the introduction of a far more sophisticated and comprehensive measure under the auspices of the 1910 Finance Act which introduced four types of duty on land, which were:

1 *increment value duty*, a levy of 20 per cent on the increase in value of land upon conveyance
2 *undeveloped land duty*, at the rate one half-penny in the £ every year on the site value of undeveloped land
3 *reversion duty*, a tax of 10 per cent payable by the lessor on the value of the reversion at the end of the lease
4 *mineral rights duty*, 5 per cent p.a. on mineral working rents.

Owing to the problems of valuation and administration, all four were abandoned by 1920.

All this time the courts were awarding the '10 per cent bonus' to allow for forced sale in cases of compulsory purchase. In 1919, however, the Acquisition of Land (Assessment of Compensation) Act introduced the 'six basic rules' which still form part of the procedure by which compensation is assessed. The main effect was to abolish the 10 per cent rule and establish open-market value as the appropriate level. The Law Society have recently advocated a return to the pre-1919 situation, a clear admission, perhaps, of our failure to adequately reconcile proprietary interests and returns from land with the requirements of comprehensive planning.

Until 1947 the only other major change in the provisions of the 1909 Act was the raising of the rate of levy from 50 per cent to 75 per cent by the Town and Country Planning Act 1932. In 1943, however, an expert committee under the chairmanship of Lord Justice A. A. Uthwatt produced a report on compensation and betterment which still represents probably the most exhaustive study on the problem to date. The principal recommendations were:

that the development rights in undeveloped land should be vested in the state. All future land required for development would be compulsorily purchased at a value reflecting its existing use, and leased back at full open market value, thus recouping betterment.

if the land was 'dead ripe' for development, plans having been prepared for it, it should still be acquired by the state but compensation would be full development value

developed land would only be acquired as and when necessary for planning schemes. The level of compensation would be assessed at full open market value as at 31 March 1939, thus, hopefully, discouraging excess speculation

a levy, for example 75 per cent, would be imposed upon all increases in the value of land as from a particular date, with five-year revaluations

central government grants should be made available to local authorities to assist in the redevelopment of central areas.

In making their recommendations the Committee had taken account of several problems that surround the issue of betterment/worsenment. First, defining the amount of the increase in the value of land that was attributable to direct public policy, and not market forces, was problematical. Second, the valuation of respective interests was difficult. Third, if compensation was to be paid for restriction, development might 'shift' elsewhere, and so one authority might collect betterment while another was forced to pay worsenment. Fourth, if compensation was to be made in full for restriction in development, the actual worsenment might 'float' over many properties and owners' claims would exceed actual damage. For these reasons the recommendations have a pragmatic rather than philosophical approach to the problem.

The 1947 Town and Country Planning Act, which draws heavily from the Uthwatt report, and a White Paper *The Control of Land Use* published in 1945, has become established as a major landmark in land use planning, and is exhaustively documented elsewhere. In

order only to achieve continuity, therefore, the principal enactments
are listed below:

planning was made subject to central control
all development rights were vested in the state
planning permission was required for all development, and a charge
   was made on the difference between the existing use value, and the
   developed value, of land
existing use value was established as the basis of compensation for
   compulsory purchase
a *global fund* of £300 million was set up to compensate those persons
   who lost existing development value. The total sum claimed
   amounted to £376 million, which after allowing for 'floating' value
   would appear to be a remarkably accurate estimate.

For a number of reasons, including the shortage of materials, and the
general restriction of development, as well as the 100 per cent development charge, the land market was stultified following the 1947
Act. A return to Conservative government resulted in the Town and
Country Planning Acts of 1953 and 1954, which abolished the
development charge, extinguished the global fund converting the
claims for loss of development rights into unexpended balances of
established development value, but anomalously still restricted the
compensation for compulsory purchase to existing use value only.
This anachronistic and manifestly unjust state of affairs whereby a
dual level of values existed side by side was rectified by the 1959
Town and Country Planning Act which re-established an open-
market value for land compulsorily acquired. This Act was
subsequently consolidated in the 1961 Land Compensation Act,
which still prevails.

The Land Commission

Arising from a pledge in a Labour party policy document *Signpost for
the Sixties* a second post-war attempt to resolve the land question
came into operation on 6 April 1967, with the setting up of the Land
Commission. The two main objectives of the Commission were first,
to ensure that the right land became available at the right time for the
implementation of national, regional and local plans; and second, to
ensure that a substantial part of the development value created by the
community be returned to the community and that the burden of the
the cost of land for essential purposes was reduced. The Land

Commission was a central government agency set up to act as a kind of national property dealing company assisting developers, particularly small private housebuilders, to obtain land in areas of high demand, and also to charge a betterment levy of initially 40 per cent on all transactions resulting in a realization of development value. Unlike the 1947 Act, therefore, the Land Commission Act allowed vendors to retain a substantial portion of development land to encourage willing disposition, although the intention was to increase the level of levy to 45 per cent then 50 per cent and even higher. The Commission possessed only selective powers of compulsory acquisition, for land had either to have a substantive planning permission or be designated for certain specific purposes. Planning permission could, however, be sought by the Commission if one of a number of acceptable purposes could be demonstrated which expedited the process of satisfactory development. Land purchased by the Commission did not have to be sold immediately. It could be serviced, improved and then disposed of by sale, lease or tenancy, and while normally it had to be sold for the best possible price, the Commission also had powers to dispose of land at less than market value on what were described as concessionary Crownhold terms for housing purposes. In the event these special powers were never used.

The total amount of land purchased by the Land Commission between 1967 and 1970 was only 1134 ha, most of which was acquired in areas of slack demand, and only 137 ha were resold. Over the same period a gross sum of £71 million was assessed for betterment levy and £47 million collected. At the time, the main criticisms directed at the Act were:

Too little land, and of the wrong sort, was acquired.

Land was held off the market by vendors unwilling to incur betterment levy.

The Commission frequently found itself in conflict with local planning authorities.

It was unsatisfactory that the final decision upon planning matters where there was disagreement between the Commission and local government was vested in the same Minister.

Betterment levy was inflationary, increasing rather than reducing the price of land.

The provisions of the Act were too complicated.

To all these criticisms counter-arguments can be advanced along the lines that: too short a period was allowed to test the performance of the Commission, during which period too much was expected; no evidence can be shown that land was held off the market; conflict with some local authorities was not only inevitable, but even desirable with the more recalcitrant councils; joint ministerial responsibility could be a positive advantage, and might avoid delay; the levy would be unlikely to be inflationary once supply was increased; and that such a piece of legislation was unlikely to be simple, if it was also to be effective. Suffice it to say that if the Land Commission had benefited from a longer period of operation, better ministerial leadership, and less sanguine political pundity, and had been divorced from taxation responsibilities, it might have fulfilled a valuable role as a land dealing agency to this day.

The community land scheme

A third major attempt to deal with the problem of land values and tenure was introduced by the White Paper *Land* (Cmnd 5730) in 1974, and again promulgated twin aims, first of enabling the community to control the development of land in accordance with its needs and priorities, and second of restoring to the community the increase in the value of land arising from its efforts. The lesson of divorcing planning and fiscal measures had, however, been learnt, and the Community Land Act 1975 and the Development Land Tax Act 1976 were separately enacted to achieve the stated aims.

In advancing the notion of 'positive planning' as being central to the spirit of the community land scheme and affirming the view that market forces do not, of themselves, arrive at satisfactory solutions regarding the use and development of land, it was also argued that land was the planners' resource and that they, on behalf of the community, were restricted by the proprietary nature of present land ownership. A contrary case can be put that land is not the planners' resource but rather the developers', and that land ownership does not automatically lead to development. Moreover, high land values are not necessarily a deterrent to development, but more a reflection of the need for it. Whatever the respective merits, the Community Land Act came into operation on April 6th, 1976, known as the *first appointed day,* when local authorities were charged with the duty of considering the desirability of acquiring 'relevant' development land over the proceeding ten years, and given the power to purchase land suitable for development. It was intended that as time went by and local authorities gained experience in the field of land acquisition, management and disposal, this power would become a duty, area by area and sector by sector. While local planning authorities were designated as the proper authorities for operating the scheme in England and Scotland, in Wales the responsibility was vested in a newly created body, the Land Authority for Wales, whose future remains undecided at the time of writing.

With the return of a Conservative government in 1979 committed to repeal the Community Land Act it seems senseless to recount the detailed provisions of the scheme, but the following synopsis should serve to outline the most salient features.

1   Three stages to the full implementation of the scheme were envisaged. From the *first appointed day* local authorities could, but did not have to, acquire relevant development land. Then as time went by certain incidents of relevant development would be designated by a 'relevant date order' served by the Minister, by kind and by locality, when authorities would be obliged to purchase land. After these orders had been served across the entire country on all forms of relevant development the *second appointed day* would be declared when all authorities would have a duty to acquire all development land, and at existing use value.

2   Three categories of development were identified: *exempt development,* being minor proposals which would always remain outside the scope of the Act; *excepted development,* of a more significant nature but still not normally suitable for public acquisition, and while authorities could purchase land for such development, there was no duty to do so, and, in fact, there was a presumption against; and *relevant development,* being the kernel of the scheme and covering all other forms of development, for which local authorities had at first a power, and were eventually intended to have a duty, to acquire.

3   Having prepared *land acquisition and management schemes* indicating the respective acquisition, management, planning, development and disposal functions of adjoining authorities in the light of their previous experience and existing expertise, local authorities were also expected to produce *land policy statements* showing a policy link between their planning objectives and their financially oriented rolling programme.

4   The *rolling programme* was intended to be an annually revised, eighteen-month programme of development land planning policy and funding based upon a five-year perspective, and submitted

before the yearly public expenditure review conducted by the treasury.

5   Relevant development land could be identified in one of two ways – either by designation by the local authority or by a privately initiated planning application, in which case it was known as an opportunity purchase. Following the first appointed day, but before the service of a relevant date order, all applications for planning permission on land suitable for relevant development were suspended until the local authority decided to purchase the land or abandon their right to so acquire, within certain time limits.

6   In selected areas, where there was thought to be a degree of planning and development uncertainty, an authority had the power to declare a *disposal notification area,* within which landowners considering the sale of their land for development had first to offer it to the authority.

7   Local authorities were allowed to purchase land net of development land tax before the second appointed day, never designated, after which compensation was to be calculated at current use value and not development value.

8   Any profits on the community land accounts were to be shared between the local authority concerned, central government and other needy local authorities.

9   The other prong of the community land scheme, Development Land Tax, remains in force, but at a lower rate of 60 per cent as opposed to the original levels of 66.67 per cent on the first £150,000 and 80 per cent on the remainder.

As with its predecessors there were a number of criticisms levelled at the community land scheme, such as: the objective of positive planning could be equally well achieved irrespective of who owns the land; the scheme discouraged development and stultified the land market; local authorities were the wrong agencies to operate the scheme; there was a built-in temptation to concentrate upon the more profitable sites which could equally well be developed by private owners; the rate of tax was too high and unfairly levied; the scheme increasingly became 'finance' as opposed to 'planning' led; and it was costly and time-consuming to administer. Once again, however, too little time was allowed to make a proper judgement about the scheme's performance and too few funds were available to promote its effective operation.

Land values and the inner city

In 1978 the Royal Town Planning Institute produced a report on land values and planning in the inner areas that set out to consider the extent to which land prices and other land market problems exacerbate inner city conditions and impede regeneration, and to make recommendations on what action should be taken, with special reference to the planning system. Their main conclusions can usefully be summarized as follows:

1   Great caution must be taken in accepting that the price paid in the market for a site measures its utility to the purchaser in any precise way, or its usefulness to society.

2   The notion of cost is clearly distinct from that of value in respect of land, especially where purchase is undertaken by a public authority who depend upon the basis of valuation laid down in the various statutes which constitute the compensation code.

3   The cost of inner city land to local authorities has in the past been considerably higher than the price it can command on disposal for such uses as industry and housing, as well as the notional price for the allocation to non-market uses such as open space and schools.

4   The gap between price paid and price fetched depends upon the context and location of the site; the planning assumptions upon which the valuations are based, some being out-of-date and unrealistic; the social objectives set and attained; and the cost of clearance and infrastructure provision, which may itself often exceed the price of green field sites.

5   The extent of private-sector demand for land in inner city areas depends upon the economic situation, the relative attractions of green field sites in physical and financial terms, and the efforts of the public sector to recreate confidence in the inner city.

6   A more active land market could result in the gap between public land assembly costs and the prices obtained upon disposal gradually being narrowed, and the selective land transactions of local authorities could assist this process.

7   Nevertheless, the cost of modernizing the infrastructure of the city would appear to be such that the physical regeneration of inner areas will remain a loss-making operation, and that this loss will continue to fall on the shoulders of local authorities as the main agents for renewal.

8   The compensation code causes serious financial difficulties to local authorities, since the cost at which they acquire land is largely determined by legal requirements that tend to push costs above what might be expected on the basis of the level of investment demand and the presence or absence of alternative purchasers.

From their investigations the RTPI working party responsible for the report made a number of recommendations. Some of these related to the community land scheme, with proposals for its improvement, and are now redundant, but among the others are:

1   In respect of compensation law, that 8th-schedule rights should cease to qualify as a basis for valuation once the formerly established use of the site had been discontinued for say five years; unexpended balances of established development value created under the 1947 Act should no longer be paid; and that more use should be made, where appropriate, of the provision of the Land Compensation Act 1961 whereby increases in acquisition cost due to the existence of a scheme can be avoided.

2   From the viewpoint of planning practice, all surveys and consultations undertaken as a basis for plans should include studies of the local land market including the attitude of investors and developers, influences and trends in the market, and ways of encouraging desirable private- and voluntary-sector contributions towards inner city regeneration.

3   With particular regard to plan implementation, inner city local authorities should review their total land holdings to see how they can best contribute to regeneration, publish their conclusions, and keep a record of their holdings open to public inspection. Similar public reviews and statements should be made by central government and statutory bodies in the area; and all these documents should be subject to co-ordinated planning between all the agencies concerned with a view to forward budgetary planning. Further, that local plan preparation should be more closely integrated with the production of programmes for land, infrastructure, environmental improvements, project appraisals and development briefs, and be reviewed continuously with them.

4   All price and transaction data for England and Wales presently held in the Land Registry should be made open for public inspection as occurs already in Scotland.

Alternative solutions to the betterment/worsenment problem

One immediate solution is to do nothing, but to allow the fortuitous and unrestricted reallocation of land values due to public authority activity, wherever and whenever it occurs. In respect of betterment this is virtually the current situation, with the burden falling upon no one but the planning agencies. The corollary to this, however, is that no compensation for worsenment should be paid, which is obviously politically, and perhaps morally, unacceptable. The authority responsible must therefore, in effect, pay a double cost. This policy must inevitably detract from efficient and effective land use planning. The remaining variety of positive alternatives ranges from the arbitrary application of partial taxes, charges and levies, to immediate and comprehensive nationalization of land. The following text briefly represents the majority of suggested reforms.

Nationalization

The principal problems that beset the viability of land nationalization as an acceptable solution are the political implications of endeavouring to change the whole character and tradition of land ownership and tenure in this country; and the financial repercussions implicit in the payment of vast sums of compensation that might be unleashed upon the economy in any transitional arrangements introducing nationalization.

1   *Total nationalization.* Despite the inherent financial difficulties, and the political stigma, it would at least provide an instant panacea to the betterment problem. The task of valuation, however, would be stupendous and there is no reason why the process should not be made more gradual.

2   *Unification of the reversion.* This would avoid the problem of massive payments of compensation, for it would convert existing freehold tenure into long leaseholds of approximately the same value, which upon subsequent effluxion would revert to the state. It thus has the same effect as nationalization but mitigates the political and financial impact. The Uthwatt Committee made reference to such a scheme in paras. 348 *et seq.* whereby

all land in Great Britain be forthwith converted into leasehold interests held by the present proprietors as lessees of the state at a peppercorn rent for such uniform term of years as may reasonably, without payment of compensation, be regarded as equitable, and subject to such conditions enforceable by re-entry as may from time to time be applicable under planning schemes.

3 *Lifing.* A scheme incorporating the unification of the reversion was proposed by *Socialist Commentary* in 1961 and described by Lichfield in *Land Values* in 1965. In this system all buildings would be surveyed and given a 'life' of up to 80 years depending upon their physical condition. Undeveloped land would be given a 'life' of 80 years subject to rent reviews and building leases granted upon development. During the statutory life of a building an increased rental would be levied by the state to reflect any change in value. Leases could be conveyed as would normally be the case, and for changes of use or upon redevelopment new leases could be arranged with revised rents. At the end of the lease the building would belong to the state, and compensation would be limited to the original site value plus 50 per cent of any site value increase. There have been many criticisms of this scheme and it probably compares unfavourably with the Uthwatt proposals.

Partial solutions to the betterment/worsenment problem

1 *The unification of development rights.* The purpose of this scheme is to vest all development value in the state while leaving land in the ownership of individual owners to change hands at existing use value, and was the basis of the 1947 Town and Country Planning Act. The chief criticism levelled at this method is the stultifying effect it can have on development, particularly if a change in political control and associated repeal is expected. Moreover, although all betterment is collected, the administrative problems concerning the assessment and payment of compensation are not reconciled.

2 *Land management and levy.* Similar to the recent Land Commission, whereby some central authority is charged with the responsibility of co-ordinating land development in this country. It would be vested with powers of compulsory purchase and exempt from any tax, charge or levy, thus placing it in a favourable position and capable of ensuring a steady supply of land coming on to the market, particularly in crisis areas. Once again worsenment is neglected and betterment collection is only partial, and the higher the level of levy the greater the discouragement of development.

3 *Site value rating.* This scheme is a principal plank in the party political platform of the Liberal Party. It has its roots in the Ricardian theory of economic rent, Adam Smith had proposed a tax on the

returns from land, John Stuart Mill put forward a programme for taxing 'the future unearned increase of the value of land', and in 1879 Henry George advocated a 'single tax on land', intended to replace all other forms of taxation.

Site value rating is essentially an annual tax on the site value of land. It is not levied on any improvement to the land, but is based on the optimal use to which the land can be put. It is, therefore, maintained that landowners would be encouraged to release vacant land because they are taxed on its development potential irrespective of whether or not the development has taken place. A similar argument is advanced in respect of redevelopment. It is also stated that the burden of the rate will fall upon the landowner since he is the person who receives the benefit of site value, but this idea is open to debate. The proportion of betterment collected depends upon the level of the site value rate decided upon. Revaluations would occur at appropriate intervals as with the present rating system, at least in theory. In one guise or another this approach has been adopted in New Zealand, Australia, Jamaica, Denmark and South Africa.

The major difficulties inherent in such a scheme are as follows: the revaluations tend to be postponed; the valuation task might be extremely complex, although the Whitstable study undertaken in 1964 to test the viability of site value rating proved otherwise; the decision as to optimal use might be open to question and review leading to uncertainty, blight and conservatism; and the problem of worsenment is poorly covered.

Part Four

Development and control

22 The development control system

A system of comprehensive control over all developments was introduced under the provisions of the 1947 Town and Country Planning Act which required for the first time that all future building development and any material change in the use of a building would, henceforth, be subject to the need for planning permission from a local planning authority. The twenty-five years which followed this radical step, however, did not see many advances made in respect of the measures adopted to implement it. As a result more and more shortcomings in the development control system became apparent. It was criticized as being too slow, too meticulous and lacking a uniform procedure. How long the calls for reform would have gone unheeded is a matter of conjecture, but matters came to a head with what has become known as the development control crisis of the early 1970s.

The development control crisis

Between 1962 and 1971, the number of decisions did not fluctuate very widely. The period was one of modest peaks and troughs with an annual average number of decisions made of around 428,000. In no year was the total more than 9 per cent higher or lower than this figure. The two years of least activity were 1962 (397,000) and 1969 (402,000) while the peaks occurred in 1964 (462,000) and in 1971 when 463,000 decisions were made. The annual average rage of increase from 1963 to 1971 was only 1.8 per cent.

Against this relatively peaceful background the years of 1972 and 1973 were traumatic. After the 1971 level of 483,000 decisions there was a spectacular leap to 615,000 in 1972, almost one-third higher than that recorded the previous year (itself the highest for ten years) and 45 per cent higher than the average for the preceding ten-year period, followed by a further rise (albeit of only 1.3 per cent) to 623,000 in 1973.

A breakdown of planning decisions by class of development reveals that the largest increases were in the two categories of 'residential – new development and redevelopment' (up 87 per cent in three years) and 'all other classes' (up 69 per cent). By comparison, the number of industrial and storage/warehousing decisions actually declined, the number of shop decisions rose by only 11 per cent, and the number of office decisions rose by 23 per cent.

Unfortunately, the government statistics provide no breakdown of the 'all other classes', which account for over a quarter of all decisions, but it seems probable that a major factor was the rise in the number of house extensions and conversions at about this time.

Over the same period the proportion of planning applications which were refused rose from about 15 per cent in 1969 to about 20 per cent in 1972. The refusal rate in fact increased in all classes except two (health/welfare and amusement/recreation) which perhaps indicated a general tightening up of development control over these years. However, it is evident that the refusal rate rose faster in some categories than in others. Thus the percentage of applications for new residential development which were refused rose from twenty-four to thirty-two, and for office development from about eleven to sixteen. The increasing number and proportion of decisions which were refused put an increasing strain upon the Department of the Environment, since it led to an upsurge in the number of planning appeals. In 1971 the number of appeals determined amounted to 9818; in 1972 it rose to 14,808. During the first half of 1973 the number of appeals lodged was 80 per cent higher than during the first half of 1972, and by mid 1973 the backlog of undecided appeals totalled 15,000. As a result, the time between an appeal being lodged and an inquiry date fixed had lengthened considerably. By mid 1973 the gap was thirty-eight weeks on average, as compared with thirteen weeks two years previously.

Three factors combined to bring about this massive increase in planning applications. First, whereas funds for house purchase were restricted during the late 1960s, they became much more freely available in 1971; not only was it easier to borrow money, but the money itself was cheaper. Second, the rapid escalation of house prices (which on average doubled in little more than two years) coincided with a period of continuing inflation. Third, the 1969 Housing Act, which introduced higher grants for the improvement and conversion of older properties and extended their availability over a wider range of works, led to a significant increase in the number of applications for house conversions. Furthermore, The development control workload is determined not only by the volume of applications but also by the nature of the procedures which have to be followed, and in preceding years these had undoubtedly become more complex and time-consuming. One contributory factor was the growth in public consultation on planning applications urged on local authorities both by the government and by an increasingly articulate public, particularly by local residents' associations and community groups.

It must also be said that many development agencies took an optimistic, if not bullish, view of potential development opportunities, and excessive speculation led to even greater pressure upon planning control machinery. As a result of these difficulties and consequent criticism George Dobry, QC, was appointed in October 1973 to review the whole system of development control, including the arrangements for appeals, and to advise on the lines along which it might be improved.

The Dobry report

An interim report was published in January 1974 and a final report *Review of the Development Control System* in February 1975.

The reports endorsed the basic features of the established system in so far as these related to decision-making by local authority elected members, the exercise of development control within a framework of firm plans and policies (though with due allowance for special cases), preservation of a right of appeal to the Secretary of State, and retention of the planning inspectorate under the all-embracing shield of the Department of the Environment. Mr Dobry also appears to have been impressed by the line of argument used by many professional planners and amenity societies to the effect that the quality of decision is more important than speed, and that a reasonable time should be allowed to consider an application for a building which, once erected, may stand for 100 years.

The final report remains the most thoroughgoing piece of research on development control to date, examining the detailed operation of the system as well as proposing recommendations for reform. Its aims were to give greater freedom to harmless development, but, at the same time, guard against harmful development by retaining applications for all cases; separate from the main stream all applications which might cause harm; dispose of applications in the main streams by rapid and routine procedures; and apply the same approach to appeals. The principal recommendations contained in the report can usefully be summarized as:

1 Applications for planning permission should be divided into two categories. Class A applications should comprise all simple cases, all applications conforming to an approved development plan, development that only just exceeds that permitted by the General Development Order, and the approval of reserved matters where outline permission was previously granted under class A. Class B should include all other applications. Class A cases would be dealt with speedily and planning permission deemed to be granted if a decision was not made within forty-two days or transferred to class B within twenty-eight days. Class B cases would attract a time limit of three months but without the deemed consent procedure. In all cases strict compliance with the time limits would be demanded.

2 There should be a uniform procedure for dealing with applications, a model code, standard forms, a single procedure for publicity, time limits for consultations should be enforced, and quarterly returns should be made by local planning authorities to the Department of the Environment recording their processing of applications.

3 In cases of special significance applicants should submit an 'impact study' describing the proposal in detail and explaining the likely effects upon its surroundings.

4 Meetings with applicants should be more productive with a greater use of committee interviews, section 52 agreements and independently chaired meetings.

5 Local planning authorities should distinguish more clearly between grounds of refusal in principle and objections of detail capable of resolution by negotiation; in class B cases there should be a statutory duty to give reasons for a deemed refusal; and upon refusal of a permission the applicant might be given the right to a hearing.

6 As the distinction between outline and detailed planning permission was unclear and inflexible there should be four types of application – outline, illustrative, detailed and guideline.

7 A stamp duty or charge for planning applications should be considered.

8 Control of detailed design should be retained but facilitated by greater use of design guides and briefs.

9 More delegation to subcommittees and officers must take place.

10 Only minor amendments to the General Development Order should be made but more use of article 4 directions should occur.

11 Better communication between planning authorities and the public should be encouraged by better use of the media, educational promotion, more extensive co-option, involvement of parish, community and neighbourhood councils, establishment of information centres, and the introduction of a planning aid scheme.

12 Appeals should also be divided into two classes along similar lines to applications, and the appeal system should be streamlined with more accent upon written representations.

Despite qualified support from most quarters few of the major recommendations proposed by the Dobry report were enacted. Times had, however, changed between the commissioning of the report and the final publication, and this was accepted by George Dobry who acknowledged in his introduction that the task had been complicated since his appointment by several factors, notably by the dramatic changes in the economic situation of the country as a whole; by the related fact that no increase in resources for planning could be expected in the near future; and by the uncertainty as to the effects of the proposed community land scheme.

The present position

Since the publication of the Dobry report there have been a number of other investigations into the workings of the development control system including a report of the Environmental Subcommittee of the House of Commons Expenditure Committee and a study by the Royal Town Planning Institute. Criticism still surrounds the process of development control, however, and some of the most common complaints can be listed as follows:

1 Delay remains the recurring theme of critics and while a tardy response on the part of planning authorities can sometimes be put down to a developer's poor presentation of an application or a legitimate bargaining device in negotiations, it is often caused by the dilatoriness of planning departments or inexpertly applied without an appreciation of the financial repercussions.

2 Counties and districts have still not sorted out certain and reliable development control schemes between themselves.

Duplication of effort and conflict of view has frequently resulted from a lack of county–district understanding.

3 The development plan framework is often inadequate for the needs of development control, and applications are decided on an *ad hoc* basis according to their peculiar merits or the current whims of the planning authority. As local plans are produced the situation improves but reliance is still placed upon non-statutory documents which lack a coherent base.

4 Many members of planning committees are not able to distinguish the significant from the trivial, and the proverbial town centre goes by on the nod while the rear extension is hotly debated.

5 Some local planning authorities are tempted to refuse politically contentious but properly acceptable decisions so that a sensitive decision is seen to be made at appeal and not by them.

6 Planning officers commonly resort to meaningless cliches in framing their grounds for refusal of planning permission and occasionally attach a number of make-weight reasons which are either irrelevant or wrong.

7 Many authorities strive for what they consider to be a perfect solution on an imperfect site, when almost any form of development would be an improvement.

8 There does not always appear to be a real appreciation of the economics of conservation resulting in an undue restriction upon the inclusion of commercial uses in many schemes of rehabilitation.

9 A more flexible attitude towards 'non-conforming' development is needed where employment could be retained or expanded.

10 Tension is often created between small firms and a local authority because of inadequate consultation, discussion and information.

11 General development orders and use classes orders are crude and insensitive instruments of control.

12 The appeals system remains lengthy, uncertain and expensive.

On the other side of the coin, however, it has been argued that since local government reorganization in 1974 a number of improvements have been made to the development control process within planning authorities. Larger teams of more qualified planning staff have been established in district councils. Better support services have been obtained which facilitate the administrative procedures involved in handling applications. A higher level of job satisfaction from working in development control departments has been perceived by planners, whereas previously it was frequently seen as the Cinderella of the profession. A closer integration of local plan and development control staff has been achieved, to the extent, in some authorities, of the same staff doing both jobs. The actual processing of applications has been better co-ordinated and the mechanics of administration have been improved by having one authority largely responsible for development control, committee cycles at frequent intervals, more delegated powers to officers and more specialist advice available to officers and members.[1]

At the time of writing in November 1979 a new Local Government Planning and Land Bill is proposed but already the Secretary of State has outlined a number of intended reforms, including placing the responsibility for all development control decisions upon district authorities; expediting the preparation and approval of development plans; charging for planning applications according to the size of the development; ensuring quicker decisions upon appeal and experimenting with instant decisions followed by a subsequent legal paper; relaxation of the General Development Order; and a speeding up of consultative and participatory procedures. The stated aim of the government is to change the accent of development control from negative to positive.

Common cases

Constant changes in legislation and administrative guidance make the field of planning law a positive labyrinth of statute and case law, a detailed examination of which is way beyond the scope of this book, and while a broad outline of the legal framework of development control is provided in a later chapter, it might be helpful to give a brief description of the major areas of dispute. In doing so, the following section draws heavily upon an excellent series of publications on planning appeals.[2]

Housing

By far the largest number of planning appeals relate to a refusal of planning permission for housing development. These cases can be conveniently grouped into edge of settlement, infill, open countryside, extension and alteration, and change of use developments.

Proposals for *edge of settlement* housing development range from a few units on a small site to a vast estate of several hundred dwellings. The most usual grounds for refusal are related to either broad policy or practical considerations. Arguments as to broad policy throughout the mid 1970s frequently centred around the provisions contained in DoE Circulars 102/72, 122/73 and 24/75 regarding land availability for housing and suitable densities for development. Rounding-off within a 'village envelope' to achieve 'the completion of a compact area of development by building up of vacant areas to conform with a logical and recognizable boundary'[3] is a common reason for permitting housing development, but where the scale or impact of the scheme is such as would cause social strain or a poor environment it can often be rejected. Development within an area of green belt is usually viewed with disfavour, but may occasionally be allowed where the site is already surrounded by buildings or of particularly poor amenity value. Land availability is invariably the most contentious issue at appeal, with local authority site identification at odds with that of the developer, but as the number of approved local plans increases so the likelihood of success on the grounds of conflicting assessments of availability diminishes. Practical considerations for the refusal of permission normally relate to such matters as the lack of social facilities, unacceptable levels of noise, inadequate means of access, excessive traffic generation on to overloaded road networks, insufficient sewerage and drainage services and inappropriate layout or design. Despite exhortations by central government, a characteristic of edge of settlement development proposals has been the large number refused because the density was thought to be too high although many of these applications prove successful at appeal.

Again, with *infill developments* the most common ground for refusal has been too high a density, and where this can be supported because the site would be overcrowded, out of character with the surrounding area, or burdensome upon the road system or other services and utilities, it may be upheld. The sensitive and least predictable area of development control is that of design. Where a housing scheme lies in, or close to, a conservation area, an area of outstanding natural beauty or an area with special features, or is manifestly out of sympathy with surrounding buildings, a strong case for strict design control exists. Otherwise it is debatable how far a local authority should scrutinize design. It frequently happens that a proposal to develop housing competes with alternative uses for the land such as open space, allotments or a road scheme, and much depends upon the circumstances of the particular case as to the outcome. Access is also an important consideration for infill sites, especially when an application is made in respect of 'backland' development, and road capacity, traffic generation, sight lines, speed limits, parking and lighting will all be taken into account in making a decision.

A vast number of applications are made in respect of isolated housing in the *open countryside,* most of which attract a refusal from local authorities, who, in turn, find substantial support from the Minister at appeal. Policies for strictly regulating housing in the countryside have become progressively more rigorous over the past few years, whether proposals relate to new houses in green belts and areas of great landscape value or merely to the conversion of old farm buildings and rehabilitation of disused agricultural cottages elsewhere. The main justification for relaxing this strict control has tended to be that the dwelling would be used in connexion with farming, but even here the viability of the agricultural unit is closely investigated and a standard condition restricting occupation to an agricultural worker imposed.

Housing *extensions and alterations* cause a considerable amount of aggravation in development control, and, at the time of writing, the government are proposing to extend the provisions of the General Development Order so that fewer applications will be forthcoming from this category. The most common matters relate to development in front of the building line, development of roof spaces with dormers, side extensions, rear extensions, facing materials, windows, garages and access to the highway, but others such as car ports, pigeon lofts, stables, swimming pools and radio masts have all been the subject of regular control.

A number of appeals occur where occupiers wish to use part of their house or garden for *business purposes* and local authorities either refuse planning permission or serve an enforcement notice. The most typical instances are to do with light industry, professional offices, sales and repairs of cars, commercial storage, kennels, surgeries, child-minding and hairdressing, and the outcome of any appeal usually depends upon the nature, scale and degree of the activity. Noise, safety, visual intrusion, visitors, parking, deliveries, smell, local need and general disturbance are the normal criteria by which such cases are judged.

The other main area of development control in housing is the *conversion* of one dwelling house into two or more self-contained flats or use for multi-occupation. The location, nature and arrangement of the accommodation are the key factors in such cases.

Town centre shops

Apart from large-scale mixed-use planned shopping centres, which tend to be of such a special nature in specific locations that they are often treated as one-off schemes, the principal aspects of urban retail development control are those relating to large stores, infill shops, shop fronts and non-retail shop uses.

The main issues connected with the possible development of *large stores* are traffic, parking, design and the effect upon small traders. Proposals to erect in-town superstores or department stores frequently conflict with local authority policies towards traffic constraint and parking restrictions. Where suitable parking facilities already exist or can readily be provided, and the scheme is well placed in relation to the present and future major highway network, applications are more favourably received. It is likely, however, that where conflicts with commuter parking are feared, conditions regulating the opening hours and tariff charges will be imposed to ensure short-term visitors. Access for service and delivery vehicles, together with adequate unloading facilities, are also important transport considerations. Where the suggestion is to place a large store on the fringe of a town centre, traffic arguments might well work in its favour. An emotive issue in respect of the location of large stores is the possible effect they might have upon local small shops. The sheer volume and prominence of superstores, combined with the stark frontage they sometimes disport, can have too dominant an effect upon old high streets, although most multiple supermarket chains have shown a more sensitive approach towards design over recent years.

The attitude of most local authorities to individual applications for the development of *infill shops* in existing shopping areas is usually fairly sympathetic. Only where redevelopment in conservation areas is proposed, or a policy towards rear servicing might be breached, are problems usually encountered. Growth of employment, increased traffic and loss of residential accommodation can, however, be advanced as reasons for refusal, but require a clear case on the part of the local authority at appeal.

Unless changes to *shopfronts* are proposed within a conservation area, or are clearly in conflict with normal advertisement control, the Secretary of State is usually reluctant to oppose them on purely design grounds. Nevertheless, if the building is listed any shopfront would be expected to reasonably be in keeping with the appearance and character of the building.

Controversy has raged recently around the development of *non-retail shop uses* in high street locations, particularly building societies, estate agents, banks, insurance brokers, betting offices and launderettes. A spate of appeals dealing with applications from building societies have taken place over the past few years. The principal objection to them is that they create a 'dead frontage' in shopping streets, affecting pedestrian flow and the shopping efficiency, and are better grouped with similar commercial activities in an off-pitch business quarter. Until about 1978 local authorities were notably unsuccessful at appeal, but since then it would appear that a stricter appraisal is given to the effect of a building society branch office upon the continuity of shopping frontages and the town's trading potential. An unofficial quota system is often applied. Estate agents offices attract similar refusals to those of building societies, but the relative attraction afforded by their window display seems to mitigate in their favour. Likewise the activity generated by banks is often seen as sufficient reason for allowing their appeals in shopping streets. Betting offices on the other hand do not appear popular with local authorities, although it has been suggested that they are often refused on moral grounds dressed up as planning reasons.

Out-of-town shopping

Many of the advantages and disadvantages of *out-of-town* shopping have been discussed eleswhere. In respect of policy issuing from the Department of the Environment a great deal of uncertainty persisted throughout the 1970s as to the criteria by which large superstores situated on the outskirts of towns or in the open countryside would be assessed at application and appeal. Nevertheless, it has become clear from decisions at appeal that the Secretary of State is anxious to protect the green belt and safeguard the economic performance of existing town centres. The place of out-of-town superstores in the overall shopping hierarchy has, however, become accepted, as has their role in alleviating historic and congested city centres by the relocation of convenience goods shopping outside. Prematurity to the production of approved structure and local plans has been a frequently cited ground for refusal, otherwise applications are typically resisted for reasons of environmental intrusion, traffic, and shopping need and impact.

A number of applications for superstores on *industrial estates* have been made, but, owing to conflicting pressures on the road network, service roads and parking space, have generally been resisted.

The development of *district centres* based upon a supermarket but comprising a wider range of retail outlets and associated with an identifiable residential area are often received more favourably so long as social, economic, visual and infrastructure criteria are met.

The recent growth of retail sales from *industrial or warehouse premises* has not attracted much support from local authorities and the majority of appeals have been dismissed, commonly on the grounds that the land should be retained in industrial use, a poor environment for shopping is created, inadequate car parking facilities are available, a detrimental effect upon local and main shopping centres will result, or an unacceptable level of traffic would be generated. Where permission has been granted or appeals allowed it is usually because the goods involved are bulky, the type of sales are so limited or specialized that no precedent is created, there is a lack of suitable retail premises in the nearby town, or retailing is already established and no harm can be discerned.

Other out-of-town retailing activities which have attracted attention over the past few years have been the growth in retail sales from petrol filling stations, which is generally disapproved of; the sale of agricultural produce from farm shops, which, if home grown, is normally viewed as ancillary to the farming function, so long as reasonable access can be gained; the development of garden centres, sometimes linked to do-it-yourself centres, applications for which are again largely determined on traffic grounds; and the use of car parks, racecourses, sports grounds and the like for weekly markets, whose success mainly depends upon residential amenity and traffic problems.

Offices

It is even more difficult to generalize about office development than the other sectors described in this section. By and large, most appeals are decided upon their individual merits and against a background of regional location policy, the now defunct office development permit controls, local user conditions, scale and design. One of the most contentious aspects of office development, however, has been the desire to change the existing use of a building to offices. Those applications seeking to change from residential to office use have a low success rate at appeal, except in certain instances where it has been shown that such a conversion might preserve a listed building. Small shops also tend to be safeguarded from a change to offices.

Warehousing and industry

Because of rising unemployment, industrial development proposals have been greeted with comparative acclaim. Strong political pressures have frequently outweighed compelling planning arguments. The main considerations for *industry*, apart from the usual zoning traffic and infrastructure criteria, are noisy or noxious uses, although the Secretary of State will often seek to control potential pollution by means of conditions rather than refuse permission outright. Problems frequently arise over what actually constitutes industrial development where a change of use is involved, but the details of such cases are legally complex.

The more problematic cases usually refer to *warehousing*. Commercial storage proposals are far less enthusiastically received by local authorities than are industrial. This category of development covers not only purpose-built warehouses, but also the change of use of existing buildings to warehousing and the use of open land for storage. The relaxation of industrial development certificate control has reduced the number of applications for warehouse development made with an ultimate view of factory use, and with changing industrial processes and methods of distribution the relative employment ratios between warehouse and factory premises are not so sharply divided as they have been. Most commonly warehousing is rejected because of interference with residential amenity, the overloading of existing road networks, or inadequate access from the highway.

Minerals

This category is taken to include the tipping and disposal of waste materials as well as the extraction of minerals. Since the Control of Pollution Act 1974, however, the nature of materials to be tipped and the operation of tips are now the responsibility of the relevant waste disposal authority on receipt of an application for a disposal licence.

The principal considerations regarding mineral extraction and waste disposal are the degree of visual intrusion, length and duration of working, highway access, noise, fumes, alternative sites, landscaping after use, toxicity of materials and proven need. Many cases relate to applications for the extraction of sand and gravel, and the argument generally revolves around national aggregate requirements against environmental objections, with reference usually being made to the reports of local sand and gravel working parties, such as the Middle and Upper Thames Gravel Region Working Party, who establish areas of search and identify sites. At the time of writing an inquiry has just started into the proposal to mine coal in the Vale of Belvoir and the dichotomy of need and amenity is likely to be brought into even sharper focus.

Miscellaneous

Inevitably, the development control system attracts a wide variety of development proposals that do not fit easily into the foregoing categories or defy even the simplest generalization. This is exemplified by the field of *leisure and entertainment* where applications for hotels, pubs, restaurants, fast food shops, bingo halls, clubs and discotheques have produced a multitude of appeal cases, many of which have been determined on the grounds of either local amenity or traffic. Slightly less common, though frequently recorded, are cases relating to such sporting activities as playing fields, golf courses, sports centres, stables, rifle ranges, marinas, flying clubs and squash courts. Where the use of good farming land is involved the loss of agricultural value is normally weighed against the needs of recreation and the availability of alternative sites.

Similarly, where it is proposed to establish *caravans* in the countryside, the loss of agricultural land together with the degree of visual intrusion are the two most important considerations. Caravans have been responsible for a large body of appeals covering holiday homes, gypsy sites, residential estates, agricultural and other workers' accommodation, and winter storage.

Another prodigious category of appeals is that of *advertisements,* and shop signs, illumination, hoardings, for-sale boards, window displays, flags and garage advertisements have caused much dispute. Among other forms of development which have been the subject of frequent appeals are agricultural uses and buildings, hospitals, hostels, churches, tree preservation and listed building consent.

Again, it should be stressed that it is not possible to more than touch upon the general areas of policy in reviewing the most common cases experienced in the development control system, and a fuller exposition of individual cases can be found elsewhere.

Development briefs

Sundry interpretations have been placed upon the term 'development brief' by local planning authorities, depending on the type and complexity of the proposal, the respective ownerships involved, the time available for preparation, the relative attractiveness of the scheme, the resources of the planning authority and the recourse they have to consultants' advice.

A common definition might be that a development brief is a non-statutory written statement and site plan, sometimes with supporting maps and illustrations, indicating a local authority's policy and aspirations towards a specific site, or clutch of related sites, possessing development or redevelopment potential, outlining the probable constraints upon such development and the likely terms and conditions by which it will be approved and executed. Frequently the term 'development brief' is used interchangeably with that of planning brief; mistakenly, for it goes much farther. Whereas a planning brief is usually restricted to matters of planning policy and urban design, a development brief will normally have regard to the basis of tenure, the possible financial arrangements between the parties, the kind of development agency thought suitable to take responsibility for implementation, and the way in which they might be selected. Nevertheless, much of this text applies equally to both planning and development briefs. Neither should be confused, however, with design guides, which give general design advice across an entire planning area, although reference may be made in a brief to them.

In the main, most development briefs have been drawn up for commercial development, particularly town centre redevelopment schemes, where the privileged powers of land assembly open to local authorities, and the consequent position of landowner, has enabled them to impose conditions upon developers not normally available under planning legislation. This is not to say that they are not employed in the initiation and regulation of residential development, for a number of housing development briefs have been produced.

Apart from focusing a council's mind wonderfully upon the ingredients of successful development, the principal objectives of the development brief have been succinctly described elsewhere[4] as being to:

Give the local authority reasonable control over the form and content of the scheme.

Provide a clear basis for the design of the scheme on which developers can work.

Set out the main financial terms required by the local authority.

Clearly show the procedure to be adopted by the local authority in selecting their development partner.

Inform the developer of what plans and written material should be submitted.

Provide a common basis for comparing developers' proposals.

Minimize the scope for renegotiation after the tender date.

Generally, therefore, it can be said that the twin aims of any brief are to promote and control private development, whether independently conducted or in partnership. The list set out above, however, places most emphasis upon control, and it should be recognized that in many circumstances the promotional aspect is dominant, and a much more publicity-conscious approach is required where the development brief then assumes the role of a marketing document. Furthermore, in providing guidelines and establishing a framework for suitable development, it should be the goal of every brief to create a climate of confidence between public- and private-sector planning and development agencies, within which a higher degree of certainty means more expeditious procedures for everyone concerned, and thus, by avoiding abortive expenditure on unacceptable proposals, attains a greater level of profitability all round.

Planning process

While the preparation of development briefs occupies no formal part of statutory development planning procedures, the stage in the process at which they properly appear is naturally that of implementation, where strategic policies are translated into a more parochial land use context, and to this end a number of authorities use them as insets to local plans. Their position has been highlighted by the fashionable concern for 'positive planning' originally propounded by community land scheme legislation. Indeed, the only official mention of any significance made about development briefs by central government is contained in the subsequent guidance notes to that Act. It is also worth remembering that while many development briefs are prepared at the initiative of a local authority, many are produced as a reaction to a private planning application and can cause a certain amount of chagrin if undue delay or loss of development rights results.

Because of the comparatively precise nature of development briefs they are a useful instrument in drawing together local authority policies across a wide range of municipal interests, departments and services, thereby fostering the concept of corporate planning. Their physical orientation further facilitates discussion and agreements with other public-sector agencies outside the council's direct aegis such as those public utilities, transport operators, social services and other planning authorities which might retain an interest in any development proposition. Similarly, they have been much vaunted as vehicles for public participation, being site specific, reasonably clear and comprehensible in their form, and relatively revealing in the likely impact they will make upon the surrounding area. Though this may be true, to my mind it is imperative that a local authority completes all the necessary public consultations before it issues a final development brief, and should in preference attach an outline planning permission to it, as an act of good faith if nothing else.

Form and content

Both the form and content of a development brief will vary according to the circumstances of the case. Some of the most successful briefs have consisted of a few simple stencilled pages of information identifying the site, specifying the broad purpose envisaged by the council, and seeking offers from interested parties. Many are often too long, too glossy and too detailed. The very production of the brief seems to have overtaken the purpose for which it was prepared.

While the following list of suggested contents should be seen as neither exclusive nor exhaustive it might be borne in mind that in many situations the information would also be superfluous. Nevertheless, as a general guide an effective development brief will include some of the following matters:

Prevailing planning policy; a concise explanation should be given of how the brief relates to other planning documents for the area.

Site characteristics: a description of the boundaries of the site together with any topographic information such as known tipping, mining, flooding, subsidence or underground services.

Intensity of development: an indication of the suggested minimum and maximum superficial areas of such components as shopping, offices, housing, factories, warehouses and parking, together with perceived tolerances to allow for possible future expansion.

Development control standards: such as building heights, materials, distance between dwellings, carrying distances for refuse disposal, local user conditions, permitted noise levels, sunlight and daylight standards, and any other relevant parking and density standards.

Design standards: such as elevational treatment, roof pitches, disposition of building groups, open space, landscaping, integration of surrounding buildings, focal views, access points, highway standards, and reference to any relevant design guides.

Special features: some for inclusion, such as pedestrian segregation, certain types of shop or recreational facility; others for retention, such as notable trees, views or buildings.

Planning gain: where not included above, mention might be made to any 'tithes' the council seek to extract, for example housing accommodation in commercial schemes, off-site infrastructure works or civic amenities.

Disposal terms: including the contemplated period of any lease, expectation of ground rent, desirability of a premium, prospective equity share and anticipated intervals of review. A further consideration might be the developer's continuing responsibility for management and maintenance.

Financial support: with the complexity of public finance it is always helpful to try and indicate the possible sources of any loans, grants or other financial incentives that might be available, particularly in the field of industrial development.

Selection procedure: although this important aspect is dealt with in more detail below, the brief should always identify who can be approached for more information, which other bodies are likely to be involved and what steps must be taken by an aspiring developer.

Despite this relatively full list of contents it cannot be stressed enough that it is often very dangerous for planners to be too specific regarding the proposed details of a development. Not only may the market change, but it is conceivable that they might even have got it wrong in the first place. In any case, scope should always be left for the developer to exercise his market knowledge and innovative skills; because if the brief is really perfect in every detail there is no call for the involvement of an outside development agency, merely for funds. Conversely, it should be said that if the brief does not confer a sufficient degree of physical and financial certainty then subsequent valuations performed by competing development agencies can fluctuate so widely that the selected scheme might be chosen on the basis of a bullish ground rent rather than for its social or aesthetic merit. Moreover, such over-optimistic estimates can easily lead to renegotiation so that the local authority loses in the end anyway.

Selecting the developer

Several different formulae have been devised to select a preferred developer. At one extreme is an architectural competition between prospective developers contending against a financially oriented development brief prepared by the local authority and its consultants, while at the other is a financial competition based upon a similar brief, but with the accent upon design. Understandably the most usual answer is a combination of both, and a commonly adopted procedure aimed at attracting a wide range of development agencies, avoiding unnecessary and abortive work, ensuring an open-handed and equitable impression, and allowing the local authority to test the market and work-up the best solution, is as follows:

1   A preliminary outline brief is prepared in broad principle, the site is advertised in one of the property journals and potential developers are invited to make application registering their interest by a particular date.

2   From the total number of applications, which may be as many as fifty or more for an especially popular site, ten or a dozen are selected for interview. It is often advisable to choose a representative mix of agencies drawn up from large and small property development companies, financial institutions, construction firms and commercial operators so as to explore all possible opportunities. This interview stage binds no one, involves little expense by any party, and permits the local authority to sound out its ideas against the variety of commercial developers and learn from them.

3   Following these interviews a detailed development brief can be drawn up and a short-list of between three and six developers selected to tender against it, one or two of whom will invariably drop out. Most reputable developers are willing at this stage to bear the cost of preparing a full submission, even though the cost can quite quickly reach £10,000 and more, as the chances of success seem reasonably fair.

4   In determining the successful submission the council and their advisers will not only pay regard to the physical design and financial offer, but may also look to see if the reduced coterie of developers have achieved any pre-letting agreements or become otherwise associated with prospective occupants. Moreover, they can visit and examine previous schemes completed by the various applicants in order to judge their degree of experience and line of approach, as well as to take the opportunity of closely exploring their current financial position and probable collateral.

There are occasions when an open competitive tender or selective tender are inappropriate, and a negotiated deal with a single developer is struck. Such circumstances are, however, rare, and only usually occur where the developer concerned is already a substantial landowner of part of the site, where there is a strictly limited demand, or where the task is especially complex and the developer uniquely qualified. In this event it is normal for the local authority to prepare the initial development brief as before, but for the final detailed brief to be worked up together and recourse had to external consultants as confirmation of propriety or to resolve any disputes.

Enforcement

It has already been stated that the development brief is an informal non-statutory document and, therefore, has no status in law. For the terms of the brief, and any subsequent agreement made between the local authority and the developer, to be enforceable they must rely upon some other form of legal relationship drawn from planning, private, property or company law.

The most common method of enforcement is that provided under planning law through the system of development control. Withholding detailed planning permission upon the submission of reserved matters, or the attaching of conditions to either an outline approval or a detailed permission, are familiar controls to all those involved in the development process, as are the enforcement procedures available to ensure compliance. Although the statutory power exists for local authorities to impose such conditions 'as they think fit' it should be remembered that the courts have successively circumscribed this right, so that a planning condition must be certain, must not be manifestly unreasonable, must fairly relate to the permitted development, and must never require the payment of money. The efficacy of conditional planning permission is always slightly uncertain given the administrative character of the appeal system, but judicial thinking would appear to be moving against allowing a developer to challenge the validity of conditions once he had already been seen to accept them.[5]

Because of doctrinal difficulties associated with privacy of contract, whereby a contract is only enforceable between the original parties to it, and consideration, by which some *quid pro quo* between the parties must take place, contract law is not immediately the most suitable legal mechanism for enforcing a development brief. Moreover, the vague and descriptive nature of the brief is unlikely to be sufficiently precise to form the proper basis of a contract. Nevertheless, there exist several types of statutory contract which, when used alongside a development brief and prior to the grant of a full planning permission, can surmount these problems. Most notable of these are section 52 agreements made under the Town and Country Planning Act 1971, and agreements made under section 126 of the Housing Act 1974. Section 52 agreements, often called planning agreements, are made for the purpose of restricting or regulating the use or development of land and may impose obligations upon a developer that would otherwise be *ultra vires* in a planning condition. Being directly enforceable by the courts they also avoid the lengthy business of serving enforcement notices and conducting appeals. While they can clearly be enforced against negative covenants some doubt has been expressed regarding their binding effect on positive clauses, and though section 52 agreements have not been the subject of wide litigation it has been suggested that 'Provided that the main clear purpose of an agreement is to restrict or regulate use or development, that purpose may be achieved through positive or negative consequential or incidental terms'.[6] Since the introduction of the 1974 Housing Act, however, even positive covenants to carry out particular works in respect of land subject to a registered agreement may be enforced by the courts if specifically made under section 126, and they do not have to relate specifically to residential development.

The landlord and tenant relationship between local authority and developer, which results from many partnership schemes based initially upon a development brief, invokes the power to enforce agreements by reference to property law. While a straightforward building agreement will normally be used during the construction period of a development project, so that the local authority retains ready powers of repossession if for any reason the developer defaults, a lease will usually be granted upon completion. Its position as landlord then affords the local authority much more effective control over the use, occupation and management of a development than that provided by planning law, as well as conferring the right to sue for damages for any breach of contract, or even proceed for forfeiture in certain circumstances, not only against the original tenant but also against third parties to the contract, unless the terms are purely personal.

A much less common arrangement to secure the execution of a development brief undertaken in partnership between a local authority and private developer is the formation of a trust for sale. The principal advantage of a joint company to a local authority is that by creating a separate legal *persona* bureaucratic constraints are loosened and greater use can be made of private capital. Conversely, one of the main problems is the possibility of further delays in the process of development owing to the inherent conflicts of interest that might face the council in trying to serve both community and company. Similarly the trust for sale resembles a tenancy in common or vertical partnership arrangement, but is again better suited to parties sharing mutual interests and objectives, and more frequently employed for joint investment in the market rather than development in partnership.

The above summary of the various legal methods available to enforce the implementation of development based upon a brief is, of necessity, cursory and simplistic, but while the most appropriate means will depend upon the nature of the covenant to be enforced, the party it is intended to control, the length of time for which enforcement has to run and the degree of equity participation that is required, it should be appreciated that different methods will be applied to different parts of the same brief, as fit.

Problems

Experience has shown that one of the principal problems bedevilling action upon a development brief from the developer's point of view is the changing nature of local government policy. It is, therefore, important to ensure that full and proper public participation and consultation with other agencies concerned with the execution of a project have been conducted and agreement reached before the final detailed brief is produced. Another obstacle that impedes progress and deters developers is the over-elaborate form and content of so many briefs, where the purpose of the brief, and the need to produce it simply and quickly, is submerged by the fervour of those producing it. It is not unknown for development companies either to lose interest or actually to withdraw preliminary submissions in the face of a brief rigidly sated with a surfeit of information. The trouble with a number of briefs is that their demands are frequently unrealistic, not merely in terms of the cost of compliance but also in respect of marketing problems or the need to fulfil institutional design requirements in order to secure funding.

A common dichotomy facing local authorities is the choice that often lies in selecting between the best architectural design and the best financial offer, and while they do not necessarily have to accept the highest monetary bid, the pressures of accountability can sometimes weigh very heavily upon elected members. The difficulty is heightened when it is not always easy to assess the reliability of financial offers made by developers in response to a brief, especially with the volatility of costs and rents displayed in our inflation-prone economy. Consequent upon this changeability in the market, and given the comparatively long gestation period of most major development schemes, local authorities are well advised to retain a certain amount of flexibility in the financial arrangements, so that either the brief, or more likely the final partnership agreement, should contain a predetermined procedure by which amendments can take place and resulting financial adjustments be made.

Notwithstanding the hurdles that have to be overcome in producing effective briefs, their role in reducing the polarity between public planning authorities and private development agencies in their task of promoting and managing change in the urban property market cannot be understated. The keynote, however, must be certainty with flexibility.

23 Planning standards

Having established the broad goals and objectives of the development plan for a particular area it is necessary to translate this overall strategy into specific land use and space requirements. The various professions concerned with the planning process have therefore devised a set of codes, regulations and specifications by which to judge the performance of the constituent elements that compose the plan, and to assist in the optimum allocation of resources. Thus certain standards are set to control the physical setting of the urban area and to contribute in ensuring safety, health, amenity welfare, convenience, efficiency and public interest.

Although no definitive or comprehensive list of standards exists, a widely acceptable range have emerged from a variety of sources. There are legislative standards such as the Building Regulations, the Use Classes Order, the Control of Advertisement Regulations and a host of local byelaws that relate to development. There are central government administrative standards, often the result of commissions, reports and committees, that advise, recommend and guide local authorities in the implementation of their policy. These include the design and planning bulletins, the development plans manual and the vast number of memoranda, circulars and handbooks that again aim to assist both public and private development and planning agencies. There are also empirical standards, those gained from experience and observation in practice.

Zoning

Whether this device for expressing land use proposals is best described as a form of control rather than as a planning standard is a matter of conjecture; it is, however, desirable that it should be mentioned in the same context. Zoning is a method by which the development plan segregates parcels of land or areas of towns and ascribes to them broad classifications of appropriate use, for example residential, industrial, commercial or educational. Combinations of uses can also be indicated. A set of characteristic notations is provided by the Ministry to secure consistency among authorities in the preparation of plans; thus commercial uses are shown in blue, educational in red and open space aptly in green.

The indication of suitable land use by means of zoning is but one technique amongst many for influencing change and deterring non-conforming uses in this country. In the United States of America it provides the basic planning instrument and is called the *zoning ordinance*. Closely associated with the ordinance is the *performance standard* which is based upon the use of different tests to determine whether or not a particular land use conforms with certain established basic criteria regarding aspects of locational suitability such as noise, fumes, pollution, glare and congestion. This performance approach is intended as a more sophisticated and sensitive alternative to groupings like heavy, light and general manufacturing industries. It has yet to be applied in this country but its merits are enhanced with the increasing amount of research that is being undertaken on the measurement of noise, pollution, overcrowding and so on.

The designation and allocation of land for specific uses under the 1947 Town and Country Planning Act code tended to be static and rigid, and all too often merely reflected existing land use distribution, whereas the 1971 Act sets out to create a more flexible yet positive framework for the distribution of resources at the structure plan level, and a more precise and certain indication at the local plan level.

Density control

It can be argued that the very basis of planning lies in the functional relationship between land and the various competing uses to which it is put. What is required, therefore, is some form of index which equates both the demand for, and supply of, land and allocates it in such a way as to ensure a maximization of existing resources. To this end a range of density standards have been established relating to residential and commercial activities. Essentially, density is the amount of some factor divided by the area that the factor occupies. The resultant figure expresses the average intensity in that area. In the sphere of plan preparation, monitoring and control there exists a variety of density standards in respect of different areas and different representative units of intensity within those areas. The following definitions are extracted from the Ministry publication *The Density of Residential Areas.*[1]

Residential density

Residential density is a system of measurement expressing in mathematical terms the number of people (population density) or the amount of housing (accommodation density) in a specified area of land. From this are devised several other measures which depend on what particular area of land is being measured.

Overall residential density

This is applied to a town as a whole. It is the residential population of the town divided by the number of hectares it occupies, regardless of how the land is used. It excludes undeveloped or agricultural land but includes industrial land, all public open space, all schools, and all other types of development. It is not generally used for local planning purposes but it does have a significance in national and regional planning where the intensity of development of one town can be compared with another. Today 175 bedspaces per hectare is considered to be a low intensity of development, 175–300 about average, and over 300 high.

Gross residential density

This is applied to a neighbourhood as a whole, or what is described in development plans as a *gross residential area.* It is the population of the area divided by the number of hectares, including all the land covered by dwellings and gardens, roads, local shops, primary schools and most open spaces, but excluding all other urban uses such as industrial land, secondary schools, town parks and town centres. It is of no direct relevance in development control but is used in the preparation of development plans where areas of high or low intensity can be identified.

Net residential density

This is applied to a particular housing layout or zone on a development plan and is regarded as being a normal basis for development control. It is the population or accommodation divided by the number of hectares including dwellings and gardens, any incidental open space, and half the width of surrounding roads up to a maximum of 6 metres, but excluding local shops, primary schools and most open space, and all other types of development.

There are several ways of expressing net residential density. It can either be done in terms of the number of people themselves or in terms of the accommodation they occupy, as follows:

dwellings per hectare
persons per hectare
habitable rooms per hectare
bedspaces per hectare
floorspace

The most accurate measure is thought to be bedspaces, as it most closely reflects the demand for accommodation, the way in which it is supplied, and the degree of overcrowding; as such it is frequently adopted in cost analysis work and in cost yardstick calculations.

Population density can be readily converted to accommodation density and vice versa by making certain assumptions about the average number of people occupying a separate dwelling, or a separate habitable room, that is a room normally used for sleeping or living in. This is called the *occupancy rate* and is used to gauge the level of overcrowding or under-occupation, with one person per habitable room being widely applied as a maximum above which overcrowding exists. Many authorities seek to attain a rate considerably below this with 0.75 being considered comfortable.

The residential density controversy

Over time, and from various sources, the main functions of residential density control can be listed under the following headings:

the preservation and economy of land use
to ensure scope exists for variety of development
to give reasonable minimum requirements for comfort and a satisfactory environment
to confine urban sprawl and prevent low suburban densities
to ensure an adequate provision of community facilities
to recognize and control both overcrowding and under-utilization, aid decentralization and control growth, guiding both the location and intensity of new development.

The preservation and economy of land use
The town planner is charged with ensuring that no more land is used

for urban purposes than is absolutely essential; a great premium is currently placed upon the preservation of agricultural and other land in non-urban use. One of the most obvious ways of achieving this aim is to raise the density of urban development, and a great debate has taken place in recent years regarding the relative merits of various forms of high-density living. In this vein the Joint Parliamentary Secretary to the Minister of Housing informed Parliament in April 1962 that 'by raising the net density of an area from 24 persons per acre to 40 persons per acre, and the number of houses from 8 to 13 per acre it is possible to save 17 acres of land per 1000 population or enough to house another 500 persons'. This proportionately high saving only occurs, however, where existing densities are at the lower end of the scale, because in circumstances where it is raised from 484 persons per hectare to 551 persons per hectare there is only a saving of 0.73 hectares, for as the numbers of persons increases so too does the amount of land required for community facilities and services.[2]

In this context it is worthy of note that it is unlikely that densities can be increased in existing suburban locations, so that adjustments are limited to the replacement of obsolescent housing in the inner city, where densities are probably considerably in excess of development plan maxima, and new estates of the urban periphery where densities have been increasing anyway. It is a common fallacy that building high saves land, for the savings in site and public utility costs with high-density development are less than the rise in maintenance and servicing costs which arise from the use of high buildings.[3]

Despite the Malthusian prophets of doom, the need to save land is perhaps not so axiomatic as is often asserted. Even in the highly urbanized region of London only about 30 per cent of the total area is developed, and in the outer ring of suburbia, where the gross residential density is only about 5 persons per hectare, some 80 to 85 per cent of the total area is under agriculture or woodland. It has been calculated that to replace the produce all of land lost to urban development between 1950 and 1970 it would require an increase in net output on the remaining land of only £3 per hectare, whereas intensification schemes had been yielding £10 per hectare in a 5-year period. Furthermore, output in terms of calories increased on average by nearly 2.5 per cent per annum, or enough to offset in one year the expected loss of land over a period of 20 years.[4] A further analogy often quoted is on the urban scale of *Lebensraum,* that is 125 persons or approximately 30 families per hectare, West Germany alone could house the entire present population of the earth. At this same density the entire population of the United States could be accommodated on the Pacific coast with nearly everyone having a view of the ocean. About 70 per cent of the population of the United States is now concentrated in urban and suburban communities occupying in total a little more than 1 per cent of the nation's land area. Even in England only 4 per cent of the land is occupied by as much as 40 per cent of the people.

These statistics are rather trite and say little about the real problems and causes of urban congestion and the need for density standards. The matter is put into perspective by J. R. James when analysing the merits or employing gross densities as a planning yardstick:

One main aim is to economize the use of land, and this can best be done not by raising gross densities to high levels but by keeping it above low levels. To crowd development closely and to build high does not produce an important saving in land. On the other hand great savings are achieved by preventing sprawl.[5]

To ensure scope exists for variety of development
The mere application of density controls does not of itself guarantee the nature and form of development. The results can, in fact, be disastrously monotonous and regular. It is only when these standards are enforced with a measure of flexibility and discretion that any variety or mix can be achieved. It is essential that while a net residential density is valuable as a guideline, the actual planning permission should take account of the physical condition of the site, the purpose of the dwellings, the architectural quality, and all the other factors that dictate satisfactory development. Although an overall standard might be appropriate to a particular area it is likely that a range of densities above and below that mark, related to specific sites, might produce the best result.

This approach is further supported by the demand for different forms of accommodation based upon varied social need. Housing estates with their predominantly two-storey three-bedroom dwellings appear to cater almost exclusively for the family with children under sixteen who, after all, make up but 40 per cent of total households. Special provision, based upon a survey of requirements for each separate planning area, should therefore be made in respect of mixed development, because although the residential space needs of substantial communities are fairly similar, the space needs of individual households vary enormously.

To give reasonable minimum requirements for comfort and satisfactory environment

A stated consideration in implementing density standards is to achieve 'compactness without congestion' and 'spaciousness without sprawl'.[6] The means of creating this and the resultant densities are matters of great controversy. Of recent years the 'high-rise, high-density', school of thought has tended to give way to that of 'low-rise, high-density'. The reasons why the slab and point high-rise blocks of the 1950s and 1960s have fallen out of favour become apparent when the advantages of low-rise construction are set out. The major benefits are as follows:

there is greater supervision of play space and therefore greater safety
  for children
there is more private open space
greater accessibility to the street is available to all; there is no
  dependence on lifts
two- and three-storey high-density development can be introduced to
  existing street patterns and based upon existing services
there is greater speed of construction
it is generally more economic
a wider range of dwelling size can be built
phasing is easier, redevelopment can be undertaken piecemeal
it can be applied to smaller and narrower sites.

It must be emphasized, however, that although density standards are fine for sorting out numbers of rooms, people, dwelling, schools and other services, the visual and environmental effects can be calamitous. They might give a measure of the intensity at which people live on land, but they do not provide a comparative basis of living standards or a measure of aesthetic control.

To confine urban sprawl and prevent low suburban densities
It has been maintained that around all towns

there has been a tendency for villages and new settlements to grow haphazard and produce a spoiled semi-rural, semi-urban background, an 'urban' area which if linked in the envelope of the town will show a dropping of density which is not a healthy sign either for the town or the countryside.[7]

The main problem, therefore, is preventing excessively low densities in suburban areas which can easily become grey areas secluded from city services with populations too thin to generate public life. This proclaims the need for minimum controls as well as maximum, and a number of county planning authorities enact just such controls.

To ensure an adequate provision of community facilities
It is important that dwellings should be conveniently sited in relation to shops, schools, open space and other land uses normally associated with the general convenience of residents. It has been asserted that without density controls it is quite impossible to ensure adequate provision of such facilities.[8] Although they might provide an invaluable check or yardstick, particularly in respect of new development, density levels rarely reflect actual intensity of occupation in existing areas. Other means of ensuring the provision of community services are therefore required. It can be argued that at higher densities there is an increased loss of private facilities and therefore further provision of communal facilities should be made, thus demanding a more complex relationship between density standards and public services.

In the United States they employ the zoning ordinance which governs land use, and an associated subdivision regulation which governs the design of streets and provision of utilities. Approval of subdivision design can control the layout of an area, and in some instances approval can also control the placing of community facilities such as schools, parks and playgrounds, since the large land developer is required to set aside certain portions of his land for such purposes. Professor Denman has suggested a similar method, which he describes as an 'amenity percentage', for use in this country, giving a more flexible approach to the problem.

To recognize and control both overcrowding and under-utilization
There are several bases for the bulk measurement of accommodation as mentioned previously.

The dwelling: commonly used before the war but suffers from the fact that it does not indicate the actual amount of accommodation owing to the variety of house size and type that exists. It is, however, used in rural areas as a minimum standard.

The habitable room: the definition of what constitutes a habitable room can vary between local authorities. Also the size of rooms and occupancy rate can vary enormously, depending as they do on socio-economic group and age. When applied the desired occupancy rate is used to translate habitable rooms per hectare into persons per hectare and vice versa.

The bedspace: although not always used as such, this base should provide an indication of use and intensity.

Floorspace: this is difficult to measure, unnecessarily precise, and again subject to wide variations in different economic and social circumstances.

As the Ministry points out, however,

density control is often expected or believed to serve many purposes which in fact it can only accomplish within very broad limits, if at all. For example, overcrowding within dwellings cannot be prevented by density control since it cannot limit household size or determine living habits, although it can influence the number of people who can live in an area by controlling the number of rooms or dwellings.[9]

An argument could in fact be advanced that the converse is true and that density control, by limiting the number of rooms or dwellings in areas of high demand for accommodation, stifles redevelopment and in fact causes overcrowding.

Certainly as an instrument for assessing overcrowding or under-utilization the social survey provides a far better measure.

Commercial density

The purpose of establishing commercial density standards is aimed at achieving a form and distribution of commercial activity which allows the town centre, or urban area, to function at its most efficient level, ensuring a balanced pattern of growth, and acting as a guide for future new development. Once again there exists no common standard for measuring and controlling the intensity of shop and office use. There are, however, two very similar methods that are widely acceptable, the floor space index and the plot ratio.

The floor space index (FSI)

This is based upon the total area of permitted floorspace expressed as a proportion of the site plus half the width of surrounding roads. It is intended to take into account the need to provide a system which allows for all the service facilities implicit in development such as roads, parking, access and footpaths. Thus, if a local planning authority, having considered existing and potential traffic and pedestrian flows, and the availability of other services and utilities, would allow twice the equivalent amount of floorspace as that area covered by the site and half the width of the adjoining roads, the FSI is said to be 2:1. The developer is then able to decide whether he will construct three storeys over the whole site, assuming the road widths are 50 per cent of the site area, or six storeys on half the site, or perhaps twelve storeys on a quarter of the site. There will, of course, be other controls that inhibit his decision and dictate the final form such as daylight and sunlight factors, car parking, access, height and materials.

Plot ratio

This is mainly used in London and is similar to the floor space index but excludes half the width of the roads. It provides a more consistent standard for controlling development on individual sites, because where the FSI is employed corner sites might benefit unduly and

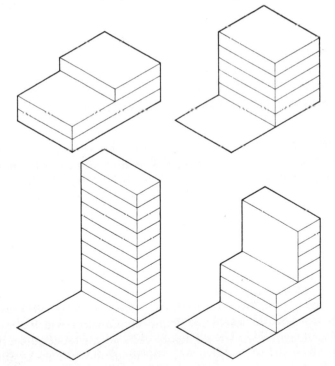

Figure 25   *Alternative methods of developing a site at a plot ratio of 2.5:1*

become over-developed and these are often the locations where congestion is at its worst (Figure 25).

It can be said that both the floor space index and the plot ratio provide a comparatively equitable assessment between respective sites, prevent over-intensification, and work against spiralling land values. Conversely they do not relate the amount of space available with the use to which it is put: a large block of offices given over to insurance companies, with their vast personnel, places a very different burden in terms of urban congestion upon a town than does a computer firm with its few operators. Their application can also lead to awkward, ugly and inefficient design and in no way ties in with parking, space or height standards. Furthermore, it does not differentiate between sites in the same area but has contrasting accessibility characteristics. For example, a case can be made out for permitting considerably greater intensity of development over and around transport termini as happens abroad.

An attempt has been made to devise an *environmental standard* control of the bulk of buildings in central areas based upon the size, population, pedestrian space on the ground, and capacity of transportation.[10] The result is a formula which states the amount of floorspace in a building that can be permitted for a given amount of pedestrian footpath space fronting the building. A certain sophistication is added to existing procedures, but the amount of survey and analysis work involved detracts from its usefulness.

Industrial density

Unlike residential and commercial development no easily applied numerical standards exist for controlling industrial location, intensity and growth. The only broad measure sometimes employed is that of *site coverage* whereby the cover of buildings upon a site is expressed as a percentage of the site area. A coverage of around 45 to 50 per cent is usually adopted, although this may sometimes be a little higher on inner urban sites. Otherwise each case is judged on its individual merits. The principal constraints imposed are chiefly statutory, such as the Use Classes Order which distinguishes between various forms of industry such as light, heavy and special, the various Acts that relate to development and employment which control industrial location, and the Factory Acts which relate to specific layout, design and construction of industrial premises. Some methods of quantitative assessment are mentioned in the following chapter on industrial site development.

Conclusion

Of necessity, density standards are negative in character. They cannot, of themselves, generate a development of a particular kind of character, although to some extent they can prevent improper or inefficient land use. Traditionally population density controls – those standards concerned with measuring the capacity of land in terms of persons – have been associated with residential development. More recently in the United States the notion of controlled population densities has been extended to the work areas of the community, the central business district and the industrial and commercial concentrations. In this extension of the concept, the criterion of density becomes the number of people present in an area during peak hours of congregation as opposed to place of residence. The densities are expressed in persons per million feet and provide a serviceable technique for preparing, implementing and monitoring plans.

Also in the United States they have initiated, under the auspices and direction of the Federal Housing Administration, a measuring device known as the *land use intensity rating* which is described as 'the overall structural mass and open-space relationship in a developed property, which correlates the amount of floor area, open space, livability space, recreation space and car storage space of a property with the size of its site or land area'. Its approach is not entirely dissimilar to gross residential density but it takes into account a wider field of planning factors, providing what is described as a more reliable and less variable standard.[11] It is interesting to note that the French award a 'density bonus' to schemes which in outline appear to have potential aesthetic quality.

Finally, great concern has always been given by planners and planning authorities to net densities, but a plea has been made by J. R. James for them to pay greater attention, in the context of density and urban development, to gross densities which he describes as

an important and useful planning concept. Within big urban subdivisions, forming the appropriate envelope, standards of density can be set that permit the proper planning of housing with local facilities and ensure the economical use of our national stock of land.[12]

Daylighting and sunlighting indicators

The daylighting indicator

This is a method recommended by the Ministry in their handbook

The Density of Residential Areas for controlling the spacing of
residential buildings on a site. It provides a quick and approximate
means of ensuring that buildings are so placed in relation to each
other that it would be possible to attain the daylighting standards
recommended in the *British Standard Code of Practice* provided that
in the design of the dwellings themselves the windows are properly
positioned and of adequate size.[13]

Two basic types of indicator are employed, one for testing
adequate daylight provision from surrounding streets and plot
boundaries, and the other for testing from one building to another on
the same site. Each indicator ignores daylight reaching a window at a
horizontal angle with the plane of the window of less than 45° because
it provides insufficient illumination. The remaining light is assessed
for suitability through a possible range of wide to narrow angles.
Separate sets of indicators are provided for residential and non-
residential buildings (Figure 26).

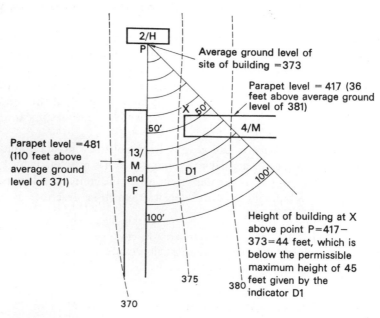

Figure 26   *The use of one of the range of daylight indicators*
Source: *Planning for Daylight and Sunlight*, planning bulletin 5 (HMSO 1964).

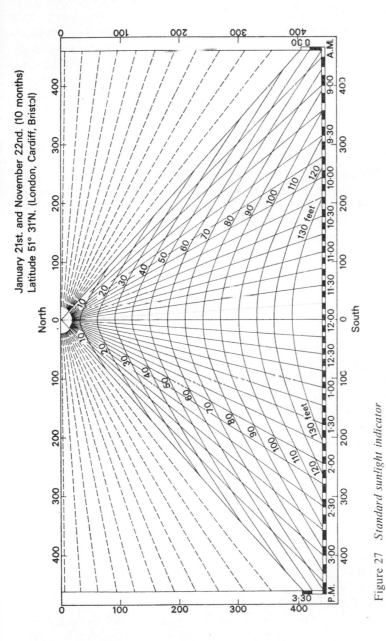

Figure 27 *Standard sunlight indicator*

Source: *Planning for Daylight and Sunlight*, planning bulletin 5 (HMSO 1964).

The sunlighting indicator

A *standard sunlight indicator* (Figure 27) has been devised which can be used as a ready check to ensure that from 21 January to 22 November, at particular latitudes, buildings are so placed that sunlight can enter as many main windows in as many main rooms for at least an hour at some time of the day. Sunlight is not considered as having entered a room if the horizontal angle between the sun's rays and the plane of the window is less than 22.5°, and if the sun has an altitude of less than 5° above the horizon.

Sets of indicators are available for latitudes 51° 30'N, approximately that of London, Cardiff and Bristol; 52° 30'N, approximately that of Birmingham; 53° 30'N, approximately that of Liverpool, Manchester and Leeds, and 55°N, approximately that of Newcastle.

An explanation of exactly how both these indicators are applied in practice is beyond the scope of this book, but is lucidly described in the Ministry's planning bulletin number 5, *Planning for Daylight and Sunlight*. They appear to have provided a valuable tool at the preliminary design stage of site layout.

Noise

It has already been mentioned, in looking at pollution, that a great deal of research has been directed towards the measurement of traffic noise, the establishment of acceptable standards, and the means of reducing the level of intrusion. Statutory control of vehicle noise was introduced by the Ministry of Transport in 1968 under the Motor Vehicles (Construction and Use) Amendment Regulations whereby new vehicles are limited to a noise level of 92 dBA, which represents decibels (dB) weighted on a special scale A for use in assessing traffic noise. On this weighting an increase of 10 dBA corresponds approximately to a doubling of loudness.

With regard to the total amount of noise produced by traffic on urban roads, there is currently no outdoor environmental noise standard, but the Greater London Council have adopted the recommendations of the Wilson Committee on the problem of noise in respect of acceptable indoor noise levels that should not be exceeded for more than 10 per cent of either day-time or night-time. Table 15 lists suggested standards for various building types. When compared with typical noise levels in Inner London as described in Table 16 it can be seen that a great deal of work remains to be done in

Table 15 *Indoor noise standards for various building types*

| | Maximum indoor 10% noise level (dBA) | |
	Day	Night
Quiet suburban areas	45	35
Busy urban areas	50	35
Lecture theatres	30	
New classrooms	45	
Private offices	45–50	
General offices	55–60	

Source: *GLC Urban Design Bulletin on Traffic Noise* (1970).

Table 16 *Typical noise levels in Inner London*

| | 10% noise level (dBA) | |
Area	Day	Night
Residential	65	53
Industrial	66	54
Shopping	76	58
Offices	69	58

Source: *GLC Urban Design Bulletin on Traffic Noise* (1970).

terms of reducing traffic noise. Both the Building Research Station and the National Physical Laboratory have carried out experimental work on constructing indices to measure noise pollution. Further, as an aid to the land use and transportation planner the Greater London Council has created a set of transparent protractors that assist in calculating the effect of distance and screening in reducing noise levels.

The above standards are relatively simple to use, and give a fair indication of the annoyance caused, but they do not take into account the frequency of noise and the difference between peak foreground noise and general background noise, and they cannot be applied to aircraft or railway noise.

Car parking standards

To any motor vehicle owner it scarcely requires stating that the urban areas, and in particular the town centres, of this country are facing a crisis regarding traffic congestion and the ever-increasing demand for parking space. In controlling development it is incumbent upon the planner to decide how much parking space each individual development should provide, where, and of what kind.

It has long been established that with residential development each house should have at least one car parking space and a further proportion should be set aside throughout the estate for visitors' parking. The Parker Morris report in 1961 suggested that an extra 25 per cent should be provided for visitors' cars, but the Road Research Laboratory estimates that there will soon be an average of one car per family, or almost three times the number of cars on the road. There is also an increase in the ownership of bicycles, scooters, boats and caravans, all of which must be catered for and stored. Most local planning authorities are therefore insisting upon one visitors' space per dwelling in addition to the household space.

There exists a great disparity between authorities regarding the standards they impose, particularly in respect of non-residential development. Table 17 should be taken as an indication only.

Cars are such space-hungry devices that all these standards are probably insufficient. The crude application of standards can also lead to a haphazard distribution of small, privately owned, poorly located, under-utilized car parks. It is far better strategically to site fewer but larger public car parks available at all times to all people. For this reason some local authorities conclude arrangements with developers whereby the latter make financial contributions towards the cost of providing spaces in public car parks as an alternative to supplying parking on the particular site which is to be developed.[14]

Table 17   *Car parking standards*

Land use	*Parking spaces*
Residential	2 per dwelling
Offices	1 per 35 m^2 of gross floorspace
Central area shops	5.75 per 100 m^2 of gross floorspace
Suburban shops	5 per 100 m^2 of gross floorspace
Out-of-town shops	8.5 per 100 m^2 of gross floorspace
City hotels	1 per 10 bedrooms
Other hotels	1 per 3 bedrooms
Hospitals	1 per 12 beds
Theatres	1 per 30 seats
Restaurants	1 per 10 seats
Industrial	1 per 50 m^2 of floorspace

Parking standards, as such, tend to be inflexible in practice if discretion is not exercised on the part of the planning authority concerned. Some developments require very much less provision than others but may well fall within a general category of control. What is perhaps required is a complete revolution in urban transportation and parking policy. The imposition of flexible discriminatory road pricing and the wider introduction of park-and-ride schemes may not be far off.

Open space

The various recommended standards for individual activities such as rugby, cricket, parks, allotments, school playing fields and incidental spaces are detailed elsewhere.[15] They have changed little over the years but recent research has indicated that if anything they tend to be over-generous. At any rate the character of leisure and recreation is changing to such an extent that a demand is growing for completely different facilities.

The old Greater London Plan proposals in 1944 recommended that for every 1000 population there should be 10 acres of open space, 6 for playing fields, 1 for parkland, and 3 attached to schools. Based upon extensive survey work undertaken by Essex County Council in 1965 it has been suggested that, excluding land attached to schools, only 3.5 acres of open space would be sufficient in built-up areas as opposed to 7 acres previously proposed.[16]

In Table 18 there are some interesting contrasts between American cities in their provision of community open space.

A roughly similar survey was undertaken by F. T. Burnett during 1966 of ten of the established English new towns which demonstrated

Table 18 *Open space in US cities*

Cities	Open space (%)	Gross population density	Net population density
Detroit	5.5	16.1 p.p.a.	35.2
Pittsburgh	6.1	7.6 p.p.a.	14.8
Philadelphia	8.6	14.3 p.p.a.	27.4
Los Angeles	9.1	7.9 p.p.a.	20.6
Cleveland	14.8	10.6 p.p.a.	23.9
Chicago	20.5	14.4 p.p.a.	44.7
New York	28.0	10.6 p.p.a.	26.1

amazing discrepancies in the provision of major open space, ranging from 5.9 acres per 1000 population in Basildon to a staggering 39.2 acres in Peterlee. The latter was due mainly to a high proportion of woodland within the designated area of the town. The average provision was in the region of 18 acres per 1000 population.

These broad figures in isolation do not paint a true picture of the quality and usefulness of the open space. It might not be accessible to large sections of the community, or it might be heavily wooded or liable to subsidence or flooding. In a period of worsening urban pressures, greater concentration of development, and increasing leisure time, it is imperative that further consideration should be given to the nature, form and distribution of open space and the standards that control it.

24 Site layout and development

The preparation of detailed site plans at the local scale is a skill which appears to attract ever-diminishing attention from town planners in both training and practice. The stigma of 'physical determinism' discourages great premium being placed upon this part of the planning process. Admittedly, in the past, perhaps too much weight was attached to the design and layout of buildings, and the conformity to regulations and standards, but any policy for the social and economic development of a particular community must inevitably possess a physical expression. The determination of the precise form of the physical environment draws upon a variety of skills including those of the architect, engineer, surveyor, economist, landscape architect, lawyer, sociologist and town planner. It is unreasonable to expect an individual discipline to maintain a comprehensive view of the whole, while practising a specialist role in all parts. It is necessary, however, for the town planner to have an understanding of the principal factors that influence the method of site planning. Only in this way can he effectively fulfil his responsibilities regarding the control of development implicit in the implementation of his policy. In this context, it is worth remembering that a considerable proportion of a local authority's time and resources in respect of their town planning duties is taken up with the processing of applications for planning permission of a detailed and local nature.

Site planning has been described as 'the art of arranging the external physical environment to support human behaviour. . . . Site plans locate structures and activities in three-dimensional space and, when appropriate, in time'.[1] The preparation or consideration of a site plan will often relate to a detailed design for a specific use such as housing, shops or offices in a particular area. Sometimes it might involve mixed development, but always the nature of the use and the form of its layout will be governed by the relevant provisions of the development plan, the general accessibility and location of the area, the requirements of the client and the topography and characteristics of the site.

The experience of the author and confines of the text preclude any profound appraisal of design techniques or architectural merit; the general purpose is to outline some of the factors that warrant attention in assessing development.

Residential

Of paramount importance in deciding the form and layout of any site plan is an understanding of the exact needs and desires of the client for whom it is being prepared or considered. The nature of the plan will almost certainly vary according to whether the proposed development is public or private, high or low income, central, suburban or rural. Although each site and every situation will deserve individual treatment, broad elements that are common to all can be identified.

Density

The various ways in which the density of residential development is measured, dwellings, persons, habitable rooms, and bedspaces per hectare, is fully discussed elsewhere.[2] It remains, however, a useful concept in assessing the intensity of development and regulating the impact in respect of the provision of community services and facilities. As in all other planning matters it provides a quantitative measure permitting comparison, judgement and control; it says little, however, about the actual coverage or use of land. The most appropriate density for a particular site is determined by, first, the provisions of the development plan – any amendment amounting to a 'substantial departure' might require ministerial confirmation; second, the area itself and the character of surrounding development; third, the nature of the site, its topography and landscape; fourth, the prevailing demand regarding income, design and size; and fifth, the availability of services, because scattered low density layout can prove extremely expensive to service.

Having examined these factors, various types of construction possess their own density margins. Detached housing rarely exceeds 20 dwellings per hectare, semi-detached 30, and terraced 50. To achieve levels above this, elements of high-rise housing types in the form of maisonettes or flats are required. In this connection, density standards can be employed as a gauge of performance: for example, above 30 dwellings per hectare problems of noise and loss of privacy emerge; as a general rule at about 50 dwellings per hectare the returns derived from private development reach a 'break-even' point; above this the provision of adequate space and amenity combined with low-rise construction becomes incompatible; in excess of 100 dwellings per hectare the process of design becomes difficult and costly; and over 200 dwellings per hectare everything becomes congested and almost overriding problems of lack of space for recreation, parking and servicing are faced; even accommodation becomes cramped.

In deciding suitable levels of residential development a certain variation in the needs, and consequent size, of constituent households should be allowed for. A certain proportion, perhaps 10 per cent of one-bedroom dwellings should be provided; similarly, about 20 per cent two-bedroom and another 10 per cent four-bedroom dwellings would more closely approximate to real household demand as opposed to the universal supply of the standardized three-bedroom 'family' house. Given the current conditions of the housing market, especially the methods of financing individual purchase, it is unlikely that the private-sector developer would be able to cater for this range of choice. Nevertheless, there remain many thousands of households who live in dwellings which are either too big or too small for their requirements.

Dwelling types

Closely associated with the density of residential development is the type of development involved, each possessing its own peculiar characteristics, whether they be laid out in courts, avenues or cul-de-sacs, on a rectangular, Radburn or patio basis (Figure 28).

The advantages of detached houses are almost too obvious to state; they form the ideal unit to which most people aspire, having both light and access all round, the minimum of noise and intrusion, and possessing independent support. On the other hand they impose low densities of around 10 dwellings per hectare. Requiring a frontage over 35 feet they contribute greatly towards urban sprawl, and, with ever-increasing pressures upon land for various uses, are rapidly becoming an impracticable form of development in this country. They are at their best, however, when individual treatment can be afforded to their design and layout, and while they tend to be visually unrelated, unless built at high densities, coherence and unity can be achieved with careful landscaping by way of fairly dense planting or open-frontage layout.

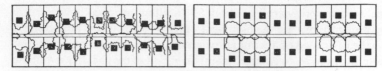

Figure 28   *Alternative detached housing layouts*

Source: Lewis Keeble, 'Principles and practice of town and country planning', *Estates Gazette* (1969).

The characteristic semi-detached residence which epitomizes so much of British suburban development also typifies the renowned art of compromise. They are comparatively cheap to build, give the illusion of being detached, and have reasonable access and orientation, but with frontages of 40 to 50 feet for a pair of houses, and a height of around 30 feet, their layout is considered to 'lack repose through the absence of long horizontal lines' and when 'ranged in a row, have very ragged and irregular shaped spaces between them producing the effect known as tooth-and-gap'.[3]

The growing preference for terraced housing is as much a matter of expedience, through force of economic circumstance, as it is a reflection of taste or fashion. Nevertheless, their facility for unity and continuity of design frequently bestow a most acceptable and satisfying form of urban development (Figure 29). The expression 'terraced' includes any three or more dwellings joined together with frontages of anything upwards of 18 feet. Their individual design can be identical or dissimilar. Even some of the famous Georgian terraces provided for different styles in the same row, achieving unity by ensuring that each was kept in proportion to the whole, with the storey and window line running through the block and the materials and style remaining constant. Their public image is again improving; perhaps the title 'town house' has helped. Having few external walls they provide the most space at the least cost, heat loss is reduced, advanced acoustic insulation has ameliorated the problem of noise, and the ease and flexibility of layout that their design allows readily appeals to the planning and architectural professions. The difficulty of private covered parking is overcome either by the popular, but unsightly, apparent return to 'mews living' with the car occupying the ground floor, or by the provision of communal garage courts conveniently situated nearby.

Variations on these low-rise dwelling themes are possible. Chain houses can be constructed whereby dwellings and garages are staggered alternately, thus affording a better visual rhythm than tooth-and-gap semis, and permitting the valuable estate agents description of detached. Mediterranean style patio houses can be developed allowing densities of up to 300 persons per hectare to be attained, but producing formidable problems of orientation, access and privacy (Figure 30).

To accomplish higher densities, over and above 250 persons or 185 habitable rooms per hectare, some proportion of the dwellings must be provided in the form of flats. Judging by their selection of residence in the private sector of the housing market, the vast majority of the population of this country display a marked disdain of flatted accommodation. This is in distinct contrast to the custom and conditions prevailing on the Continent, where in many cities

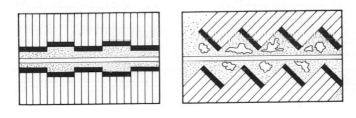

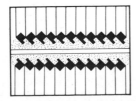

Figure 29   *Alternative terraced housing layouts*

Source: Lewis Keeble, 'Principles and practice of town and country planning', *Estates Gazette* (1969).

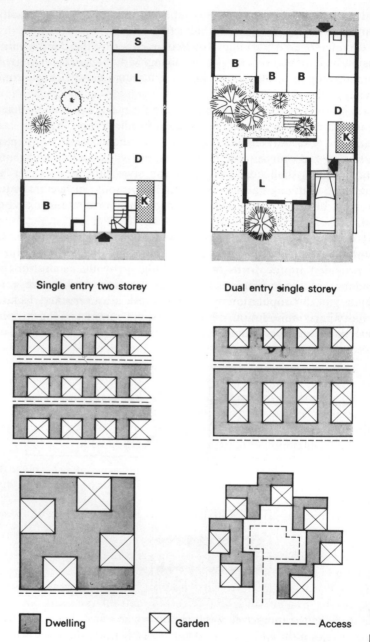

Single entry two storey   Dual entry single storey

☐ Dwelling   ☒ Garden   ----- Access

Figure 30   *Some alternative forms of patio layout, internal and external*

upwards of 80 per cent of the population are housed in apartment buildings of one kind or another.

Characteristic advantages and disadvantages of flat development are immediately apparent. On the one hand they provide a compact arrangement of dwellings; a considerable saving of land up to certain levels; permit more people to live in proximity to central areas; allow for a convenient grouping of social facilities; encourage collective and economic provision of such services as central heating, hot water and refuse disposal; favour the supply of a greater variety of different sized dwellings for single people, those without children and those who prefer to deny themselves the joy of gardening; assist in the redevelopment of high-density slum areas without resort to excessive overspill schemes; and provide points of interest in the skyline that break up the drab monotony of low-rise urban areas. On the other hand flats can be said to impose greater costs of construction per dwelling, particularly in respect of combating the increased structural stress, the supply of lifts, sound insulation, rubbish chutes, fire escapes, and general maintenance of common parts; induce danger to children, old people and the infirm; cause inconvenience, lack of privacy and, increasingly, mental stress; encourage vandalism, and promote wind traps and unwelcome shadows. Even at densities of up to 300 persons per hectare about three-quarters could be accommodated in two- and three-storey houses and the remainder in flats. This provides a balanced form of layout, assists in the satisfactory development of corner sites, and might actually reflect the suppressed demand for flats from certain sectors of the community. Sir Frederick Gibberd gives a rational and authoritative explanation of the national reluctance to accept high-rise development.

If we set aside blind prejudice, the answer is that the objections are not to the flat dwelling as such, but to its abuse when combined into a building type, and abuse in the way the flat building is sited. . . . The object has been to cram as many dwellings on the site as possible, irrespective of light, air and amenities of planning.[4]

There are two principal forms of high-rise flat development – the point and the slab block (Figure 31). The point block can be used to great advantage as a focus of attention in urban development, particularly for exaggerating the effect of natural contours and for minimizing the impact of building upon open space. Their full effect is often lost if they are dispersed haphazardly throughout a town; far better that they should be clustered 'into bold groups in contrast to a

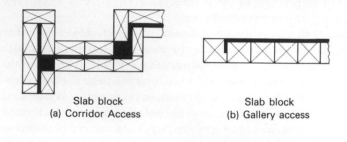

Slab block
(a) Corridor Access

Slab block
(b) Gallery access

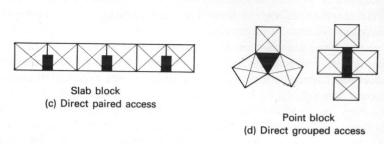

Slab block
(c) Direct paired access

Point block
(d) Direct grouped access

Figure 31   *Some forms of flat development*

horizontal setting and, with such groupings, there is also the interplay of one form against another in space which, even with two towers, has more than twice the significance of a single block'.[5] The slab block can be employed to surround and give definition to areas, to open out and provide perspective to areas, and also to give shelter. The wide variety of flatted accommodation, the scope, layout and design, is fully described in Sir Frederick Gibberd's outstanding book *Town Design*.

Space and orientation requirements

The placing of buildings in relation to one another, and with due regard to sun and wind, commands considerable attention in judging the layout of residential development. The traditional approach attempted to idealize the orientation of dwellings, but in temperate climes and with modern designs a greater flexibility can be allowed for. The objective in respect of sunlight and daylight is to maximize the amount of light penetrating the dwelling. In estate development this entails a certain amount of compromise to ensure that this benefit is shared among the whole community. Nevertheless, as a general rule of thumb, a layout which attempts to align the frontages on the dwellings in an approximately north to south direction is infinitely preferable to one whose orientation is west to east. In this way both the back and the front of the buildings will receive sunlight, one in the morning, the other in the afternoon and early evening. The light in the south at midday is not really lost, because it has least penetration owing to its elevation in the sky. The internal arrangement of the house should aim to get as much sunlight into as many rooms as possible, as indicated in Figure 32, but in any event should take account of popular preference for early morning sun in the kitchen. In circumstances where it is not possible to secure north to south road layouts the use of houses situated in echelon, or the introduction of courts or cul-de-sacs leading off, will often secure a satisfactory aspect. Although not a matter of great moment in this country, the prevailing wind should also be considered in selecting the most propitious plan.

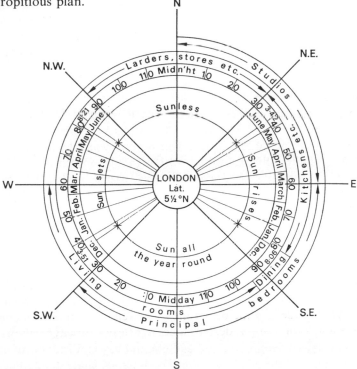

Figure 32 *Orientation for residential layout and design*

This factor of orientation assumes even more importance in the location of high-rise, high-density development where not only the penetration of sunlight but also the effect of shadow and wind become significant. This is especially so where slab blocks of flats are under consideration, for, often having only one central corridor, the individual flats will necessarily have only one aspect. Correct siting is therefore critical.

The degree of daylight and sunlight received by a dwelling is also affected by the space between buildings. To ensure adequate provision in this direction the government publication *Design of Residential Areas,* produced as long ago as 1952, sets down particularly useful guidelines. It estimates that proper penetration is only secured where there is an uninterrupted sight line of 25° from the horizontal. As demonstrated in Figure 33 this produces minimum distances of 48 feet between two-storey houses and 68 feet between three-storey houses. This is supplemented by the time-honoured *70-foot rule,* which is selected as a satisfactory separation of dwellings, asserting that at this distance the outline of the human body becomes blurred and actions indistinguishable, thus preserving personal privacy. Perhaps the radical notion of curtains, by no means a modern invention, might permit a certain flexibility in the interpretation of this rule. It still serves, however, as practical indication for the spacing of buildings.

In this context another standard which regulates the layout of development is the *building line.* This prescribes a line at a given distance from the middle of the road beyond which the erection of buildings is normally prohibited. Although it is sometimes varied to allow for outstanding features, it is inclined to produce a rather drab, uniform and monotonous perspective if rigidly applied. Many of the new towns adopted a more imaginative approach towards the control space requirements and either ignored or waived the adherence to building lines.

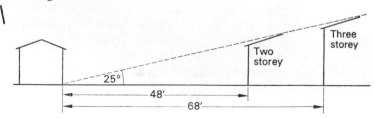

Figure 33   *Space required between buildings to allow adequate daylight*

One final element of orientation that is frequently overlooked is the opportune and skilful use of existing features of note or views worth preserving and enhancing.

Road layout

The layout of roads in residential areas not only provides the framework for development and the channels of communication between respective land uses, but also carries the facilities and utilities that service the dwellings, both above and below the ground, as well as playing a prominent part in determining the very character and environment of the neighbourhood. It is an element of the overall plan where the town planner exercises extensive control, and although the detailed construction is essentially the province of the traffic engineer, the function and location of roads and their relationship with other activities is of great consequence in the planning process.

Different roads obviously fulfil different purposes and the individual design and the general layout should take account of and reflect this. The concern here is for local roads in residential areas. Two extreme forms of site layout present themselves. First, the old-fashioned grid network where the land is divided up into squares or rectangles of approximately the same size. While this leads to an economic use of building land it also gives rise to a large number of intersections between roads of equal importance which pose great accident hazards. The overriding uniformity also creates extremely monotonous vistas, disregard of topography, and lack of differentiation between roads, and, despite the blocking-off of certain links in the grid and the formation of cul-de-sacs, the network remains inefficient and dangerous. Second, an alternative form of layout is developed in which roads radiate or branch out from a single distributor road, again forming a large number of rather long cul-de-sacs. This system is comparatively rigid and dictates a single direction of movement, and while the problem of through traffic is eliminated it is at unnecessary cost to the provision of services, which must be run longer distances, and the uneconomic delivery of goods. For these reasons the city of Philadelphia has forbidden the creation of cul-de-sacs more than 150 m long[6] and in this country 180 m is considered a maximum length. Although no ideal form of layout can be established for comprehensive application, each site has unique characteristics and deserves special treatment. Certain guidelines common to all residential estates can be suggested:

1   It is important to seek the development of an 'environmental area' through which no extraneous traffic flows, the principle of which is illustrated in Figure 34.

2   The road layout should discourage short cuts being taken through the area.

3   Long straight stretches of road which might lend themselves as racetracks should be avoided either by a constantly changing road pattern or by the use of 'speed bumps' built into the surface.

4   Crossroads should be excluded, particularly at the intersection of roads comparable in the hierarchy. The use of T-junctions is preferable.

5   Junctions should be staggered wherever possible, a suitable distance between neighbouring junctions being about 45 m.

6   Roads should intersect at right angles to ensure adequate vision and safety.

7   While depending upon the design speed of the roads, the sight lines provided at intersections should normally allow 90 m of clear unobstructed vision from 9 m at the junction of a local access road with a distributor and 60 m at the junction of two access roads.

8   The total length of roads should be kept to a minimum in the interests of economy; thus an attempt should always be made to secure a double frontage of dwellings.

9   To ensure satisfying perspectives and vistas the views at the ends of roads should be closed by the skilful positioning of interesting features such as churches or trees, or the careful layout of houses square to the road alignment.

10   Roads with house frontages are best designated in a north to south direction to permit satisfactory orientation.

11   The length of cul-de-sacs should be kept within reasonable limits and never more than 180 m long. Similarly, care must be taken not to inadvertently create a cul-de-sac out of a network of access roads. Most estates of any significant size should always provide more than one entrance and exit.

12   The construction of houses fronting on to distributor roads should be avoided.

13   The segregation of motor traffic and pedestrians should be considered.

14   The overall layout of the road system should not be too complex,

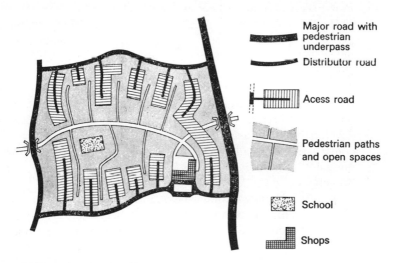

(a) The principle of traffic separation

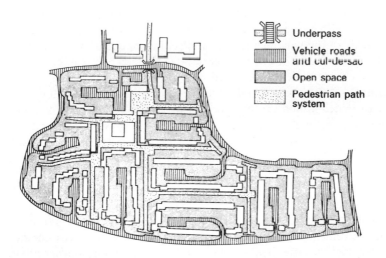

(b) An example of traffic segregation at Beeston, Notts.

Figure 34 *Traffic segregation*

Source: *Cars in Housing*, design bulletin 10 (HMSO).

so that visitors and delivery vehicles can find their way around the estate.

15   Plot shapes should be kept as regular as possible.

16   In low-rise residential development the provision of ample private open space in the form of back gardens should be given precedence over the supply of public open space and front gardens.

17   The treatment of corner plots should merit special attention; the requirement for adequate vision often necessitates the setting back or total restriction of development and subsequent loss of developable frontage. This can often be overcome by the construction of small blocks of flats, maisonettes or old peoples' bungalows where the demands for private open space are not so pressing.

18   To ensure adequate drainage throughout the road system, there must be a minimum gradient of 1:200 everywhere. A slope of over 1:10 becomes dangerous when freezing occurs and one in excess of 1:17 precludes use by service vehicles of any size.

The actual nature and dimensions of the respective estate roads warrants some consideration. The distributor roads which convey traffic around the residential area should be about 7 m wide and flanked with pavements about 3 m wide; the access roads which carry vehicles to the various individual dwellings require to be 5 m wide with pavements 2 m wide; the cul-de-sacs, which by their very nature carry no through traffic, need only be 4 m wide with pavements again 2 m wide. At the end of cul-de-sacs turning points will need to be provided which are big enough to accept the largest of service vehicles; turning circles are out-of-date and wasteful of land, the tendency being to employ hammer heads. If a great deal of kerbside parking is anticipated it might prove necessary to provide a separate parking lane which can be of a lighter construction, about 2.5 m wide and designed in bays approximately 6 m long so that it is only used for the desired purpose and vehicles park singly.

The use of grass verges separating the road and pavement is not just for convenience, safety and visual relief but can also accommodate services and utilities below the ground in an economic and accessible manner that causes least disturbance. Where laid, these verges should be at the very least 1 m and, where trees and bushes are planted, 2 m wide. At any point where poles are placed on the kerbside for street lighting, telephone wires or bus stops, they should ideally be placed 0-

0.75 m back from the kerb,; regrettably, however, they are often less.

Another feature that is rarely incorporated into residential estate layout in this country is the cycleway. The merits of this form of transport are said to include 'quietness, economy, no pollution, good exercise, ease of parking and safety to others'.[7] When provided they should be approximately 4 m wide with a generally curving alignment and easy gradients, and can be combined with separate pedestrian ways.

Parking

The phenomenal increase in private-car ownership over recent years has placed a great responsibility upon residential estate developers and local planning authorities in ensuring that as many vehicles as possible are attracted off the already congested and cluttered roads when stationary. Although on-street parking is convenient for the householder during the day, and inevitable for the delivery of goods and supply of certain services, it should be realized that apart from being a constant source of danger to children, hindering refuse collection and street cleaning, one parked vehicle reduces the capacity of a road for 90 m in both directions; this can restrict the flow of traffic in a residential area at peak hours by over 50 per cent. Although the provision of parking spaces sometimes appears inadequate, Figure 35 portrays a variety of approaches to the problem selected from *Cars in Housing,* a Ministry publication.

The travelling allowance of one off-street parking space per dwelling is extremely dated and in many areas the provision of one private space and one visitors' space is totally insufficient. Many developers are finding that in higher-income-group estate houses a double garage is being demanded as an absolute necessity, on top of which free off-street standing space for visitors is still required. In areas of higher density where the construction of terraced houses is employed it is possible to provide communal garage courts, well-drained, screened, carefully located off distributor roads, possessing good angles of vision in both directions, and with adequate space for cleaning and the carrying out of repairs. These garage courts, however conveniently placed in relation to the dwelling, are nevertheless unpopular; people demand a garage within the curtilage of the dwelling house, hence the advent of the three-storey 'town house' (Figure 36).

Apart from private vehicles and visitors' cars, a third category

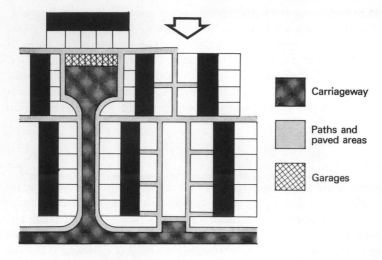

(a) The vehicle cul-de-sac

■ Carriageway

▢ Paths and paved areas

▨ Garages

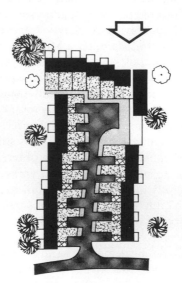

(b) The vehicle cul-de-sac with individual garages

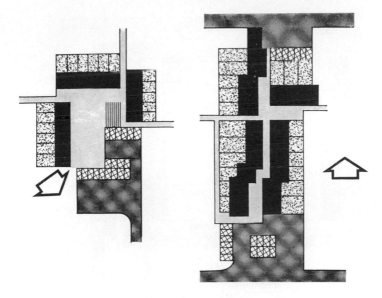

(c) Pedestrian courts and passageways

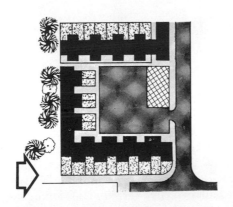

(d) Garage court (Laindon, Essex)

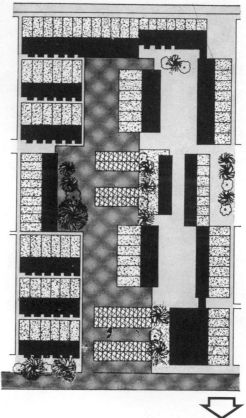

(e) Pedestrian and garage courts (Hook proposed new town)

Figure 35   *Examples of Radburn layout groupings*
Source: *Cars in Housing*, design bulletin 10 (HMSO).

must be provided for, the delivery of goods and public service traffic, otherwise known as 'tradesmen traffic'. These are normally only parked for a short period of time and must therefore be accommodated at the kerbside. When such traffic is particularly heavy, and is forced to compete with the private car, special parking bays laid out in echelon can be incorporated in the layout.

As an interesting and attractive variation on sloping sites, garages can be set into the ground or hillside, and where this relates to communal courts the roofs can be pleasantly planted or landscaped.

Services and utilities

Apart from pedestrians and motor vehicles there are a number of other critical flows in and out of residential areas that are essential to the welfare and serenity of community life. These include the flow of energy, information and waste.

Drains and sewers

Drains are essentially those pipes, channels and culverts within the individual property boundary which convey water and waste to local authority sewers. There are three basic systems of waste disposal; *combined,* which takes all domestic waste and surplus water together; *separate,* in which one pipe carries domestic waste and another surface water; and *partially separate,* where one pipe carries all domestic waste and surplus water from on and around the dwelling while another receives all other surface water. The separate and partially separate systems provide a more assured method of catering for excessive surface water imposed by rainstorms. Theoretically all land surfaces should be designed in such a way as to permit the flow of water away to drains and sewers. The appropriate gradient around residential dwellings to ensure this process is 1:50 but on other open spaces it can decrease to 1:100 and even 1:200 on specially constructed and engineered surfaces such as roads. In order to introduce a satisfactory system a knowledge of the total amount of water naturally entering a site, its possible velocity and its capacity to drain are prerequisites to the planner and engineer. The general configuration and geology of the site will govern the nature of the most appropriate system of drainage and sewerage. This is a major factor, albeit one of several, that should be taken into account in establishing the pattern of roads. The ideal situation is found where the roads can run along broad, gently sloping valleys along the line of natural fall. Roads which run parallel with the contours will cause problems because dwellings both sides of the same street will not be able to naturally drain into intermediate sewers; pipes will have to be laid through the intervening plots. Roads which run at right angles to the contours might facilitate the disposal of sewage but surface drainage is often difficult.

All sewers must be buried to prevent damage; the actual depth varies according to the susceptibility of the area and the soil to freezing. Naturally the deeper they are laid the more expensive becomes both the initial operation and any possible future inspection

365ft

370ft

0 50 100   200   300   400   500   600ft

Figure 36   *Housing estate layout as Warley, Essex, illustrating various form*

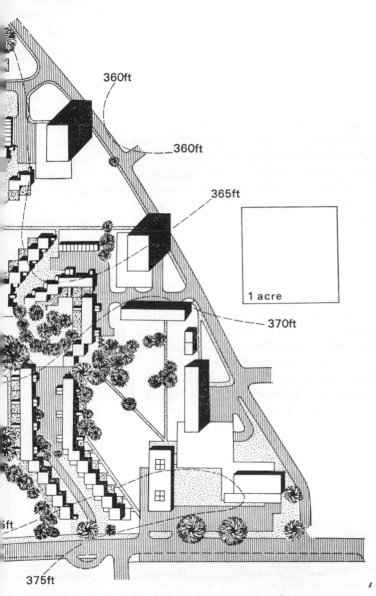

360ft

360ft

365ft

1 acre

370ft

375ft

residential development and different kinds of car parking treatment

and repair. As a general rule 1 to 2 m is considered sufficient; below about 3 m the task becomes very costly. At the same time, however, it must be recognized that the main sewers must be laid at a sufficient depth to allow the flow of waste from neighbouring houses. In this country sewers must be laid in straight lines, although more advanced systems in the United States are laid in gentle horizontal curves with a radius of never less than 30 m.[8] In their vertical alignment the sewer pipes must have a minimum grade to maintain constant flow and permit self-cleansing. As always, it is more economic to take advantage of the natural contours of the site and the ideal gradient largely depends upon the size of the pipe and the expected flow. In most circumstances a slope of 1:200 will ensure a flow of 1 m/s when operating at maximum capacity, which is satisfactory. The minimum acceptable gradient is about 1:300, while at the other extreme the velocity should never exceed 3 m/s, otherwise damage to the pipe as a result of scouring might occur. For uneven ground of extreme slopes, sudden changes in gradient can be made at manholes performing roughly the same function as locks on a canal. In any event these should be placed at intervals of between 90 to 150 m in order to facilitate inspection, entry, repair and cleansing.

The size of pipe varies according to the function it performs and the number of dwellings it serves. In practice 'run-off coefficients' and other formulae are used to calculate the requisite diameter, but as a rough guide it can be said that domestic pipes are approximately 100 mm to 150 mm wide and main sewers start at around 200 mm, being sufficient to serve an estate of 100 houses, and for each additional 100 houses an extra 75 mm in width is required. In this context another important rule is that pipes must always discharge into larger ones, for fairly obvious reasons.

In assessing a site for residential development, flat or swampy land can cause serious problems. Pumping is always possible but is extremely costly. If the surface water is merely localized 'ponding', the planting of moisture-absorbing plants can ease the situation.

Water

The quantity, quality, pressure and general availability of water exercises a material control over the feasibility of residential development. While, however, it plays a prominent part in determining location it is not such an important influence over layout, although the water pipe is the most susceptible to frost. Because water is distributed under pressure a much greater degree of flexibility can be introduced in respect of gradients, curves and overall design. The size of pipe is normally about 200 mm in diameter, and, to equate the maintenance of a minimum of pressure with maximum of potential demand, a pressure of 137,880 newtons per square metre at the hydrant or house is required. There are two basic methods or systems of piping water: first, like branches of a tree running off from a main stem, which minimizes overall length and is therefore cheaper to install, and second, as a series of loops, which is initially more expensive but virtually eliminates extensive reduction in pressure owing to breakage and subsequent interruption of the whole system to effect repair.

Electricity
On a national basis electricity is distributed at high voltage, being stepped down for local use at transformers and connected from there with dwellings at low voltage. These low-voltage secondary lines are wasteful and costly; therefore their length must be kept to a minimum, preferably about 120 m.[9] It is this location of transformer stations that concerns the site planner at the local scale, although considerable discretion and flexibility can be exercised in their exact positioning. It is often the case that in any residential estate development there will be small, irregular and awkwardly shaped plots of land left over within the layout. These readily lend themselves for use as transformer sub-stations. They should have access to the road system and be suitably screened.

Electricity cables, whether for power or telephone, are best situated underground. This operation is initially more expensive but breaks are less frequent, although when damage does occur repairs are very costly to effect. There is marked tendency, especially in new town development, to erect one communal television aerial to which everybody has access and prohibit the use of separate individual antennae, a practice to be applauded and encouraged.

Gas
The provision of gas is based on approximately the same principle as that of water, with either a branching or a loop system of distribution. The pipes, however, are considerably smaller, and almost the only matter of concern for the site planner is to ensure that, because of the great danger caused by leakage, electricity and gas pipes are not laid in the same conduit.

Refuse disposal

Naturally provision must be made in the overall layout and internal design of the buildings for the collection of domestic refuse. The estate roads must be of sufficient dimensions to allow the service vehicles access and facility to turn. The actual areas set aside for dustbins should be well-drained, adequately sheltered, conveniently situated for collection, having no steep gradients and with the route preferably paved.

Owing to the propensity for damage and leakage and the consequent need for inspection and repair, all pipes and cables should, wherever possible, be laid under a public right of way so that they are readily accessible and cause the minimum amount of inconvenience, delay and expense. To this end the arrangement of conduits under grass verges flanking the road network supplies an admirable solution.

In assessing the relative qualities of urban residential development it should be recognized that the respective services, utilities and facilities that combine in producing a satisfactory 'life-support system' also give rise to the unsightly clutter of poles, wires, aerials, lights, power lines and other such apparatus. There is no reason why the design and detail of these essential accoutrements of urban living should not attract greater attention in the process of site planning, and why a greater harmony between them and their relation to the general environment should not be achieved. A more eloquent plea is made by Lynch.

Because of the prevalent ugliness of much of our circulation equipment, we consider roads and utilities as regretfully necessary things that must be supplied but should be hidden . . . we should demand an even clearer expression of the essential elements of this system instead of camouflaging them. Power lines and highways can be an expressive component of the landscape; exposed pipes can be handsome.[10]

Landscape and planting

To achieve unity in design and coherence in layout it is necessary to supplement the bare form of buildings with a more natural and visually pleasing environment. The skill employed by the landscape architect in planning the composition and character of open spaces can be divided into two broad categories — the site itself, and the purpose to which it is put.

The site

When surveying a particular site in the preparation of a separate landscape plan it is important to take into consideration the following features:

1 An appraisal should be made of the existing vegetation, some of which might be suitable for retention or even replanting. Healthy mature trees are always worth preserving and featuring.

2 The availability of natural water on the site plays a large part in determining the amount and kind of landscaping that can be provided. The purity of the water should also be tested, as should the level of the water table and the possible effect the proposed development might have upon it. Seasonal variations in the supply of water might prove significant and should also be recorded.

3 An analysis of the microclimate should be undertaken, examining the rainfall, temperature and amount of sunshine, together with any proclivity towards mist, fog or freakish winds. The orientation of slopes should also be noted as this affects the performance of certain species.

4 The type of bedrock and the nature and condition of the soil can influence the approach towards landscaping. Although artificial fertilization can be employed it is much better if the right kind of soil is matched to the most appropriate form of vegetation.

5 Any assessment of the site should also include an appreciation of the surrounding area. It might prove necessary to screen unsightly, noisy or noxious neighbouring activities. On the other hand, buildings of architectural and historic interest or views of particular beauty can be opened up and used to advantage in siting the residential development.

The purpose

Landscaping can play a positive role in assisting the plan to fulfil its function. The following are examples of the way in which this might be achieved:

1 In an attempt to reduce the visual impact of the motor car, car parks can be screened and hidden.

2 The segregation of pedestrian and motor vehicle can be obtained by expert planting even where the two channels of communication run almost alongside. A moderately meandering pathway flanked with trees and bushes and separated by only a

few metres from the road can be both convenient and pleasant.
3 Undesired movement can be discouraged by the use of hard, rough but visually attractive surfaces such as cobblestones.
4 In residential areas of low density where development is comparatively scattered, landscaping can both ensure effective use of excess open space and act as a visual, and even physical, link between dwellings. In areas of medium density it can be used simply to break the monotony of uniform estate layout. In areas of high density it provides tremendous relief and contrast, but great care must be exercised in the choice of materials owing to the fact that such open space as does exist is subjected to intensive wear.
5 Landscaping can also be applied as a safety precaution regarding dangerous roads and water hazards.

It can, therefore, be seen that the landscape architect should be brought in at an early stage in the planning and layout of residential areas. His art is not confined, as is the popular misconception, to providing the icing on the cake, for in its widest context the expertise is required from inception to completion of estate development.

Tree planting
The planting of trees and the retention of existing vegetation within a residential estate fulfils a number of functions: it gives shelter and protection against wind, noise and fumes; screens undesirable views and safeguards privacy; directs attention to and from buildings and other objects; acts as a visual link between development; demarcates boundaries; influences pedestrian circulation; accommodates changes in ground level; creates and defines external spaces; and generally supplies visual contrast and relief. The great art of preparing and implementing a satisfactory tree planting programme lies in the ability to reconcile a number of conflicting factors such as:

1 The placing of trees close to buildings or underground services can cause extensive damage, not only directly by root growth, but also indirectly by causing moisture changes and therefore instability in the soil. Most roots lie within about a metre of the surface and can extend very approximately one-third as far again as the height of the tree; in dry soils, however, this can be even further. It should also be remembered that most trees require an

enormous amount of water; a poplar may consume as much as 12,000 gallons in a year, although a conifer might only use 2000 gallons (Figure 37).

2   The right tree must be selected for the right site. Certain species are particularly suitable for use in towns, being more resistant to the polluted atmosphere, such as poplar, plane, elm and cherry. Others are especially tolerant to coastal conditions and salt spray, including certain types of elm and oak. Some varieties, such as alder and willow, demand a waterside location.

3   The nature of the soil is important; ash, lime and elm prefer a light alkaline soil, whereas chestnut, oak and pine are happier in sandier, more acid conditions. Most varieties grow well in medium loam which has a neutral character.

4   Drainage might have to be provided in retentive subsoils such as clay. Porous formations such as sand, limestone and chalk are normally sufficiently self-draining.

5   Frequently quick results are called for and fast-growing species such as ash, birch, willow, alder or cypress must be incorporated within the layout.

6   Strongly coloured trees, such as purple maple, copper beech and golden false acacia, should be sited with great care, preferably singly as a focal point contrasting with their background.

7   Trees should always be in proportion to surrounding developments.

8   The cost of planting, although small in comparison to other facets of development, is critical, and therefore every precaution to preserve existing trees, to avoid inappropriate species that require excessive pruning, fertilizing and drainage, and the introduction of young saplings as well as mature trees, must be taken.

9   Some species, such as poplar and ash, are exceptionally invasive with excessive root growth, while others shed vast amounts of foliage which can cause dangerous slippery surfaces and clog drainage systems. Both types must be sited with great care.

Industrial estates

The scale, location and condition of industrial estates play a large part in determining the character and tone of urban areas. The squalor of some sprawling nineteenth-century developments has a depressant effect upon a whole town or region, while the savage

siting/choice

Position your trees where they won't shade windows or flower beds. (Fig. 1)

reasonably well away from buildings (especially on clay soil) to avoid damage to foundations.

clear of gutters, gulleys and underground services.

to extend the outline of the house and soften its edges. (Fig. 2)

where the colour of blossom won't clash with brickwork.

allowing for future growth, root and branch

to form groups of same species, incorporate lower shrubs to enhance effect.

avoiding mixtures of several contrasting species.

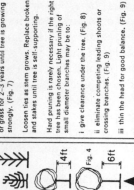

Fig. 1

Fig. 2

Choose the simplest tree for its situation – exotic flowering species may fit suburban but not village or rural surroundings.

from the following characteristics:

Shape narrowly upright, roundheaded or weeping. (Fig. 3)

Foliage deciduous or evergreen.
large leaves or small.
dense or open.
spring, summer and autumn colouring
(silver, gold and purple *summer* foliage is best used sparingly).

Blossom/fruit colour and month.
Bark colour and marking.

Fig. 3

buying/planting

You can buy trees as bushes 10/6 to 20/– each feathered 7/6 to 25/– half standards 17/6 to 40/– standards 17/6 to 40/–. (Fig. 4)

Evergreens are best bought with a good root ball. (Fig. 4b)

Order your trees in Summer and Autumn from a reliable nurseryman.

On delivery protect the roots from frost and drying wind – either place them in a trench, support stem and backfill, or if the ground is frozen, store temporarily well wrapped under frost-proof cover (e.g. in garage). (Fig. 5)

Plant normally from November to March but when the ground is not waterlogged or frozen. Evergreens may be best planted in September or April.

To plant, lift out soil from holes larger than the spread of the roots, loosen soil in the bottom. Drive in support stake and place tree at the depth it grew in the nursery. Add moistened peat and 2 handfuls of bonemeal in returning the excavated soil and firming it around the roots. Tread with the heel. (Fig. 6)

Secure tree to stake with inch wide plastic or rubber tree ties, one at top, one halfway down.

Fig. 4

4ft

6ft

Fig. 4b

Fig. 5

Fig. 6

care

Keep ground round the stem free from weeds or grass for 2–3 years until tree is growing strongly. (Fig. 7)

Loosen ties as stem grows. Replace broken ties and stakes until tree is self-supporting.

Hard pruning is rarely necessary if the right tree has been chosen. Light pruning of small diameter branches may be to:

i give clearance under the tree. (Fig. 8)

ii eliminate competing leading shoots or crossing branches. (Fig. 9)

iii thin the head for good balance. (Fig. 9)

Make cuts flush with stem or larger branch and apply Stockholm Tar, Arbrex or similar. (Fig. 10)

Fruit trees see appropriate literature.

Fig. 7

Fig. 8

Fig. 9

Fig. 10

Botanical Name	Common Name	Special Characteristics	Eventual size in feet on good site Height × Spread	Remarks	Form (Evergreens shaded)
Acer negundo	Box Elder	Fresh green summer foliage	40 × 25–30	Variety variegatum has white and green leaves	
Amelanchier canadensis	June Berry	April – white blossom Autumn colour	20–30 × 20–30		
Betula pendula	Silver Birch	Small leaves – gold in Autumn – silver stem	40–60 × 25	Fast growing on light soils. Plant small.	
Betula pendula youngii	Weeping Silver Birch		20–30 × 30–35	Slow growing	
Chamaecyparis lawsoniana Varieties	Lawson's Cypress and Varieties	Green, grey or gold-foliaged varieties	15–60 × 6–20	Some varieties not for smoky areas	
Crataegus oxyacantha plena	Double White Thorn	Double flowers in May. No fruit	20–25 × 20–25	Also pink and crimson varieties	
Crataegus X carrieri	Hybrid Thorn	White blossom, June. Large leaves and orange red berries into New Year	20–25 × 18–20		
Ilex aquifolium and varieties	Holly	Foliage and winter berry	40 × 25–30	Slow growing	
Laburnum alpinum and L. vossii	Laburnum	May–June – yellow blossom	20–30 × 20–25	Seeds poisonous. The variety watereri has fewer seeds	
Malus floribunda	Flowering Crab Apple	April–May – profuse apple blossom. Densely twiggy habit	20–25 × 25–35		
Picea omorika	Serbian Spruce	Slender elegant evergreen. Good as a Christmas tree	60–80 × 20	Accommodating as to soil and situation	
Prunus amygdalis	Almond	Pink blossom in March before the leaves	20–25 × 20–25	Best on loam. Plant against dark background	
Prunus cerasifera nigra	Purple Leaf Plum	Pink blossom in March before the leaves. Purple Summer foliage	20–25 × 20–25	Not for smoky areas	
Prunus cerasus rhexii	Flowering Cherry	Beautiful double white flowers – April–May	20–25 × 20–25	Also single white variety P. serrulata affinis	
Prunus hilleri spire	Flowering Cherry	Soft pink blossom April–May Autumn tints	25–30 × 6–8		
Prunus X Okame	Flowering Cherry	April – small rosy pink flowers	18–25 × 18–25		
Prunus rosea pendula	Cheal's Weeping Cherry	April–May. Double pink blossom on arching branches	15–20 × 15–20	Also known under Shidare-zakura	
Prunus subhirtella autumnalis	Winter Flowering Cherry	Semi-double white flowers in mild Winter periods	20–25 × 25–30		
Prunus padus and the variety Watereri	Bird Cherry	May – fragrant white flowers in long racemes	30–40 × 25–30	Accommodating as to soil and situation	
Pyrus salicifolia pendula	Weeping Pear	Dense silver grey oliage on arching branches	15–25 × 15–25	Willow-like leaves	
Robinia pseudoacacia fastigiata	Fastigiate Locust	Feathery foliage, bright green throughout Summer	25–30 × 6–8	Good on light soils	
Sorbus aucuparia and variety asplenifolia	Rowan or Mountain Ash	May–June. White blossom— red berries. Autumn tints	30–50 × 25–40		
Sorbus discolor	form of Mountain Ash	Similar, with fine Autumn colour	25–35 × 25–35		
Sorbus pinnatifida gibbsii	Hybrid Service Tree	Grey green leaves – bright red berries	20–30 × 10–15		

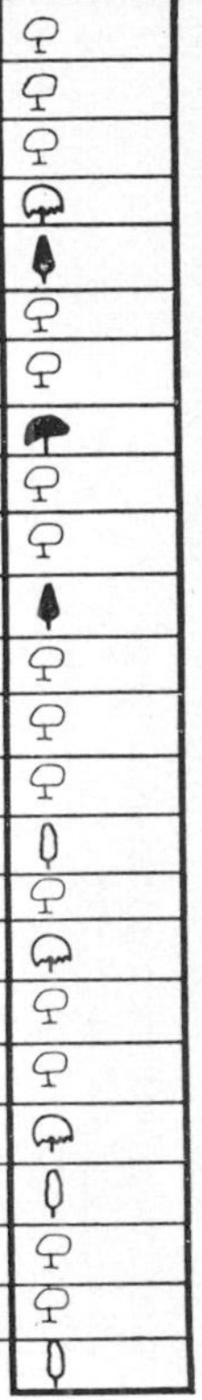

Figure 37 *Trees in estate layout*

Source: Michael Kennett, 'Safeguarding our trees', *Official Architect and planner* (September 1968).

forms of some industrial buildings possess a certain splendour all of their own, enhancing the quality of an area.

Location

Most industrial activities form only part of a complete process, and a major locational factor becomes the proximity and accessibility to other related activities. This complementarity and demand for continuity can be extended beyond production and applied to the sharing of services and facilities as well as the desire for prestige location. Extractive industries, by their very nature, must be sited on the source of their raw materials. Others, such as shipbuilding, are also inextricably bound to particular locations. The need for water in vast quantities is a principal requirement in a number of other processes, demanding sites alongside rivers and canals. These include paper mills, bleach and dye works, and tanneries, which form a kind of incursive riverside ribbon development.

Although the demand for labour and the call for urban concentration suggest the need to establish industrial estates in the approximate vicinity of residential areas, great care must be taken to ensure that the traffic to work does not conflict with the rush-hour traffic travelling to the town centre. Some degree of separation is also occasioned because of the noise, fumes and unsightly appearance often associated with such development. With the prevailing wind in this country blowing from the south-west it is common practice to locate industry in the north-east sector of a town, especially where noxious operations such as brick and cement works are concerned, unless variations in topography or local microclimate dictate otherwise.

Another principal factor influencing industrial location is accessibility. The use of rail has largely given way to road transport with only about 20 per cent of industrial concerns requiring access to the railway network. As these tend to be the bigger concerns the presence of railway sidings is no longer a prerequisite to the siting of smaller industrial estates, although such a facility is always an advantage. It has recently been discovered that even airports attract certain specialized light industry; however, as yet, no direct runway links have been formed as occurs in the United States. One of the problems that has to be faced wherever an industrial estate is placed is the sudden disgorgement of vehicles on to the public road system at certain hours. If possible the most satisfactory method of dispersal is by way of several exits on to a number of secondary roads, but where this cannot be effected peak-hour traffic control at major intersections must be introduced.

One of the greatest misconceptions in respect of industrial location is the fact that not all operations are automatically non-conforming and must therefore be isolated from residential areas. Certain activities can be beneficially mixed with other uses including housing, the criteria being that 'they should not be detrimental to the amenity of the area by reason of noise, vibration, smell, fumes, smoke, soot, ash, dust or grit'.[11]

Layout

It is impossible to lay down a format that governs the preparation of all plans for industrial estates in all circumstances. A number of simple rules common to most layouts can, however, be identified:

1   The size of industrial estates varies considerably, from as little as 10 hectares to well over 200 hectares (Figure 38). A crude but convenient way of assessing the appropriate size for a particular urban area is to adopt a figure of 1.5 hectares per 1000 population. This produces an estate of 100 hectares for a

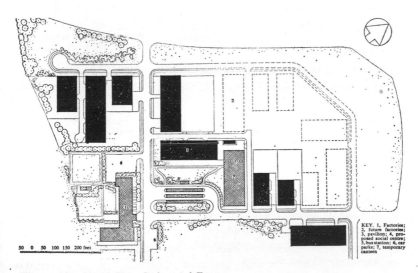

Figure 38   *North Tees Industrial Estate*
Source: Frederick Gibberd, *Town Design* (Architectural Press 1970)

theoretical new town of around 65,000, which represents what appears to be a reasonable provision.[12]

2   Another method of calculating the size of estates, but more usually employed to regulate the extent of industrial development, is the application of the relevant density standards. In this country levels of between 125 and 175 workers per hectare have prevailed, but in recent years there has been a marked tendency towards lower levels of around 75 to 125 workers per hectare.

3   The intensity of development and ground coverage can be controlled by the use of the floor space index, more popularly applied in office development. This relates the permitted amount of industrial floor area to the total plot size with some allowance for surrounding roads and is commonly put at around 0.5.

4   The site should be as flat as possible and under no circumstances have a slope in excess of 1:20.

5   The size of individual plots should vary to accommodate factories from 200 m² to 20,000 m².

6   The shape of plots and the provision of services should be so designed as to permit consolidation if necessary.

7   The most suitable plot shape is usually square or rectangular served by a gridiron or loop network of access roads. The principal system of access roads should preferably be one-way with a number of cul-de-sacs branching off to individual plots or groups of plots.

8   A generous provision of land should be reserved for any future potential expansion both on individual plots and throughout the overall layout.

9   The roads should be of liberal proportions to allow for the continual passing of heavy vehicles. Each traffic lane requires to be about 3.5 m wide, good sight lines are required, a clear indication of the entrance and exit to the estate should be provided, extra lanes for accelerating and decelerating should be supplied on neighbouring arterial roads, the minor access roads within the estate should intersect at T–junctions, and the more important ones at roundabouts.

10   Heavy delivery and service traffic should be separated from employees' private cars.

11   If the construction of factory premises is undertaken they should permit flexibility of use with ample service and delivery bays.

Single-storey straight-line buildings are more popular than multi-storey developments, having more uniform and effective natural lighting, less structural obstruction, being cheaper to erect, and easier to relet or sell. Certain concentrated processes such as confectionery and flour milling are best suited to multi-storey buildings, but they are rare.

12 Industrial concerns having the same characteristics or requirements should be grouped together. In this way noxious or noisy activities can be segregated, and parking, canteen, medical and recreational facilities can be shared.

13 Sports fields surrounding industrial estates not only provide a physical or spatial barrier but are also compatible uses in that sporting pursuits and industrial production often take place at different times, thus not impinging upon one another and permitting the sharing of parking facilities.

14 The amount of parking space provided in connection with industrial premises must obviously be related to the number of workers employed, the availability of public transport, and the frequency and duration of delivery trips. The number of spaces supplied should normally be between 0.75 and 1.0 per worker; this allows for the overlapping of shifts. This is an ideal and perhaps excessive requirement. The number of spaces is usually related to the amount of factory floorspace, a crude and arbitrary standard, and varies enormously throughout the country, averaging approximately one space for every 25–30 m^2 up to 250 and closer to one space for every 100 m^2 beyond that. As workers know where their destination is, and will remain parked for up to 8 hours, it is reasonable to expect them to walk up to 100 m. In this way central parking facilities can be provided for small concerns.

15 Industrial processes place a heavy burden upon local services and utilities; high-capacity power, water and waste disposal equipment will be required and occasionally gas, steam and compressed air. The location, layout and development of industrial estates should take account of existing facilities, surplus capacity and future requirements. Consideration should also be given to the recent demands for recycling of waste products within the industrial process. An examination of the size, location, density and character of existing industrial estates demonstrates the point that there are no absolute acceptable conventions currently applied. The magnitude of Park Royal in

West London, covering well over 1000 ha, and Trafford Park near Manchester, stretching over approximately 500 ha, bears little or no relation to the garden city estates of Welwyn and Letchworth, each of about 70 ha, let alone the smaller trading estates associated with so many urban areas today. It has been suggested that the most suitable size for such estates lies between 20 and 60 hectares, below which only very small concerns will be attracted and the benefits of scale will be lost, and above which it is difficult to relate to other areas of the town. There is no reason why small estates should not be designed in conjunction with overall residential and neighbourhood layout, not as a substitute for the larger industrial estate of the town but in addition to it. These sites need only be about 6 hectares in size and accommodate small single-storey factories, preferably those which employ a high proportion of women who could then work close to their homes. Such a development was planned as an integral part of the Caldwell Estate at Nuneaton.[13]

One further aspect of industrial layout and design is the need to introduce a more positive approach towards landscape and environmental quality. In the past control has tended to be of a negative kind, directed at layout, density and materials to the virtual exclusion of all else. There is a need to create a planned landscape structure as with all other forms of development, because, as Lynch, asserts

Industrial areas, like roads, are not simply unpleasant necessities to be kept as neat and reticent as possible. Roads, dams, bridges, pylons, cooling towers, stacks, quarries and even spoil heaps are magnificent objects if well shaped. They are big enough and meaningful enough to take their place in large landscapes. They explain the industrial basis of our civilization; they contrast handsomely with hills, trees and lakes.[14]

Neighbourhood shopping centres

Over the past twenty years a minor revolution in shopping habits has taken place – the ascendant success of the supermarket, the movement out of town, the advent of discount trading, the beginnings of bulk buying and the creation of the modern covered centre. Despite these developments there remains a need for convenient local retail facilities grouped together with other community services and forming a neighbourhood centre. The dominant activity of the neighbourhood centre will continue to be shopping, therefore the most suitable location will be determined by the retailing potential which is heavily dependent upon the available catchment area. Thus, in selecting a site for locating a neighbourhood centre, it is necessary to consider the size, age and character of the local population, the capacity of existing utilities, the availability of public transport facilities, the nature of the surrounding road system, the direction and pattern of the pedestrian network and the proximity of competing centres. Accessibility is all-important. Although a support population of 5000 is sufficient to warrant the existence of a small centre, one of 10,000 will permit the introduction of a wider range of trades and even a certain element of competition.

Layout

In brief the material considerations which govern the layout of neighbourhood shopping centres are as follows (Figure 39):

1   The size of the site depends entirely upon the locational factors and the economics of demand. With the greater mobility conferred upon shoppers by increased car ownership, the tendency in neighbourhood centres is likely to be towards fewer shops and smaller sites. To give some indication, however, a centre of twelve to fifteen shops plus ancillary services and adequate car parking would require something just less than 1 hectare of land.

2   As with all other forms of development, sites with excessive slopes should be avoided. Greater flexibility does exist in this respect, however, with shopping layouts; careful, and for that matter interesting, designs can be introduced whereby split-level basements can be constructed and used for extra selling space, storage or car parking. If car parks are laid out on sloping ground it is imperative that the parking spaces lie across the slope, not up and down.

3   The site should be a focal point in both the road and pedestrian network.

4   Good visibility and sight lines are required, not only for reasons of safety and circulation but also to attract passing custom.

5   The shops can be laid out as a strip running alongside an existing road, with or without a front service road. Before the Second World War this was the traditional form of development. For

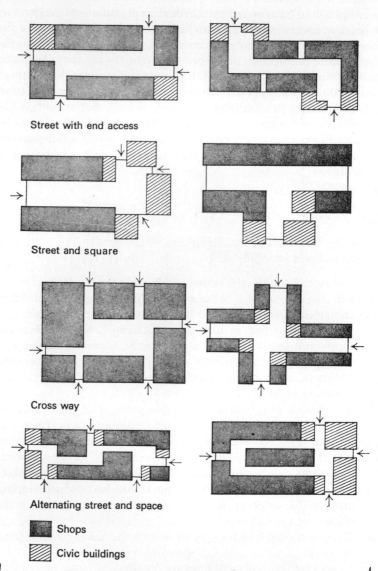

Street with end access

Street and square

Cross way

Alternating street and space

■ Shops

▨ Civic buildings

Figure 39   *Some examples of neighbourhood shopping centres*
Source: Frederick Gibberd, *Town Design* (Architectural Press 1970)

obvious reasons of safety, inconvenience and poor visual quality, it is to be avoided. Where local conditions dictate this approach, however, parking should be provided in front of the shops, care being taken to avoid dangerous turning or reversing on to a main road. Rear access for service deliveries should be provided wherever possible, and the key tenant or magnet should be placed in the middle of the strip. A more suitable form of this development places the strip at right angles to the road with the shops facing the direction of the source of greatest trade, making an allowance of about 15 m for rear servicing and ensuring that walking distances from car parks are kept to a reasonable minimum, certainly less than 120 m.

6 Another form of layout is the U- or L-shaped centre which reduces the overall walking distances, permits custom to be drawn from two roads, and bestows a pleasing sense of enclosure. It is most suitably applied to square or rectangular sites with the shop fronts facing away from main roads and surrounding an open landscaped forecourt or parking area. The key tenants should be placed at the junction.

7 Yet another form is the construction of compact pedestrian malls which consists of two lines of shops directly opposite one another separated by a narrow pathway. This mall may be covered and built on more than one level. It is more appropriate to large-scale development where there are a number of competing magnets which should be sited at either end of the pedestrian way to stimulate circulation. These malls may in fact be arranged in a variety of shapes according to site, market or design requirements.

8 The distribution, mix and precise location of shops, while not critical at the local neighbourhood level, is nevertheless important enough to merit the planner's attention. The aim is to construct a layout that encourages pedestrians to circulate around as many shops as possible with the minimum of inconvenience. At this scale the supermarket will provide the main attraction and should be positioned so as to create the greatest movement around the centre.

9 In the above context the siting of car parks and their access to the shops, the placing of the bus stop and the design of any staircases within the centre can be all-important.

10 Although the size of different shops varies according to their respective trades, the average neighbourhood unit in this

country has a frontage of between 5 and 7 m with a depth of about 12 to 15 m. The supermarket might require anything from 300 to 800 m² depending upon the local market, with a frontage of not less than 12 m, and readily lending itself to an internal corner site.

11   Rear access to each shop for deliveries and other services is almost essential, as is adequate staff parking and turning space.

12   The movement of private cars, service vehicles, and pedestrians requires thoughtful planning and segregation.

13   Car parks should be well signposted, with good lines of vision from the entrance and exit and no dangerous turns or junctions on to the neighbourhood roads. The circulation should ideally be one-way, in which case a 45° herringbone layout of spaces can be provided which maximizes space; otherwise bays must be laid out at 90° angles. The amount of parking space required largely depends upon the availability and frequency of public transport, although a standard provision of 3 to 5 spaces for every 100 m² of

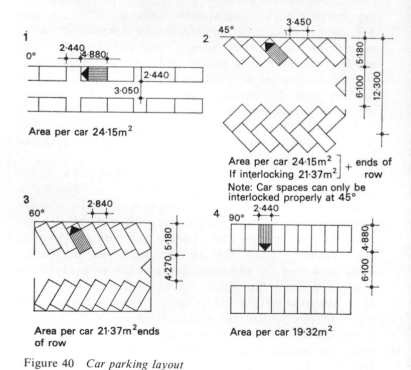

Figure 40   *Car parking layout*

selling space has been suggested. The car parks should be designed to cater for maximum peak-hour capacity, and because of the rapid turnover an efficient circulation system, separate entrance and exit, and generously sized bays should be supplied (Figure 40).

14 It must be remembered that a neighbourhood centre is intended to fulfil a social and community, as well as a retail, function. To achieve this the planner should consider the incorporation of a clinic, church, public house, cafe, bank, library, cinema, hall and

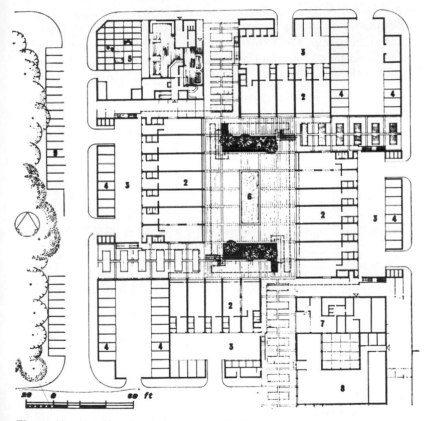

Figure 41 *Neighbourhood shopping precinct*

1	Public buildings	6	Ornamental pond
2	Shops	7	Clinic
3	Delivery area	8	Offices
4	Garages	9	Visitors' car parking
5	Patio		

public lavatory within his layout, taking account of the peculiar locational and servicing requirements of each. The centre should also provide telephones, a pram park, perhaps a crèche and seats (Figure 41).

15   As with other forms of urban development the various services of drainage, electricity, gas, water and refuse disposal must all be provided and the orientation and aspect of the layout taken into account.

An object lesson in obtaining a simple inexpensive yet highly effective neighbourhood layout can be seen halfway between Winchester and Southampton in the Fryern Arcade at Chandlers Ford. Eighteen shops are grouped in a U-formation on a site of 0.8 hectare with the open end facing the road and enclosing a one-way circulation car park as shown in Figure 42. The site slopes away from the road and an

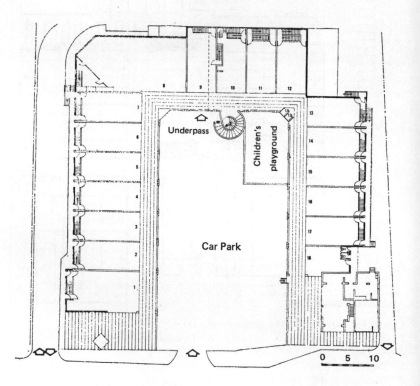

Figure 42   *General shopping level plan of Chandlers Ford*

overflow car park is provided at the rear with an access tunnel in the middle of the development; this is, however, too low for service vehicles, which have separate partially segregated side and rear access. Good lines of vision are provided from the service road and car park. Storage space and a number of flats are provided on a second storey and because of the sloping nature of the site a third floor has been created in the middle section of the U and is used for storage, lavatories and a tenants' conference room. A children's play area, telephone kiosk and a restaurant are included in the scheme which is superbly constructed and tastefully finished. A perfect balance between the needs of the motorist, the demands of the pedestrian, and the general convenience of the shopper has been established.

Other forms of site development

Every form of development, be it private, commercial, industrial or civic, possesses its own particular characteristics and poses its own problems. Whereas the building regulations control the construction and performance of buildings, there exists no general convention, code or set of standards to govern the location and layout of various types of land use activity. Their formulation would present a formidable, if not impossible, task, and to do so would be to impose an excessive degree of conformity upon urban development. Each individual application must be judged on its merits, for only in this way can vital private-sector involvement be stimulated and the rich pattern and variety of British townscape be preserved. Certain proposals, however, are endowed with common elements that influence the nature of their siting. To illustrate the matters that might warrant consideration by a local authority planning committee in assessing an application for planning permission, a brief outline of several different kinds of development and their distinctive features is included. It must be remembered, however, that no hard and fast rules can be laid down, for circumstances alter cases.

Service industry

This type of operation represents those very small commercial and industrial concerns catering for the needs of a neighbourhood and concerned with the maintenance, repair and servicing requirements of that community. It includes shoe repairs, bakery, laundry, car repairs, builders, decorators, plumbers, window cleaners and even scrap merchants.

1 They do not need to be in the middle of a residential area but they do require to be accessible to it. Approximately 1 hectare of land for a neighbourhood of 10,000 persons is sufficient space for service industry.

2 They occupy fairly substantial sites which often tend to be rather untidy. For this reason, and because of the call for accessibility, they are best located adjacent to the neighbourhood shopping centre, ideally on the rear service road.

3 Some degree of separation from the immediate vicinity of residential dwellings is required, a certain amount of disturbance being inevitable.

4 The volume and type of traffic associated with the particular service industry commands attention. The frequency should not be excessive, the surrounding roads should be of suitable construction and sufficient dimension to permit convenient access, and the lines of vision at entrances and junctions should be adequate.

5 Provision for parking employees', clients' and delivery vehicles should be made.

6 The amount of noise, fumes and vibration should be taken into account, as well as the times of incidence. A baker, for instance, might commence work and delivery at 3 or 4 o'clock in the morning, and apart from the clamour even the smell of freshly baked bread can begin to pall.

7 Because of their frequent proximity to residential areas the control of advertisements demands special consideration.

Petrol filling stations

1 The major considerations governing site layout relate to matters of traffic flow and road safety. The final solution is nearly always an uneasy compromise between commercial viability and satisfactory planning.

2 From an economic point of view an ideal location is the intersection of major traffic routes. The greater the flow the better the business. The prime position, however, must be at a spot where the flow is comparatively slow, in order to attract the attention and entice the custom of passing motorists.

3 From a satisfactory planning point of view a petrol station should not be sited opposite a break in a central reservation between dual carriageways, as it is likely to encourage traffic to cross the road, nor should it be close to a road junction or roundabout, but it could with advantage be placed where traffic is already slowing down provided it does not interfere with turning or weaving traffic.[15] The encouragement of right turns is generally to be avoided.

4 A service road layout provides an acceptable solution with two points of access and possibly more than one station. Ideally, stations should be paired on opposite sides of the road to serve traffic from both directions, and so located that the nearside station comes into view first.

5 A petrol filling station should be designated to cater for customers well away from the road. The entrance and exit should both give clear lines of vision, a one-way system of service is preferable, a deceleration lane is a great advantage, and plenty of space should be allowed for queuing during peak periods.

6 Apart from traffic considerations extra control might have to be exercised over ancillary activities that are associated with petrol fillings stations, such as car repairs and the sale of goods. These can often cause additional disturbance and congestion inappropriate to a particular area.

7 The design and appearance of a station are important, not only in its structure and layout but also in the display of advertisements, which with this type of development can reach absurd and visually disastrous proportions.

Hotels

Over the last decade tourism has developed as a major growth industry but the provision of accommodation to cater for the rise in tourists has consistently lagged behind the demand for hotel space. Great pressure is being exerted upon local planning authorities, not only in London but throughout the country, to release land for hotel construction, and a vast number of applications for planning permission are continually being received. Certain factors common to most applications can be discerned.

1 As a general rule hotel developers seek to obtain sites that optimize their position in terms of accessibility. They wish to be

as close as possible to transport termini, entertainment facilities, shopping centres and places of interest. Naturally these are also the areas of greatest congestion and conflict between other activities.

2   Adequate provision must be made for car parking. One space for every five beds and a further space for every forty daily visitors, depending upon the amount of conference and banqueting facilities, is considered to be sufficient. In central areas, however, with increased dependence upon public transport these standards are found to be extravagant.

3   One of the major problems in determining hotel location is assessing and controlling the amount of traffic generated by the proposed development. Congestion of varying degrees is likely to be caused throughout the day with exceptional peaks at particular times. This problem is again further aggravated where public room facilities are provided. In a traffic survey of the Hilton Hotel in London, well over 1000 vehicles were counted setting down and picking up passengers during a twelve-hour period. Although hotel staff generate little traffic, tending to live close to work and travel in off-peak hours, the amount of service vehicles visiting hotels, while varying considerably, can cause great pressures on the transport network. The same Hilton Hotel survey indicated sixty vans and forty lorries calling within the twelve-hour period. Another serious aspect is the growing volume of coach traffic associated with hotels, for few establishments have off-street facilities for parking and disembarking.

4   The control over the intensity of hotel development is exercised by way of plot ratio. Most central area zones permit densities of between only 2:1 and 4:1. This level is proving increasingly uneconomic for many developers and it is worth noting in this context that established hotels such as the Grosvenor and the Cumberland have plot ratios of approximately 11:1. Some flexibility in the exercise of density regulations is probably required.

5   Another contentious element that has emerged in recent years is the creeping or surreptitious development of hotel accommodation whereby existing purpose-built blocks of residential flats, having certain communal facilities and common entrance hall, have been gradually converted into hotels. A number of enforcement notices alleging a material change of use without planning permission have been served during the last few years.

6   In the case of large-scale hotel development the effect of staff
    moving into a particular area might have a debilitating effect
    upon local conditions, especially the provision of low-cost
    housing. Conversely hotels can act as great stimulants within the
    local economy, providing a valuable source of trade for service
    and entertainment industries. Furthermore, with careful planning
    and design a dual use can be made of hotel facilities for conference
    or university accommodation during off-peak seasons, thus
    promoting productivity and protecting local employment.

25 Town planning law

To be truly effective, any administrative system that seeks to plan the nation's resources and regulate the use and development of land requires the full rigour of a statutory code to ensure compliance and control. The history and administration of town planning and the responsibility for the preparation of development plans have already been described. These tend to accentuate the functions of central and local government, and the respective duties with which they are charged.To permit the proper and efficient execution of planning policy, however, it is necessary to devise and enforce a competent method of planning control. Thankfully the law relating to town planning has largely been consolidated in the 1971 Town and Country Planning Act.

General planning control

Generally speaking all development requires planning permission which can be obtained from the local planning authority. The definition of what actually constitutes 'development' is at the very nub of planning control and is described in section 22 of the Act as 'the carrying out of the building, engineering, mining or other operations in, on, over or under land, or the making of any material change in the use of any buildings or other land'.Thus there are basically two broad categories of development, first, anything in the nature of a building operation, and second, any material change of use. Problems naturally arise in determining whether or not certain activities on land fall within these categories and thus require planning permission. To assist in clarifying the position the Act expressly states that:

1   *The following are development* (section 22):
    the use of one house for two or more dwellings

the depositing of refuse on an existing dump if the area is enlarged or the height increased above surrounding land

the display of advertisements on the outside of a building not normally so used

2 *The following are not developments* (section 22):

works of improvement, alteration or repair, except for building below ground level, which do not materially affect the external appearance of the building

maintenance or improvement of existing highways, sewers, pipes, and cables undertaken by the local authority or other statutory undertakers

the use of any buildings or land within the boundary of a house for any purpose incidental to the enjoyment of the house as a house

the use of land for agriculture, forestry and associated buildings.

3 *The following may be development but do not require planning permission* (section 23):

the resumption before 6 December 1968 of the normal use of land which was temporarily used for another purpose on 1 July 1948, when planning control commenced

the occasional use of land for a purpose apart from its normal use, so long as there has been at least one such occasional use before 6 December 1968

the use of land unoccupied on 1 July 1948 for the purpose last used before that date but after 7 January 1937

the resumption to a previous use on the expiration of a limited planning permission or enforcement notice provided that use is not itself in contravention of planning control

the display of certain types of advertisement for which planning permission is deemed to be granted under the Town and Country Planning (Control of Advertisements) Regulations 1969, as amended

certain development by local authorities and statutory undertakers sanctioned by central government under a development order.

Apart from town and country planning legislation, a vast body of case law has been decided in an attempt to further define the act of development. A building operation has been held to mean work normally undertaken by a builder, such as rebuilding, alteration and addition to any structure or erection, excluding plant and machinery.

This has included the construction of Bekonscot model village[1] and even the demolition of part of a building.[2] The expression 'material change of use' is nowhere defined as such, but the change must be substantial.[3] This can be caused by the nature, intensification or frequency of the change. A full discussion of the relevant case law is beyond the scope of this text.[4] Statute has, however, sought to provide some guidance in the form of the 1963 Use Classes Order, as amended. This order sets out nineteen classes of land use activity such as shops, class one; offices, class two; light industry, class three; general industry, class four; certain chemical operations, class five; and so on. When, in the event of a change of use taking place from one use to another falling within the same use class, it does not amount to a 'material' change of use, and does not constitute an act of development, and therefore does not require planning permission. It says no more. It does not make any statement regarding a change of use from one use class to another; this may or may not constitute development according to the individual circumstances. Exemptions are made in certain classes, such as the sale of fried fish and motor cars in class one, and expressions such as 'shop' and 'office' are further defined in both statute and case law; a shop, for example, is a building used for retail trade and includes a hairdresser, undertaker, ticket agency but not betting office, garage, hotel or public house.

Development control

As previously mentioned, most acts of development require prior consent from the relevant local planning authority. If any doubt exists in the potential developer's mind whether a particular act constitutes development or not, the matter may be determined by an application to the local planning authority under section 53 of the 1971 Town and Country Planning Act. One notable exception to the general requirement to obtain planning permission is the power conferred upon the Secretary of State under section 24 of the 1971 Act to introduce *development orders* which automatically grant permission to particular kinds of development known as *permitted development.* These are introduced in an attempt to rid the public and the planning authorities alike of the mundane trivia that might otherwise clog the planning machine. The most important of these orders is the General Development Order 1973. This sets down twenty-three categories of development for which planning permission is automatically granted, and includes the enlargement of existing dwelling houses within prescribed limits, the construction of fences and walls to certain heights, the external painting of buildings, the erection of selected temporary buildings, and specified material changes of use. There are certain standard conditions relating to highways and road traffic which apply to all categories. Moreover, if for any special reason permitted development is thought inappropriate, the Secretary of State may direct or approve the withdrawal of deemed permission, either for a particular category or for a chosen area. This is done by issuing an *article 4 direction* and is accepted practice in conservation areas and areas of outstanding natural beauty. The General Development Order also lays down the procedure involved in applying for planning permission.

Application for planning permission

Application must be made to the local planning authority on the forms provided, and to save unnecessary expenditure outline planning permission can be sought prior to a detailed submission. Once outline permission is granted the authority are obliged to allow the development in some form or other but may reserve their judgement on such matters as siting, layout and design. An applicant does not have to possess an interest in the land, but in such circumstances he is required to serve notice of his intention upon the owners and complete certain certificates to this effect in accordance with section 27 of the 1971 Act. Certain classes of 'bad neighbour' development such as knacker's yards, public conveniences, cinemas, dance halls and refuse disposal operations must be publicized in the local press, and by a notice on the site, to enable third parties to make representations for consideration by the local planning authority when coming to their decision. Under section 28 this provision also now applies to proposals that might affect the character of a conservation area.

Having received the application the local planning authority must notify the applicant of receipt and make their decision within two months, unless a trunk road is affected, in which case the period is three months. These periods may, however, be extended by agreement between the parties. If no decision is reached within this time the application is deemed to be refused. To expedite the procedure of planning control in this country some critics favour the adoption of the French system whereby permission is deemed granted after the effluxion of the statutory time limit.

In making their decision the local planning authority must have regard to the provisions of the development plan and any other considerations thought material. The decision itself must be made in writing and may refuse permission, grant it unconditionally, or grant it subject to conditions. If permission is refused or conditions are imposed, reasons must be given. A register of all applications and decisions is kept by the authority and is open for public inspection. Since 1968 certain decisions may now be given by a named officer if the local planning authority has delegated the power to him so to do. In exceptional circumstances where matters of national concern or extreme controversy are involved the Minister may under section 35 of the 1971 Act 'call in' an application and determine it himself.

Duration of planning permission

Under section 41 of the 1971 Act all planning permissions are subject to a time limit of five years, although this may be extended or reduced in individual cases. Outline permission, however, is only valid for three years, and development must be started within two years of any reserved matters being dealt with. The beginning of development is defined in section 43 of the 1971 Act. These provisions limiting the duration of planning permission were introduced to facilitate the process of development control, combat the speculative holding of land off the market, and prevent a number of out-of-date permissions from accumulating upon a piece of land which might involve considerable compensation to revoke. In the same context the ability to limit the time allowed for the completion of development has been conferred upon local planning authorities who are now empowered to serve a *completion notice*. This terminates the permission relating to development already begun but which has not been finished within the time specified by the permission, and which appears unlikely to be completed within a reasonable time. The notice, which is served upon the owner and occupier, must be confirmed by the Minister and allows twelve months for completion before the planning permission ceases. Any development finished before that date is considered permissible.

Conditional planning permission

The local planning authority may impose such conditions 'as they think fit' upon a permission (section 30). These may relate to the regulation of any land within the control of the applicant, the removal of buildings and discontinuance of use at the end of a specified period, the length of the permission and the time by which it must be started, as well as the design, layout and materials of any buildings. Any condition must, however, be 'fit' from a planning point of view. It must be reasonably certain, intelligently and sensibly related to the particular planning scheme and the prevailing policy for the area, made in good faith, and not attached for an ulterior motive. The condition restricting occupation of cottages to agricultural workers has been held valid,[5] but the obligation to construct a road which was not just for service but gave a public right of way,[6] the payment of money as security against fulfilment of conditions, and the restriction of occupation of industrial premises to firms already within the county,[7] have all been held to be invalid. If a condition is invalid it is a matter of common sense whether or not it strikes at the root of the whole permission and thus renders it invalid. If it is incidental and not fundamental to the decision then the original planning permission can still be valid.

Appeal

Appeal against refusal of permission or the imposition of conditions lies to the Secretary of State under section 36 and must be made within six months of receipt of the decision. The Secretary of State may reject or allow the appeal, or may alter the terms of the conditions, but before doing so he must afford both sides, if they so desire, either a private hearing or a local public inquiry before one of his inspectors. To save the expense of a hearing, appeal proceedings can be conducted by way of written submissions. To expedite matters certain appeals are not only heard by the Secretary of State's inspector but may also be determined by him. The Secretary of State is further empowered to refer an appeal relating to the design or external appearance of a particular building to an independent tribunal by way of a development order. Certain matters of exceptional importance may be referred to a planning inquiry commission consisting of a chairman and several other members. All appeals to the Secretary of State are otherwise final except on a point of law which lies to the High Court and must be made within six weeks of the appeal decision.

Revocation and modification

If, owing to a change of policy, circumstance, or even error, a local planning authority wishes to retract or alter a planning permission they have previously granted they may do so by means of an order made under section 45 of the 1971 Act. Such a revocation or modification order must be served before any change of use has taken place or any building operations have been finished and does not affect completed work. Unless the orders are unopposed or unlikely to give rise to claims for compensation the Secretary of State's consent to the service of the order is required. Compensation is payable for any abortive expenditure incurred such as the preparation of maps and plans and for any loss directly attributable to the order.

If a local planning authority desires the removal or alteration of an existing authorized, but non-conforming, development they must serve a *discontinuance order* under section 51, which again requires confirmation by the Secretary of State and attracts full compensation for any loss and disturbance caused by the service of the order.

Control of advertisements

Owing to the large number of applications and their special nature, a separate code has been devised for the control of outdoor advertisements under the Town and Country Planning (Control of Advertisements) Regulations 1969, now authorized by section 63 of the Town and Country Planning Act 1971. Although the display of advertisements is considered to be a building operation, thus constituting an act of development requiring planning permission, the regulations confer a wide range of 'deemed consent'. Among those included within these classes of permitted development or deemed consent are temporary advertisements such as for-sale boards, the functional advertisements of local authorities and statutory undertakers such as bus stops and street name plates, those relating to certain business premises such as trade signs or professional plates, and flags bearing the emblem or name of the person occupying the building over which they fly. Certain standard conditions are laid down in the regulations which apply to all these categories in respect of siting, dimension, safety and cleanliness. It can be seen that the definition of the term 'advertisement' is fairly broad; it applies to 'any word, letter, model, sign, placard, board, notice, device or representation, whether illuminated or not, in the nature of and employed wholly or in part for the purposes of advertisement, announcement or direction'. The regulations do not apply, however, to those advertisements which are not readily visible to the public, are inside a building and more than one metre away from any opening, form part of the fabric of a building or are carried on a vehicle. Where other proposed advertisements do not fall within the classes of permitted developments they naturally require planning permission.

If it is thought appropriate, a local planning authority can require that advertisements currently displayed with deemed consent should be made subject to control by the authority and 'express consent' obtained from them in order to secure continued display. This practice is known as the *challenge procedure* and is operated in the interests of amenity or public safety. Any such grant of express consent must be for a fixed term of not more than five years.

Stricter control over the display of advertisements is exercised in areas of special control which are normally designated in the development plan or created by means of an order confirmed by the Secretary of State. The general rule is that no advertisements should be displayed in these areas apart from essential public signs; those that are permitted are treated as exceptions to the rule. Over one-third of the country is now covered by *special area control.*

Control of caravans

Because of the inordinate amount of litigation caused by this particular form of development in the years proceeding the 1947 Town and Country Planning Act, the general code of law relating to the control of caravans was reinforced by the Caravan Sites and Control of Development Act 1960. In general, the development of land for the siting of caravans requires both planning permission and a site licence. Application for planning permission is made to the local planning authority and must be obtained before a site licence can be granted. The site licence is issued by the local borough or district council who are obliged to grant one if planning permission has been obtained. They may, however, impose conditions which they consider to be necessary or desirable in the interests of both the caravan dwellers and the public at large. These conditions may relate to the number of caravans permitted, their size, layout and state of repair; and the sanitation, safety and amenity of the site. Appeal against the conditions attached to a site licence lies to the Magistrates Court and must be made within twenty-eight days of issue.

There are a number of circumstances in which exemption for a caravan site from the provisions of the 1960 Act is given; these include the use of land within the curtilage of a house so long as it is incidental to the enjoyment of the house; the use of land for not more than twenty-eight days in the year for a single caravan not exceeding two nights at any one time; the use of more than five acres of land for not more than three caravans at any one time for a period not exceeding twenty-eight days in the year; and the use of land for exempted caravan organizations, agricultural, construction and entertainment workers.

Another provision relating to caravans and concerning town planning, albeit somewhat peripherally, is the Caravan Sites Act 1968, which places a responsibility upon local planning authorities to consider the provision of caravan sites for, and protect the interests of, 'gypsies and other persons of nomadic habit'.

Protection of trees and woodland

Under section 59 of the 1971 Act a *tree preservation order* can be served by the local planning authority on an individual tree, groups of trees, or woodlands, the only criterion being that it is 'expedient so to do in the interests of amenity'. The confirmation of the Secretary of State is required unless no objection is raised, and in any event no order can be made on Forestry Commission or Crown land without their consent. The procedure for making an order is laid down in the Town and Country Planning (Tree Preservation Order) Regulations 1969 and covers the form of the notice, the persons to be served, and time limitations regarding appeal. Once in operation a tree preservation order prohibits the cutting down, topping or destruction of protected trees without the consent of the authority unless they are dead, dying, diseased or dangerous. Even then it is possible that the owner may be required to replace the felled trees.

If certain trees appear to be in imminent danger the local planning authority are empowered under the Civic Amenities Act 1967 to issue a provisional tree preservation order operative for six months which takes immediate effect. This same Act has introduced fines of up to £250 or twice the value of the tree, whichever is the greater, for contravention of an order.

Protection of buildings

The Secretary of State for the Department of the Environment is charged under section 54 of the 1971 Town and Country Planning Act with compiling a list of buildings of special architectural and historic interest. The details of such protection is dealt with in the chapter on conservation (Chapter 17).

Enforcement of planning control

If a local planning authority considers that any development has been carried out without the grant of planning permission, or that any condition or limitation to which such permission was subject has not been complied with, an *enforcement notice* can be served in accordance with section 87 of the 1971 Town and Country Planning Act. The notice can also be served by the Secretary of State for the Department of the Environment. It must be served on both the owner and the occupier, and, if the authority think fit, on any other person having an interest in the land who might be affected. If the alleged breach of planning control is a building operation, or a change of use to a single residential dwelling house, the notice must be served within four years of the breach occurring. If the breach amounts to any other material change of use a notice may be served at any future time. Since the four-year rule also used to apply in cases alleging a material change of use and was only abolished in 1968, a person having an interest in land which was subject to a change of use taking place before 1964, and still continuing, may apply to the local planning authority for a *certificate of established use* which if granted precludes subsequent enforcement proceedings.

Although there is no prescribed form for an enforcement notice it must specify the alleged breach, describe the steps required to remedy the breach, the time allowed for the necessary steps to be taken, and the date from which the notice becomes effective, being not less than twenty-eight days. It must be served to take effect on all the parties at the same time. Care must be taken in the preparation and service of an enforcement notice because, although the Secretary of State can correct any informality, defect or error which is not material on appeal, a false statement of fact as the basis upon which the notice is served can render it a nullity.

Within the twenty-eight days before the notice takes effect an appeal may be lodged with the Secretary of State who, if the appellant or the local planning authority desire, must afford each an opportunity of appearing before an inspector appointed by him. An appeal can only be made on certain grounds, which are, that planning permission for the alleged breach ought to be granted, has been granted or is not required, the time limit has expired, no development is involved, the requirements of the notice are excessive, or that the period of compliance is too short. The notification of appeal need only indicate the general grounds upon which it is made; in fact for safety all can be stated, but the Secretary of State discourages mere recital and usually requests amplification. Unlike most other planning appeal proceedings the burden of proof is placed firmly upon the appellant and evidence is usually given under oath. The Secretary of State has a wide discretion to allow or reject the appeal, grant planning permission, or vary attached conditions, and except on a point of law where further appeal lies to the High Court, his decision is final. Once the appeal has been rejected the notice immediately becomes effective. If the terms are not then complied with, several other remedies are available to the local planning authority; in certain circumstances they may enter the property to ensure compliance and recover expenses, apply to the High Court for an injunction against persistent breach, and even prosecute the occupier of the land when he is not directly responsible, who may himself in turn make recovery from the owner at fault.

Because development in contravention of planning control was frequently pursued during appeal proceedings, to the general detriment of the public interest, a new procedure called a *stop notice* was introduced in 1968, now re-enacted in section 90 of the 1971 Act, which has the effect of halting the alleged breach almost immediately. This notice can be served by the local planning authority upon any person who appears either to have an interest in the land or be concerned with carrying out the alleged breach. It can only be issued following the service of an enforcement notice and in respect of a building operation or the deposit of refuse specifying the date from which it is to take effect, being not less than three days and not more than fourteen. Failure to observe the notice is a criminal offence punishable by a fine. If, however, the enforcement notice to which it relates is subsequently withdrawn or quashed on appeal the stop notice automatically ceases to have effect and full compensation for any loss incurred can be claimed.

Compensation for planning restrictions and proposals

As a general rule the circumstances in which compensation is available for refusal of planning permission or the imposition of onerous conditions are severely curtailed. In respect of *new development*, which if defined as any development not falling within the 8th schedule of the 1971 Act, compensation is limited under part 7 of the Act to those applications where an 'unexpected balance of established development value' is attached to the land. This refers to the established claim made under the 1947 Town and Country Planning Act as amended by the 1953 and 1954 Acts and reduced by the value of any subsequent development. Even if this condition is fulfilled, compensation is still not available in accordance with section 147 of the 1971 Act if the refusal or condition relates to a material change of use, access to a highway, the working of minerals, the display of advertisements, the number, design or layout of dwellings, premature development, development of land liable to subsidence or flooding, or where permission exists for residential, commercial or industrial development. This precludes payment in the vast majority of cases. Compensation does, however, arise when restrictions apply to development that falls within part 2 of the 8th schedule, often referred to as *existing use rights*. It may also be claimed, as previously intimated, in situations where planning permission has been revoked, modified or discontinued.

The other main categories in which compensation becomes payable are when individuals suffer as a result of an adverse planning decision or proposal and are able to compel the local planning authority to purchase their interest. Where planning permission is refused or onerous conditions are attached which 'render the land incapable of reasonable beneficial use in its existing state' an aggrieved owner may within twelve months of the decision, under section 180 of the 1971 Act, serve a *purchase notice* on the local authority requiring them to acquire the land affected by the decision. The notice may only apply to the land in the original application, not more and not less. The local authority must serve a counter-notice within three months, either accepting, in which case notice to treat is deemed to be served, or refusing, giving reasons which must be communicated to the Secretary of State. He can confirm or reject the notice, with or without modifications, confirm the original planning permission, grant alternative planning permission, or substitute an alternative purchaser, notifying the parties accordingly and affording them an opportunity of a hearing before an inspector. Apart from the refusal of planning permission or imposition of onerous conditions, a purchase notice can also be served in connection with revocation, modification, discontinuance and tree preservation orders, as well as the control of advertisements, listed buildings and industrial premises.

If an individual is affected by an adverse planning proposal, as opposed to decision, he may serve a *blight notice* upon the local planning authority in accordance with section 192 of the 1971 Act, so long as the land concerned is indicated in a statutory plan as being required for one of the purposes described in the Act. These include highway development, compulsory purchase, public facilities and services. In other words, the eventual loss of the land is a prerequisite to serving a purchase notice. The class of owner who can claim is, however, restricted to resident owner–occupiers of residential dwelling houses, owner–occupiers of farms, and non-resident owner–occupiers of hereditaments with an annual value below £750. Before the owner can serve a blight notice he must show that he has made reasonable attempts to sell his interest and has been unable to do so except at a price substantially below the normal market value. The authority upon whom the notice is served may, within two months, serve a counter notice under section 194 denying blight, refusing the owner's attempts to sell, or claiming that they do not propose to compulsorily acquire the land for at least fifteen years, which exempts them from purchase. Appeal lies within a further two months to the Lands Tribunal.

References

Chapter 1: The need to plan

1 L. Keeble, 'Principles and practice of town and country planning', *Estates Gazette* (1969).
2 Thomas Sharp, *Town Planning* (Penguin 1940).
3 J. B. McLoughlin, *Urban and Regional Planning: A Systems Approach* (Faber 1969).
4 P. Hall, *Urban and Regional Planning* (David & Charles 1975).
5 D. Foley, 'British town planning: one ideology or three?', *British Journal of Sociology*, vol. 2 (1960) p. 211.
6 W. Solesbury, *Policy in Urban Planning* (Pergamon 1974).
7 M. Webber, *Beyond the Industrial Age and Permissive Planning*, CES working paper 18 (1968). Quoted in Solesbury.
8 G. Cherry, *Town Planning in its Social Context* (Leonard Hill 1970).
9 Solesbury, *Policy in Urban Planning*.
10 D. Eversley, *The Planner in Society* (Faber 1979).
11 McLoughlin, *Urban and Regional Planning: A Systems Approach*.
12 J. F. Q. Switzer, 'The surveyor in society', *Chartered Surveyor* (August 1969).
13 A. E. Weddle, *Technique of Landscape Architecture* (Heinemann 1967).
14 Cherry, *Town Planning in its Social Context*.
15 J. Western, 'The role of the sociologist in town planning', *Royal Town Planning Institute Journal* (May 1971).
16 F. S. Chapin, *Urban Land Use Planning* (University of Illinois Press 1965).

Chapter 2: The emergence of modern town planning

1 C. Bell and R. Bell, *City Fathers: The Early History of Town Planning in Britain* (Barrie & Rockcliff 1969).
2 R. Owen, *A New View of Society* (1813).
3 M. Hillman, *Towards a Linear New Town. Essays in Local Government Enterprise* (Merlin 1965).
4 C. Perry, *Housing for the Machine Age* (Russell Sage 1939).

5   P. Willmott, 'Housing density and town design in a new town: Stevenage', *Town Planning Review*, vol. 34.
6   Ministry of Housing and Local Government, *Green Belts* (HMSO 1962).
7   L. Keeble, 'Principles and practice of town and country planning', *Estates Gazette* (1969).
8   D. R. Mandelker, *Green Belts and Urban Growth* (University of Wisconsin 1962).

Chapter 3: The foundations of town planning legislation

1   E. Jones, *Notes to the People* (1851).
2   T. C. Horsfall, *The Example of Germany* (Manchester University Press 1904).
3   W. Ashworth, *The Genesis of Modern British Town Planning* (Routledge and Kegan Paul 1954).
4   Ministry of Housing and Local Government, *Town and Country Planning* (HMSO 1967).
5   Ministry of Housing and Local Government, *Development Plans: A Manual on Form and Content* (HMSO 1970).
6   Department of the Environment, *Structure Plans: The Examination in Public* (HMSO 1973).
7   ibid.
8   Department of the Environment, *Structure Plans*, Circular 98/74 (HMSO 1974).
9   Department of Environment, *Structure Plans*, Circular 55/77 (HMSO 1977).
10   C. Fudge, 'Local plans, structure plans and policy planning', *The Planner* (September 1976).
11   Institute of Local Government Studies, *Tackling Urban Development* (Birmingham University 1977).
12   J. Ratcliffe, 'Local plans: a time for realism', *Built Environment Quarterly* (June 1977).

Chapter 4: The organization and administration of town planning

1   J. Stewart, 'Corporate planning', in M. Bruton (ed.), *Spirit and Purpose of Planning* (Hutchinson 1974).
2   R. Hambledon, *Policy Planning and Local Government* (Hutchinson 1977).
3   ibid.
4   J. Stewart, *The Responsive Local Authority* (Charles Knight 1974).
5   Hambledon, *Policy Planning*.
6   Department of the Environment, *Area Management*, Consultation Paper (1974).
7   Hambledon, *Policy Planning*.

Chapter 5: The planning process

1 J. B. McLoughlin, *Urban and Regional Planning: A Systems Approach* (Faber 1969).
2 G. McDougall, 'A critique of the systems view of planning', *Oxford Working Papers in Planning Education and Research*, no. 9 (1971).
3 D. Couts, 'What is forecasting?' in G. Yewdall (ed.), *Management Decision Making* (Pan 1969).
4 J. Seeley, 'What is planning? Definition and strategy', *Journal of the American Institute of Planners* (May 1964).

Chapter 8: Employment and industry

1 E. Hoover, *The Location of Economic Activity* (McGraw Hill 1948).
2 A. Lösch, *The Economics of Location* (Yale 1954).
3 L. C. Hunter, 'Planning and the labour market', in J. B. Cullingworth *et al.* (eds.), *Regional and Urban Studies* (Allen & Unwin 1969).
4 J. N. Jackson, *Surveys for Town and Country Planning* (Hutchinson 1963).
5 J. T. Hughes, 'Employment projection and urban development' in Cullingworth *et al., Regional and Urban Studies.*
6 H. W. Richardson, *Elements of Regional Economics* (Penguin 1969).
7 C. M. Law, 'Employment growth and regional policy in north west England', *Regional Studies*, vol. 4 (1970).
8 Richardson, *Elements of Regional Economics.*
9 M. Camina, 'Local authorities and the attraction of industry', *Progress in Planning*, vol. 3, part 2 (Pergamon 1974).
10 D. Eversley, 'Social and psychological factors in the determination of industrial location', in T. Wilson (ed.), *Papers on Regional Development* (Blackwell 1965).
11 P. Blythe, 'Small firms' (Unpublished thesis, Polytechnic of Central London, 1978).
12 G. Bannock, *The Smaller Firm in Britain and Germany* (Wilton House Special Study 1976).

Chapter 9: Housing

1 *Commission of Inquiry into the Impact of Rates on Household Formation,* Cmnd 25/82 (HMSO 1965).
2 J. B. Cullingworth, 'Housing analysis' in *Regional and Urban Studies* (Allen & Unwin 1969).
3 P. Gray and R. Russell, *The housing situation in 1960* (Central Office of Information 1962).

Chapter 10: Offices

1   P. Daniels, 'Office policy problems in Greater London', *The Planner* (July 1977).
2   ibid.

Chapter 11: Shopping

1   G. Lomas, 'Retail trading centres in the East Midlands', *Town Planning Institute Journal* (March 1964).
2   R. C. Nelson, *The Selection of Retail Locations* (F. W. Dodge Corporation, New York 1958).
3   R. K. Cox, *Retail Site Assessment* (Business Books 1968).
4   C. S. Jones, *Regional Shopping Centres* (Business Books 1969).
5   National Economic Development Office, *Urban Shopping Models* (HMSO 1970).
6   Jones, *Regional Shopping Centres.*
7   R. Davies and D. Bennison, 'The planning repercussions of in-town shopping schemes', *Estates Gazette* (8 April 1978).
8   B. Wade, 'Hypermarkets and superstores: their characteristics and effects' in *Hypermarkets and Superstores* (URPI 1976).
9   ibid.

Chapter 12: Transportation

1   J. Grant, *The Politics of Urban Transport Planning* (Earth Resources 1977).
2   ibid.
3   K. Button, 'Transport policy in the United Kingdom 1968–74, *Three Banks Review* (September 1974).
4   A. Aldous, *Battle for the Environment* (Fontana 1972).
5   M. Hudson, *The Bicycle Planning Book* (Friends of the Earth 1978).
6   ibid.

Chapter 13: Leisure and recreation

1   M. Dower, *Fourth Wave: The Challenge of Leisure* (Civic Trust 1965).
2   J. E. Palmer, 'Recreational planning: a bibliographic overview', *Planning Outlook* (Spring 1967).
3   Countryside Recreation Research Advisory Group, *Countryside Recreation Glossary* (Countryside Commission 1970).
4   J. Patmore, 'Recreation', in J. Dawson and J. Doomkamp (eds.), *Evaluating the Human Environment* (Edward Arnold 1973).
5   T. Burton, *Experiments in Recreation Research* (Allen & Unwin 1971).
6   M. Roberts, *An Introduction to Town Planning Techniques* (Hutchinson 1974).

Chapter 14: Evaluation

1   N. Lichfield, 'Evaluation methodology of urban and regional plans – a review', *Regional Studies* (August 1970).
2   ibid.
3   A. R. Prest and R. Turvey, 'Cost Benefit Analysis: a survey', *Economic Journal* (December 1966).
4   ibid.
5   N. Lichfield, 'Cost benefit analysis in urban expansion: a case study – Peterborough', *Regional Studies*, vol. 3 (1969).
6   ibid.
7   M. Hill, 'A goal achievement matrix in the evaluation of alternative plans', *American Institute of Planners Journal*, vol. 34 (1968).
8   B. Malisz, *The Economics of Shaping Towns* (Polish Academy of Science 1963).
9   *Grangemouth – Falkirk Regional Survey and Plan,* vol. 2 (HMSO Edinburgh 1968).
10 *Central Borders Study*, vol. I (HMSO, Edinburgh 1968).
11 J. Kozlowski and J. T. Hughes, 'Urban threshold theory and analysis', *Town Planning Institute Journal* (February 1967).
12 N. Lichfield and P. Wendt, 'Six English new towns: a financial appraisal', *Town Planning Review*, vol. 40 (1969).

Chapter 15: Associated planning techniques

1   L. Marsoni, 'On the use of models as tools for planning', *Arena* (September 1968).
2   I. S. Lowry, *Model of Metropolis* (Rand Corporation 1964).
3   M. Batty, 'Recent developments in land use modeling. A review of British research', *Urban Studies* (June 1972).
4   R. A. Garin, 'A matrix formulation of the Lowry model for intra-metropolitan activities', *American Institute of Planners Journal*, vol. 132 (1966).
5   Batty, 'Recent developments in land use modeling'.
6   M. Batty, 'Models and projections of the space economy', *Town Planning Review*, vol. 41 (1970).
7   M. Batty, 'An activity allocation model for the Nottingham–Derbyshire sub-region', *Regional Studies*, vol. 4 (1970).
8   M. Echenique, 'A spatial model of urban stock and activity', *Regional Studies*, vol. 3 (1969).
9   F. S. Chapin, *Urban Land Use Planning* (University of Illinois 1970).
10 N. Lichfield, 'Evaluation methodology of urban and regional plans: a review', *Regional Studies* (August 1970).
11 A. Potter, 'The methodology of impact analysis', *Town and Country Planning* (1978) p. 400.
12 ibid.

Chapter 16: Rural planning

1   Because of this the chapter draws heavily upon: G. Cherry, (ed.), *Rural Planning Problems* (Leonard Hill 1976).
2   M. Dunn, 'Population change and the settlement pattern' Cherry, *Rural Planning Problems.*
3   Dunn, 'Population change'.
4   I. Martin, 'Rural communities', in Cherry, *Rural Planning Problems.*
5   A. Rogers, 'Rural housing', in Cherry, *Rural Planning Problems.*
6   R. Pahl, *Whose City?* (Longman 1970).
7   Pahl, *Whose City?*
8   A. Gilg, 'Rural employment' in Cherry, *Rural Planning Problems.*
9   ibid.
10 ibid.
11 D. Robinson, 'Rural landscape' in Cherry, *Rural Planning Problems.*
12 I. Laurie, *et al., Landscape Evaluation* (Centre for Urban and Regional Studies 1976).
13 P. Hall, *et al., Containment of Urban England* (Allen & Unwin 1973).
14 Centre for Agricultural Strategy, 'Land for agriculture' (CAS Report 1, 1976).
15 E. Braley-Smith (ed.), *Constructional and Other Bulk Materials* (Oxford University Press 1974).
16 M. Nicholls, *Dereliction* (Unpublished dissertation, South Bank Polytechnic, 1978).
17 Ministry of Housing and Local Government, *The Use of Conditions in Planning Permissions*, Circular 5/68 (HMSO 1968).
18 Ministry of Housing and Local Government, *The Control of Mineral Working* (HMSO 1960).
19 Nicholls, *Dereliction.*

Chapter 17: Conservation

1   D. Eversley, 'The planner in society: the changing role of a profession' (Town and Country Planning Association, Summer School 1975).
2   M. Thorncraft, *The Economics of Conservation* (Royal Institution of Chartered Surveyors 1975).
3   A. Youngson, 'Britain's historic towns', in P. Ward (ed.), *Conservation and Development in Historic Towns and Cities* (Oriel 1968).
4   R. Worskett, 'Great Britain: progress in conservation', in S. Cantacuzino, *Conservation in Europe* (Architectural Press 1975).

Chapter 18: Resource planning and pollution

1   P. A. Stone, 'Resources and the economic framework', in P. Cowan (ed.), *Developing Patterns of Urbanisation* (Oliver & Boyd 1970).

2 P. Ehrlich, *The Population Bomb* (Ballentine 1968).
3 ibid.
4 I. Simmons, *The Ecology of Natural Resources* (Edward Arnold 1974).
5 A. Edwards and G. Wibberley, 'An agricultural land budget for Great Britain' (Wye College, 1971).
6 *Natural Resources: Sinews for Survival* (HMSO 1972).
7 M. Allaby, 'British farming: revolution or suicide?', in J. Barr (ed.), *The Environmental Handbook* (Ballentine 1972).
8 D. Robinson, 'Rural landscape', in G. Cherry (ed.), *Rural Planning Problems* (Leonard Hill 1976).
9 *Natural Resources* (HMSO 1972).
10 Department of the Environment, *The Human Environment: The British View* (HMSO 1972).
11 H. Richardson, 'Economics and the environment', *National Westminster Bank Quarterly Review* (May 1971).
12 Department of the Environment, *The Human Environment*.
13 The Ecologist, *A Blueprint for Survival* (Penguin 1972).
14 P. Odell, *Energy Needs and Resources* (Macmillan 1974).
15 P. Chapman, *Fuel's Paradise* (Penguin 1974).
16 J. Edington and M. Edington, *Ecology and Environmental Planning* (Chapman & Hall 1977).

Chapter 19: The inner city

1 R. Llewellyn-Davies *et al., Unequal City*, final report of the Birmingham inner area study (HMSO 1977).
2 D. Eversley, 'Semi detached view', *Built Environment Quarterly* (September 1977).
3 Department of the Environment, *Inner Area Studies* (HMSO 1977).
4 G. Shankland, *et al., Inner London: Policies for Dispersal and Balance*, final report of the inner area study (HMSO 1977).
5 Institute of Local Government Studies, *Tackling Urban Deprivation: The Contribution of Area Based Management* (1977).
6 Shankland, *Inner London*.
7 Lewellyn-Davies *et al., Unequal City*.
8 M. Haxby, 'Inner city problems – a role for local planning'(Unpublished dissertation, Polytechnic of the South Bank, 1978).
9 ibid.
10 J. Burrows, 'Vacant urban land', *Planner* (January 1978).

Chapter 20: Planning and public participation

1 D. Lock, 'Legal aid funds for planning aid', *Planner* (January 1978).
2 J. Kelly, 'Community action' (Unpublished dissertation, Polytechnic of the South Bank, 1978).

3   J. Cox, *Cities: The Public Dimension* (Penguin 1976).
4   R. Bailey, *The Squatters* (Penguin 1973).
5   Cox, *Cities*.

Chapter 22: The development control system

1   D. Vickery, 'Development control: a new sense of purpose', *Planner* (January 1978).
2   G. Holt (ed.), *Planning Appeals* (Ambit Publications 1979).
3   Department of the Environment, Planning Appeal Ref. APP 5280/A/ 76/4928.
4   H. Couch, *RICS Planning and Development Division Study Day on Development Briefs* (Royal Institution of Chartered Surveyors 1979).
5   Holt, *Planning Appeals*.
6   M. Grant, 'Enforcing the brief', Conference on Development Briefs, Polytechnic of the South Bank (6 June 1979).

Chapter 23: Planning standards

1   Ministry of Housing and Local Government, *The Density of Residential Areas* (HMSO 1952).
2   Ministry of Housing and Local Government, *Residential Areas: Higher Densities* (HMSO 1963).
3   P. Hall, *London 2000* (Faber 1969).
4   G. P. Wibberley, *Agriculture and urban growth: a study of the competition for urban land* (Michael Joseph 1959).
5   J. R. James, Paper given to the Town and Country Planning Association, Conference on residential densities and housing layouts (1967).
6   L. Keeble, 'Town planning at the crossroads', *Town Planning Institute Journal* (August 1961).
7   James, Conference paper.
8   Keeble, 'Town planning at the crossroads'.
9   Ministry of Housing and Local Government, *Residential Areas, Higher Densities*, Planning bulletin 2 (HMSO 1963).
10 G. Rosenburg, 'A standard for the control of building bulk in business areas', *Town Planning Institute Journal* (September 1969).
11 United States Department of Housing and Urban Development, land planning bulletin 7.
12 James, Conference paper.
13 Ministry of Housing and Local Government, *Houses and Flats* (HMSO 1958).
14 A. Strachan, 'Car parks and shopping', *Estates Gazette* (October 1971).
15 L. Keeble, 'Principles and practice of town and country planning', *Estates Gazette* (1969).

16 D. Winterbottom, 'How much space do you need?', *Town Planning Institute Journal* (1967).

Chapter 24: Site layout and development

1 K. Lynch, *Site Planning* (Massachusetts Institute of Technology 1971).
2 See pages 398–9.
3 F. Gibberd, *Town Design* (Architectural Press 1970).
4 ibid., p. 297.
5 ibid., p. 310.
6 K. Leibbrand, *Transportation and Planning* (Leonard Hill 1970).
7 Lynch, *Site Planning*, p. 139.
8 ibid., p. 169.
9 ibid., p. 184.
10 ibid., p. 133.
11 Ministry of Housing and Local Government, *Industrial and Commercial Development*, development control policy notes (HMSO 1969).
12 L. Keeble, 'Principles and practice of town and country planning', *Estates Gazette* (1969).
13 Gibberd, *Town Design*, p. 225.
14 Lynch, *Site Planning*, p. 343.
15 Ministry of Housing and Local Government, *Industrial and Commercial Development*, petrol filling stations.

Chapter 25: Town planning law

1 *Buckinghamshire County Council v. Callingham*, 1952.
2 *Coleshill and District Investment Co. Ltd. v. Ministry of Health and Local Government* (1968).
3 *Palser v. Grinling* (1948).
4 See D. Heap, *An Outline of Planning Law* (Sweet & Maxwell 1979).
5 *Fawcett Properties Ltd. v. Buckinghamshire County Council* (1959).
6 *Hall and Co. Ltd. v. Shoreham-by-Sea Urban District Council* (1964).
7 *Allnat London Properties Ltd. v. Middlesex County Council* (1964).

Recommended further reading

Chapter 1: The need to plan

Bruton, M. (ed.), *The Spirit and Purpose of Planning*, Hutchinson 1974
Burke, G., 'Town planning and the surveyor', *Estates Gazette* (1980)
Cowan, P., *The Future of Planning*, Heinemann 1973
Faludi, A., *Planning Theory*, Pergamon 1973
Faludi, A., *A Reader in Planning Theory*, Pergamon 1973
Hall, P., *Urban and Regional Planning*, Penguin 1974
Hall, P., *Great Planning Disasters*, Weidenfeld & Nicolson 1980
Harloe, M., *Captive Cities*, John Wiley 1977
Harvey, D., *Social Justice and the City*, Edward Arnold 1973

Chapter 2: The emergence of modern town planning

Aldridge, M., *The British New Towns*, Routledge & Kegan Paul 1979
Burke, G., 'Towns in the making', *Estates Gazette* (1971)
Gillingwater, D. and Hart, D. (eds.), *The Regional Planning Process*, Saxon House 1978
Glasson, J., *An Introduction to Regional Planning*, Hutchinson 1978
Morris, A., *History of Urban Form*, Godwin 1979
Osborn, F. and Whittick, A., *The New Towns*, Leonard Hill 1977
Thomas, R. and Cresswell, P., *The New Town Idea*, Open University Press 1973

Chapter 3: The foundations of town planning legislation

Fudge, C. (ed.), *Approaches to Local Planning*, Bristol University SAUS Working Paper 3, 1978
McAuslan, P., *The Ideologies of Planning Law*, Pergamon 1980
Roberts, N., *The Reform of Planning Law*, Macmillan 1976

Chapter 4: The organization and administration of town planning

Blowers, A., *Limits of Power*, Pergamon 1980
Cockburn, C., *The Local State*, Pluto 1977

Cullingworth, J., *Town and Country Planning in Britain*, Allen & Unwin 1976
Dearlove, J., *The Politics of Policy in Local Government*, Cambridge University Press 1973
Friend, J. *et al.*, *Public Planning: The Intercorporate Dimension*, Tavistock 1974
Gyford, J., *Local Politics in Britain*, Croom Helm 1976
Hepworth, N., *The Finance of Local Government*, Allen & Unwin 1980

Chapter 5: The planning process

Chadwick, G., *A Systems View of Planning*, Pergamon 1978
Royal Town Planning Institute, *Planning and the Future*, RTPI 1976

Chapter 7: Population

Cox, P., *Demography*, Cambridge University Press 1970
Cullingworth, J. B. and Orr, S. C. (eds.), *Regional and Urban Studies*, Allen & Unwin 1969
Jackson, J. N., *Surveys for Town and Country Planning*, Hutchinson 1963
Kesall, R. K., *Population*, Longman 1967
Stone, P. A., *Urban Development in Britain: Population Trends and Housing*, Cambridge University Press 1970

Chapter 8: Employment and industry

Bale, J., *The Location of Manufacturing Industry*, Oliver & Boyd 1976
Keeble, D., *Industrial Location and Planning in the UK*, Methuen 1970
Sant, M., 'Issues in employment', in P. Hall and R. Davies (eds.), *Issues in Urban Society*, Penguin 1978
Slough Estates Ltd, *Industrial Investment*, Slough Estates Ltd 1979
Tym, R. *et al.*, *Time for Industry*, HMSO 1979
URBED, *Industrial Estates and the Small Firm*, Research Report 1, 1977
Walker, D. (ed.), *Planning Industrial Development*, Wiley 1980

Chapter 9: Housing

Cullingworth, J., *Essays on Housing Policy: The British Scene*, Allen & Unwin 1979
Kirby, D., *Slum Housing and Residential Renewal*, Longman 1979
Lambert, J. *et al.*, *Housing Policy and the State*, Macmillan 1978
Lansley, S., *Housing and Public Policy*, Croom Helm 1979
Murie, A. *et al.*, *Housing Policy and the Housing System*, Allen & Unwin 1976
Paris, C., *Not Much Improvement*, Heinemann 1979
Smith, M., *Guide to Housing*, Housing Centre Trust 1977

Chapter 10: Offices

Alexander, I., *Office Location and Public Policy*, Longman 1979
Daniels, P., *Spatial Patterns of Office Growth and Location*, Wiley 1979
Department of the Environment, *The Office Location Review*, HMSO 1976

Chapter 11: Shopping

Davies, R., 'Issues in retailing' in P. Hall and R. Davies (eds.), *Issues in Urban Society*, Penguin 1978
Davies, R. (ed.), *Retail Planning in the European Community*, Saxon House 1979
Northen, I., *Shopping Centres*, CALUS 1977

Chapter 12: Transportation

Department of Transport, *Policy for Roads*, HMSO 1978
Faulks, R., *Principles of Transport*, Allan 1973
Grant, J., *The Politics of Urban Transport Planning*, Earth Resources Research Ltd 1977

Chapter 13: Leisure and recreation

Coppock, J. and Duffield, B., *Recreation in the Countryside*, Macmillan 1975
Miles, C. and Seabrooke, W., *Recreational Land Management*, Spon 1977
Patmore, J., *Land and Leisure*, Penguin 1972

Chapter 14: Evaluation

Hawkings, C. J. and Pearce, D. W., *Capital Investment Appraisal*, Macmillan 1971
Institute of Municipal Treasurers and Accountants, *Cost Benefit Analysis*, Institute of Municipal Treasurers and Accountants 1969
Laurie Carr, J., *Investment Economics*, Routledge & Kegan Paul 1969
Lichfield, N. *et al.*, *Evaluation in the Planning Process*, Pergamon 1975
Merrett, A. J. and Sykes, A., *The Finance and Analysis of Capital Projects*, Longman 1965
Mishan, E. J., *Cost Benefit Analysis*, Allen & Unwin 1971
Pearce, D. W., *Cost Benefit Analysis*, Macmillan 1971
Peters, G. H., *Cost Benefit Analysis and Public Expenditure*, Hobart Paper, Institute of Economic Affairs 1965

Chapter 15: Associated planning techniques

Baxter, R., *Computer and Statistical Techniques for Planners*, Medical and Technical Publishing 1974
Lee, C., *Models in Planning*, Pergamon 1973

Chapter 16: Rural planning

Ashton, J. and Long, W., *The Remoter Rural Areas of Britain*, Oliver & Boyd 1972
Davidson, J. and Wibberley, G., *Planning and the Rural Environment*, Pergamon 1977
Gilg, A., *Countryside Planning*, David & Charles 1978
Shaw, J. (ed.), *Rural Deprivation and Planning*, Geo Abstracts 1979
Woodruffe, B., *Rural Settlement Policies and Plans*, Oxford University Press 1976

Chapter 17: Conservation

Binney, M. and Hanna, M., *Preservation Pays*, SAVE 1978
Cormack, P., *Heritage in Danger*, Quartet 1978
Dobby, A., *Conservation and Planning*, Hutchinson 1978

Chapter 18: Resource planning and pollution

Arvill, R., *Man and Environment*, Pelican 1967
Dawson, J. and Doomkamp, J. (eds.), *Evaluating the Human Environment*, Edward Arnold 1973
Foley, G., *The Energy Question*, Pelican 1967
Jacobs, J., *The Death and Life of Great American Cities*, Penguin 1962
O'Riordan, T., *Perspectives on Resource Management*, Pion 1971

Chapter 19: The inner city

Greater London Council, *Inner London Must Live*, GLC 1978
Jones, C., *Urban Deprivation and the Inner City*, Croom Helm 1979
Loney, M. and Allen, M., *The Crisis of the Inner City*, Macmillan 1979
McKean, C., *Fight Blight*, Kaye & Ward 1977

Chapter 20: Planning and public participation

Civic Trust, *The Local Amenity Movement*, Civic Trust 1976
Davies, J., *The Evangelistic Bureaucrat*, Tavistock 1972
Dennis, N., *Public Participation and Planner's Blight*, Faber 1972

Nicholson, S., *Community Participation in City Decision Making*, Open University Press 1973
Pateman, C., *Participation and Democratic Theory*, Cambridge University Press 1974
Thornley, A., *Theoretical Perspectives on Planning Participation*, Pergamon 1977

Chapter 21: Planning and land values

Hagman, D. and Misczynski, D., *Windfalls for Wipeouts*, University of Chicago Press 1978
Lichfield, N. and Darin-Drabkin, H., *Land Policy and Planning*, Allen & Unwin 1980

Chapter 22: The development control system

Royal Institution of Chartered Surveyors, *Investigations of a Local Authority's Planning Policies and Proposals*, Practice Note 1, RICS 1977
Royal Institution of Chartered Surveyors, *Enforcement of Planning Control and Surveying, Valuation and Planning Investigations*, Practice Note 4, RICS 1978
Royal Town Planning Institute, *Development Control into the 1980s*, RTPI 1979

Chapter 24: Site layout and development

Rubenstein, H., *A Guide to Site and Environmental Planning*, Wiley 1980

Chapter 25: Town planning law

Heap, D. (ed.), *The Encyclopaedia of Planning Law and Practice*, Sweet & Maxwell updated quarterly
McAuslan, P., *Land, Law and Planning*, Weidenfeld & Nicolson 1975
Telling, A., *Planning Law and Procedure*, Butterworth 1977

Index